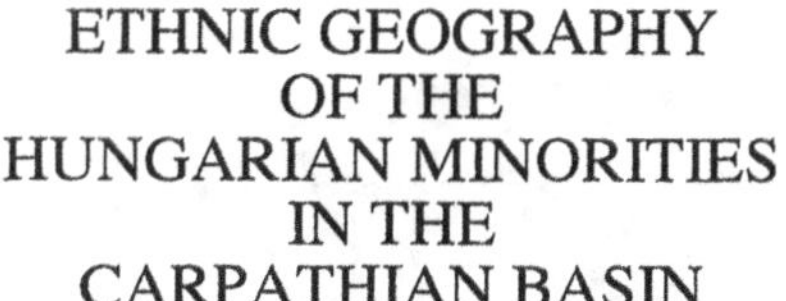

ETHNIC GEOGRAPHY
OF THE
HUNGARIAN MINORITIES
IN THE
CARPATHIAN BASIN

ETHNIC GEOGRAPHY
OF THE
HUNGARIAN MINORITIES
IN THE
CARPATHIAN BASIN

by

KÁROLY KOCSIS
ESZTER KOCSIS-HODOSI

GEOGRAPHICAL RESEARCH INSTITUTE
RESEARCH CENTRE FOR EARTH SCIENCES
and
MINORITY STUDIES PROGRAMME
HUNGARIAN ACADEMY OF SCIENCES
Budapest, 1998

Layout: ZOLTÁN KERESZTESI

Translation by: LÁSZLÓ BASSA

Translation revised by: MARION MERRICK

Cartography: LIVIA KAISER, ZSUZSANNA KERESZTESI

Technical board: MARGIT CSAPKA-ĹACZKÓ, ISTVÁN POÓR

ISBN 963 7395 84 9

Preparation for printing carried out
at the Geographical Research Institute Research Centre For Earth Sciences
Hungarian Academy of Sciences (Budapest, Hungary)

The preparation of the manuscript was sponsored
by the Illyés Közalapítvány (Foundation) and
by the Hungarian National Research Fund (OTKA, Project T 22831), Budapest

Printed in Hungary
by EXEON Bt.

To
our children
Ágnes, Levente and Attila

CONTENTS

LIST OF FIGURES

LIST OF TABLES

INTRODUCTION

Since the 17th and 18th centuries, the Carpathian Basin[1] has become one of the most diverse and conflict-ridden macroregions of Europe from both an ethnic and religious perspective. During the last century no social or ideological system has succeeded in easing the tensions which have arisen from both the intricate intermingling of different ethnic groups, and the existence of the new, rigid state borders which fail to take into account the ethnic, cultural and historical traditions, economic conditions, and centuries-old production and commercial contacts. Not even communist internationalist ideology (from 1948 to 1989) was able to solve this problem. On the contrary, the ethnic tensions that had been concealed or denied for forty years have since surfaced with an elemental force.

As a result, in the years since the collapse of communism, nationalist governments sensitive only to the interests of state forming nations (ethnic groups) gained power. National minorities reacted in self-defence by reorganising and establishing their cultural organisations and political parties. Following the collapse of the former socialist economic system and an upsurge of nationalism and chauvinism, minorities have once again become the source of both interethnic tensions and inter-state conflicts. This is especially true of the Hungarian minorities in the Carpathian Basin. The majority of countries which gained Hungarian territories in 1920 continue to consider them as the main supporters of Hungarian irredentism and revanchism.

The need for geographical research on the Hungarian national minorities in the Carpathian Basin can be explained not only by the enormous thirst for information in academic, governmental and general public circles, but also by the political events of the recent past. Geography, since its beginnings, has played and continues to play an important role in the education and formation of national self-consciousness both in Hungary and abroad. Right up to the end of World War I, when the Hungarian Kingdom that had extended throughout the entire Carpathian Basin for almost one thousand years was partitioned, geographical research and the education of the nation corresponded to that of the actual country. After the 1920s, however, the relationship of Hungarian geography to the Hungarian nation and state was divided into two main eras.

The first era lasted from 1920 until 1945. With one sudden blow, the Peace Treaty of Trianon (1920) forced one third of the Hungarian nation to live as minorities as foreigners. In this era, ethnic, political and economic geography became the main scientific source of revisionist and irredentist demands. As a result, the study of the geography of the lost territories and their Hungarian populations played an exceptionally important role in scientific research and education.

---

[1] The Carpathian Basin is a synonym for the territory of historical Hungary in the everyday language of Hungary. From a geographical point of view it includes at least three great basins: Little Hungarian Plain (Kisalföld), the Great Hungarian Plain (Alföld) and the Transylvanian Basin

During the four decades following the 1940s, in order to avoid conflict with neighbouring Communist allied countries, and in accordance with the proletarian internationalist ideology of the region, the relationship of geography with the Hungarian national minorities was characterised by totally opposite principles. Study of the nation was equated with a study of the Hungarian state. Fear of accusations of nationalism, chauvinism or irredentism led to a consideration of the Hungarians of the Carpathian Basin living outside the borders of Hungary as being almost non-existent. The centuries-old Hungarian names of regions and settlements inhabited by Hungarians were also omitted, intentionally or by ignorance, both in the press and in school-books. Unfortunately, this fact contributed to increasing national despair in society as well as to a fall in the amount of literature written in Hungarian. From this point of view, the situation has improved considerably since then, but school books still hardly mention the Hungarian minorities of several millions living over the border. For this reason, several generations have grown up in the last decades for whom Hungarian geographical names such as Csallóköz, Gömör, Párkány, Beregszász, Nagykároly, Sepsiszentgyörgy and Zenta sound just as exotic as Buenos Aires, Capetown, Teheran or Peking. During their trips to neighbouring countries people are genuinely surprised by the local population's knowledge of Hungarian and by the presence of the several hundreds of thousands of Hungarians.

This has, of course, only increased the thirst for information regarding Hungarians living outside the borders. In recent years, a considerable number of people have voiced the demand that after seven decades of extremist attitudes, the millions of Hungarians living next door should finally be offered a place in Hungarian science and education, as they deserve.

The first chapter outlines the position of Hungarians in the Carpathian Basin among European minorities, the relationship between changes in population and political events in the 20th century, and the present ethnic geographic, demographic and social situation of the Hungarian minorities in the Carpathian Basin. In the remaining chapters the natural environment and changes in the territory of Hungarian settlement is explored further between the 15th and 20th centuries.

Chapter 1

HUNGARIAN MINORITIES IN THE CARPATHIAN BASIN

General Outline

Out of a total 14,1 million ethnic Hungarians in the world — a number corresponding to the population of Australia — 92 % live in the Carpathian Basin on the historical territory of Hungary *(Tab. 1)*. There are 3.2 million European Hungarians living outside the borders of present-day Hungary, forming the largest minority in Europe[1], apart from the 15.1 million ethnic Russians, and having the same size as the population of Ireland while outnumbering the population of 87 countries in the world (e.g. Mongolia, Libya) *(Tab. 2)*.

If the number of people of minority status is compared to the number of their entire ethnic group, then Hungarians are among the first with a rate of 25.9%. In Europe, only the Albanians and the Irish are above the Hungarians on the list — with a proportion of 30-42% of the ethnic group living outside the borders of their country *(Tab. 3)*.

During the period following the Hungarian Conquest of the Carpathian Basin (896), its natural environment and capacity to support a large population were the most decisive factors influencing the limits of the area populated by the forefathers of the Hungarians. At this time, Hungarians mainly inhabited the steppes and lightly-forested areas, the strategically important valleys and the hills, which reminded them of the landscape of their previous homeland, while it suited their half-nomadic way of life. Later, with a change in lifestyle to an agricultural way of life, and with a demographic rise, the Hungarian ethnic borders were extended to the verge of the high mountainous regions *(Fig. 1)*.

In the times of the Ottoman (Turkish) occupation demographic losses were proportionate to the geopolitical and geographical position of the population. The diminishing Hungarian ethnical area and its shrinking borders were mainly felt in southern parts, that is in the neighbourhood of the Ottoman Empire, and in the flatlands and strategically unfavourable zones like in some valleys or basins (such as the Transylvanian Basin). The present-day Székely[2] ethnic area owes its existence to its favourable geographical position as well as its former autonomous status.

---

[1] Excluding the Turkish and Italian migrant-workers ("Gastarbeiters") of 3 million each.

[2] Székelys (Hungarian: Székelyek, German: Szeklers, Rumanian: Secui, Latin: Siculi). Hungarian ethnographical group in the middle of Rumania, in Southeast Transylvania. Their ethnic origin is a controversial question. During the 10th and 11th centuries they lived as border guards and

Table 1. Hungarians in different regions of the World (around 1990)

Country, region	Total	Carpathian Basin
1. Hungary	10,222,000	10,222,000
2. Slovakia	608,000	608,000
3. Ukraine	180,000	168,000
4. Rumania	1,640,000	1,620,000
5. Yugoslavia	350,000	345,000
6. Croatia	20,000	19,000
7. Slovenia	9,000	8,000
8. Austria	33,000	7,000
2–8. total	*2,840,000*	*2,775,000*
9. Czech Republic	20,000	
10. Germany	120,000	
11. Netherlands	5,000	
12. Belgium	10,000	
13. United Kingdom	25,000	
14. France	50,000	
15. Switzerland	20,000	
16. Italy	5,000	
17. Sweden	25,000	
18. Russia	20,000	
19. other European countries	17,000	
2–19. total	*3,157,000*	*2,775,000*
20. Europe total	*13,379,000*	*12,997,000*
21. USA	450,000	
22. Canada	73,000	
23. Latin American countries	100,000	
24. South Africa	10,000	
25. Other African countries	10,000	
26. Israel	27,000	
27. Other Asian countries	30,000	
28. Australia	36,000	
29. New Zealand and Oceania	5,000	
21–29. total	*741,000*	
30. World total	**14,120,000**	

Sources: 1–8. Census data (native tongue). 22., 26., 28. Britannica. Book of the year 1992, 9–21., 23-25., 27., 29. Estimations of K. Kocsis and of the organizations of the Hungarian minorities (Databank of the World Federation of Hungarians, Budapest).

---

auxiliary troops in disperate groups along the borders of the Hungarian settlement area (e.g. Banat, Syrmia, Southwest Transdanubia (Dunántúl), present-day South Slovakia, Bihar county). In the 12th and 13th centuries the majority of them were concentrated in the eastern bordeland of Hungary. This was a very underpopulated, wooded area endangered by Patzinak and Mongol invasions. As a border guard, privileged population they have lived till the 14th century in "clan" organisation, after that in seven districts ("szék") under the leadership of the bailiff (Hungarian: "ispán") of all Székelys, of the local representative of the king of Hungary in power. Since the Middle Ages their increasing, by economical and political reasons motivated emigration from the overpopulated and underdeveloped Székely Region to Moldavia demographical reinforced the Roman Catholic Csángó-Hungarians of Moldavia.

Table 2. National minorities of Europe by population size (around 1990)

National minorities	Total number
1. Russians	15,120,000
2. Hungarians	**3,157,000**
3. Turks	3,000,000
4. Italians	2,600,000
5. Germans	2,445,000
6. Albanians	2,390,000
7. Irish	2,300,000
8. Poles	1,669,000
9. Ukrainians	1,528,000
10.Portugueses	1,030,000
11.Serbs	983,000
12.Spanish	953,000
13.Belarussians	860,000
14.French	670,000
15.Greeks	564,000
16.Rumanians, Moldavians, Vlachs	540,000

Sources: Geografichesky Entsiklopedichesky Slovar. Ponyatia i terminy. (Treshnikov, A.F. /ed./1988, Moscow, pp. 420-426., Census data: 1989 (USSR), 1992 (Rumania), 1991 (Yugoslavia, Croatia, Slovenia, Macedonia, Czechoslovakia), Britannica. Book of the Year 1991, London, pp. 758-761.
Remarks: The national minorities include "Gastarbeiters (migrant workers)" on the territory of Europe excluding Russia and Turkey. The state borders of 01.01.1993 are considered.

Table 3. Percentage of Europe's national minorities compared to the total population of their ethnic groups (around 1990)

National minorities	Percentage
1. Albanians	42.0
2. Irish	30.3
3. Macedonians	25.2
4. Hungarians	**20.3**
5. Muslimans	18.7
6. Slovenes	13.6
7. Serbs	10.7
8. Russians	10.3
9. Slovaks	9.4
10. Croats	8.7
11. Belarussians	8.4
12. Portugueses	7.6
13. Finns	6.4
14. Turks	5.7
15. Bulgarians	5.0

Sources, remarks: see Table 2.

The next stage in the history of ethnic Hungarian territory is characterised in the mass migrations of the 18th century, following an evening out in number of the

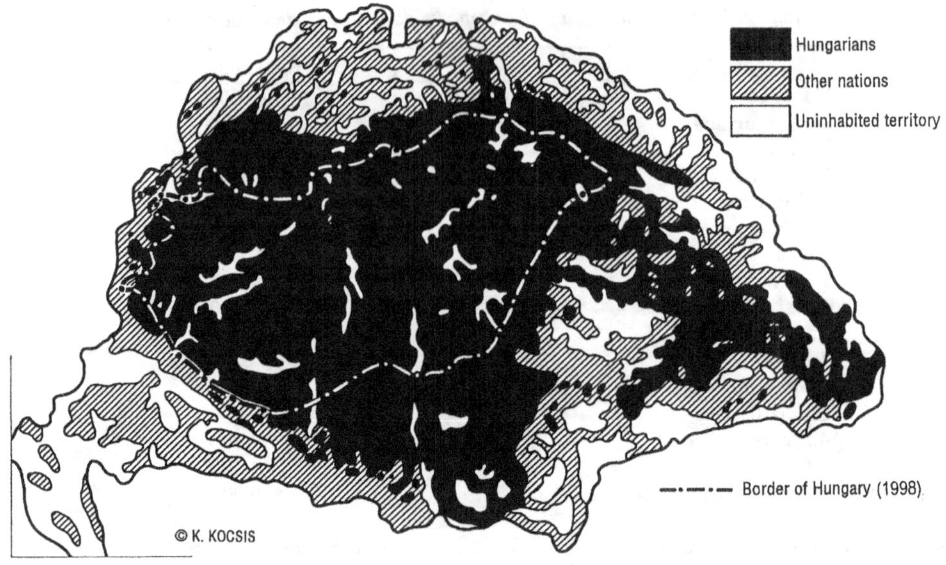

Figure 1. Ethnic map of Hungary (late 15th century)

population. Masses of people from the ethnic peripheries moved to the great basins located in the Great Hungarian Plain or the Transylvanian Basin which were formerly almost depopulated or sparsely inhabited, but offered great productivity and were rich in different natural resources.

The result of this process was the dislocation of the Hungarian-Slovak, Hungarian-Ruthenian, Hungarian-Rumanian ethnic borders at the expense of the ethnic Hungarians *(Fig. 2.)*. The present-day area of Hungarian rural settlement did not change significantly after the 18th century, only occasionally was it violently modified (e.g. deportations between 1945-1948, genocide in 1944, etc.) or slightly changed by both natural and forced assimilation.

We cannot speak of Hungarian minorities in the Carpathian Basin until 1920, the year of the peace treaty of Trianon and the partitioning of the historical territory of Hungary. The detached areas had constituted an organic part of Hungary from the 10th century up to 1920. From then on, Hungarians lived first in five, then from 1991 in eight different countries: Hungary, Slovakia (starting in 1993), Ukraine (Transcarpathia), Rumania (Transylvania), Yugoslavia — Serbia (Vojvodina), Croatia, Slovenia (Transmura Region) — and Austria (Burgenland). During the past seven decades their "dismembered" situation determined their destiny and their statistical numbers as registered by the Czechoslovak, Rumanian, Yugoslav etc. official censuses.

According to the last Hungarian census (1910) in the total territory of historical Hungary, 33% of the total number of Hungarians living in the Carpathian Basin — approximately 3.3 million people — lived on the territories that are now outside the new

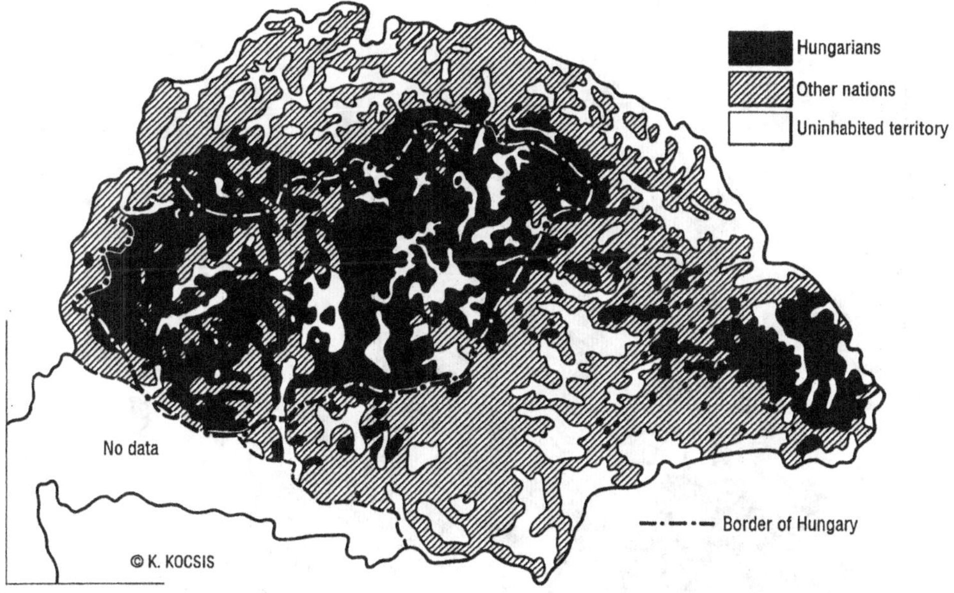

Figure 2. Ethnic map of Hungary (1773)

Hungarian national borders. In the period following the peace treaty of Trianon these people experienced a change of status from that of a majority to one of a minority for the first time in history. Thus, they became the target for anti-Hungarian revenge by Slovaks, Rumanians, and Serbs. Their geographical position also changed fundamentally, since the areas they inhabited — with the one exception of the Székely regions — had all formerly been in the central area of the Hungarian state. After 1920 these areas became heavily militarised frontier zones on the periphery of the neighbouring countries *(Fig. 3.).* According to the data of the National Office for Refugees (Budapest) about 350,000 Hungarians fled to the new territory of Hungary in the period between 1918 - 1924. The greatest number (197,035) left territories annexed to Rumania, others (106,841) came from areas given to Czechoslovakia, and the rest (44,903) emigrated from their native lands which then belonged to the Kingdom of the Serbs, Croats and Slovenes[3].

Ethnic status is a very subjective social structural element. It relies on the personal beliefs of the individual, and is much influenced by the prevailing ideological and political system. For this reason the number of individuals making up the various ethnic groups is determined by many factors: natural increase or decrease of population and migration, fluctuations in the declaration of ethnicity at censuses, demographic proc-

---

[3] Petrichevich-Horváth E. 1924 Jelentés az Országos Menekültügyi Hivatal négy évi működéséről (Report about the activity of the National Office for Refugees) , Budapest

19

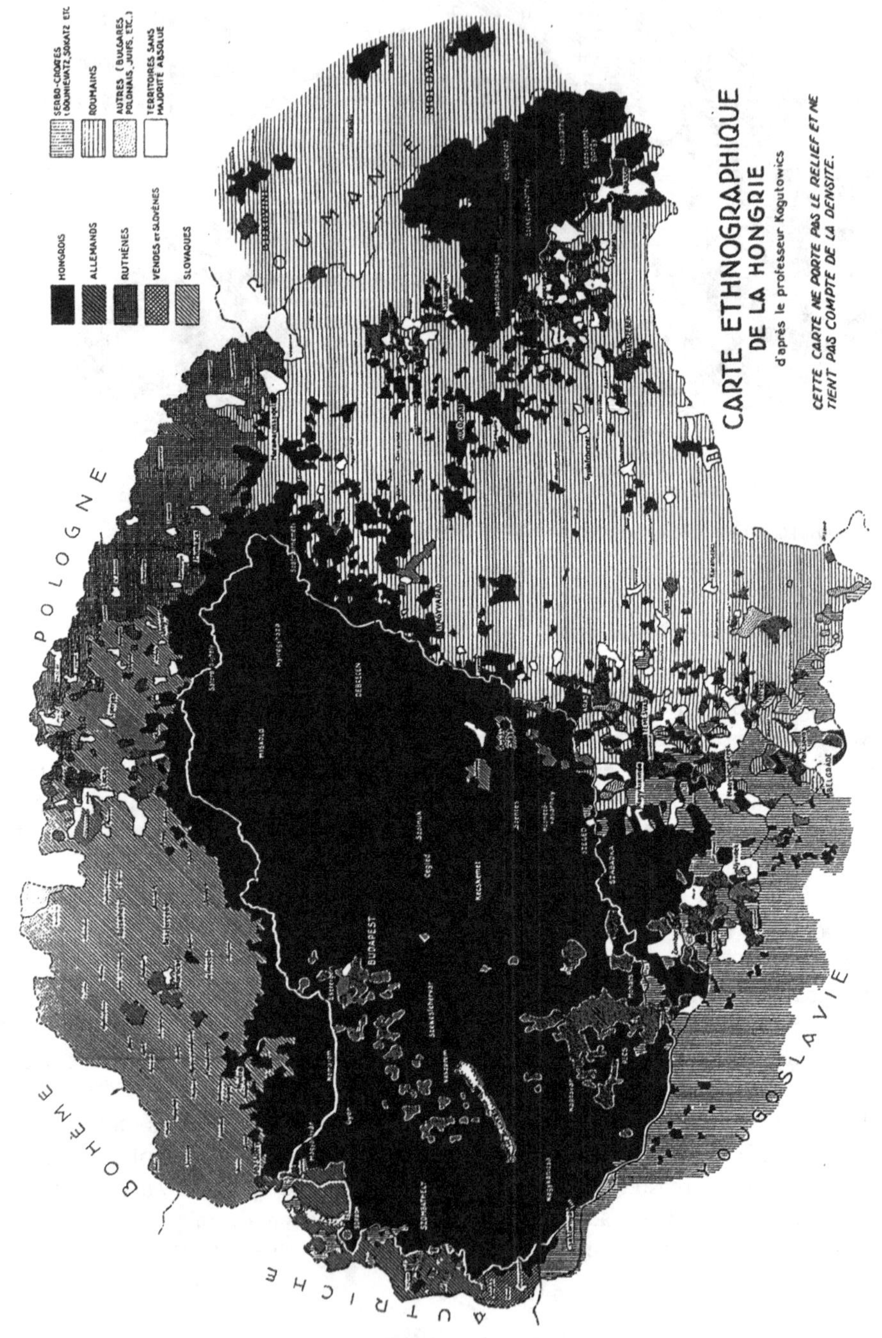

Figure 3. Ethnic map of Hungary (1910) and the Trianon border (1920)
Source: Dami, A. 1929 La Hongrie de Demain, Paris

esses such as assimilation, and differences in data relating to the mother tongue, the language used at home, ethnic origins, etc. Between the two wars the most striking phenomenon in this respect was that Jews and Gypsies were listed in different categories in Czechoslovakia and Rumania. This diminished the number of those people who considered themselves to be Hungarian primarily in Transcarpathia, Slovakia and Transylvania, as compared to the statistics of 1910 *(Tab. 4., Fig.4.)*. An important factor in the rapid statistical decrease in the number of Hungarians now living in minority groups was the fact that the many bilingual and bicultural groups living along the borders declared themselves to be Slovaks, Ruthenians (now Ukrainians), Rumanians, Serbs or Croats, but not Hungarians. This was the case with the population in the areas around Nyitra, Érsekújvár, Léva, Kassa and Tőketerebes in Slovakia, the western part of the Nagyszőlős district in Transcarpathia, and certain areas in the counties of Szatmár and Szilágy in Rumania. Compared to these places, the decrease in the number of Hungarians living in smaller communities (in Burgenland or Slavonia) was less dramatic. These phenomena led to a fall in the number of Hungarians firstly in Transylvania and Slovakia, and to some extent in Croatia, Burgenland and Transcarpathia.

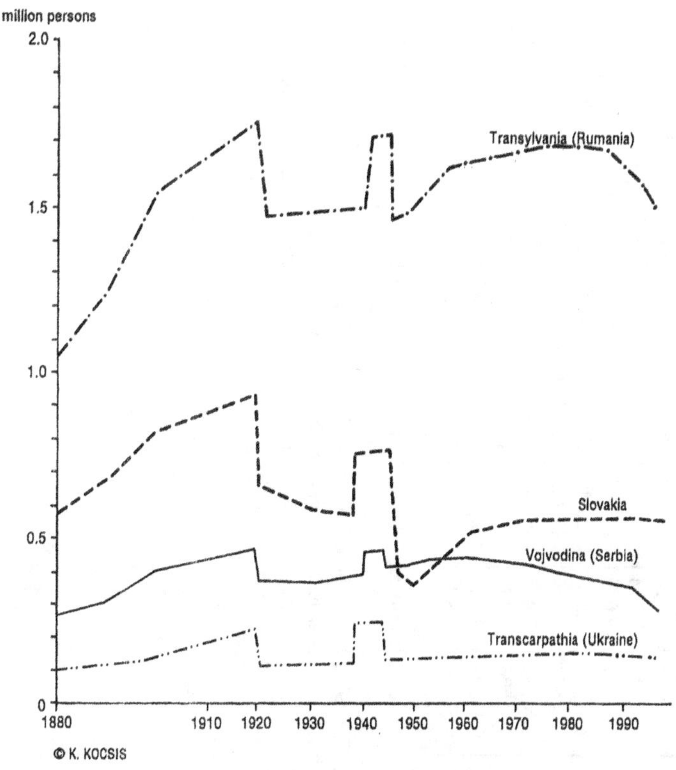

Figure 4. Change in the number of ethnic Hungarians in Transylvania, Slovakia, Vojvodina and Transcarpathia according to the census data (1880–1990)

Table 4. Change in the number and percentage of the Hungarian minorities in different regions of the Carpathian Basin (1880–1991)

Year	Slovakia		Transcarpathia (Ukraine)		Transylvania (Rumania)		Vojvodina (Yugoslavia)		Croatia		Transmura Region (Slovenia)		Burgenland (Austria)	
	number	percent.	number	percent.	number	percent.	number	percent.	number	percent.	number	percent.	number	percent.
1880	574,862	23.1 M	105,343	25.7 M	1,045,098	26.1 M	265,287	22.6 M	49,560	1.9 M	13,221	17.7 M	11,162	4.2 M
1910	881,326	30.2 M	185,433	30.6 M	1,658,045	31.7 M	425,672	28.1 M	119,874	3.5 M	20,737	23.0 M	26,225	9.0 M
1930	585,434	17.6 N	116,584	15.9 N	1,480,712	25.8 M	376,176	23.2 M	66,040	1.7 M	15,050	–	10,442	3.5 M
1941	761,434	21.5 M	233,840	27.3 M	1,711,851	28.9 M	456,770	28.5 M	64,431	–	16,510	20.1 M	–	–
1950	354,532	10.3 N	139,700	17.3 N	1,481,903	25.7 M	418,180	25.8 N	51,399	1.4 N	10,246	10.8 N	5,251	1.9 U
1961	518,782	12.4 N	146,247	15.9 N	1,616,199	25.9 M	442,560	23.9 N	42,347	1.0 N	9,899	11.0 N	5,642	2.1 U
1970	552,006	12.2 N	151,122	14.5 N	1,625,702	24.2 M	423,866	21.7 N	35,488	0.8 N	9,064	10.0 N	5,673	2.1 U
1980	559,801	11.2 N	158,446	13.7 N	1,691,048	22.5 N	385,356	18.9 N	25,439	0.6 N	8,617	9.5 N	4,147	1.5 U
1991	567,296	10.8 N	155,711	12.5 N	1,604,266	20.8 N	339,491	16.9 N	22,355	0.5 N	7,636	8.5 N	6,763	2.8 U

Sources: Census data (Slovakia: 1880, 1910, 1930, 1941, 1950, 1961, 1970, 1980, 1991; Transcarpathia:1880, 1910, 1930, 1941, 1959, 1969, 1979, 1989; Transylvania : 1880, 1910, 1930, 1941, 1948, 1956, 1966, 1977, 1992; Vojvodina, Croatia, Transmura Region: 1880, 1910, 1931, 1941, 1948, 1961, 1971, 1981, 1991; Burgenland: 1880, 1910, 1934, 1951, 1961, 1971, 1981, 1991).
Remark: Hungarians include the Székelys (Secui) and Csángós (Ceangãi).
Abbreviations: M– mother (native) tongue, N– ethnicity,   E– ethnic origin, U– every-day language ("Umgangssprache")

Between 1938 and 1941 there was a lull in the rapid fall in the number of Hungarians in the Carpathian Basin when areas with a compact Hungarian population were given back to Hungary e.g. present-day Southern Slovakia, Transcarpathia, Northern Transylvania, Bácska, Southeast Baranya, and the Transmura Region. In these territories the number of Hungarians increased considerably, especially in the present-day territories of Transcarpathia, Slovakia and Transylvania. This followed the appearance of Hungarian government officials (civil servants, a police force and army), an influx of Hungarian colonists from Bukovina and the fact that the majority of Jews also belonged to the Hungarian ethnic community.

After the Second World War, according to census data from the neighbouring states, the total numbers in the Hungarian minorities shrank from 3.2 million (in 1941) to 2.4 million. Among the main factors contributing to this decrease between 1944-48 were migration (fleeing their homes, expulsions, or deportations). 125,000 Hungarians fled to present-day Hungarian territory, or were deported from Rumania; 120,500 from Czechoslovakia; 45,500 from Yugoslavia; and 25,000 from Transcarpathia (belonging then to the Soviet Union, and now to Ukraine). At the same time the Czechoslovakian government deported 44,000 Hungarians to the Czech regions between 1945-1947, from where Germans had fled or had been deported, in order to press for a gradual Czechoslovak-Hungarian "population exchange". Besides emigration and the casualties during the war, came the annihilation of Jewish Hungarians — the numbers of Hungarians in neighbouring countries was mostly diminished by the fact that those groups, whose awareness of nationality was not very strong continually vacillated and now declared themselves to belong to the majority population. In South Slovakia, there was a process of "re-Slovakization", while the general anti-Hungarian atmosphere also contributed to the diminishing number of Hungarians, especially in Slovakia, Transcarpathia and Transylvania.

In areas belonging to former Yugoslavia (Bácska, Bánát), in spite of the vendetta of the Serbs in October-November 1944, which claimed approximately 20,000 civilian casulaties, the number of Hungarians was dropping far slower. This fact is partly explained by the fact that the Germans preferred to declare themselves Hungarian from fear of persecution. During the last 40 years the number of minority Hungarians in statistical reports was greatly influenced by the specific socio-economic system of the different countries, their various policies towards ethnic minorities, and the "maturity" of the majority population in each country.

In Serbia (Vojvodina), Croatia and the Transmura Region of Slovenia, the number of Hungarians either increased or remained unchanged up to the 1960s. From then on with the chance of working in the West, or with the appearance of the "Yugoslav" category in the ethnic statistics, the number of Hungarians in the former Yugoslavia started to diminish dramatically. The natural increase of Hungarians in Transylvania was counterbalanced — first of all in the important towns and cities — by the "nation-state" programme of the Rumanian government and the resulting policy towards minorities, as well as distortions of the statistics. In Slovakia, with the fading of the memory of the shocking events of the late 40s, the number of those who dared to declare themselves Hungarian increased greatly during the 1950s. To this was added a high rate of natural increase, but this growth suddenly dropped from the 1970s on. The greatest Hungarian demographic increases in the Carpathian Basin were registered in the following regions during the period from 1970 to 1980: Beregszász district (12.7%), Hargita and Kovászna counties (respectively 11.7% and 10.5%) and Dunaszerdahely district (18.7%).

An outline of the present ethnic geographic, the demographic and the social situation of the Hungarian minorities in the Carpathian Basin

According to the different censuses from the 1990s, the number of ethnic Hungarians in the Carpathian Basin is 13 million, out of which 2.8 million are living outside the borders of the Republic of Hungary. Minority organisations, however, estimate that the number of Hungarians in the area is 3.2 million. This makes up 24.9% of the total number of Hungarians in the Basin.

The majority of Hungarians living in a minority are found in Transylvania (1.6 million people), followed by Slovakia with 567,000 people, and Vojvodina in Serbia (339,000). When speaking about the number of Hungarians living in different neighbouring countries, it is worth touching upon the much used term of "ethnical reciprocity". This is very important because the situation of the respective minority in Hungary has played, and still does play, an immense role in the granting of rights for Hungarians in the neighbouring states.

As can be seen from *Table 5.*, one can speak about ethnical reciprocity in the case of Hungary only with Croatia, Slovenia and Austria, for only in these cases are their numbers and their demographic and ethno-geographic situations comparable. At the same time, the latest census shows that the Hungarian minorities in Serbia, Rumania and Slovakia are 189, 151, and 54 times greater respectively than their corresponding minorities in Hungary. Apart from the different historical developments of each minority this great disproportionateness makes a comparison between the situation of Hungarians in Slovakia, Rumania and Serbia with that of the Slovaks, Rumanians and Serbians in Hungary impossible. Moreover, this lack of symmetry in number has further increased the vulnerability of Hungarians in Czechoslovakia, Rumania and Yugoslavia. Their political situation has become similar to that of a political hostage during the past 70 years. Although the number of Ruthenians and Ukrainians is very small in Hungary, the lack of balanced ethnical reciprocity does not in any way influence the good relations between the young Ukrainian state and Hungary. What is more, the Ukrainians have realised that in pursuit of an approach to Western Europe, there is a need for a western bridge (Transcarpathia) without ethnic tensions, and for good political and economic relations with Hungary, which can be achieved with the Hungarian minority inside the Ukrainian borders.

According to the censuses of around 1990, on the territory of the Carpathian Basin beyond the borders of Hungary, 2,703,176 persons declared themselves to be ethnically Hungarian and 2,773,944 persons were native Hungarian speakers. The num-

Table 5. Ethnic reciprocity in the countries of the Carpathian Basin (around 1990)

Hungarians in Slovakia	567,296 (653,000)	Slovaks in Hungary	10,459 (80,000)
Hungarians in Ukraine	163,111 (210,000)	Ukrainians in Hungary	657 (..)
Hungarians in Rumania	1,627,021 (2,000,000)	Rumanians in Hungary	10,740 (15,000)
Hungarians in Serbia	343,942 (365,000)	Serbs in Hungary	2,905 (5,000)
Hungarians in Croatia	22,355 (40,000)	Croats in Hungary	13,570 (40,000)
Hungarians in Slovenia	8,499 (12,000)	Slovens in Hungary	1,930 (5,000)
Hungarians in Burgenland	6,763 (7,000)	Germans in West-Hungary	1,531 (17,000)

Source: Census data /Ukraine 1989, Hungary 1990, Slovakia, Serbia, Croatia, Slovenia, Austria 1991, Rumania 1992/ according to the ethnicity (in Austria: every-day language). In parentheses are the estimations – according to the language knowledge and ethnic origin – of the organizations of the minorities and the calculations of K.Kocsis (1988). Hungarians in Transylvania include the Székely- and Csángó-Hungarians.

ber of the latter exceeded that of ethnic Hungarians by 80,500 in Hungary; 40,900 in Slovakia; 15,800 in Transylvania; 11,600 in Transcarpathia, and 5,200 in Vojvodina. The number of native Hungarian speakers surpasses that of ethnic Hungarians almost everywhere, mainly due to the fact that the Gypsy and German populations „Magyarized" their language but have recently undergone a revival of ethnic awareness in areas with a Hungarian majority. Moreover, along the Hungarian language border (e.g. in towns like Pozsony, Kassa, Ungvár and Munkács and in their environs), and in Szatmár County in Rumania this difference had reached between 12 and 48 %. On the other hand, an accelerated lingual assimilation of Hungarians in Slovak, Ruthenian, Serbian and Croatian majority territories means that the number of native Hungarian speakers remains below those of Hungarian ethnic affiliation (e.g. in the overwhelmingly Ruthenian parts of Bereg and Máramaros counties by 14 -27 %, in Croatia by 12 %, in the Transylvanian counties of Szeben, Hunyad, Krassó-Szörény, Beszterce-Naszód - by 5-10 %).

The 1980's, decisive in present population trends, found that the number of ethnic Hungarians had decreased by 4.67 % within the borders of Hungary and by 4.57 % beyond them. In Central Eastern Europe the only areas with a growing number of Hungarians were Burgenland (63.1 % growth due to a significant Hungarian influx following the fall of the "iron curtain"), in the Székely Region, and in Slovakia (as a result of the not unfavourable trends in the birth rate, where there was a 2.1 % and 1.39 % growth, respectively). As a consequence of an increasingly unfavourable birthrate and distorted demographic structure of the Hungarian population, the irreversible assimilation of its diaspora, a national revival among the previously „Magyarized" Gypsies and persons of German origin in the new political situation, the number of those declaring themselves to be ethnic Hungarians decreased by 7.6 % in Transylvania (without the Székely Region), and by 11-12 % in Vojvodina, Croatia and the Transmura Region. The macro-regional ethnic discrepancy at the expense of Hungarians is indicated by the fact that during the same period there was a 3.2 % to 5.2 % population growth in the neighbouring countries (e.g. 5.2 % in Slovakia, 5 % in Yugoslavia[4]).

In the first half of the 1990's the negative trends in demography of the Hungarian minorities (decreasing birth rates and increasing mortality rates, a negative balance of migration for political and economic reasons) had led to a drop in the number of Hungarians living in the Carpathian Basin beyond the borders of Hungary, below an estimated 2.6 million by the end of 1995. At the same time ethnic Hungarians within the present territory of Hungary decreased to "a mere" 10 million. The number of people declaring themselves to be ethnic Hungarians living in the neighbouring states and regions at the end of 1995 might have been as follows (in thousands): Slovakia 572, Transcarpathia 154, Transylvania 1,565, Vojvodina 280, Croatia 15, the Transmura Region 7, and Burgenland 7. The losses were especially severe - mainly due to the flight provoked by the Serbo-Croatian War in 1991 - among Hungarians who lived in Croatia (approx. 33 %) and Vojvodina (approx. 17 %).

According to the censuses of around 1990, 27.3 % of the 2.7 million persons constituting Hungarian minorities in the Carpathian Basin (722,000 people) live in ethnic blocks along the border with Hungary (South Slovakia, Ung-Bereg-Ugocsa Border-Zone in Transcarpathia, Szatmár-North Bihar Zone in Rumania and Tisza Region in Vojvodina); 26.8 % of them (723.000 people) populate the Székely Region in eastern Transylvania *(Fig.5.)*. At the same time, in a chain of towns (an ethnic "contact zone"[5]) linking Pozsony-Ungvár-Szabadka, where Hungarians have lost their majority during the past fifty years, they now constitute 13 % (350,000), while the remainder (32.9 %) form language islands or are scattered (858,000). In the 1980's, there was a 2.1 % increase in the number of Hungarians living in the Székely Region, and a 4.7 % growth rate in the towns in the "contact zone". This can be attributed to a 4.3 % decrease within the neighbouring ethnic blocks and a 13.3 % loss due to the diaspora, i.e. due to migration associated with the trends of urbanisation. The loss from ethnic blocks was the most severe (-8.2 %) in the Tisza Region (Vojvodina) as a consequence of a low birthrate and high emigration, and the most moderate (-1.3 %) in southern Slovakia. In spite of this, the towns in the contact zone experienced the highest gain (+17.8 %) during this period, together with southern Slovakia, as a result of migration fed by the relatively favourable demographic trends in the ethnic blocks. Hungarians who are dispersed and who make

---

[4] A relatively significant increase in population of Yugoslavia between 1981 and 1991 was primarily due to the 27.9 % increase of Albanians and 14.6 % increase of Muslimans (Serbian speakers of Islamic faith) of still high fertility. During the same decade the number of Serbs increased by 4.9 %, and that of Montenegrins dropped by 5.1 %.

[5] This ethnic "contact zone" includes the following settlements presently with Hungarian minority populations, neighbouring ethnic blocks along the border: Pozsony, Szenc, Diószeg, Galánta, Vágsellye, Érsekújvár, Nagysalló, Léva, Nagykürtös, Losonc, Osgyán, Rimaszombat, Rozsnyó, Jászó, Nagyida, Kassa, Szlovákújhely, Ungvár, Munkács, Nagyszőlős, Szatmárnémeti, Margitta, Nagyvárad, Szabadka.

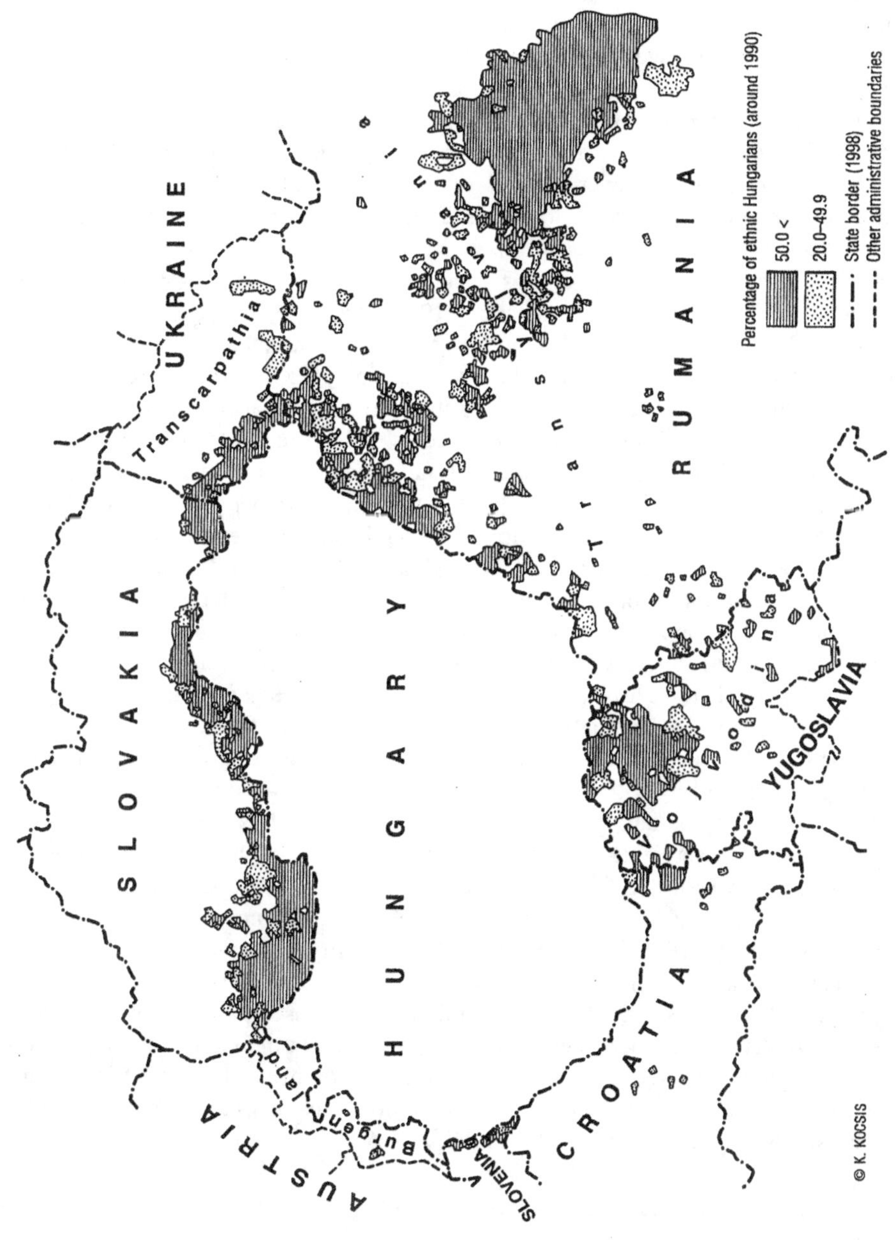

Figure 5. Percentage of the Hungarian minorities in the Carpathian Basin (around 1990)

up an ageing group of people suffering from the effects of emigration and growing lingual assimilation diminished by 8-9 % in Slovakia, Transcarpathia and Partium[6] and by 16.1 % in Vojvodina.

1.6 million Hungarians (61.5 % of the national minority) are in a favourable position to retain their ethnic identity. This represents an absolute majority (above 50 %), and amounts to 1410 such settlements in the Carpathian Basin. An overwhelming majority of Hungarians in Slovakia, Transcarpathia and the Transmura Region (77.1 %, 71.8 % and 71.9 %, respectively) and slightly more than half of the Hungarians in Transylvania and Vojvodina (56.9 % and 56.1 % resp.) live in such ethnically (for them) favourable environments. However, 54.8 % of Hungarians inhabiting Croatia and 54.2 % of those in Burgenland are trying to preserve their identity in settlements where their proportion does not reach 10 %. The above-mentioned conditions and characteristic features of areas inhabited by Hungarians resulted in the following distribution of settlements with a Hungarian majority in about 1990: Transylvania 786, Slovakia 432, Vojvodina 80, Transcarpathia 78, Transmura Region 23, Croatia 9 and Burgenland 2.

From the above it follows that there are considerable differences between conditions in the settlements system in regions of the Carpathian Basin populated by Hungarians. The proportion of those living in settlements with more than 5,000 inhabitants is the highest in Vojvodina (72.9 %), with small and medium-sized towns and large villages, and in Transylvania (57.2 %) which otherwise has extremely diverse conditions. Among Hungarian minorities the proportion of urban dwellers in centres with more than 100,000 inhabitants is also the highest in Transylvania (25.5 %). In Slovakia, Transcarpathia and Vojvodina this proportion reaches 4.6 - 5.6 %. In settlements of less than 1,000 inhabitants, the population faces serious problems in providing an infrastructure and consequently in offering favourable living conditions, and suffers from increasing emigration. This is characteristic of Hungarians in the Slovenian Transmura Region (73.6 %), Croatia (33.9 %), Burgenland (29 %) and Slovakia (22.8 %).

Conditions in settlement system are closely connected to the level of urbanisation of Hungarian minorities. So it is not surprising that the proportion of urban dwellers is the largest in Vojvodina and Transylvania (58.7 % and 56.1 %, resp) exceeding the national average (Yugoslavia 45.7 %, Rumania 54.3 %). Although the number of Hungarians inhabiting towns in the Carpathian Basin is on the increase as a whole, the rate of growth has remained far below that of the state-forming nations which is also due to accelerated assimilation. (E.g. figures show +4.2 % growth for Hungarians and +33.9 % for Rumanians in Transylvanian towns between 1977 and 1992; the corresponding data was +0.2 % for Hungarians and +24 % for Ukrainians in Transcarpathian towns between 1979 and 1989). As a result there has been a steady decline in the Hungarian population in the overwhelming majority of towns in neighbouring countries. This trend is particularly striking in big towns with the largest communities of Hungarians (Marosvásárhely, Kolozsvár, Nagyvárad, Szatmárnémeti) *(Tab. 6., Fig. 6.)*.

---

[6] Partium: historico-geographical region denoting West Rumanian counties Arad, Bihar, Szatmár, Szilágy, Máramaros.

Table 6. The largest Hungarian communities beyond the borders of Hungary in the Carpathian Basin, according to census data (around 1980 and 1990, thousand persons)

Settlements	1980	1990
1. Marosvásárhely / Târgu Mureş R	82.2	83.2
2. Kolozsvár / Cluj-Napoca R	86.2	74.9
3. Nagyvárad / Oradea R	75.1	74.2
4. Szatmárnémeti / Satu Mare R	47.6	53.9
5. Sepsiszentgyörgy / Sfântu Gheorghe R	34.0	50.0
6. Szabadka / Subotica Y	44.0	39.7
7. Székelyudvarhely / Odorheiu Secuiesc R	27.7	38.9
8. Csíkszereda / Miercurea Ciuc R	25.5	38.0
9. Temesvár / Timişoara R	36.2	31.8
10. Brassó / Braşov R	34.0	31.6
11. Arad / Arad R	34.3	29.8
12. Nagybánya / Baia Mare R	25.6	25.9
13. Komárom / Komárno S	20.0	23.7
14. Pozsony / Bratislava S	18.7	20.3
15. Kézdivásárhely / Târgu Secuiesc R	13.9	19.4
16. Dunaszerdahely / Dunajská Streda S	15.1	19.3
17. Gyergyószentmiklós / Gheorgheni R	15.7	18.9
18. Zenta / Senta Y	18.7	17.9
19. Újvidék / Novi Sad Y	19.2	15.8
20. Beregszász / Berehove U	15.7	15.1
21. Nagybecskerek / Zrenjanin Y	16.8	14.3
22. Nagykároly /Carei R	10.4	13.8
23. Zilah / Zalău R	9.7	13.6
24. Óbecse / Bečej Y	14.7	13.5
25. Érsekújvár / Nové Zámky S	9.4	13.3
26. Nagyszalonta / Salonta R	13.6	12.6
27. Bácstopolya / Bačka Topola Y	12.6	11.2
28. Szászrégen / Reghin R	10.9	11.1
29. Kassa / Košice S	8.0	10.8
30. Magyarkanizsa / Kanjiža Y	10.5	10.2
31. Ada / Ada Y	10.3	10.0

Abbreviations: R = Rumania (1977, 1992), S = Slovakia (1980, 1991), Y = Yugoslavia / Serbia (1981, 1991), U = Ukraine (1979, 1989)

Of the 344 towns of the Carpathian Basin located beyond the Hungarian border only 24 showed a modest increase in ethnic Hungarian population during the 1980's. Most of them are small or medium-sized towns (14 in Slovakia and 7 in Transylvania), with a Hungarian-populated hinterland, from where a gradual emigration of the population of nations forming states and a simultaneous immigration of Hungarians modified the ethnic relations favourably for Hungarians[7]. Hungarians give preference to villages

---

[7] The proportion of ethnic Hungarians showed an increase in the following towns. In Slovakia (1980-1991): Dunaszerdahely, Nagymegyer, Diószeg, Galánta, Vágsellye, Komárom, Ógyalla, Érsekújvár, Párkány, Ipolyság, Szepsi, Királyhelmec, Nagykapos, Tiszacsernyő; in Transylvania (1977-1992): Székelyudvarhely, Szentegyházas, Gyergyószentmiklós, Tusnádfürdő, Barót, Érmihályfalva, Nagykároly, Segesvár, Erzsébetváros (The two former due to the rapid

in the Transmura Region (86.1 %), Croatia (64.2 %), Transcarpathia (62.3 %) and Slovakia (60.5%) offering relatively lower living standards, (and for this reason neglected by other ethnic groups and favourable for preserving the original ethnic structure - compared to towns).

Besides emigration and immigration due to sudden changes in the political scene (e.g. in Croatia or Austria), the present demographic structure and situation has been determined by other statistics (birthrate, mortality rate, natural increase and decrease). Demographic parameters of Hungarians living beyond the borders - since it ceded its territories - are basically associated with socio-economic factors, and conditions created by the population policy of the given state. At the same time, changing patterns of natural reproduction of certain groups, rooted in history, still survive. Though there are no detailed ethnic demographic statistics for all the eight countries over the past several decades, and to compile such statistics seems to be unfeasible, partial data show that the decline in the birth rate and a growing mortality rate - or at least its stabilisation - has been a general trend for all the ethnic groups of the Carpathian region. Regretfully, the above demographic parameters show the most unfavourable statistics for ethnic Hungarians. As a result, at the beginning of the 1990's, birth rates for the Hungarian minorities exceeded mortality rates only in southern Slovakia and Transcarpathia, securing a natural increase for their communities for a couple of years, which is today a rarity in areas inhabited by Hungarians.

Based on the statistics of Hungarians in Slovakia, Transcarpathia, Transylvania and Vojvodina, the average birth rate of Hungarian minorities in the Carpathian Basin in 1991/92 is even lower (10.2 %) than that of Hungary (12.2 %). Hungarians in Transcarpathia stand out with a birthrate of 15.4 %, surpassing the average of all neighbouring countries. Hungarians in Slovakia show a rate close to that of Hungary (15.4 %), but for those in Transylvania and Vojvodina the birthrate has dropped drastically, down to 9 % and 9.9 %, resp.). The mortality rate of Hungarian minorities (14.3 %) is close to that of Hungary (14.1 %) which is very high in comparison with the average of neighbouring countries, and less favourable than for the total population of Slovakia (10.1%), Transcarpathia (9.4 %) and Transylvania (12 %). Death rates were relatively lower for the Slovakian and Transcarpathian Hungarians (11.1 % and 10.9 %, resp.) with relatively younger populations and it was more severe for those of Vojvodina (19,3 %), abandoned by younger elements of the Hungarian population and now in a disastrous demographic position.

Thus, a natural decrease in numbers of Hungarians beyond the borders (-4.1 %) exceeds that within the boundaries of Hungary (-1.9 %). The accelerating natural shrinkage of the population is primarily due to the trends affecting Hungarians in Transylvania (-5.8 %) and Vojvodina (-9.4 %) and can not be counterbalanced even by Transcarpathian (+4.5 %) and Slovakian (+1.5 %) Hungarians who retain their former dynamism of population. One of the most serious problems for Hungarians in the Carpathian Basin is an alarming natural decrease in population (-5.8 % in 1992) as a result of a drastic fall

---

outmigration of Germans.); in Burgenland (1981-1991): Felsőőr (As a result of the dissimilation of part of the formerly Germanised Hungarians and of an immigration from Hungary.).

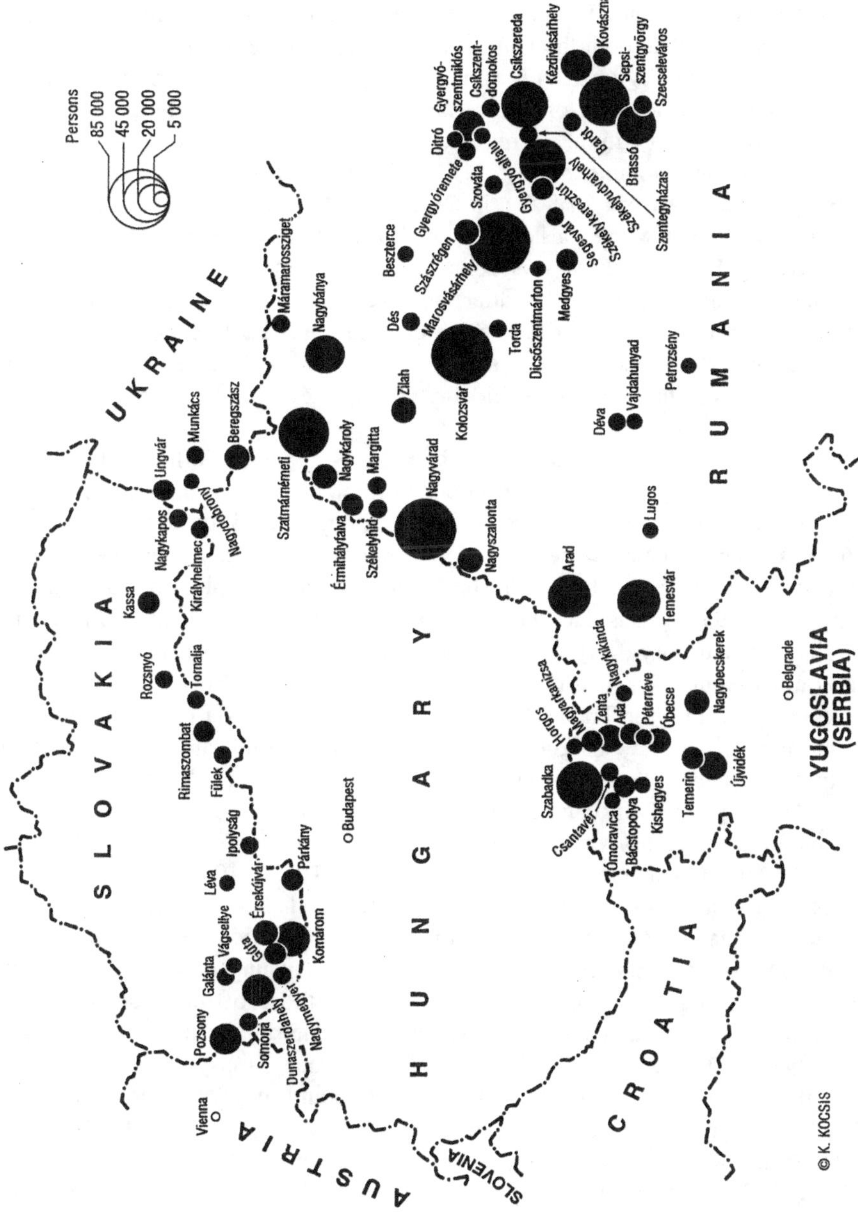

Figure 6. The largest Hungarian communities beyond the borders of Hungary (around 1990)

31

in births and a similar growth in mortality. (In the 1980's natural change was similar to the Slovakian and Transcarpathian-Hungarian trends, approx. +4 %). It should be mentioned however that the Hungarian population of Transylvania is far from uniform as far as demography is concerned. Hungarians of the Székely Region have more positive demographic statistics than both the Hungarians and the whole of Transylvania (natural increase for the Székely Region +3.4 %, for Transylvania +2.7 % in 1990). To compare the above demographic features of Hungarians with other ethnic groups it should be mentioned that by 1992 a natural decrease was typical not only among the Hungarian minorities (-4.1 %) and in Hungary (-1.9 %), but in the Vojvodina province of Serbia (-1.8 %), Burgenland in Austria (-1.8 %), in Croatia (-1.1 %) and Transylvania (-0.7 %), and a natural increase in Slovenia had dropped to 0.3 %. At the same time, from the regions bordering Hungary there was considerable natural growth in Transcarpathia (+6.6 %) and Slovakia (+4%). In the latter, however, national and Hungarian averages disguise significant regional disparities which emerged in the 19th century. A traditionally low level of fertility and a severe ageing of population have led to a dominating trend of natural loss in the vicinity of Párkány, Zseliz, Léva, Ipolyság, Nagykürtös and Losonc.

Demographic structure according to gender is generally influenced by several factors. As a rule the ageing of a given population, emigration from a region and war casualties diminish the proportion of males, while a higher fertility rate increases it. In the former case this can be attributed to a higher mortality of men, a greater share in the migration process and in war losses, in the latter case, to a surplus of males at birth. According to the 1990 census data the male/female ratio was similar for the Hungarian minorities and for Hungary (93.1 and 92.5 males resp. per 100 females). Apart from the data for Transcarpathia (85.7) still affected by the consequences of World War II, this figure is lower than that for Transylvania (97.1) and for Slovakia (95.3). Of the Hungarian minorities living in the neighbourhood, gender proportions are the most balanced in Slovakia (93.5) and in Transylvania (93.4), while in the case of Hungarian minorities in Croatia (83.4) and the Transmura Region (87.3), particularly affected by the war, they are most distórted. In Transylvania there was a curiosity in Hargita County, where high fertility resulted in a positive male/female ratio in 1992 (100,1 / 100.0).

The age distribution of Hungarian minorities, the degree of their ageing - due to both the alarming natural and other demographic and assimilation trends (e.g. low natural reproduction and fertility, accelerating emigration of young people, loss of ethnic self-awareness and lingual assimilation) - is similar to those of the population of the Transmura Region, Vojvodina and Hungary. The proportion of children (up to 14 years old) was between 19.1 - 20.5 % for Hungarians in Hungary, Transylvania and Slovakia, exceeding the ratio of children in Burgenland, Croatia and the Transmura Region with extremely low fertility rates (9.5 %, 11.1 % and 12.1 % resp.). The percentage of elderly people (60 years and over) showed the opposite: Hungarian minorities, and those elderly people living in Hungary were 19.7% and 18.9% respectively. They were surpassed by the ratio of elderly Hungarians in Burgenland, Croatia, the Transmura Region and Vojvodina (44. 7 %, 29.8 %, 26.3 %, 24.1 %, resp.). From the above it follows that a frequently -used demographic parameter, the index of ageing (elderly/100 children) shows balanced average values for the Hungarian minorities as a whole (103.1), the Transmura Region (99.9), Vojvodina (95.1) and Hungary (92.2). The populations of Transcarpathia and Slovakia are quite young (47.9 and 59.6, resp.), while Burgenland's is rather old (496.6!). Comparing the aggregated index of ageing for Hungarians in the Carpathian Basin (94.4), with that of Yugoslavia (68.7), Rumania (72.2), Slovenia (79) and Ukraine (83.3) the latter indicate a much more favourable age distribution.

As a consequence of four decades of socialism with its anticlerical and anti-religious policies, the minorities' attitude to religion, the Church and religious identity, especially attitudes of the younger generations who grew up under a totally new political system, underwent a profound change. Hungarians beyond the borders, being minorities, adhered to the Church and religion as symbols of ethnic identity, and were less affected by secularisation than the state forming ethnic groups of the Carpathian Basin. This is proven by the fact that the proportion of those declaring themselves to be atheists (non-religious) or not responding to the question in the censuses of around 1990, only reached 5.2 % for the Hungarian minorities, while the same value was much higher for Slovakia, Slovenia, Hungary and Austria (27.2 %, 23.5 %, 14.9 %, 12.1 % resp.). Nevertheless, these people without any religious affiliation (an average of 5.2 %) showed considerable disparity with regard to the "index of secularisation", from Transylvanian Hungarians (0.3 %) struggling for survival in an Eastern Orthodox Rumanian environment, to Slo-vakian Hungarians (19.5 %) with a similar religious structure to state forming nation (Slovaks).

The distribution by denomination of Hungarians declaring themselves religious during the last census has been modified by objective and subjective circumstances influencing over the past half of a century ethnic relations (natural change and mobility, socio-political conditions, processes of assimilation, etc.). Presently the religious com-position of Hungarians in the Carpathian Basin shows the following pattern: 57.6 % (7.4 million) Roman Catholics, 22.8 % (2.9 million) Reformed (Calvinists), 3.6 % (470 thou-sand) Lutherans, 2.2 % (290 thousand) Greek Catholics and approx. 13 % (1.7 million) without or with unknown religious affiliation. Compared with the above average values, there are relatively more Roman Catholics and Lutherans among the Hungarians of Hungary, while beyond the borders Calvinists and Unitarians have a higher ratio[8]. At the beginning of the 1990's religious denominations of Hungarian minorities were as fol-lows: 51.8 % Roman Catholics, 34.2 % Calvinists, 2.7 % Unitarians and 2.1 % Greek Catholics. Roman Catholics prevail (65 % to 88 %) among the Hungarians of Vo-jvodina, the Transmura Region, Burgenland, Croatia and Slovakia. A relative majority of Transylvanian and Transcarpathian Hungarians (47.4 % and 46.9 %, resp.) belong to the Calvinist Church. Communities with a Calvinist majority are to be found in southern Slovakia in the environs of towns like Nagymegyer, Komárom and Zseliz; in the Gömör region they are strongly mixed with Roman Catholics, while they constitute a minor

---

[8] Distribution of the population of Hungary by denomination in 1989: 57.8 % Roman Catholics, 2.2 % Greek Catholics, 19.3 % Reformed, 4.1 % Lutherans, 13.1 non-religious, atheists, with no religious affiliation, etc. (Gesztelyi, T. /ed./ 1991, Egyházak és vallások a mai Magyarországon (Churches and Denominations in Hungary), Akadémiai Kiadó, Budapest, 20. p.)

denomination in the Gömör-Torna (Slovakian) Karst Region. Within the other groups of Hungarians along the border, from Nagykapos in Slovakia through to Beregszász in Transcarpathia, and from Szatmárnémeti, and Érmihályfalva up to Nagyszalonta in Rumania, the Calvinist Church is prominent among local Hungarians (in spite of a high number of Roman Catholics living in the valley of the Ung River, and in Szatm r County and of Greek Catholics in the Bereg and Ugocsa regions). Even more Calvinists live among the Hungarians of Szilágyság, Kalotaszeg, Mezőség and in the southwestern part of the Székely Region. In the latter, most religious Hungarians belong to the Calvinist and Unitarian churches along the western and southern margins of Udvarhelyszék. The main bases of the Roman Catholics in Transylvania are in the northern third of the Udvarhelyszék, Gyergyó, Csík, Kászon and Kézdi regions, and there are scattered communities in Bánát, in the environs of Arad. Among the Hungarians of Serbia, Croatia and Slovenia the population is overwhelmingly Roman Catholic. The Calvinist Church has a majority in only 3 - 4 villages[9].

In spite of the scanty and scarce data available, investigations into the structure of Hungarian families living outside the borders shed light on fertility, natural changes and assimilation phenomena which make it possible to make forecasts for the future. The proportion of incomplete families owing to mortality and divorce is slightly lower in Hungarian families in Transylvania and Slovakia (12.7 % and 13 % resp.) than in those of Hungary (15.5 %). A higher extent of ageing, a lower fertility rate,and the later age of having children has meant the ratio of families without dependent children among the Hungarian minority is higher compared with the national average of not only the neighbouring countries, but of Hungary with its notorious demographic trends: Hungarians in Slovakia (43.6 %), Transylvania (35.6 %), Vojvodina (42.3 %); Slovakia as a whole (39.6 %), Transylvania (32.3 %), Hungary (34.3 %). An overwhelming number of Hungarians in an environment occupied by a majority of the same religious affiliation, similar cultural background and mentality already live in ethnic mixed families. The proportion of these people (married to a person of a different ethnicity and with a different mother tongue) has reached 30.3 % in Slovakia and 42 % in Burgenland. Here, owing to a change to another language of their children, and a loss of their national awareness, there may follow a demographic erosion of the affected ethnic community and put under question its very survival.

The social stratification of Hungarian minorities related to their economic activity (work, occupation) shows a correlation with several other factors (e.g. distribution of population by gender, age, educational level - qualifications, skills - physical and social environment of settlements, historical background, and traditions). Nearly half (44 - 49 %) of all women are active earners due to a steady ageing of the population, a growing proportion of those of productive age and an increased proportion of working

---

[9] The mentioned villages are the following. In Vojvodina (Serbia): Bácsfeketehegy, Bácskossuthfalva (Ómoravica), Pacsér, in Baranya (Croatia): Kopács, Laskó, Várdaróc, in East Slavonia: Haraszti and in Transmura Region (Slovenia): Szécsiszentlászló, Kisszerdahely, Csekefa. In Croatia the East Slavonian Kórógy and Szentlászló used to be communities with Calvinist Hungarian majority until the flight of their population during the Serbo-Croatian War in 1991.

women, formerly working in the home. However, as a result of an alarming decline in natural reproduction, ageing and emigration, a decrease in the number of people of active age in the present grave economic circumstances might involve a drop in the employment level of women and an increased number of forced retirements to avoid unemployment. As a consequence, a rise in the proportion of the non-working population may occur at the expense of Hungarian active earners, putting an increasing burden on them in the near future.

The geographic environment and economic background of Hungarians living beyond the borders are to some extent reflected in their occupations and economic groups. Social grouping is following international trends (albeit delayed), and has led from the primary sector (e.g. agriculture) to secondary sectors (e.g. mining, construction, manufacturing), and from secondary sectors to tertiary ones (e.g. commerce, transport and telecommunications, culture and other non-productive activities). Together with the natural environment, the character of the settlement and the economic and regional development policy of the given state, agriculture still plays a relatively significant role in Hungarian communities. The contribution of this sector is especially high in the case of Hungarian minorities in those regions where 60 - 86% of the population live in rural settlements: in Croatia (41.8 %), the Transmura Region (32.1 %), South Slovakia (23.8 %) and Vojvodina (26.7 %), the latter being considered the bread box of Yugoslavia. The average number of people actively engaged in agriculture in the Carpathian Basin varies between 14 and 26 %; with a figure for the Hungarians of Transylvania (16.2 %) showing the maximum. This has resulted in a particularly high involvement of active earners in the secondary (i.e. industrial) sectors (52.7 %) well above the Rumanian average (44.7 %). This can be attributed partly to the hastened industrialisation of Transylvania during the past decades, and partly to the geographical environment of the area of Hungarian settlement. Due mainly to the Székely Region, the Hungarian share in certain branches of light industry (timber processing, furniture making, leather and textile industries) and construction is well above average. The building industry has traditionally been important among Hungarian workers living in peripheral regions, with a scarcity of non-agricultural employment and a high ratio of commuting workers (e.g. South Slovakia, Transcarpathia). The proportion in the tertiary sector - used recently for measuring the level of economic development - remains below national average figures (32 - 59 %) and those of Hungary (46.5 %) for Hungarian minorities everywhere. In certain categories of employment requiring a high level of skill and qualifications, those belonging to the spheres of education, culture, science and administration, the proportion of Hungarians is below average. For example, in Slovakia where the figure for Slovakians is 1.5% in science and education, it is only 0.5% for Hungarians; in Rumania, where the Rumanian average is 2.4%, it is 1.5%.

The level of education and qualifications of Hungarian minorities has developed closely alongside the above trends. Hungarians beyond the state borders are seriously handicapped compared with the majority nations as far as education and qualifications are concerned, which basically influences their marketability and job opportunities. The "knowledge industry" (system of education) which produces human capital and resources is being upgraded all over the world, and this causes a grave situation for the

Hungarian minorities in the Carpathian Basin who have not been provided with a modern education system. In certain neighbouring countries there have been (open or disguised) moves to eliminate education in Hungarian, so in some communities the ratio of persons with higher qualifications within the population of over 24 years only reaches a maximum half of the national average: this figure is 4.7 % for Hungarians in both Slovakia and Transylvania, 5.9 % for those of Vojvodina, 10.1 % for Hungary, 9.8 % in Slovakia, 6.9 % in Rumania, and 10.8 % in Yugoslavia. These unfavourable statistics for Hungarian minorities are due to various factors. In the case of Hungarians in Slovakia historical circumstances are responsible (removal and deportation of the Hungarian intelligentsia between 1945 and 1949, a complete elimination of the school system after 1945 and a postponement of Hungarian education till the 1950's etc.) In the case of minorities in Transcarpathia, Transylvania and Vojvodina alarmingly large-scale emigration of Hungarian "human resources" has taken place over the past ten years. A mediating factor in the generally frustrating picture of the educational level is that Hungarian minorities are underrepresented in the lower sections of the "educational pyramid". The rate of illiteracy among Hungarians in Transylvania and Vojvodina (1 % and 2.4 % resp.)[10] is well below that the of Rumanians and Serbs (3 % and 4.9 %) in the same regions.

The fact that regions with a majority Hungarian population are found not further than 60 - 70 km from the borders, can be regarded in more ways than one. For the Hungarian minority this is favourable, since ethnic identity and the purity of the mother tongue can be best preserved in close proximity to Hungary through permanent — and most of the time exclusive — relations (personal, mass communication, etc.).

The advantage to the Hungarian minority, as compared to the Ruthenians, Rumanians or Slovaks who live in the same areas together with them, manifested itself during the last few years in the development of a market economy along the borders, especially in Transcarpathia, Transylvania and Slovakia. This results from their permanent relations with the mother country, and their being bilingual. Through their strong political organisations and parties, Hungarians play an important role in the political life of Slovakia, Transcarpathia, Rumania (Transylvania), and Serbia.

In the case of Slovakia, Rumania, and Serbia (Yugoslavia) the existence of frontier zones with a majority Hungarian population can be judged in two ways. From the point of view of the (Slovakian, Rumanian, Serbian) nationalist forces, which are aspiring to create a homogeneous national state, these areas are incredibly dangerous and unstable. They regard them as the "fifth column" of Hungarian irredentism and revanchism, and thus as areas inhabited by the inner enemy. The ethnical loosening up and the homogenisation of these geopolitically dangerous areas is a most urgent mission. According to the other view — as yet not very widespread — these areas will not be the scenes of redrawing the borders or of nationalistic fights in the near future. On the contrary, following the examples of Western Europe, they will be — must be — a means of international integration (based on their bilingual population), and encourage ever-closer

---

[10] Rate of illiteracy is referred to people over 12 years for Hungarians of Transylvania and over 15 years for those of Vojvodina.

co-operation between the different national economies. Such tendencies have been observed lately in Slovenia, with its minorities living in Austria and Italy, and even in the Ukraine, along the border with Hungary.

In our opinion, the over 3 million European Hungarians who live outside the territory of the Republic of Hungary and are bilingual and bicultural, will play an important role as mediators in political and economic co-operation among the nations in the Carpatho-Pannonian area. Hopefully, this will happen in the not too distant future.

Chapter 2

THE HUNGARIANS OF SLOVAKIA

In the Slovak Republic's most recent census (March 3rd, 1991) 567,296 people declared themselves to be ethnically Hungarian, while 608,221 said they were Hungarian native speakers. Similar to census data of Hungary and other countries, the above-mentioned figure differs from the estimated size of the given ethnic group, or in this case, the number of people claiming and cultivating Hungarian national traditions and culture. In Slovakia, according to ethno-historical, demographic and migration statistics, but not including linguistic assimilation, the estimated number of Hungarian native speakers could well have been 653,000 in 1991in our opinion. This figure corresponds to the population of the Hungarian counties of Győr-Moson-Sopron and Komárom. According to the latest census data, the Hungarian national minority represents 10.7% of Slovakia's population, 4.4% of the total number of Hungarians in the Carpathian basin and 22.3% of Hungarians in the Carpathian Basin living beyond Hungary's borders.

THE NATURAL ENVIRONMENT

The majority of the Hungarian national minority of Slovakia live on the plains (62%). Their settlements can be found along the Danubian (55%) and East-Slovakian (7%) lowlands. With the exception of the alluvial soil alongside larger rivers, the Hungarian-inhabited plains which are almost exclusively used for agriculture are characterised by meadow soil (southern part of Csallóköz[1], along the river Dudvág and in Bodrogköz[2]), and chernozem (northern part of Csallóköz, the regions between Vág-Nyitra and Zsitva-Garam). From the viewpoint of the Carpathian Basin, the Danubian Lowland can be considered as a part of the Little Hungarian Plain (Kisalföld). Its most important rivers are the Danube, Little-Danube and Vág, their floodplains are bordered by groves. The Nyitra, Zsitva and Dudvág considered as tributaries of the Vág, are also worth mentioning. Csallóköz and the territory between the Little Danube and Vág are excellent for agricultural production and play a significant role in the republic's food-supply. *(Fig. 7.)*

---

[1]Csallóköz (Slovak: Žitný ostrov, German: Große Schütt-Insel). Region almost exclusively by Hungarians inhabited in Southwest Slovakia between the Danube (Hungarian: Duna, Slovak: Dunaj) and Little Danube (Hungarian: Kis-Duna, Slovak: Malý Dunaj) rivers.

[2]Bodrogköz (Slovak: Medzibodrožie). Region almost exclusively by Hungarians inhabited in Northeast Hungary and Southeast Slovakia between the Tisza, Bodrog and Latorca rivers.

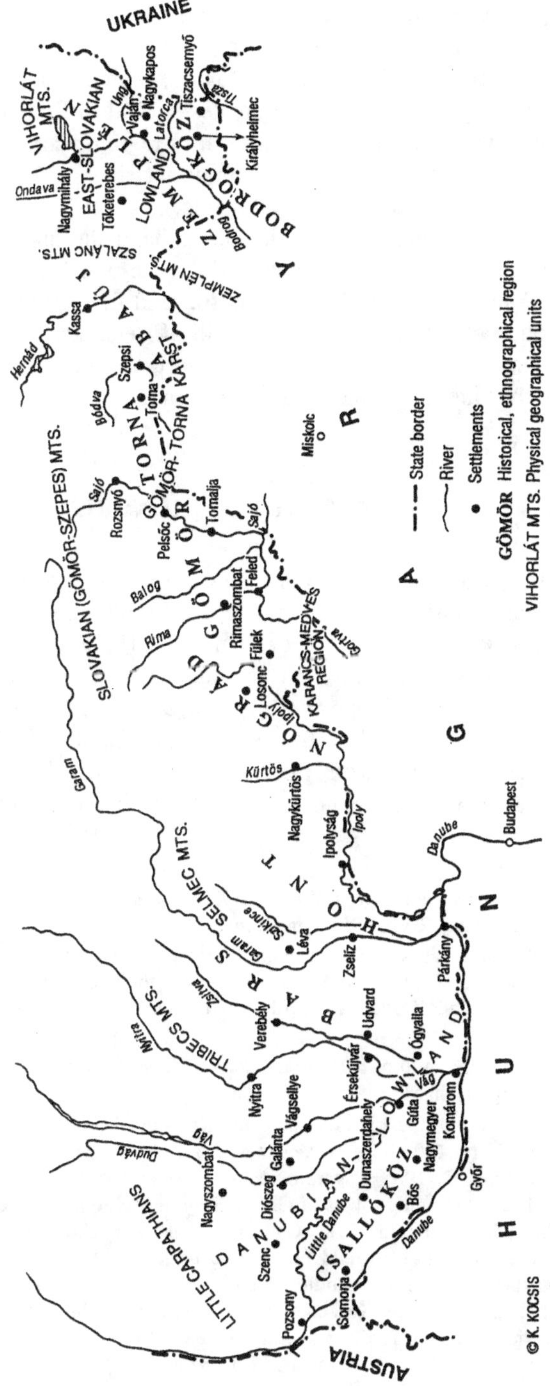

Figure 7. Important Hungarian geographical names in South Slovakia

One third of Hungarians inhabit the hills (along the Garam and Ipoly Rivers) and the Ipoly, Losonc, Rima and Kassa basins. In adapting to the hilly environment, the majority of settlements in these regions (Bars, Hont, Nógrád, Gömör and Abaúj) remained in the "small and tiny village" category. This creates special difficulties in supplying communities with fundamental institutions. These hilly regions, covered mostly by brown earth and brown forest soil, contain a few important rivers (Garam, Ipoly, Sajó, Hernád) and streams (Szikince, Kürtös, Rima, Balog, etc.).

Only one of out of twenty Hungarians in Slovakia inhabit the highlands. The majority of them live among the rendzina soil covered dolomite and limestone cliffs such as Gömör-Torna (Slovakian) Karst, the Rozsnyó basin, and the Karancs-Medves Region with basalt cones (Somoskő Mt., Ragács Mt., the hill of Béna etc.) in the southern corners of Nógrád and Gömör in Slovakia. The most important water sources of the above-mentioned regions are the Gortva, Torna and Bódva streams.

ETHNIC PROCESSES DURING THE PAST FIVE HUNDRED YEARS

By the end of the Middle Age, at the time of the taxation census of 1495, in the territory of the Upper Hungarian counties[3] there were at least 413,500 people[4], probably 45 % were Slavs[5] (Slovaks and Ruthenians) 38 % of them were Hungarians and 17 % Germans *(Tab. 7.)*. Of the counties investigated an absolute majority was formed by Germans in the counties of Pozsony and Szepes and by Hungarians in Gömör, Abaúj, Torna and Zemplén. All of the ten most populous towns which had 1,500 – 4,500 people (Pozsony, Kassa, Nagyszombat, Eperjes, Bártfa, Besztercebánya, Selmecbánya, Lőcse, Késmárk és Körmöcbánya)[6] had a German majority, but the Hun garian and Slovak

---

[3] Upper Hungary included the counties of Pozsony, Nyitra, Bars, Hont, Trencsén, Turóc, Árva, Liptó, Zólyom, Gömör, Szepes, Abaúj, Torna, Sáros and Zemplén.

[4] Source of national and county data on population at the time of the 1495 census: Kubinyi A. 1996 A Magyar Királyság népessége a 15. század végén (Population of the Kingdom of Hungary at the end of 15th century), Történelmi Szemle XXXVIII. 2-3.pp.135-161. Data on ethnic composition are estimations by the author.

[5] According to our estimates the ratio of Hungarians and of Slovaks could be around 38 % each in the area of the counties of Upper Hungary.

[6] Population numbers at the turn of the 15th and 16th centuries: 4,000-5,000: Pozsony, Kassa, about 3,500: Nagyszombat, Eperjes, Bártfa, 3,000: Besztercebánya, 2,500: Selmecbánya, 2,000: Lőcse, 1,500: Körmöcbánya. Sources: Paulinyi, O. 1958 A garamvidéki bányavárosok lakosságának lélekszáma a XVI.sz. derekán (Population of the minig towns of Garam Region (Pohronie) in the middle of 16th century), Történelmi Szemle 1958. 3-4.pp.351-378., Gácsová, A. 1974 Niektoré aspekty počtu majetnosti obyvateľov vychodoslovnských miest v stredoveku (Some aspects of the number of possessions of inhabitants of East Slovakian towns in the Middle Ages) — in: Spišské mestá v stredoveku, VV, Košice, Iványi, B. 1941 ibid., Fügedi, E. 1956 Kaschau, eine osteuropäische Handelstadt am Ende des 15. Jahrhunderts, Studia Slavica II.1-4.pp.185-213., Granasztói Gy.1980 A középkori magyar város (The medieval Hungarian town), Gondolat, Budapest, 157.p., Szabó, I. 1941 A magyarság életrajza (Biography of the Hungarians), Magyar Történelmi Társulat, Budapest,

Table 7. Ethnic structure of the population of Upper Hungary (1495 - 1919)

Year	Total population		Hungarians		Slovaks		Ruthenians		Germans		Jews		Others	
	number	%	number	%	number	%	number	%	number	%	number	%	number	%
1495	413,500	100	157,000	38.0	186,000	45.0	←	←	70,500	17.0				
1720		100		22.9		67.6		←		9.5				
1787	1,974,483	100									34,086	1.73		
1840	2,454,223	100	539,083	22.0	1,459,870	59.5	203,312	8.3	163,329	6.7	88,375	3.5	254	0.0
1850	2,262,663	100	462,561	20.4	1,401,066	61.9	113,132	5.0	160,254	7.1	116,490	5.1	9,160	0.5
1857	2,286,641	100	672,126	29.4	1,346,802	58.9	141,603	6.2	126,110	5.5				
1869	2,471,739	100	598,180	24.2	1,474,936	59.7	183,498	7.4	215,017	8.7			108	
1880	2,458,273	100	602,525	24.5	1,512,991	61.5	80,342	3.3	241,381	9.8			21,034	0.9
1890	2,571,896	100	673,812	26.2	1,555,177	60.5	83,906	3.3	232,220	9.0			26,781	1.0
1900	2,777,663	100	801,897	28.9	1,642,252	59.1	83,828	3.0	216,539	7.8			33,147	1.2
1910	2,904,657	100	937,768	32.3	1,613,891	55.6	90,643	3.1	198,877	6.8			63,478	2.2
1919-20	2,917,204	100	758,422	26.0	1,859,173	63.7	86,105	3.0	148,954	5.1			64,550	2.2

Sources: **1495**: Estimation of Kocsis K. based on Fig.9. and Kubinyi A. 1996 A Magyar Királyság népessége a 15. század végén — Történelmi Szemle XXXVIII. 1996. 2-3. pp.135-161., **1720**: Acsády I. 1896 Magyarország népessége a Pragmatica Sanctio korában 1720 - 21. — Magyar Statisztikai Közlemények XII. /Új folyam/, Budapest **1787**: Danyi D. - Dávid Z. 1960 Az első magyarországi népszámlálás (1784-1787), KSH, Budapest **1840**: Fényes E. 1842 Magyarország statistikája I., Pest **1850**: Hornyánsky, V. 1858 Geographisches Lexikon des Königreiches Ungarn, G. Heckenast, Pest **1857**: Fényes Elek 1867 A Magyar Birodalom nemzetiségei és ezek száma vármegyék és járások szerint, Pest **1869**: Keleti K. 1871 Hazánk és népe a közgazdaság és a társadalmi statistika szempontjából, Athenaeum, Pest **1880**: A Magyar Korona országaiban az 1881. év elején végrehajtott népszámlálás ...Országos Magyar Királyi Statisztikai Hivatal, Budapest 1882 **1890**: Jekelfalussy József (szerk.) 1892 A Magyar Korona országainak helységnévtára, Országos M. Kir. Statisztikai Hivatal, Budapest, **1900**: A Magyar Korona országainak 1900. évi népszámlálása 1. rész. 1902. A népesség általános leírása községenkint, Magyar Statisztikai Közlemények I., **1910**: A Magyar Szent Korona országainak 1910. évi népszámlálása 1. rész. 1912 Magyar Statisztikai Közlemények 42. **1919-20**: Soznam miest na Slovensku podľa popisu ľudu z roku 1919., Ministerstvo s plnou mocou pre spravu Slovenska, Bratislava, 1920, Az 1920.évi népszámlálás I. A népesség főbb demográfiai adatai .. 1923, Magyar Kir. Központi Statisztikai Hivatal, Budapest
Remarks: Upper Hungary = Territory of Pozsony, Nyitra, Bars, Hont, Trencsén, Turóc, Árva, Liptó, Zólyom, Gömör-Kis-Hont, Szepes, Abaúj-Torna, Sáros, Zemplén Counties (1914). Slovaks include Ruthenians in 1495 and in 1720.

minorities were numerous. Apart from the above-mentioned towns the German ethnic region extended to the area situated between the German towns of Somorja–Szenc–Nagyszombat and the Little Carpathians and to the northern and southern foreland of Pozsony *(Fig. 8.).* The German (Saxon) ethnic area also included most of Szepes County, but they had been increasingly losing ground to both the Goral-Polish ethnic group and Ruthenians in the northern areas (Szepesi Magura, Dunajec), and to Slovaks in the Hernád Valley and in a strip along the Poprád-Lőcse-Szepesvár main road. Beside the Szepes and Pozsony German ethnic blocks there were a number of ethnic pockets of Germans in the counties of Sáros (Eperjes, Bártfa, Kisszeben), Abaúj (Kassa, Abaújszina, Szepsi), North Gömör (Rozsnyó, Dobsina, Csetnek, Alsósajó) and in present-day Central Slovakia (Besztercebánya, Zólyom, Korpona, Selmecbánya, Újbánya, Körmöcbánya, Nyitrapróna and their surroundings).

In this period the northern "boundary" of the Hungarian ethnic area (more precisely a Hungarian-Slovak, or in some places a Hungarian-German contact zone) had stabilised along the line stretching between Somorja-Nagyszombat-Galgóc-Nyitra-Léva-Losonc-Rimaszombat-Rozsnyó-Jászó-Kassa-Gálszécs-Nagymihály. It could by no means be considered a rigid ethnic bundary, for sizeable Hungarian and Slovak minorities lived north and south of this line, especially in the central areas of Nyitra, Hont, and Zemplén[7] counties. Similar to the Slovaks, most of the Hungarians of Upper Hungary were rural dwellers at the end of the 15th century. They formed significant urban blocks only due to their penetration of towns founded by Germans (e.g. Eperjes, Kassa, Korpona, Bélabánya, Nyitra, Galgóc, Nagyszombat, Pozsony). Within the area of Hungarian settlement – besides the above-mentioned market towns – only the Hungarians in Komárom had a sizeable population.

At that time the Slovak ethnic area extended mainly to the inter-mountain basins, river valleys and the southern foreland of the Western Carpathians. The mountain regions of Árva and North Trencsén, the High and Low Tatras and Gömör-Szepes (today Slovak) Ore Mountains were uninhabited dense woodland. Along the northeastern borderland, on the northern periphery of Zemplén and Sáros counties and in the marginal areas of Szepes and Gömör a gradually expanding ethnic area of Ruthenians pursuing a pastoral way of life was being established.

The victory of the Ottoman Turks at Mohács (1526) not only signalled the fall of the Hungarian Kingdom considered at that time to be a middle-sized European power, but initiated a profound transformation in the ethnic patterns in the southern and central areas of the country. Military operations and destruction had soon reached territories now belonging to Slovakia (1529, 1543)[8]. Even prior to this, a massive flight of Hunga-

---

[7] Bakács, I. 1971 I. 1971 Hont vármegye Mohács előtt (Hont County before 1526), Akadémiai Kiadó, Budapest,33.p., Kniezsa I. 1941 Adalékok a magyar-szlovák nyelvhatár történetéhez (Contributions to the history of the Hungarian-Slovak ethnic boundary), Budapest, pp.18-24.,51-52.

[8] Mainly after the Ottoman campaign against Vienna in 1529 and after the fall of Esztergom (1543), the centre of the Hungarian Catholic Church.

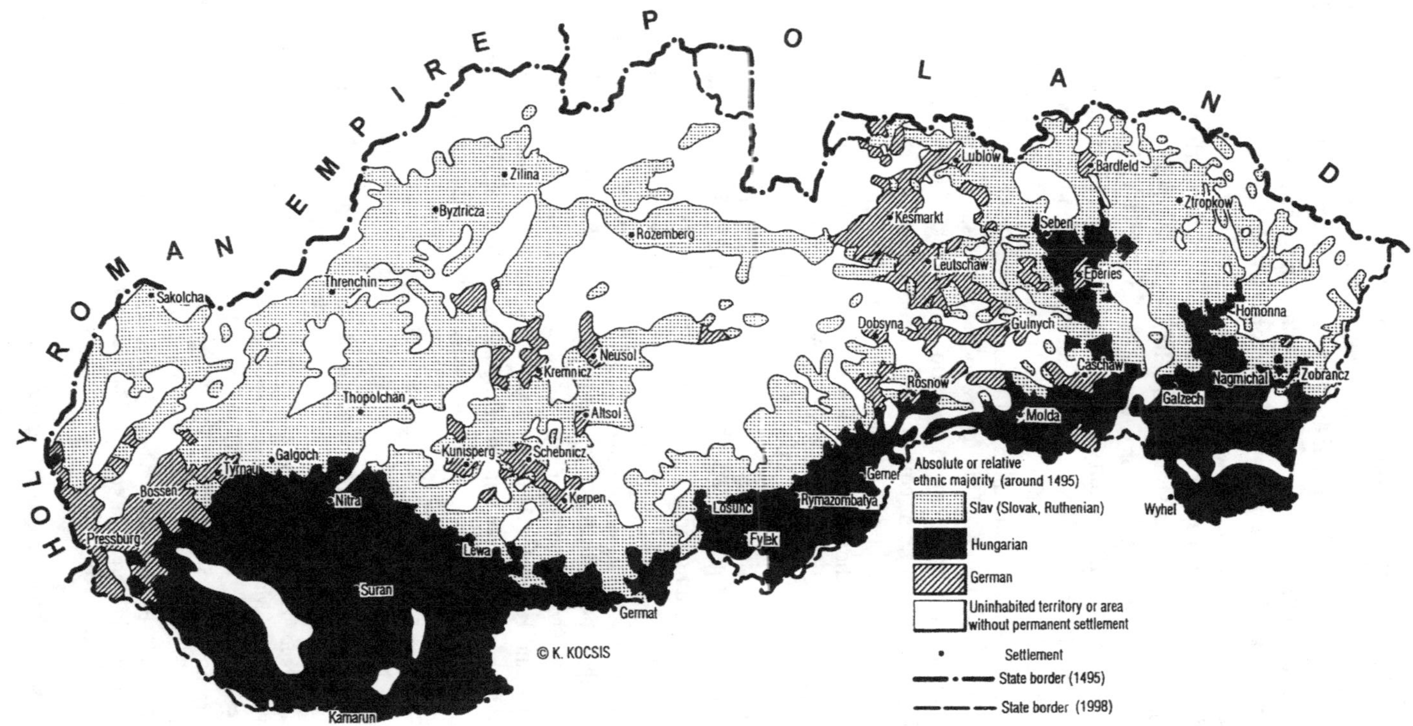

Figure 8. Ethnic map of the present-day territory of Slovakia (late 15th century)

Main sources: Bakács I. 1971 Hont vármegye Mohács előtt, Akadémiai Kiadó, Budapest, Fekete Nagy A. 1934 A Szepesség területi és társadalmi kialakulása, Budapest, Fügedi E. 1938 Nyitra megye betelepülése, Budapest, Ila B. 1976, 1944, 1946, 1968 Gömör megye I-IV., MTA, Budapest, Kniezsa I. 1941 Adalékok a magyar-szlovák nyelvhatár történetéhez, Athenaeum, Budapest, Marsina, R. - Kušík, M. 1959 Urbáre feudálnych panstiev na Slovensku I., Vydavateľstvo SAV, Bratislava, Varsik, B. 1964, 1973, 1977 Osídlenie Košickej kotliny I-III., SAV, Bratislava, Varsik, B. 1984 Nemecká kolonizácia na území bratislavskej stolice v 13.-14. storočí — in: Varsik, B. 1984 Z osídlenia západného Slovenska v stredoveku, Veda, Bratislava, Vlastivedný slovník obcí na Slovensku I-III. Veda, Bratislava, 1977-1978

rians and Croats[9] had started. Refugees from Croatian-Slavonian territories occupied by the Turks inhabited nearly 20 villages, primarily around Pozsony and Nagyszombat[10], from where the German population had perished or escaped between 1529 and 1553, due to the destruction and intimidation of the Ottoman and Habsburg troops. These depopulated German villages became repopulated not only by Croats but by Slovaks (in the vicinity of Nagyszombat, Bazin, Modor) and Hungarians (e.g. in Pozsonyivánka, Cseklész, Éberhard, Szenc and Németgurab). In this period, particularly following the surrender of Esztergom (1543) a massive move of Hungarians started to Nagyszombat, to where the seat of the Hungarian Roman Catholic archbishop was transferred. As a result,until the beginning of the 18th century this town became a settlement with a relative Hungarian majority . Between 1543 and 1575, after the surrender of fortresses and castles which had protected the counties of Komárom, Esztergom, Bars, Hont, Nógrád and Gömör against the Turks[11] large numbers of Hungarians[12] fled the river valleys and hill regions, depopulating these areas. This followed the war losses, the carrying off of some of the population, the heavy burden of taxation, and a lack of both personal security and that of their property. As a consequence, between 1495 and 1598 the population of counties such as Komárom, Hont and Gömör had dropped by one third. The number of existing settlements between the mid-15th century and 1598 in the present-day Slovakian counties of Komárom and Esztergom decreased from 106 to 55, and between 1427 and 1572 in Gömör County the number fell from 340 to 213[13].

Apart from the destruction caused by warfare, in these borderland areas between the Habsburg Empire and the Ottoman Empire a doubling of taxation (imposed on the population by Habsburg-Hungarians and Ottoman-Turks) also contributed to accelerating depopulation and to the large-scale exodus of predominantly Hungarian and to a lesser extent, Slovak serfs. Owing to Hungarians fleeing northwards and a Hungarian majority prevailing within the outskirts of towns in the second half of the 16th century, there was an intensifying "Magyarization" of towns with a German character such as Kassa, Eperjes, Szepsi and Rozsnyó. At the same time, in towns situated far away from the Hungarian ethnic areas the proportion of Hungarians (mainly arriving as refugees) within the local population, which was predominantly Slovak and German, was rela-

---

[9] Refugees from Croatia first appeared in present-day Slovakia in 1529. (Ritig-Beljak, N. 1986 Gradišćanski hrvati Croats of Burgenland - in: Enciklopedije Jugoslavije 4., Zagreb, 485.p.

[10] The villages repopulated by Croats: e.g. Horvátjárfalu, Dunacsún, Oroszvár, Lamacs, Pozsonyhidegkút, Dévényújfalu, Mászt, Zohor, Németbél, Horvátgurab, Nagysenkőc, Kárpáthalas, Felsőhosszúfalu, Nahács, Selpőc.

[11] e.g. Esztergom (1543), Ság, Drégely, Gyarmat, Szécsény (1552), Salgó, Fülek (1554), Ajnácskő (1566), Divény (1575).

[12] Csapodi Cs. 1942 Bars megye Verebélyi járásának nemzetiségi viszonyai az újkorban (Ethnic structure of the District of Verebély -Vráble of Bars County in the New Age), Magyar Történettudományi Intézet, Budapest, Ila B. 1976 Gömör megye (Gömör County) I., Akadémiai Kiadó, Budapest

[13] Žudel, J. 1984 Stolice na Slovensku (Counties in Slovakia), Obzor, Bratislava, 70., 107.p., Ila, B. 1976 ibid. 266.p.

44

tively high e.g.[14] Sztropkó 35.7 %, (1569), Garamszentkereszt 26 % (1573), Bát 36 % (1664), Bakabánya 32 % (1664), Nagytapolcsány 21 % (1664). On the other hand, in Hungarian towns situated within the Hungarian-Slovak ethnic contact zone, which was particularly prone to the destruction caused by military operations, the proportion of Hungarians (or at least taxpayers bearing a Hungarian name) dropped considerably during the 16th and 17th centuries owing to a massive resettlement of Slovaks from the surroundings: Léva 72 % (1554), Losonc 63 % (1596), Rimaszombat 82 % (1596), Tőketerebes 69 % (1601) and Gálszécs 83 % (1601)[15].

In the 16th and 17th centuries i.e. at the time of military campaigns[16] especially affecting southern areas of the present-day Slovakia which were inhabited by Hungarians, high intensity colonisation took place in the more protected mountain regions. Slavs pursuing a pastoral lifestyle settled here who had a Vlach right. The number of these settlements reached 200[17] by the end of the 17th century. This colonisation by Goral-Poles and Slovaks was especially typical in the counties of Árva, Trencsén, Liptó and Szepes[18]. In this colonisation with its Vlach right system Ruthenians only formed a minority in the 17th century while Slovaks retreated to the mostly uninhabited alpine meadows and mountain woodlands which provided security in time of war[19]. Starting in the 16th century the area of Slovak settlement expanded, not only with the colonisation of Vlach shepherds, but also with the formation of many scattered settlements (for example: in Slovak "kopanice, rale, štále, lazy, samoty") in the mountains - called "kopaničiarska kolonizácia" in Slovakian. These were particularly in the Trencsén (e.g. White Carpathians) and Nyitra counties (e.g. Miava Hills) and along the boundary between Zólyom and Nógrád (e.g. in the vicinity of Gyetva)[20]. This latter process resulted in an abundance of scattered mountain settlements colonised by Slovak farmers who had escaped from areas affected by war (mainly by the Turks), who were seeking areas to cultivate. In the western region, a gradual shrinking of the German ethnic area and its Slovakisation was somewhat counterbalanced by the massive settlement of German-

---

[14] Marsina, R. - Kušík, M. 1959 Urbáre feudálnych panstiev na Slovensku (Urbars of the feudal estates in Slovakia) I-II., SAV, Bratislava

[15] After Marsina, R. - Kušík, M. 1959 ibid.

[16] E.g. the 15 and 30 years wars (1593-1606, 1619-1645), a military campaign of the Turks in 1663-64, a struggle led by Prince I. Thököly (a vassal of the Ottoman Empire) against the Habsburgs (1682-1685).

[17] Verešík, J. 1974 Osídlenie Slovenska (Settlement of Slovakia) - in: Slovensko, Ľud - I. Časť, Obzor, Bratislava, 460.p.

[18] A 16-17th century expansion of Gorals was especially typical in the northern margin counties of Trencsén, Árva and Szepes. However, in the 16th century on the estates of the Zápolya and Podmaniczky families (e.g. around Trencsén, Ilava, Kasza, Zsolnalitva, Lednic, Ugróc) most of the Vlachs were considered Slovaks (Ratkoš, P. 1984 Rozvoj valašského ovčiarstva a jeho prírodné podmienky v 14.-17. storočí (Development of Vlach shepherdship and its natural conditions), Nové obzory 26., 142.p.).

[19] Ila B. 1976 ibid. 320.p.

[20] Verešík, J. 1974 ibid. pp. 467-469.

speaking Habans[21] in the mid-16th century in the vicinity of Szakolca in Nyitra County (e.g. Ószombat, Gázlós, Holics, Sasvár, Szentistvánfalva and Kátó). In the course of the counter-reformation (the re-catholisation of the 17th century), most of them were expelled, and the rest gradually underwent Slovakisation.

Between 1495 and 1598 due to the migration of Slovaks, Hungarians and Gorals mentioned above and relatively low war losses, the population increased for the counties of Árva (+200 %), Sáros (+ 127.9 %), Nyitra and Trencsén (both 110 %) [22]. In the period between 1598 and 1640 – chiefly during the 15 and 30 year wars – when the total population of the Upper Hungarian counties dropped from 644 thousand to 608 thousand (-5.6 %), the above-mentioned colonisation by Slavs continued (Vlachs i.e. Slovaks, Ruthenians, Gorals) in the relatively protected environment of the mountains. As a result, the population increased by 27.7 %, to 249 thousand in the counties of Trencsén, Zólyom, Árva, Szepes and Zemplén with their Slavic ethnic majority, which offered a fairly protected environment.

In the second half of the 17th century, after the surrender of the Érsekújvár fortress (1663), most of the Hungarian ethnic area north of the Danube captured by the Turks became a terrain for military operations until 1685. In spite of a massive exodus, and the carrying off and killing of the Hungarian population, by the 1664 Turkish tax census of the Érsekújvár eyalet (province)[23], most people liable to taxation living in the heavily depopulated area between the Danube and the hilly region were Hungarians (roughly up to the Galgóc - Appony - Lédec - Léva - Palást line). The most populous towns with 95-100 % Hungarians were Nagysalló, Verebély, Szőgyén, Sempte and Komját (with 411–127 taxpayers)[24]. Despite wars and epidemics, the Hungarian ethnic block maintained its previously solid extension of the 15th and 16th centuries in the eastern part of Upper Hungary. Moreover, on the basis of the analysis of surnames, of the 676 registered burgers living in the present-day city of Kassa in East Slovakia, which had had a German ethnic majority until the mid-16th century, 72.5 % may have been

---

[21] Habáns: Anabaptist religious community, the members of which escaped from Switzerland through Austria and Moravia and settled in Upper Hungary after 1547. During the counter-reformation of the 17th century the majority fled to Transylvania, then abroad. Among the Habáns there were especially skilled artisans and those who produced faiance ceramics.

[22] For the same period the combined population of the West Hungarian counties of Vas and Sopron received many refugees, German and Croatian colonists, increased by a mere 42.9 %. (Kubinyi A. 1996 ibid. pp.135-161., Bakács I. 1963 A török hódoltság korának népessége (Population of the Hungarian territories under Ottoman-Turkish authority)— in: Kovacsics J. (Ed.) Magyarország történeti demográfiája, Budapest, 129.p.

[23] Blaskovics J. 1989 Érsekújvár és vidéke a török hódoltság korában (Érsekújvár and its environs in the time of the Turkish occupation), Állami Gorkij Könyvtár, Budapest, 841p.

[24] Nyitra, Léva towns of Hungarian ethnic majority and taken back from the Ottomans in 1664 did not figure in the Turkish tax statistics (defter). At that time Érsekújvár as the most important fortress of the region accommodated mainly moslem garrison troops (Bosnians, Turks). At the same time of 583 heads of household paying tax in Galgóc 48.9 % were Slovaks, 4,1 % Germans and 47 % Hungarians.

Hungarian, 13.2 % German and 14.3 % Slovak or of uncertain origin (1650)[25]. Starting with the second half of the 17th century, the Turkish campaigns, incursions and wars of independence led by princes I. Thököly (1682 -1685) and F. Rákóczi II. (1703-1711) were a serious blow to Hungarian ethnic blocks almost everywhere in Upper Hungary[26]. Conditions were created for the spontaneous movement or settlement in places abandoned by Hungarians of the large population of Slovaks from the mountains. This was also instigated by the landowners.

Following the failure of the war of independence led by F. Rákóczi II., the territory of the Hungarian Kingdom lay in ruins (and the Carpathian Basin in general). There was a movement to restore a balance between the relatively overpopulated northern and western peripheries and the depopulated central and southern regions. This was controlled by the geographic distribution of fertile land which was to be cultivated and resulted in a massive southward migration of Hungarians and Slovaks. There had been a movement of Slovaks (and some Ruthenians) in increasing numbers from the mountainous regions which had provided shelter during wars and epidemics to the areas where Hungarians had died or emigrated.

At the beginning of this enormous migration, tax censuses were taking place in 1715 and 1720[27]. During the first 69,704 households paying tax on the territory of present-day Slovakia were registered, and 61,084 such households were recorded in the counties of Upper Hungary. Although I. Acsády (1896) and his colleagues were often mistaken in their population estimations and their ethnic composition [28], in the case of Upper Hungary their calculations seem to have been quite reliable: 67.6 % Slavs, 22.9 % Hungarians, 17 % Germans and 2 % others. In 1720 of the 63 largest towns on the territory of present-day Slovakia with at least 100 taxpaying households 40 had a Slovak majority, 14 a German and 9 a Hungarian majority[29]. The greatest number of taxpaying households were registered among Hungarians in Komárom (657), Rimaszombat (228), Kassa (205), Léva (191) and Rozsnyó (180), and of Slovaks in Szakolca (430), Selmecbánya (424), Besztercebánya (211) and Ótura (202), and of Germans in Pozsony (704), Körmöcbánya (584), Selmecbánya (360), Lőcse (338) and Késmárk (268). A

---

[25] Kerekes L. 1940 Polgári társadalmunk a XVII. században (Our civil society in 17th century - Košice), Kassa, pp.49-57. The population of Kassa in 1661 according to Evlia Cselebi, the famous Turkish traveller was composed by "...Hungarians, Germans, Upper Hungarians..." (Slovaks? comment by the author). See Karácson I. (Ed.) 1904 Evlia Cselebi török világutazó magyarországi utazásai (Travels of the Turkish world traveller, Evlia Chelebi in Hungary) 1660-1664, MTA, Budapest, 102.p.

[26] Kniezsa I. 1941 ibid. 29., 54.p., Csapodi Cs. 1942 ibid. 21.p.

[27] Acsády I. 1896 Magyarország népessége a Pragmatica Sanctio korában (Population of Hungary in 1720-21), Magyar Statisztikai Közlemények XII. Budapest, 288p.

[28] Petrov, A. 1928 Příspěvky k historické demografii Slovenska v XVIII.-XIX. století (Contributions to the historical demography of Slovakia in 18th - 19th centuries), Praha, pp.57-59., Dávid Z. 1957 Az 1715.-20. évi összeírás (The census of 1715-1720) - in: Kovacsics J. (Ed.) A történeti statisztika forrásai, Közgazdasági és Jogi Könyvkiadó, Budapest, pp.145-199.

[29] Towns of Hungarian ethnic majority in 1720: Somorja, Komárom, Udvard, Nyitra, Érsekújvár, Léva, Rimaszombat, Rozsnyó, Kassa.

picture of the rapidly-changing rural ethnic pattern in the first half of the 18th century, together with intense migration and mobility – as regards the Hungarian-Slovak relationship - was attempted by M. Bél[30]. The Slovak-Hungarian ethnic boundary had, from the second half of the 17th century, extended to the mountain foreland. As a result of the accelerated southward migration of Slovaks deep into the flatland, in the first half of the 18th century the border had stabilised along the line of towns with a Hungarian ethnic majority: Pozsonypüspöki-Cseklész-Szenc-Szered-Nyitra-Léva-Losonc-Rimaszombat-Sajógömör-Pelsőc-Rozsnyó-Jászó-Szepsi-Nagyida-Zemplén-Nagykapos.[31]

In an unpopulated area between Érsekújvár-Nyitra-Léva, including the estate at Surány, a large Slovakian ethnic pocket had formed by the second half of the 17th century. This came as a result of resettlement encouraged by landowners[32]. Along the periphery (mainly in the environs of Verebély, Léva, Nagysalló), due to the mixture of Hungarians and Slovaks (mixed marriages, everyday communication) the local population became bilingual and with two cultural identities.

War losses, the southward migration and linguistic assimilation of Hungarians to Slovaks, caused the destruction of the Hungarian "ethnic corridor" along the Hernád and Tarca valleys. Mainly due to this the earlier Hungarian ethnic block near Eperjes had shrunk by the early 18th century to three main ethnic pockets (Eperjes-Nagysáros-Pécsújfalu – Nagyszilva - Kapi; Somos - Radács; Girált – Cselfalva - Magyarraszlavica-Margonya). It had disappeared virtually without any trace by the middle of the same century. After the Hungarians who were scattered in the counties of Sáros, Abaúj, Zemplén and Ung had been Slovakized, the Hungarian-Slovak ethnic border retreated to the Jászó – Nagyida – Abaújszina – Hernádtihany – Magyarbőd – Szilvásújfalu – Hardicsa – Deregnyő – Pálóc - Ungvár line. In this vicinity – especially in Kassa and to the east, between Gálszécs, Tőketerebes and Sátoraljaújhely – an extremely mixed, Hungarian-Slovak bilingual population with an uncertain ethnic identity had come into being, similar to the situation in the above-mentioned Érsekújvár – Nyitra – Verebély - Léva area.

By the end of the 18th century regions formerly underpopulated, and thus presenting economically attractive areas had reduced in number through repopulation and the mobility of the population had been curbed, thus the ethnic stability had grown. At about the time of the first population census in Hungary (1784-1787) the ethnic pattern

---

[30] Bel, M. Notitia Hungariae novae historico geographica. See Petrov, A. 1928 ibid., Žudel, J. 1992 Národnostná štruktúra obyvateľstva na južnom Slovensku v 1. polovici 18. storočia (Ethnic structure of the population in South Slovakia in the first half of 18th century), Geografický Časopis 44. 2. pp. 140-148.

[31] Žudel, J. 1992 ibid.

[32] Kniezsa I. 1941 ibid. pp. 29-32. To the Surány estate being a property of the counts Kaunitz between 1701 and 1730 a great number of peasants from Moravia were settled as well (e.g. Tótmegyer, Nagysurány, Bánkeszi, Zsitvafödémes, Özdöge, Malomszeg). Károlyi L. 1911 A gróf Károlyi-család összes jószágainak birtoklási története (History of the whole properties of Count Károlyi Family), Budapest, 323 p.

in the present-day territory of Slovakia – based upon contemporary sources[33] – can be outlined as follows *(Fig. 9.)*. Compared with the first half of the 18th century the position of the Hungarian-Slovak ethnic border had not much changed, apart from the dissolution and Slovakization of the Hungarian ethnic block at Eperjes. Comparing the data of M. Bél, the Lexicon.., J.M. Korabinszky and A. Vályi it can be stated that the Slovakization of Hungarian villages[34] along the Hungarian-Slovak ethnic contact zone and the appearance of additional pockets of Slovaks[35] and Ruthenians[36] were ethnic processes worth mentioning during the 18th century.

The Ruthenians progressively penetrating from Polish and Ukrainian areas beyond the Carpathians since the 13th century, had created a settlement area of considerable size by the 18th century. This was primarily in the Lower Beskids, Lőcse Mountains and Pieniny under the aegis of the so-called colonisation of Vlach rights. Besides these areas, they lived in great numbers in the Eperjes (Szalánci-) Mountains and on the plains of Zemplén and Ung counties. Those living in the latter two later merged with the surrounding Slovaks and Hungarians[37] in the following centuries. Their lingual assimilation with Slovaks and Hungarians was fostered by the fact that the Ruthenians moving in were cotters and had been eager to be accepted by the Hungarian and Slovak majority, i.e. by people of a higher social status[38]. According to a census conducted in 1773 the number of small villages with a Ruthenian majority dotted about in present-day Eastern Slovakia had reached 303[39]. By the same time (second half of the 18th century) Ruthenians of Vlach rights who lived in Central Slovakia, e.g. in North Gömör, had turned into Slovaks; this process was accelerated by the conversion of Ruthenians to being Catholics of the Byzantine rite i.e. Greek Catholics[40] (Union of Ungvár, 1646). Their mutual (Roman Catholic) religion, and aspirations to belong to a society of a higher level also accelerated the assimilation of the Goral-Polish population of Vlach rights in northern parts of Szepes and Trencsén counties. Owing to their economic inferiority and the

---

[33] Lexicon locorum Regni Hungariae populosorum anno 1773 officiose confectum, Magyar Békeküldöttség, Budapest, 1920, 335p., Korabinszky, J. M. 1804 Atlas Regni Hungariae portatilis, Wien, 60p., Vályi A. 1796 - 1799 Magyar országnak leírása I - III., Buda, 702p., 736p., 688p.

[34] E.g. Pozsonyivánka, Pusztafödémes, Cifer, Vágmagyarád, Nagysúr, Hódi, Vágpatta, Nyitraújlak, Assakürt, Óbars, Alsózellő, Osgyán, Kőhegy, Meleghegy, Pólyi, Szaláncújváros (Kniezsa I. 1941 ibid. 29., 55.p.).

[35] E.g. Deménd, Százd, Dobóca, Gömörhosszúszó,

[36] E.g. Kisdobra, Bodrogmező-Polyán, Bodrogszerdahely.

[37] Petrov, A. 1923 Kdy vznikly ruské osady na uherské Dolní zemí a vůbec za Karpaty ? (When were the Ruthenian settlements in the Great Hungarian Plain and in the Carpathians founded ?), Český Časopis historický XXIX. 3-4.

[38] Udvari I. 1990 XVIII. századi történeti-demográfiai adatok Északkelet-Magyarország görögkatolikus népességéről (Historic-demographic data about the Greek Catholics of Northeast-Hungary in the 18th century) - in: Udvari I. (Ed.) A munkácsi görögkatolikus püspökség lelkészségeinek 1806. évi összeírása, Vasvári Pál Társaság Füzetei 3., Nyíregyháza, 8.p.

[39] Petrov, A. 1924 Národopisná mapa Uher podle úředního lexikonu osad z roku 1773 (Ethnic map of Hungary based on the lexicon of settlements of 1773), ČAVU, Praha, pp.34-35.

[40] Podhradszky Gy. 1924 A tótoklakta Felföld politikai és kultúrgeográfiája (Political and cultural geography of Upper Hungary inhabited by Slovaks), Studium, Budapest, 27.p.

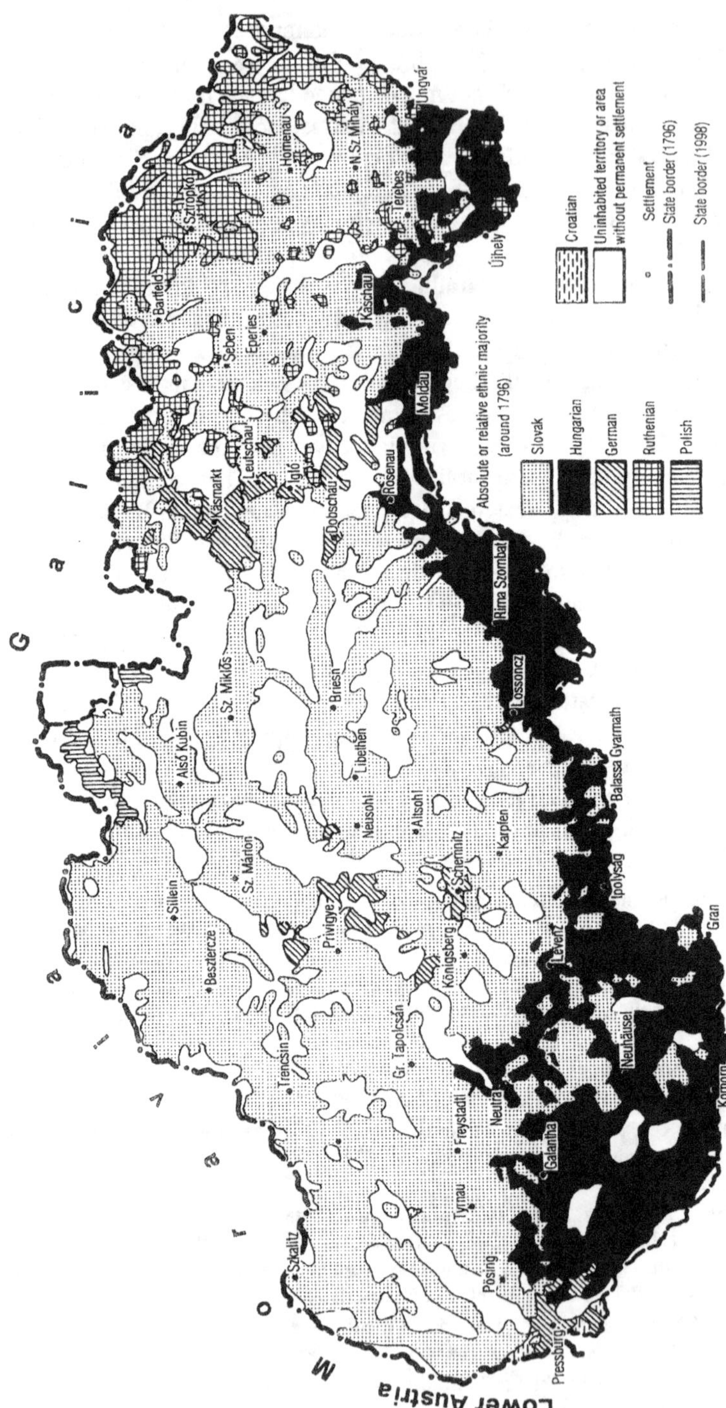

Figure 9. Ethnic map of the present-day territory of Slovakia (late 18th century)

Sources: Korabinszky, J. M. 1804 Atlas Regni Hungariae portatilis, Wien, 60p., Lexicon locorum Regni Hungariae populosorum anno 1773 officiose confectum, Magyar Békeküldöttség, Budapest, 1920, Vályi A. 1796 - 1799 Magyar országnak leírása I - III., Buda

strong pressure of the Slovakian church and of the Slovakian language they had hardly any Polish identity[41], but they were still registered as being of Polish ethnicity in the northwestern part of Árva County in 1773.

As a result of a peaceful Slovak expansion dating back to the medieval period, many areas with a German ethnic majority in the early 18th century had turned into those with a Slovak majority e.g. in towns (Bazin, Modor, Szentgyörgy and Újbánya), and in the Szepesség-Zips region (Hernád valley). In the towns of the region where rapid Slovakization was taking place between the Vág valley (Liptó County) and the Hernád-Tarca valley (Abaúj and Sáros counties), i.e. in Lőcse, Igló and Szepesváralja, the descendants of the medieval Saxon settlers became a minority by the turn of the 18th and 19th centuries. In the environs of Pozsony and Nagyszombat most of the Croats who settled there in the mid-16th century had become Slovaks by the end of the 18th century,[42] owing to a lack of ethnic replacement, a diaspora, the fact that their language was closely related to Slovakian and their common (Roman Catholic) religion.

The Jewish population, following discriminative measures taken at the end of the Middle Ages and the destruction of war in the 16th and 17th centuries, had begun to settle in Upper Hungary starting at the end of the 17th century. Parallel with the persecution of the Jews in Bohemia and Moravia in the first half of the 18th century, they moved increasingly into the western counties (Pozsony, Nyitra and Trencsén), though there had been a sizeable resettlement from the territory of Polish Galicia to the eastern counties (Zemplén, Abaúj, Sáros)[43]. The number of Jews in the counties of Upper Hungary – according to the 1787 census – had risen to 34, 086; 61,3 % of them lived in the western counties, while 34,2 % were resident in the eastern counties already mentioned.

At the time of the 1787 census[44] ethnic-religious affiliation was asked only of the Jews, so that the linguistic-ethnic composition of the 1,974,483 people living in Upper Hungary is not known exactly. However, on the basis of the distribution of serfs' declarations (fassios) by language in the course of regulating the tenements held by

---

[41] Podhradszky Gy. 1924 ibid. 25.p.

[42] Settlements with Croatian majority around 1796: Horvátjárfalu, Dunacsún, Dévényújfalu, Lamacs, Horvátgurab and Nahács.

[43] Beluszky P. 1996 A zsidó lakosság területi elterjedésének néhány jellemzője a két világháború közötti Magyarországon (Some characteristic of spatial distribution of Jews in Hungary in the interwar period) - in: Dövényi Z. (Ed.) Tér, gazdaság, társadalom, MTA Földrajztudományi Kutató Intézet, 319.p.

[44] Danyi D. - Dávid Z. 1960 Az első magyarországi népszámlálás (The first Hungarian census) (1784-1787), KSH, Budapest

socage[45] between 1767 and 1771, the ratio of Hungarians in Upper Hungary is assumed to have been 22.9 %[46].

The first ethnic data of the whole nation by county was published by E. Fényes in 1842[47]. According to this survey the total population of the counties in Upper Hungary exceeded 2.4 million, with the following ethnic distribution: 59.5 % Slovaks, 22 % Hungarians, 8.3 % Ruthenians, 6.7 % Germans and 3.6 % Jews. Ethnic proportions – apart from a slow homogeneization of the Slovak and Hungarian settlement area at the expense of the foreign diaspora – did not show any fundamental change as compared to the end of the 18th century with the exception of a sizeable influx of Jews from Galicia (*Tab. 7. *).

According to the Austrian census of 1850[48] in the combined area of the counties concerned the proportion of Slovaks had grown from 59. 5 % to 61. 9 % between 1840 and 1850 at the expense of Ruthenians (in Zemplén and Sáros), of Germans (in Szepes) and of Hungarians (in Abaúj, Gömör, Hont and Nyitra).

In the period between the Austro-Hungarian Compromise of 1867 which signalled the political emancipation of Hungarians, and the 1880 census, no significant change occurred in the ethnic spatial pattern. In 1880 in Upper Hungary and in the present-day territory of Slovakia[49] the distribution of the 2.4 million population by native language was the following: 61.5 % (61.1 %) Slovaks, 24.5 % (22.2 %) Hungarians, 9.8 % (9.3 %) Germans and 3.3 % (3.2 %) Ruthenians (*Tables 7., 8.*). By this period a trend towards southward migration which had led to a spatially balanced population had virtually ended, affected by the territorial distribution of population and the means of production (chiefly of the fertile land) together with the southward retreat of the Slovakian-Hungarian language boundary. At that time the Hungarian-Slovakian ethnic border stretched along the Pozsony-Galánta-Érsekújvár-Nyitra-Léva-Losonc-Rozsnyó-Jászó-Sátoraljaújhely-Ungvár line.

According to available data, the Slovakization of Greek Catholic Ruthenians had accelerated between 1840 and 1880; their number had dropped from 203 thousand to 80 thousand, i.e. from 8.3 % down to 3.3 %. People declaring themselves to be Ruthenian gradually became typical of the woodland areas in the Carpathians. Slovakian cultural expansion within the Roman Catholic church exerted pressure on the Polish Gorals who uniformly declared themselves to be Slovaks in 1880.

---

[45] Urbarial regulation: Regulation of the size of the tenement held by socage and of serf's services on the basis of the urbarial decree (1767) of empress Maria Theresia. See Felhő I. 1957 Data gathered in the course of the Theresian urbarial regulation - in: Kovacsics J. (Ed.) A történeti statisztika forrásai, Közgazdasági és Jogi Kiadó, Budapest, pp.454-455.

[46] Udvari I. 1996 A Mária Terézia korabeli úrbérrendezés szlovák nyelvű kéziratos forrásai (Manuscript sources of the urbarial regulation in Slovakian in the time of empress Maria Theresia), Vasvári Pál Társaság Füzetei 15., Nyíregyháza, 16.p.

[47] Fényes E. 1842 Magyarország statistikája (Statistics of Hungary) I., Pest

[48] Hornyánsky, V. 1858 Geographisches Lexikon des Königreiches Ungarn, G. Heckenast, Pest

[49] Žudel, J. 1993 Národnostná štruktúra obyvateľstva Slovenska roku 1880 (Ethnic structure of the population of Slovakia in 1880), Geografický Časopis 45. 1. pp.3-17.

The area of German settlement had remained basically unchanged: Pozsony and its surroundings, marginal areas of the Privigye district, Körmöcbánya and the Szepesség (Poprád valley and the southern part of the Igló district). In most of their medieval towns, they had however become a minority by 1880. In the Slovakian and Ruthenian territories of West and East Slovakia there lived a sizeable population of German native-speakers (5-24 %), most of whom consisted of Jews who had migrated from Bohemia, Moravia or Galicia, predominantly German native speakers.

To summarize the ethnic processes which took place between 1796 and 1880, it could be characterized primarily by Slovak ethnic expansion, starting in the second half of the 17th century[50]. In the course of this 106 Ruthenian, 63 Hungarian, 14 German, 12 Polish (Goral) and 2 Croatian settlements had a Slovakian ethnic majority by 1880. Accordingly, the Slovaks gained 145 settlements (+197 -52), the Ruthenians lost 100 (+10-110), the Hungarians 19 (+44-63), Germans 12 (+4-16), Poles 12 and Croats 2. Along the Hungarian-Slovak ethnic boundary 62 Hungarian settlements[51] changed to having a Slovak majority, 14 Slovakian villages gained a Hungarian majority (mainly in Gömör County[52]), which resulted in a further southward expansion of the ethnic border, especially in Nyitra, Abaúj and Zemplén counties. At the same time, and as a consequence of the pressure of assimilation put on the national minorities, south of the Hungarian-Slovakian ethnic boundary 23 Slovakian and 4 Ruthenian villages became Hungarian, while north of it 106 Ruthenian, 14 German[53] and 2 Croatian settlements turned into those with a Slovakian majority.

As a result of the ethnic processes outlined above, which was extremely favourable for the Slovaks, and following the Austro-Hungarian Compromise (1867), capitalist industrial development and demographic transition[54] started in Upper Hungary. People from certain regions (predominantly Slovaks and Ruthenians) in relatively overpopulated areas where agriculture could no longer support a larger population, migrated both overseas (chiefly from Zemplén, Sáros, Szepes, Abaúj-Torna counties), and to the capital Budapest (mainly from the counties of present-day Central Slovakia).

---

[50] See Kőrösy J. 1898 A Felvidék eltótosodása (Slovakization of Upper Hungary), K. Grill, Budapest, 56 p.

[51] Of the mentioned 62 Slovakized Hungarian settlements 14 were found in Nyitra, 22 in Abaúj, and 17 in Zemplén and Ung counties (e.g. Sempte, Szered, Vágsellye, Mocsonok, Ürmény, Nyitra, Nagyemőke, Újlót, Szántó, Gyügy, Ebeck, Losoncapátfalu, Pány, Abaújnádasd, Abaszéplak, Kassaújfalu, Hernádtihany, Kisszalánc, Nagyazar, Magyarizsép, Magyarsas, Nagytoronya, Pálóc, Tasolya, Ungpinkóc).

[52] Felsőfalu, Kisvisnyó, Lice, Mikolcsány, Gömörnánás, Kisperlász, Jolsvatapolca, Süvete. (See Keményfi R. 1998 A történeti Gömör és Kis-Hont vármegye etnikai rajza (Ethnic structure of the historic Gömör and Kis-Hont County), KLTE Néprajzi Tanszék, Debrecen, 296p.

[53] Towns with a German ethnic majority in the second half of the 18th century, which turned Slovakian by 1880 e.g. Igló, Lőcse, Szepesváralja, Korompa, Selmecbánya, Bélabánya.

[54] The improvement in living conditions, hygiene standards and a gradual decrease in mortality – in the beginning with high birth rates – resulted in a natural increase, in some places in considerable overpopulation.

Great numbers of non-Hungarian citizens in the Hungarian state which was celebrating its millennium, threw their lot with the Hungarians. This was especially true of those living in towns (including Jews, Germans and Slovaks) in the atmosphere of Hungarian economic prosperity. A similar voluntary process of re-Magyarization which curbed Slovakization, could be observed within the Hungarian-Slovak bilingual population of uncertain ethnic identity who were Catholic and living in the counties of Nyitra, Bars, Hont, Abaúj and Zemplén.

Aside from the process of natural assimilation which took place between the censuses of 1880 and 1910 it is worth mentioning the various Magyarization measures taken by contemporary Hungarian governments to accelerate this process, which had a negative political effect. For example, the establishment and hasty development of a network of Hungarian institutions (kindergartens, primary and secondary schools, cultural and educational societies) in regions inhabited by predominantly non-Hungarians and the nationalist excesses of local administration. The above outlined ethnic processes which were favourable for the Hungarians are still evaluated differently by Hungarian and Slovak experts. On the Slovakian side,[55] a dynamic increase in the number of Hungarians in the period at the turn of the century is considered to be forceful Magyarization, and the result of tampering with statistical data. Meanwhile, Hungarians[56] claim it was a voluntary process of natural assimilation[57]. Slovakization in the 18th and 19th centuries, and statistical data of the 1880 Hungarian and of the 1921 and 1930 Czechoslovakian censuses were treated in a similar manner by Slovak experts.

During the period between 1880 and 1910 which could be considered favourable for Hungarians and Ruthenians and unfavourable for the Slovaks from the ethnic point of view, the change of the number of settlements with the given ethnic majority showed the following picture: Hungarian settlements +64 (+76-12), Ruthenians +45

---

[55] Pl. Varsik, B. 1940 Die slowakisch-magyarische ethnische Grenze in den letzten zwei Jahrhunderten, Universum, Bratislava, Svetoň, J. 1970 Vývoj obyvateľstva na Slovensku (Change in the population number of Slovakia), Bratislava, Mazúr, E. 1974 Národnostné zloženie (Ethnic structure) — in: Slovensko, Ľud - I. Časť, Obzor, Bratislava, pp.440-457., Žudel, J. - Očovský, Š. 1991 Die Entwicklung und der Nationalitätenstruktur in der Südslowakei, Österreichische Osthefte Jg.33. 2. pp.93-123., Mésároš, J. 1996 Deformácie vo využívaní údajov sčítania ľudu v novodobých maďarsko-slovenských sporoch (Differences in the study of census data , Historický Zborník 6 (Matica Slovenska, Martin), pp. 123-135

[56] E.g. Kovács A. 1938 A magyar-tót nyelvhatár változásai az utolsó két évszázadban (Change in the Hungarian-Slovakian ethnic boundary during the last two hundred years), Századok, pp. 561-575., Kniezsa I. 1939 A magyarság és a nemzetiségek (Hungarians and the minorities) — in: Az ezeréves Magyarország, Budapest, pp. 91-114., Révay, S. 1941 Die im Belvedere gezogene ungarisch-slowakische Grenze, Veröffentlichungen der Ungarischen Statistischen Gesellschaft Nr. 14., Budapest,

[57] Experts studying ethnic processes from a nationalistic viewpoint – both in the past and in the present – have always considered ethnicity almost exclusively as determined by ethnic affiliation, although "belonging to a certain national community is not a genetic endowment but a result of a social acculturization. The consciousness, behaviour, mentality of people are heavily influenced by the cultural norms, values, models and symbols, prevailing in the society, first of all by a politically governed cultivation of the national idea" (See. Joó R. 1984 Az etnikai folyamatok és a politikai folyamatok néhány összefüggése – Some connections between ethnical and political processes), Társadalomkutatás 1984. 2. pp.98-105.).

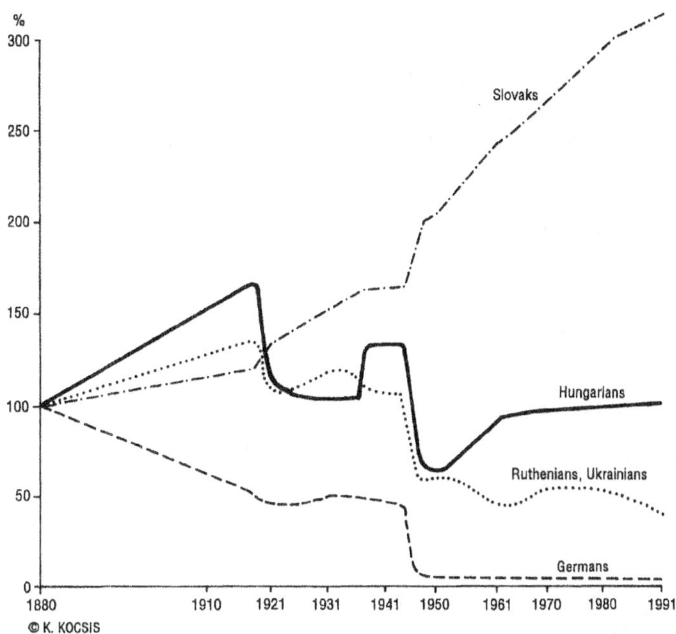

Figure 10. Change in the population number of the main ethnic groups on the present-day territory of Slovakia (1880–1991)

(+62-17), Poles +2, Slovaks -99 (+38-137). In the last case, 90 villages out of 137, reversing their former Slovakization, returned to the original ethnic majority: 62 Ruthenian, 25 Hungarian, 2 Polish and 1 German. However, the Slovakization of German settlements in the Szepesség area even in this period could not be stopped, and 7 settlements which were still German in 1880[58] had a Slovakian majority by 1910.

As a consequence of German, Jewish and Slovak assimilants declaring themselves to be Hungarians, with a higher natural increase, and relatively lower emigration, the number of Hungarians in the territory of present- day Slovakia grew by 335,000 (+61.8 %) between 1880-1910 *(Tab. 8., Fig. 10.).* The increase in Hungarians was +168.9 % north of the Hungarian-Slovak ethnic border, comprising areas of predominantly Slovak ethnicity, and it was +36,6 % in the Hungarian ethnic area[59]. There was a particularly high number of urban dwellers of Jewish, German and Slovakian origin who declared themselves to belong to the state-forming (Hungarian) nation. Due to Hungarians moving in, and to the language change of the local German and Slovak officials, and the strengthening of the bourgeois, towns like Zólyom, Aranyosmarót, Nyitra, Nagyrőce,

---

[58] Szepesbéla, Alsólehnic, Ómajor, Felka, Strázsa, Szepesszombat, Leibic.

[59] The population increase calculated for the territory of the present-day Slovakia was 18.6 % between 1880 and 1910.

Table 8. Ethnic structure of the population on the present territory of Slovakia (1880–1991)

Year	Total population		Slovaks		Czechs		Hungarians		Germans		Ruthenians, Ukrainians		Others	
	number	%	number	%	number	%	number	%	number	%	number	%	number	%
1880	2,460,865	100	1,502,565	61.1	–	–	**545,889**	**22.2**	228,581	9.3	78.402	3.2	105,428	4.2
1910	2,916,086	100	1,687,800	57.9	–	–	**880,851**	**30.2**	198.461	6.8	97,037	3.3	51,937	1.8
1919	2,935,139	100	1,960,391	66.8			**681,375**	**23.2**	145,139	4.9	92,786	3.2	55,468	1.9
1921	2,958,557	100	1,952,866	66.0	72,137	2.4	**650,597**	**22.0**	145.844	4.9	88,970	3.0	48,143	1.7
1930	3,254,189	100	2,224,983	68.4	120,926	3.7	**585,434**	**17.6**	154.821	4.5	95,359	2.8	72,666	3.0
1941	3,536,319	100	2,385,552	67.4	17,443	0.5	**761,434**	**21.5**	143.209	4.0	85,991	2.4	142,690	4.2
1947	3,399,000	100	2,888,000	85.0	37,000	1.1	**390,000**	**11.5**	24,000	0.7	47,000	1.4	13,000	0.3
1950	3,442,317	100	2,982,524	86.6	40,365	1.2	**354,532**	**10.3**	5,179	0.1	48,231	1.4	11,486	0.4
1961	4,174,046	100	3,560,216	85.3	45,721	1.1	**518,782**	**12.4**	6,259	0.1	35,435	0.9	7,633	0.2
1970	4,537,290	100	3,878,904	85.5	47,402	1.0	**552,006**	**12.2**	4,760	0.1	42,238	1.0	11,980	0.3
1980	4,987,853	100	4,321,139	86.6	55,234	1.1	**559,801**	**11.2**	5,121	0.1	39,758	0.8	6,800	0.2
1991	5,274,335	100	4,519,328	85.7	59,326	1.1	**567,296**	**10.7**	5,414	0.1	30,478	0.6	92,493	1.8
1991*	5,274,335	100	4,445,303	84.3	56,487	1.1	**608,221**	**11.5**	7,738	0.1	58,579	1.1	98,007	1.9

Sources: 1880, 1910: Hungarian census data (mother/native/ tongue), 1919, 1921,1930, 1947, 1950, 1961, 1970, 1980, 1991: Czechoslovakian census data (ethnicity), 1991*: Czechoslovakian census data (mother/native/ tongue), 1941: combined Hungarian and Slovakian census data. The data for the present territory of Slovakia were calculated by J. Žudel (Národnostná štruktúra obyvateľstva Slovenska roku 1880, Geografický Časopis 1993. 45. 1. pp.3-17.), by the Hungarian Central Statistical Office (A felvidéki települések nemzetiségi (anyanyelvi) megoszlása (1880-1941), KSH, Budapest, 52.p.) and between 1919 and 1941 by K.Kocsis.

Jolsva, Korompa, Eperjes, Varannó, Homonna, Nagymihály suddenly attained an absolute or relative Hungarian ethnic majority *(Fig. 11.)*. The increase in the number of persons declaring themselves to be Hungarian – for the above-mentioned reasons – was especially spectacular in Pozsony and Kassa *(Tab. 9.)*. In the neighbourhood of the Hungarian-Slovakian ethnic border 54 settlements turned into those with a Hungarian ethnic majority and in 11 settlements Slovaks prevailed, i.e. in 25 cases there was some re-Magyarization,[60] while in 5 cases there was re-Slovakization,[61] taking into account previous ethnic data. For a better understanding of the abrupt changes in statistical data it might be useful to analyse the ratio of the bilingual population. In Upper Hungary their proportion was 18 % among Slovaks, 33 % among Hungarians and 65 % among Germans (!), living mostly in scattered language pockets. It is notable that 21 % of Germans – especially those living in Pozsony and Szepes County – spoke German, Hungarian and Slovakian. Among the settlements with an urban status there was a particularly high proportion of bilingual (Hungarian-Slovak) people, difficult to label by one native language, as in Jolsva, Vágsellye (approx. 70-75 %), Kassa, Ógyalla, Verebély (30-40 %). Within the rural areas the proportion of these people was 35-45 % in the environs of Kassa, Tőketerebes, and Nyitra-Érsekújvár-Léva. At the later censuses they declared themselves to belong to the current nation forming a state, in this way causing significant statistical discrepancies. Although most inhabitants of the 62 Slovakized villages returned to being Ruthenian, owing to intense emigration (mainly overseas) the latter increased their share of the total population of Upper Hungary by a "mere" 23.8 %.

At the end of World War I, following the declaration of Czechoslovakia (October 28, 1918) and the formation of the Slovakian National Committee (October 30, 1918), the Czech army supported by the Entente powers occupied almost the entire area of Upper Hungary, i.e. a territory of 61,.592 km.[262] This was to be annexed to Czechoslovakia with a population of 3.5 million, 48.1 % of whom were Slovakian native speakers, while 30.3 % were Hungarian, 12.3 % Ruthenian and 7.5 % German native speakers (1910). After excluding the option of a plebiscite which would have provided an opportunity for the local population to express their opinion about the future affiliation with a state of their choice, the Entente powers in their dictate of the Trianon Peace Treaty (June 4, 1920) insisted on the detachment of the Slovak ethnic area together with the Ruthenian, northern Hungarian settlement area and the German (Saxon) blocks of Upper Hungary with a reference to the ethnic, economic and military interests of an ar-

---

[60] Re-Magyarization: e.g. Cseklész, Vágsellye, Nyitra, Gyügy, Szántó, Ebeck, Losoncapátfalva, Pelsőcardó, Pány, Hernádcsány, Kisszalánc, Csörgő, Garany, Magyarsas, Nagytoronya.

[61] Re-Slovakizattion: Kural, Jolsvatapolca, Kisperlász, Süvete, Lasztóc.

[62] The combined territory of Slovakia and Podkarpatska Rus (c. present-day Transcarpathia) as provinces of Czechoslovakia was 61,592 km^2 in 1921 and 61.623 km^2 in 1930 (Československá statistika, Svazek 98. 27x.p.). As a result of the border adjustments between 1922 and 1924 Susa (1922), Somoskőújfalu, Somoskő (1924) were returned from Slovakia to Hungary, Javorina (1923), Hladovka and Szuchahora (1924) were annexed from Poland to Czechoslovakia, receiving Nižná Lipnica (1924) in exchange. See: Houdek, F. 1931 Vznik hraníc Slovenska (Formation of the borders of Slovakia), Prúdov, Bratislava, 412.p.

Year	Total population		Slovaks		**Hungarians**		Germans		Others	
	number	%	number	%	number	%	number	%	number	%
Pozsony - Bratislava										
1880	66,122	100	14,617	22.1	**10,393**	**15.7**	37,000	56.0	4,112	6.2
1900	88,981	100	20,373	22.9	**24,500**	**27.5**	39,294	44.2	4,814	5.4
1910	104,896	100	22,708	21.7	**37,668**	**35.9**	39,818	38.0	4,702	4.4
1921	122,201	100	52,038	42.6	**26,137**	**21.4**	32,573	26.7	11,453	9.3
1930	170,305	100	87,117	51.2	**26,974**	**15.8**	41,318	24.3	14,896	8.7
1940	190,259	100	99,223	52.2	**25,394**	**13.4**	40,385	21.2	25,257	13.3
1970	305,950	100	274,294	89.7	**17,043**	**5.5**			14,613	4.8
1980	380,259	100	344,637	90.6	**18,731**	**4.9**	872	0.2	16,019	4.3
1991	442,197	100	401,848	90.9	**20,312**	**4.5**	1,266	0.3	18,771	4.3
Kassa - Košice										
1880	34,951	100	18,311	52.4	**11,162**	**31.9**	4,627	13.2	851	2.4
1900	49,885	100	17,224	34.5	**27,031**	**54.2**	3,588	7.2	2,042	4.1
1910	54,331	100	13,646	25.1	**36,141**	**66.5**	3,261	6	1,283	2.4
1921	63,063	100	40,145	63.7	**12,371**	**19.6**	2,170	3.4	8,377	13.3
1930	81,802	100	52,953	64.7	**11,711**	**14.3**	3,385	4.1	13,753	16.8
1941	79,855	100	15,367	19.2	**60,404**	**75.6**	1,703	2.1	2,381	2.9
1980	202,368	100	187,501	92.7	**8,070**	**3.9**	72	0.0	6,725	3.3
1991	235,160	100	212,659	90.4	**10,760**	**4.6**	322	0.1	11,419	4.9
Galánta - Galanta										
1880	2,844	100	854	30.0	**1,657**	**58.3**	329	11.6	4	0.1
1900	3,841	100	788	20.5	**2,810**	**73.2**	181	4.7	62	1.6
1910	4,143	100	550	13.3	**3,441**	**83.1**	128	3.1	24	0.6
1921	4,580	100	1,089	23.8	**3,233**	**70.6**	38	0.8	220	4.8
1930	5,290	100	2,284	43.2	**1,771**	**33.5**	40	1.0	1,195	22.6
1941	6,026	100	876	14.5	**5,054**	**83.9**	81	1.3	15	0.2
1970	8,954	100	6,440	71.9	**2,452**	**27.4**			62	0.7
1980	13,217	100	8,370	63.3	**4,700**	**35.6**			147	1.1
1991	16,978	100	9,810	57.8	**6,890**	**40.6**	7	0.0	271	1.6
Komárom - Komárno										
1880	13,901	100	269	1.9	**12,726**	**91.5**	766	5.5	140	1.0
1900	21,022	100	1374	6.5	**18,112**	**86.2**	1,235	5.9	301	1.4
1910	23,051	100	769	3.3	**20,636**	**89.5**	1,245	5.4	401	1.7
1921	19,075	100	2427	12.7	**14,917**	**78.2**	730	3.8	1,001	5.2
1930	22,761	100	5546	24.4	**13,951**	**61.3**	1,029	4.5	2,235	9.8
1941	23,410	100	347	1.5	**22,446**	**95.9**	338	1.4	279	1.2
1970	28,376	100	10550	37.2	**17,498**	**61.7**			328	1.2
1980	32,520	100	11900	36.6	**20,022**	**61.6**			598	1.8
1991	37,346	100	12680	34.0	**23,745**	**63.6**	10	0.0	911	2.4
Érsekújvár - Nové Zámky										
1880	10,584	100	1,526	14.4	**8,138**	**76.9**	846	8.0	74	0.7
1900	13,385	100	822	6.1	**12,197**	**91.1**	340	2.5	26	0.2
1910	16,228	100	964	5.9	**14,838**	**91.4**	377	2.3	49	0.3
1921	19,023	100	7,686	40.4	**9,378**	**49.3**	235	1.2	1,724	9.1
1930	22,457	100	9,561	42.6	**10,193**	**45.4**	256	1.1	2,447	10.9
1941	23,306	100	1693	7.3	**21,284**	**91.3**	212	0.9	117	0.5
1970	24,962	100	17,560	70.3	**7,152**	**28.7**			250	1.0
1980	34,147	100	24,200	70.9	**9,460**	**27.7**			487	1.4
1991	42,923	100	28,680	66.8	**13,350**	**31.1**	18	0.0	875	2.0

'Sources: 1880, 1900, 1910, 1941 : Hungarian census data (mother/native tongue) (except for Pozsony/
Remark: All data are calculated for the present administrative territory of the cities and towns.

Year	Total population		Slovaks		Hungarians		Germans		Others	
	number	%	number	%	number	%	number	%	number	%
Párkány - Štúrovo										
1880	3,547	100	41	1.2	**3,340**	**94.2**	54	1.5	112	3.2
1900	4,424	100	10	0.2	**4,397**	**99.4**	12	0.3	5	0.1
1910	4,578	100	26	0.6	**4,509**	**98.5**	39	0.8	4	0.1
1919	4,989	100	257	5.1	**4,703**	**94.3**	17	0.3	12	0.2
1921	5,137	100	316	6.1	**4,722**	**91.9**	31	0.6	68	1.3
1930	6,145	100	1,431	23.3	**4,046**	**65.8**	123	2.0	545	8.9
1938	5,233	100	97	1.8	**5,099**	**97.4**	5	0.1	32	0.6
1941	5,868	100	69	1.2	**5,634**	**96.0**	41	0.7	124	2.1
1991	13,347	100	3,310	24.8	**9,804**	**73.5**	3	0.0	230	1.7
Léva - Levice										
1880	7,597	100	1,316	17.3	**5,806**	**76.4**	451	5.9	24	0.3
1900	9,786	100	1,242	12.7	**8,286**	**84.7**	198	2.0	60	0.6
1910	10,816	100	948	8.8	**9,618**	**88.9**	208	1.9	42	0.4
1921	11,556	100	3,382	29.3	**7,462**	**64.6**	215	1.9	497	4.3
1930	13,975	100	6,886	49.3	**5,432**	**38.9**	216	1.5	1,441	10.3
1938	13,608	100	2,052	15.1	**11,246**	**82.6**	216	1.6	94	0.7
1941	14,150	100	1,555	11.0	**12,338**	**87.2**	162	1.1	95	0.7
1980	26,502	100	22,100	83.4	**4,010**	**15.1**			392	1.5
1991	33,991	100	28,126	82.7	**5,165**	**15.2**	6	0.0	694	2.0
Losonc – Lučenec										
1880	6,471	100	1,551	24.0	**4,449**	**68.8**	404	6.2	67	1.0
1900	10,634	100	1,441	13.6	**8,800**	**82.8**	278	2.6	115	1.1
1910	14,396	100	2,055	14.3	**11,646**	**80.9**	471	3.3	224	1.6
1921	13,798	100	6,713	48.7	**5,760**	**41.7**	594	4.3	731	5.3
1930	17,186	100	9,953	57.9	**4,411**	**25.7**	907	5.3	1,915	11.1
1941	16,641	100	1,987	11.9	**14,023**	**84.3**	335	2.0	296	1.8
1970	21,308	100	17,570	82.5	**3,514**	**16.5**			224	1.0
1980	24,770	100	20,520	82.8	**3,803**	**15.4**			447	1.8
1991	28,861	100	23,272	80.6	**4,830**	**16.7**	13	0.0	746	2.6
Rimaszombat – Rimavská Sobota										
1880	7,339	100	1,473	20.1	**5,484**	**74.7**	185	2.5	197	2.7
1900	8,048	100	741	9.2	**7,197**	**89.4**	73	0.9	37	0.5
1910	9,166	100	880	9.6	**8,014**	**87.4**	92	1.0	180	1.9
1921	9,296	100	2,750	29.6	**6,164**	**66.3**	123	1.3	259	2.8
1930	11,221	100	4,734	42.2	**4,736**	**42.2**	130	1.2	1,621	14.4
1941	9,947	100	997	10.0	**8,828**	**88.8**	50	0.5	72	0.7
1970	16,238	100	9,220	56.8	**6,770**	**41.7**			248	1.5
1980	19,205	100	11,000	57.3	**7,800**	**40.6**			405	2.1
1991	24,771	100	14,256	57.6	**9,854**	**39.8**			661	2.7
Rozsnyó – Rožňava										
1880	5,226	100	482	9.2	**4,374**	**83.7**	285	5.4	85	1.6
1900	5,748	100	369	6.4	**5,123**	**89.1**	195	3.4	61	1.1
1910	7,119	100	570	8.0	**6,234**	**87.6**	177	2.5	138	1.9
1921	6,937	100	1,163	16.8	**5,514**	**79.5**	150	2.2	110	1.6
1930	7,413	100	2,930	39.5	**3,472**	**46.8**	191	2.6	820	11.1
1941	7,676	100	530	6.9	**7,025**	**91.5**	90	1.2	31	0.4
1961	9,557	100	6,500	68.0	**3,040**	**31.8**			17	0.2
1970	10,980	100	7,380	67.2	**3,570**	**32.5**			30	0.3
1991	18,647	100	12,271	65.8	**5,826**	**31.2**	10	0.0	540	2.9

Bratislava City in 1940), 1921, 1930, 1961, 1970, 1980, 1991: Czechoslovakian census data /ethnicity/.

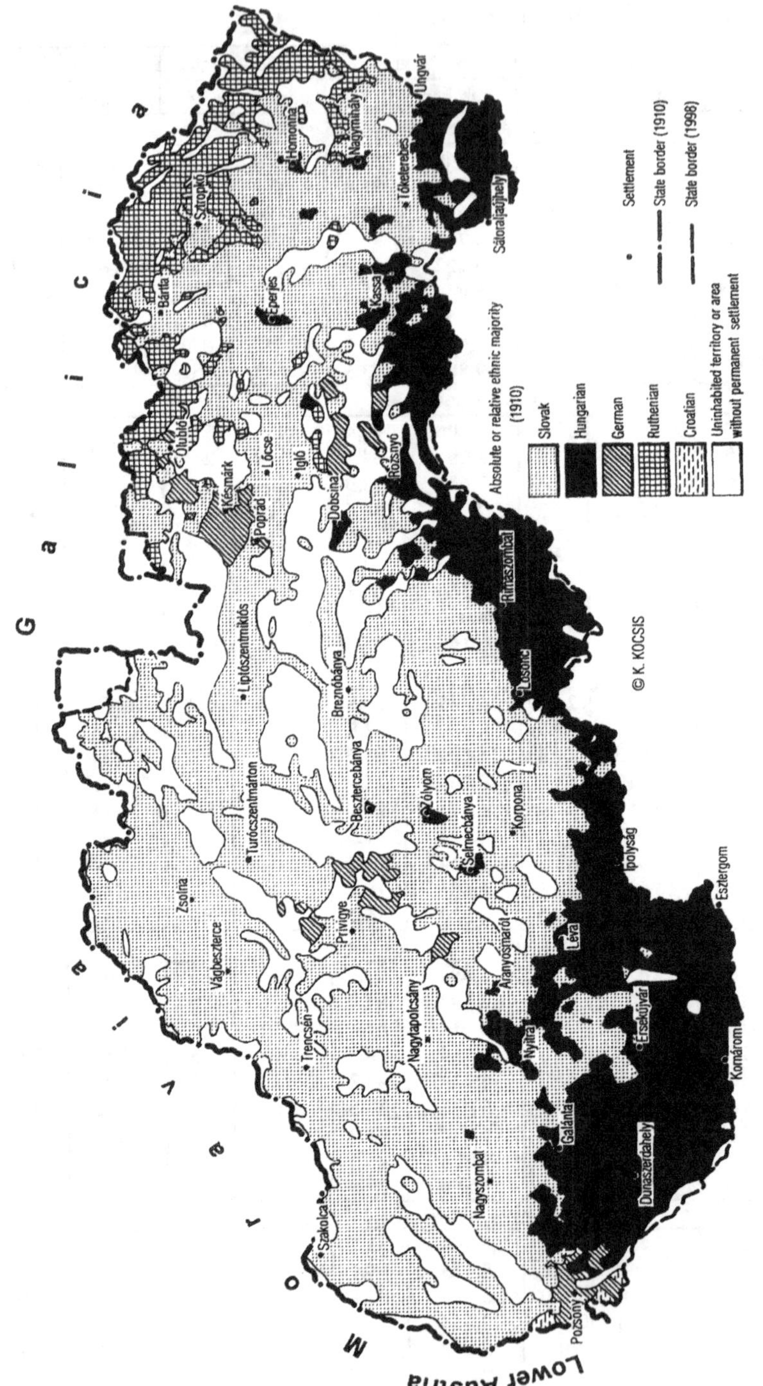

Figure 11. Ethnic map of present-day territory of Slovakia (1910)
Source: Census 1910

tificial state formation of Czechoslovakia having twice undergone disintegration since then.

From the very beginning of its existence Czechoslovak state administration – similar to that of Rumania and Yugoslavia – put a strong emphasis upon reducing the number of Hungarians in the annexed territories labelling them as enemies, and on the ethnic homogeneization and stabilization ("Czechoslovakization") of their towns and border zones. Between 1918 and 1924 following the change in the state authorities, 106,841 ethnic Hungarians (administrative and military personnel, landowners, etc.) were expelled or fled from Czechoslovakia to the new Hungarian state territory (from Slovakia approximately 88,000).[63] At the same time, approximately 70,000 Czech military personnel, civil servants and investors moved to the territory of Slovakia between 1918 and 1921. Some of the Hungarians who stayed in Slovakia (1921: 13,414, 1930: 20.349 persons[64]) were not granted Czechoslovakian citizenship, and in this way they were considered to be foreign citizens or displaced persons. The authrorities were especially eager to "Slovakize" the bilingual (Hungarian-Slovak) population with their dual identity as well as the previously Magyarized urban Slovaks, Jews and Gypsies. These two latter ethnic groups, against their own will, were classed as independent ethnic categories of Jews and Gypsies or labelled as "Czechoslovaks" at the censuses. Apart from some spectacular enforced Slovakization in education and culture, the social temptation, political pressure and statistical manipulation (e.g. the registration of military personnel not at their place of residence but at military bases) and serious abuses of authority greatly contributed to a drastic drop in the number of those recorded as Hungarians[65]. Between the censuses of 1910 and 1930 the number of Hungarians dropped from 881,000 to 585,000, that is from 30.2 % to 17.6 % on the territory of present-day Slovakia (Tab. 8.). During this period 117 settlements with a formerly Hungarian ethnic majority changed to having a Slovak majority, of these 33 were in the vicinity of Nyitra-Komárom-Léva, 25 around Kassa, and 22 in the environs of Tőketerebes, i.e. in regions characterized mainly by a population with dual (Hungarian-Slovak) identity. The Hungarian ethnic area near Nyitra became an enclave. The Hungarian ethnic territory along the Ipoly river was severed between Balassagyarmat and Nagykürtös, and the Hungarian ethnic enclaves situated east of Kassa and southwest of Tőketerebes almost completely disappeared in the Czechoslovakian statistics. At the same time as part of the Czech nationalist land reform, 69 colonies[66] (with 14,000 Czech and Slovak inhabitants) were

---

[63] Petrichevich-Horváth E. 1924 Jelentés az Országos Menekültügyi Hivatal négy évi működéséről (Report about the activity of the National Office for Refugees), Budapest

[64] Československá statistika, Svazek 9. 82.p., Sv.98. 59.p.

[65] See: Gyönyör J. 1994 Terhes örökség. A magyarság lélekszámának és sorsának alakulása Csehszlovákiában (Burdensome inheritance. Change in population number and destiny of Hungarians in Czechoslovakia), Madách-Posonium, Pozsony / Bratislava, 32-34., 58.p., Popély Gy. 1991 Népfogyatkozás. A csehszlovákiai magyarság a népszámlálások tükrében (Decrease of population. Hungarians in Czechoslovakia in census data) 1918-1945, Írók Szakszervezet Széphalom Könyvműhely - Regio, Budapest, 112. p.

[66] The most important Czechoslovakian colonies (and their Hungarian counterparts) were: Gessayov-Zálesie (Éberhard), Miloslavov, Hviezdoslavov (Csallóközcsütörtök-Béke), Bellova Ves

established in the Hungarian ethnic area between 1919-1929. In the southern areas the majority of people living in colonies which were established to break up the homogeneous Hungarian ethnic pattern were peasants, or tenants, officials or soldiers (legionaires) who had settled there from the northern, less fertile regions of Slovakia and Moravia[67].

Apart from breaking up the Hungarian rural ethnic block along the state border, which posed a danger of irredentism, another trend was the (actual or statistic) Slovakization of traditionally Hungarian towns which flanked the ethnic border. Staff in public administration were changed (Hungarians for "Czechoslovaks") by dismissing or expelling people in 1919. Hungarian Israelites were grouped into a separate category of ethnic Jews, while assimilation connected with economic considerations (statistical Slovakization) and in some cases changing of effective force of garrisons into foreign ones (e.g. those composed of Sudethan Germans)[68] together with their registration in censuses, led to a situation whereby in the towns along the Hungarian-Slovak ethnic boundary "Czechoslovaks" gained a majority[69] or equilibrium[70] was reached. There was an especially radical drop in the number of Hungarians in Kassa between 1910 and 1930 *(Fig. 12.)*. At the same time, in the territory of Pozsony, the 23,000 Slovaks of 1910 increased to 87,000 with the Czechs by 1930.

As a result of accelerated assimilation (Slovakization) the proportion of Germans and Ruthenians also decreased significantly. During this period Germans lost their majority in 10 settlements, including their traditional centres like e.g. Pozsony, Körmöcbánya, Poprád and Késmárk. Ruthenians were forced into a minority position in 44 villages owing to the dissolution of their ethnic blocks during this period. As a result of Slovakization, which accelerated during the 18th and 19th centuries, was curbed after 1867, but recurred as a state supported and enforced process following 1918, the number of Slovaks exceeded 2.2 million, that is, over 68 % in 1930. At the same time, with

---

(Tonkháza), Blahová (Nagylég-Előpatony), Vrbina (Csilizradvány), Hodžovo-Lipové (Tany), Okanikovo (Nemesócsa), Štúrová (Ekel), Violin (Megyercs), Hadovce (Örsújfalu), Nový Svet (Szenc), Hurbanová Ves (Egyházfa), Štefánikov (Taksonyfalva), Hajmaš-Nové Osady (Nagyfödémes), Trnovec-Nový dvor (Tornóc), Zelený Háj (Ógyalla), Mudroňovo (Madar), Šrobárová (Marcelháza), Mikulášov Sad (Bátorkeszi), Gbelce (Köbölkút), Bíňa-Kolónia (Bény), Čata-Kolónia (Csata), Jesenské, Kulantov (Barsbese), Bozita (Perse), Romháň-Lipovany (Fülekpilis), Šiatorská Bukovinka (Ragyolc), Rátka (Csákányháza), Čierny Potok (Várgede), Bottovo (Dobóca), Slávikovo-Orávka (Rimaszécs).

[67] As to the Czech colonization see: Karvaš, A. I. 1928 Hospodárska štatistika Slovenska (Economic statistics of Slovakia), Bratislava, Faltuš, J. - Prcha, V. 1967 Prehľad hospodárského rozvoja na Slovensku v rokoch 1918-1945 (Overview about the economic development in Slovakia in the years 1918-1945), Bratislava

[68] The ratio of military personnel within the active population in 1930: e.g. Komárom 23,7 %, Léva 6,5 %, Losonc 24,8 %, Kassa 16,8 %. The ethnic division of soldiers stationed in the Hungarian border zone in 1930: Komárom 71 % Czechoslovak, 27,4 % German, Érsekújvár: 86 % Czechoslovak, 14 % German, Kassa: 66 % Czechoslovak, 26,4 % German. See: Bene L. - Kopcsányi R. 1946 A magyar nyelvterület városai (Towns of the Hungarian ethnic territory in Slovakia) — in: A szlovákiai magyar nyelvterület városai, Budapest Székesfőváros Irodalmi és Mûvészeti Intézete, Budapest, pp.19-49.

[69] E.g. Pozsony, Nyitra, Léva, Losonc, Kassa.

[70] E.g. Érsekújvár, Rimaszombat, Rozsnyó.

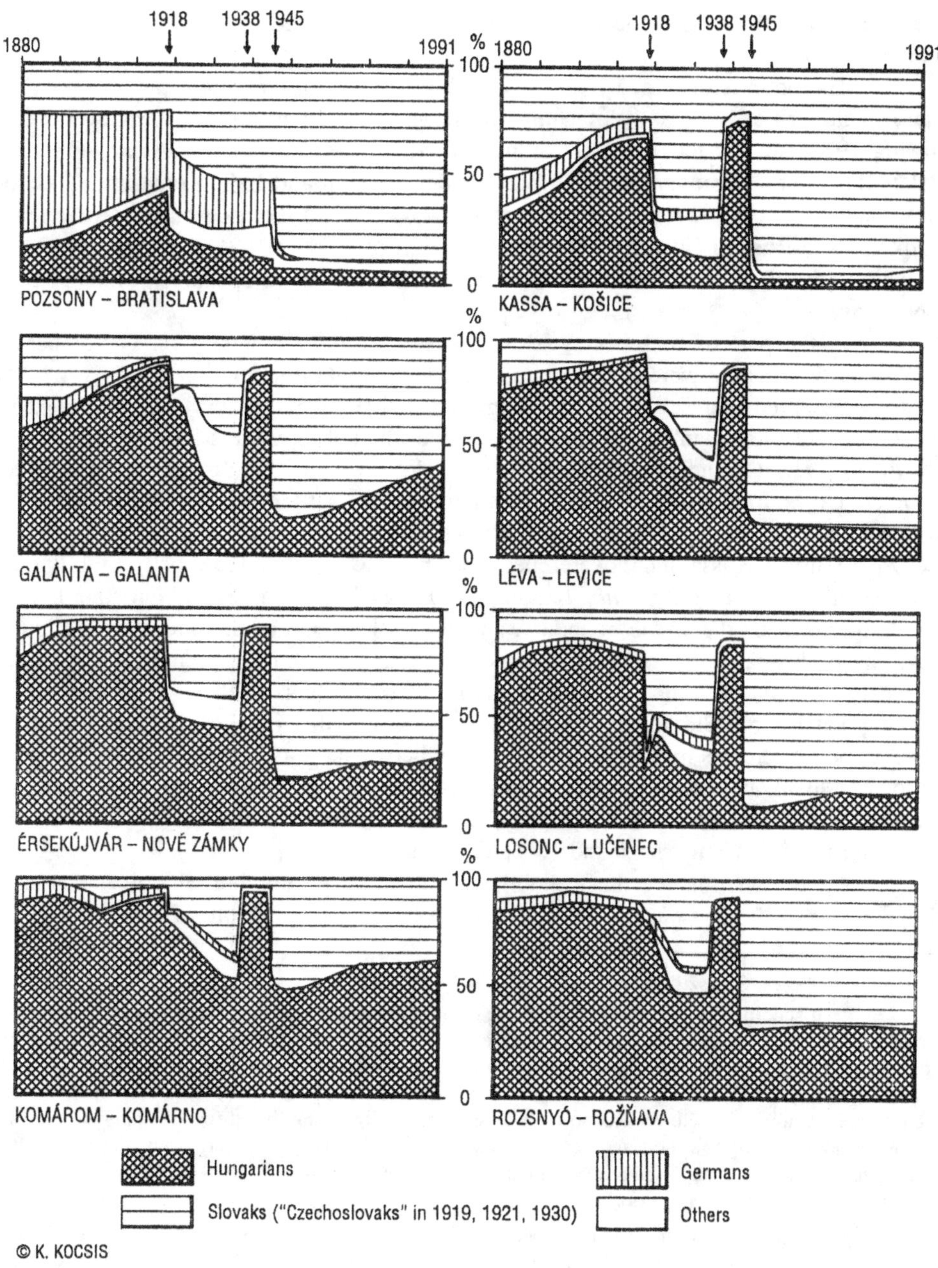

Figure 12. Change in the ethnic structure of population in selected cities and towns of present-day Slovakia (1880–1991)

the appearance of Czechs especially as civil servants and soldiers, their number rose to over 120,000.

The process of Czech and Slovak ethnic expansion and the rapid shrinking of national minorities, especially of Hungarians, was stopped by the political events following 1938 and the territorial revisions. Based on the first Vienna Award (Vienna, Palais Belvedere, February 02, 1938), and under German and Italian pressure, Czechoslovakia returned 11.927 km^2 of land from Slovakia and Transcarpathia (Ruthenia - Podkarpatska Rus) to Hungary with its population of 1,041,401 (December 15, 1938), of whom 84.4 % declared themselves to be Hungarian native speakers, while 11.9 % were Slovaks[71].

In the part of present-day Slovakia reannexed to Hungary on November 2, 1938, 857,529 people were registered at the 1941 population census. 85 % (728,904 persons) declared themselves to be Hungarian native speakers, and 13.2 % (113,619 persons) were Slovakian native speakers. Of the population of this "South-Slovakia of Belvedere" 91.4 % could speak Hungarian, 25 % Slovakian, and 16.4 % of them spoke both languages. In the returned territories there were 51 settlements which became those with a Hungarian majority but had been Slovakian in 1930, particularly in the regions of Léva-Érsekújvár, Kassa and Tőketerebes, and these were inhabited mostly by bilingual people with a dual identity *(Tab. 10., Fig. 13.)*. The Hungarian-Slovakian state border basically ran along the ethnic boundary, and some Slovakian ethnic pockets were in the environs of Kassa, north of Sátoraljaújhely and in the area between Érsekújvár and Verebély. Within the almost homogeneous northern Hungarian ethnic area there were not only some older Slovakian ethnic pockets (e.g. Kural, Újgyalla), but Slovaks colonised some settlements in Nógrád and Gömör[72] between the two world wars. The "independent" Slovakian state declared on March 14, 1939 had a territory of 37,352.9 km^2[73]. Of the 2,655,053 inhabitants 86.2% were Slovaks, 5 % Germans, 2.9 % Jews, 2.4 % Ruthenians, 1.8 % Hungarians, and 1.4 % Gypsies[74].

On the territory of the Republic of Slovakia the number of Czech residents dropped from 120,926 to 3,024[75] between 1930 and 1940 as a result of being expelled

---

[71] Magyar Statisztikai Szemle 1939. 5.szám, 456., 477.p.

[72] It should be mentioned that from the territory ceded to Hungary the overwhelming majority of Czech and Slovak civil servants who resettled during Czech rule (81,000 persons) withdrew voluntarily, using Czechoslovakian support in October 1938. (Zprávy štátného plánovacieho a štatistického úradu, Bratislava, 1946.10.01., 90.p.). Though some hundreds of Slovaks were expelled from the returned territories, but there was no collective responsibility established for the disbanding of the "common homeland of one thousand years" (Hungary) in 1918. Their Hungarian citizenship was returned and they were not deported to their home country, Slovakia.

[73] Hromádka, J. 1943 ibid. 102.p.

[74] According to the 1940 Slovakian census, the ethnic division of Slovakian citizens (2,566,984) was the following: 2,.213,761 Slovaks, 129,689 Germans, 74,441 Jews, 61,762 Ruthenians, 46,790 Hungarians, 37,100 Gypsies, 3,024 Czechs. See: Hromádka, J. 1943 ibid. 114.p.

[75] The number of Czechs living in Slovakia was 161,000 in 1937, 50,000 in 1950 /Demografická Priručka 1966, Praha, 1967, 46.p./. Their number in Pozsony dropped from 20,764 down to 4,971 between December 31, 1938 and December 15, 1940. /Fogarassy L. Pozsony város nemzetiségi összetétele (Ethnic structure of Pozsony-Bratislava City) — in: Alföld 1982.8. pp.59-74./.

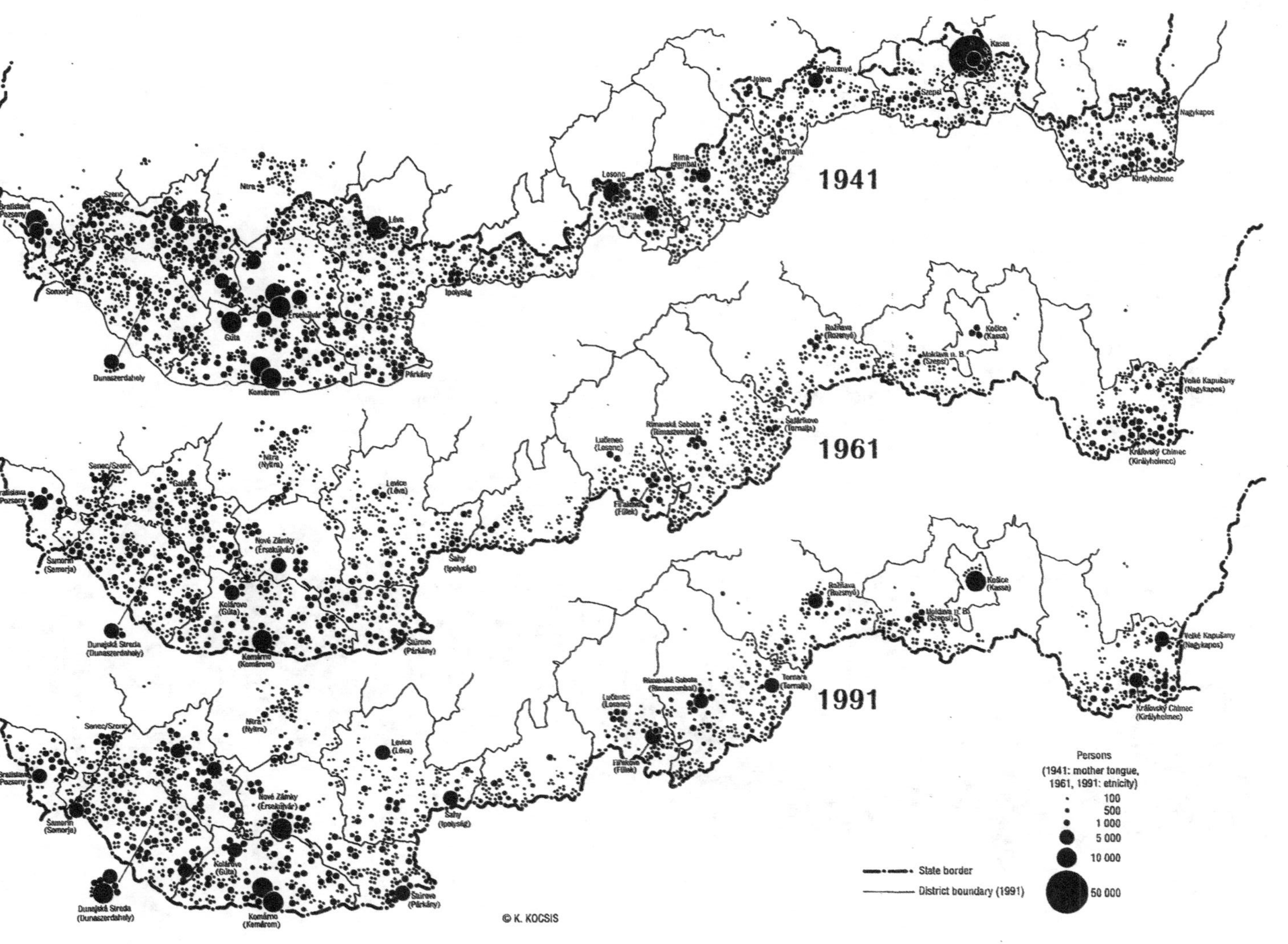

Figure 13. Bilingual (Hungarian – Slovak) population in present-day South Slovakia (1941)

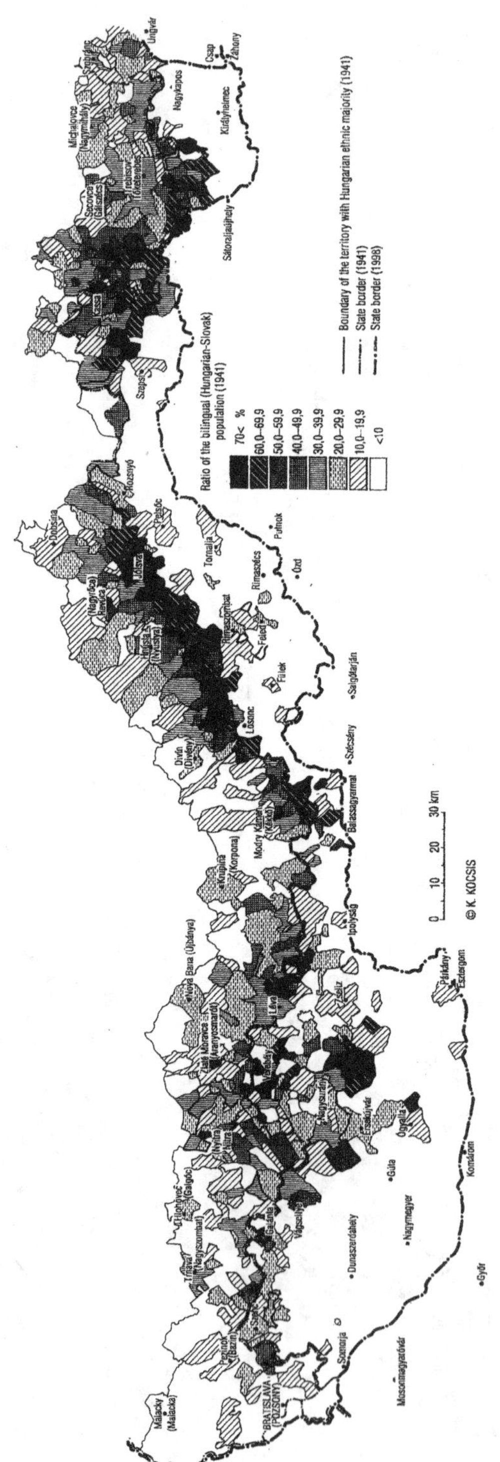

Figure 14. Hungarian communities in present-day South Slovakia (1941, 1961 and 1991)

Table 10. Changing ethnic majority of selected settlements in present-day South Slovakia (1495-1991)

Settlement	1495	1664	1796	1880	1910	1930	1941	1991
Nyitra	H	H	H	S	H	S	S	S
Nemespann	H	H	H	H	H	S	H	S
Verebély	H	H	H	H	H	S	S	S
Lüle	H		S	H	S	S	H	S
Ény	H	H	H	H	S	S	H	S
Barsbaracska	H	H	H	H	H	S	H	S
Alsópél	H	H	S	S	H	S	H	S
Fajkürt	H		S	H	H	S	H	S
Kolta	H	H	S	S	H	S	H	S
Szántó	H	H	H	S	H	S	S	S
Kassa	G	H	S	S	H	S	H	S
Pány	H	H	H	S	H	S	H	S
Saca	H	H	S	S	H	S	H	S
Enyicke	H	H	S	S	H	S	H	S
Abaújszina	G	H	H	H	H	S	H	S
Hernádzsadány	H	H	H	H	H	S	H	S
Eszkáros	H	H	H	H	H	S	H	S
Beszter	H	H	H	S	H	S	H	S
Magyarbőd	H	H	H	H	H	S	S	S
Györke	H	H	H	H	H	S	H	S
Nagyszalánc	H	H	H	H	H	S	S	S
Hardicsa	H	H	H	H	H	S	S	S
Kazsó	H	H	H	S	H	S	S	S
Garany	H	H	H	S	H	S	H	S
Magyarsas	H	H	H	S	H	S	S	S
Nagytoronya	H	H	H	S	H	S	H	S
Csörgő	H	H	H	S	H	S	H	S
Alsómihályi	H	H	H	H	H	S	H	S
Biste	H	H	H	H	H	S	H	S

Remark: Absolute or relative majority of the population: H = Hungarians, S = Slovaks, G = Germans

by the Hlinka Guard[76] and on the orders of the minister of the interior. The period between 1939 and 1945 was disastrous for Jews living in the area of present-day Slovakia, owing to discrimination against them and their extermination in the death camps. Between 1930 and 1950 the Holocaust reduced their numbers from 135,975 to 7,476[77]. The most populous Jewish communities lived (in areas under Hungarian administration) in Kassa, Losonc, Komárom, Érsekújvár, Dunaszerdahely, Galánta and Léva, in J. Tiso's Slovakia in Pozsony, Nyitra, Nagyszombat, Nagytapolcsány, Zsolna, Eperjes, Bártfa, Nagymihály and Homonna in 1941.

---

[76] Daxner, I. 1961 Ľudáctva pred Národným súdom (Ludak Party before the National's Tribunal) 1945-1947, Bratislava, 73.p.

[77] Deportation and liquidation of the majority of Jews took place in Slovakia in 1941-42, and in Hungary after March 1944. See: Gyönyör J. 1994 ibid. 219-221.p.

The above-outlined ethnic spatial structure of the "South-Slovakia of Belvedere" remained until the coming of the military front (October 29, 1944.- April 04, 1945.). There was no massive escape of Hungarians. At the same time, 120,000 out of the 140,000 Germans in Slovakia were evacuated or fled between December 1944 and April 1945[78]. In the areas along the southern border Germans stayed only in Pozsony[79] (approx. 9,000) and in Mecenzéf (Lower Zips-Szepesség, 1,600-1,800) until the appearance of the Soviet Army and the Czechoslovakian authorities.

After the change of power in 1945, within the framework of the establishment of the Czechoslovak state, ethnic cleansing, which was carefully planned and prepared, totally deprived Germans and Hungarians of their civil rights, and removed their economic foundation. They were made scapegoats for the disintegration of the state and for the war (no citizenship was granted to them, Hungarian civil servants were dismissed, their property confiscated, etc.). This was reflected in the Czechoslovak government program worked out by Gottwald in Moscow and announced in Kassa on 5 April 1945[80]. Declaring the expulsion of all Germans and Hungarians as their essential aim, the Czechoslovakian authorities expelled 31,780 Hungarians out of those in "South-Slovakia of Belvedere"[81]. At the same time the remaining German and Hungarian residents of Pozsony were transferred to two detention camps in the vicinity of the town as a first step in the urgent Slovakization of the capital. Based on estimates using census data[82] approximately 50,000 Germans and Hungarians disappeared from Pozsony between 1944 and 1950 as a result of evacuation, internment, deportation or expulsion etc. During this time about 70,000 Slovaks moved in. Population gain was also supported by a territorial annexation in 1946 so that the number rose from 138,536 in 1940 to 160,360 in 1950.

At the Potsdam Conference, on 2 August 1945, the request of the Czechoslovakian government for a unilateral resettlement of Hungarians from the country was refused (mainly thanks to the USA). As a compromise, at the behest of Czechoslovakia and with Soviet support, the Hungarian government was informed through Allied Control Commission about the possible expatriation of about 400,000-500,000 Germans. This was "unavoidable" in order to create space for Hungarians to be expelled from Czechoslovakia. Parallel with Czechoslovakian diplomatic efforts, within the framework of the land reform of 1945[83] and under the direction of the Slovakian Office of Settle-

---

[78] Dokumentation der Vertreibung der Deutschen aus Ost-Mitteleuropa Bd. IV/1. Die Vertreibung der deutschen Bevölkerung aus der Tschechoslowakei, 1957, 171.p.

[79] Dokumentation... ibid. 171,p,

[80] Dokumentation... ibid. pp.184-203., Janics K. 1993 A kassai kormányprogram és a magyarság "kollektív bûnössége" (Czechoslovak Government Programme of Kassa-Košice and the "collective guiltiness" of Hungarians), Pannónia Könyvkiadó, Bratislava, 50p.

[81] Jablonický, J. 1965 Slovensko na prelome (Slovakia in break-through), Bratislava, p.398.

[82] After Fogarassy L. 1982 ibid.

[83] The nationalist land reform was ensured by immediately confiscating land and property formerly belonging to Hungarians and Germans by decrees 27/1945 and 104/1945 issued by the Slovakian National Council (Vadkerty K. 1993 A reszlovakizáció – The Re-Slovakization, Kalligram, Bratislava-Pozsony, p.12.

ment a massive settlement of Slovaks started in the "southern zone of settlement" (the areas reannexed to Hungary between 1938 and 1945), with the support of the police. Some more successful Czechoslovakian diplomacy was considered to be the signing of the agreement on population transfer (based on parity) by Czechoslovakia and Hungary (February 27, 1946), under pressure from the Allied Control Commission. According to this agreement the same number of Hungarians living in Slovakia could be forcefully expatriated as those Hungarian citizens living in Hungary who, declaring themselves to be Slovak, were tempted to resettle in Czechoslovakia by various social promises. For the Hungarian government the expulsion of Hungarians living in their ancient settlement area - even in the form of population transfer - was unacceptable. This is why it strove to delay and postpone its implementation. In an anti-Hungarian, chauvinist atmosphere created by a planned and sophisticated manipulation, the Czechoslovakian authorities deported 43,546 Hungarians (5,422 were only six years of age) from 393 settlements in Slovakia to Czech parts of the country[84] between October 19, 1946. and February 26, 1947, where they lived in inhuman circumstances. This enforced action, deportation was labelled by a presidential decree of 88/1945. on public work as "recruitment", "involvement in public work", "labour service" or "relocation of the population". In fact it differed from the voluntary employment of Slovaks in the Czech lands by an enforced transfer of Hungarians and an immediate expropriation of their possessions and property which were distributed among Slovak colonists. As a matter of fact, this action was eventually stopped following Hungarian, American and West-European protest and was a warning to the Hungarian government about one of the possible alternatives to the Czechoslovakian solution of the Hungarian issue: either the Hungarian state was willing to receive the Hungarians from Slovakia, or the latter would be distributed more or less evenly over Czech parts of the country. This dispersion still was under way when the Allied States signed the peace treaty with Hungary (Paris, February 10, 1947.), restoring the state borders of January 1, 1938 though they ceded a further three villages (Oroszvár, Dunacsún, Horvátjárfalu) from Hungary to Czechoslovakia. The victorious powers did not agree on a territorial solution to the ethnic tensions which left national minorities in Central Europe without the protection of their collective rights, thus preserving ethnic problems for a long time. At the same time, again on the insistence of the USA, no unilateral expulsion of Hungarians from Slovakia was allowed. Anticipating the dispersion of Hungarians in the Czech lands the government of Hungary was forced to start with the population transfer (April 12, 1947.)[85]. On this day the expulsion of Hungarians from Slovakia started (from the Galánta and Léva districts)[86]. Owing to disagreements around the property rights and the missing principle of parity, it was a slow process

---

[84] Vadkerty K. 1996 A deportálások. A szlovákiai magyarok csehországi kényszerközmunkája 1945-1948 között (The deportations. The forced labour of Hungarians of Slovakia in Czech Lands between 1945 and 1948), Kalligram, Bratislava-Pozsony, pp.42-43., Kaplan, K. 1993 Csehszlovákia igazi arca (The true face of Czechoslovakia) 1945-1948, Kalligram, Bratislava-Pozsony, p.136.

[85] ibid. 31.

[86] Čas, 1947.04.03.

which lasted from April 12, 1947 to June 12, 1948 and from December 20, 1948 to September 01, 1948[87]. With this population transfer 68,407 Hungarians were forced to leave Slovakia for Hungary and about 6,000 "of their own free will". 73,273 people from Hungary declaring themselves to be Slovak, although usually without any such identity and hardly speaking the language[88], but simply eager to expropriate property that had formerly belonged to Hungarians, were resettled in South Slovakia, as this territory was called[89]. Apart from the Slovaks of Hungary and colonists from the inner mountain regions, the Czechoslovakian government had managed (with economic promises) to persuade several thousand Slovaks to repatriate from Rumania, Bulgaria, from the Soviet Union (primarily from Transcarpathia) and Yugoslavia[90]. According to our investigations, in the borderland districts 236,000 Slovaks moved between 1945 and 1950, who had previously lived in the country or abroad[91]. Within the Hungarian ethnic area the centre of Slovak colonisation (and at the same time of the expulsion of Hungarians) were towns situated along the language border (Kassa, Rozsnyó, Rimaszombat, Losonc, Léva, Érsekújvár, Vágsellye, Galánta, Szenc), the main transport zones (main roads and railways) and the most fertile rural regions (e.g. along the Pozsony-Galánta-Érsekújvár-Komárom-Párkány axis, in Garam region, and in the area between Losonc and Rimaszombat, Szepsi and Nagyida).

The ethnic composition and statistics of the population of South Slovakia were heavily influenced not only by the migrations already mentioned, but by another form of ethnic expansion, so-called "re-Slovakization" [92]. More than half of the Hungarians frightened and deprived of their rights (381,995 up to January 1 1948), especially those living in towns, in ethnically-mixed villages or who were scattered, applied to call themselves Slovaks. This meant being granted citizenship and staying in their homeland. Only 282,594 of these applications were accepted by the Commission on Reslovakization[93], obviously due to a lack of command of the language and due to "racial deficiencies". Of these, owing to the slow consolidation of the political situation, 60,000 Hungarians turned back to their original national status by 1950 and a further 80,000 by

---

[87] Szabó K. - É.Szőke I. 1982 Adalékok a magyar-csehszlovák lakosságcsere történetéhez (Contributions to the history of the Hungarian-Czechoslovak population exchange) — in: Valóság 1982.10.p.93.

[88] Obzory, 1947.10.25.

[89] Zvara, J. 1965 A magyar nemzetiségi kérdés megoldása Szlovákiában (The solution of the Hungarian ethnic question in Slovakia), Politikai Kiadó, Bratislava, p.36.

[90] Of these only the number of repatriants from Rumania was sizeable (estimated at c. 16,000).

[91] 142,000 of the 236,000 resettled Slovaks colonised the southern territories disannexed from Hungary. 80,000 moved to Pozsony and Pozsonyligetfalu, 14,000 of them settled down in villages formerly predominantly inhabited by Germans.

[92] In decree 20000/I-IV/1-1946 of the Office of Home Affairs (06.17.1946.) it was made possible for Hungarians rejecting their original ethnicity to officially declare themselves Slovaks, so getting rid of the inhuman anti-Hungarian discrimination /Vadkerty K. 1993 A reszlovakizáció, Kalligram, Bratislava-Pozsony/

[93] ibid. p.109.

1961, while the re-Slovakization of 140,000 of them (predominantly town-dwellers) became permanent.

Following these events, the ethnic composition of the "South Slovakia of Belvedere" (the so-called "resettlement area") underwent a profound change between the censuses of 1941 and 1950. The number of Hungarian native speakers (729,000 in 1941) is estimated to have fallen to 451,000[94] by 1950 (from 85 % in 1941 to 52,6 % in 1950). This was as a result of the deportation and emigration of Jews (38,000), the expulsion of Hungarians in 1945 (31,000), the resettlement of 74,000 people to Hungary, a decline following deportations to the Czech lands (20,000), and the loss through re-Slovakization. Together with the Hungarians who suddenly "turned into Slovaks" and 142,000 colonists, the number of Slovaks rose here to 370,000, that is from 13.3 % to 43.2 % (1941-1950). The organizers of ethnic cleansing managed to target towns located along the ethnic boundary with a Hungarian majority until 1945 turning them into settlements of Slovak majority[95]. There was a dramatic southward movement of the Hungarian-Slovak ethnic boundary in rural areas in the vicinity of Léva, Kassa and Tőketerebes, where the greatest Hungarian ethnic loss could be observed *(Fig. 14.)*.

To sum up: the Czechoslovakian state, in spite of the anti-Hungarian measures taken and deportations implemented between 1945 and 1948, did not manage to achieve its primary goal, the elimination of the majority of Hungarians in the south of the state. The previously uniform Hungarian character of the border region was, however, broken by Slovak colonization making it more or less mixed ethnically. The intimidation and humiliation of the Hungarian population and the nationalistic and social measures involving the resettlement of nearly 150,000 Slovaks among the Hungarians, further aggravated and conserved internal political and inter-state tensions for a long period, thus hindering the normalization of the Hungarian-Slovak coexistence.

As the shocking events of the 1940's faded, an increasing number of formerly scared and "re-Slovakized" Hungarians reassumed their Hungarian ethnicity in the census statistics. In 1970, there was already a record of 552,006 people claiming Hungarian ethnicity and 600,249 declaring Hungarian as their mother tongue. At best, the latter figure corresponds to the number recorded 80 years ago and falls far behind the 761,434 people whose native language was Hungarian in 1941.

In the past decade, the mobility of the Hungarians was increasingly determined by living conditions and the growing disparity between labour supply and demand. The contrast between the urban centre and its periphery became more marked, increasing the mobility of the increasingly open Hungarian rural society along the border. This was primarily manifested in the resettlement of young Hungarians to towns along the lan-

---

[94] In our survey, ethnic data of the Czechoslovak census of 1950 — similar to that of the 1949 Hungarian census — has not been taken into account, due to the distortions stemming from the intimidation of national minorities. In 1950 a mere 354,.532 people declared themselves to be Hungarian in the whole of Slovakia. With a slow dissolution of this fear, 518,782 persons did so in 1961.

[95] The ethnic composition of certain towns had undergone a profound change between 1941 and 1950 due to a drastic drop in the share of the Hungarians: Kassa (from 83,5 % down to 3,9), Rozsnyó (92,7 %-34 %), Rimaszombat (92,7 %-43 %), Losonc (84,5 %-16,4 %), Léva (89,4 %-17,8 %), Érsekújvár (91,3 %-31 %), Komárom (96,1 %-54 %), Galánta (87,5 %-1 4,5 %).

guage border which have a majority Slovak population, mostly in Pozsony and Kassa. As a result, the percentage of Hungarians in settlements where Hungarians comprised a minority between 1970 and 1991 increased from 17% to 22.4 %, while the percentage of Hungarians living in a predominant majority (75 % <) decreased from 63% to 52 %.

Natural assimilation, due to intermarriage between ethnic groups in territories with a Slovak majority (in 1982, 27.1% of Hungarian men and 24.7% of Hungarian women chose Slovak partners) was made even more probable by a large amount of migration. For decades, even centuries there has been significant territorial disparity in emigration and birth control. The average age of the Hungarian population is quite high in the territories between Párkány–Zseliz–Ipolyság, in the region near Ajnácskő and Pelsőc, and along the Bodrog-Latorca rivers. On the other hand, the Hungarians of Csallóköz and in part those in Pozsony and the Galánta district demonstrate the most favourable demographic indicators. Their birthrate of 6 per mille in 1983 by far exceeded not only that of the neighbouring Hungarian counties of Győr-Moson-Sopron and Komárom (-0.3 – -0.6 per mille), but also that of the demographically most fertile Hungarian county, Szabolcs-Szatmár-Bereg County (2 per mille).

Alongside a relatively modest increase and then a stagnation in the number of Hungarians, came an increasingly identity-conscious Gypsy population and the establishment of an independent Roma category at the 1991 census. Due to a high natural increase in the population of those qualifying as Gypsies, their number has risen dynamically for the past one hundred years (1893: 36,000, 1947: 84,438, 1966: 165,000, 1989: 253,943, 1996: c. 300,000)[96]. According to a survey conducted during the 1980 census 78.7 % of Gypsies declared themselves to be Slovak (slovačike roma), while 20 % of them considered themselves to be Hungarian (ungarike roma)[97]. In the 1991 census they were not described but ethnicity could be declared. 75,802 people, 28 % of the Gypsy population, declared themselves to be of Roma ethnicity, and represented the ethnic majority in 9 settlements. Gypsies live predominantly east of the Poprád-Losonc line, especially on the territory of the historical counties of Gömör, Szepes, Sáros és Abaúj, while their largest community is in Kassa City. Within the Hungarian ethnic area they live in Gömör[98] (Rimaszombat, Tornalja, Pelsőc, Rozsnyó, Krasznahorkaváralja and environs) and in Nógrád (Losonc, Fülek and environs), but sizeable communities are also to be found in western Hungarian settlement areas (e.g. Dunaszerdahely, Jóka, Komárom, Ógyalla and Sáró) and in eastern ones (e.g. Nagyida, Deregnyő, Királyhelmec and Tiszacsernyő).

---

[96] Jurová, A. 1996 Cigányok-romák Szlovákiában 1945 után (Gipsies-Romanies in Slovakia after 1945), Regio 7. 2. pp.35-56.

[97] Gyönyör J. 1989 Államalkotó nemzetiségek (State-forming nations), Madách, Bratislava, 141.p.

[98] On certain Hungarian villages in Gömör becoming Gypsy in character and changing ethnic behaviour of the Gypsies see: Keményfi R. 1998 ibid. 296p.

THE PRESENT TERRITORY OF HUNGARIAN SETTLEMENT IN SLOVAKIA

At the time of the 1991 Slovakian census, of the 5.3 million population of the country, the ratio of the members of state-forming ethnic groups were 85.7 % (Slovaks), and 1 % (Czechs). In 1910 there was a 10.4 % combined number of Germans, Ruthenians[99] and Poles (Gorals), though it dropped to 0.7 % by 1991, owing to natural assimilation and expulsion. Though the number of Hungarians (567,.296) had risen considerably compared with 1961 (518,782), their proportion, owing to a dynamic growth of Slovaks, had fallen to 10.7 %. The number of native Hungarian speakers at the 1991 population census was 608.221 (11.5 %). From the administrative perspective, 67.7 % of ethnic Hungarians in Slovakia live in the western regions (Kraj of Pozsony, Nagyszombat and Nyitra) *(Tab. 11.)*. Dunaszerdahely (87.2%) and Komárom (74.2%) can be considered the most "Hungarian" of all the districts. In the districts[100] of Vágsellye, Galánta, Érsekújvár and Rimaszombat Hungarians are balanced by the Slovaks, 40–44 % *(Tab. 12.)*.

Of the Hungarians in Slovakia a considerable number (at least 100 persons) and percentage (at least 10 %) inhabit 550 settlements. They comprise an absolute majority (50 % <) in 432 settlements and almost exclusive majority (90%<) in 164 settlements. Due to their geographic and historical preferences, Hungarians mostly inhabit large and medium-sized villages (1,000–5,000 inhabitants), but 16.7 % of them also live in small towns with 10,000-30,000 inhabitants.

Table 11. The new administrative regions (kraj) of Slovakia and the Hungarian minority

region (kraj)	total population		ethnic Hungarians	
	1991	1994	number (1991)	per cent (1991)
Pozsony-Bratislava	608,287	616,871	30,890	5.1
Nagyszombat-Trnava	562,355	547,173	136,358	24.2
Nyitra-Nitra	708,313	718,358	216,633	30.6
Trencsén-Trenčín	604,016	608,990	1,246	0.2
Zsolna-Žilina	670,850	682,983	670	0.1
Besztercebánya-Banská Bystrica	661,628	664,072	85,633	12.9
Kassa-Košice	748,722	753,849	96,021	12.8
Eperjes-Prešov	746,168	763,911	807	0.1

Sources: 1991 = Oriskó N. 1996 Coexistence-Spolužitie-Együttélés Political Movement, Bratislava, 1994 = Administratívna mapa Slovenskej Republiky (1:400,000), Vojenský kartografický ústav, š.p., Harmanec, 1996

---

[99] As a result of the ethnic expansion of Slovaks and pressure to assimilate, the number of Ruthenians decreased from 203,000 to 30,000 between 1840 and 1991 and their proportion of the population of Greek Catholics fell from 94.7 % to 14,3 %. The eventual disappearance of Ruthenians in Slovakia (similar to that of the Polish Gorals) has also been reflected by the diminishing number of villages with a Ruthenian ethnic majority from 300 to 29 on the territory of present-day Slovakia between 1773 and 1991.

[100] Data refers to the territory of districts after 1996.

Table 12. Selected new districts (okres) of Slovakia and the Hungarian minority

district (okres)	total population	ethnic Hungarians	
	1991	number (1991)	per cent (1991)
Szenc-Senec	49,868	11,893	23.8
Dunaszerdahely-Dunajská Streda	109,345	95,310	87.2
Galánta-Galanta	92,645	38,615	41.7
Vágsellye-Šaľa	54,159	21,754	40.2
Érsekújvár-Nové Zámky	153,466	63,747	41.5
Komárom-Komárno	109,279	78,859	74.2
Léva-Levice	120,703	38,169	31.6
Nagykürtös-Veľký Krtiš	46,813	14,384	30.7
Losonc-Lučenec	72,946	22,513	30.9
Rimaszombat-Rimavská Sobota	82,112	36,404	44.3
Nagyrőce-Revúca	41,765	10,256	24.6
Rozsnyó-Rožňava	59,059	21,434	36.3
Kassa-Košice-okolie (environs)	99,292	16,240	16.4
Tőketerebes-Trebišov	100,520	33,191	33.0
Nagymihály-Michalovce	104,003	13,758	13.2

Source: Our calculation based on the publication: Národnost a náboženské vyznanie obyvateľstva SR (definitivne výsledky sčítania ľudu, domov a bytov 1991), Štatistický Úrad SR, Bratislava, 1993

According to the ethnic data of the 1991 Czechoslovak census, the largest Hungarian communities are concentrated in Komárom, Pozsony, Dunaszerdahely, Érsekújvár, Kassa, Rimaszombat, Párkány, Gúta, Somorja and Nagymegyer *(Tab. 13.)*. Our estimates for 1980 differ to a certain extent: Pozsony (43,000), Kassa (35,000), Komárom (22,900), Érsekújvár (17,000), Dunaszerdahely (15,500), Léva (12,800). According to the official 1991 census data, the percentage of ethnic Hungarians exceeds that of the Slovaks only in 13 towns. Of these, the most Hungarian are Nagymegyer, Dunaszerdahely, Gúta and Királyhelmec *(Tab. 14.)*.

The inhabitants of the capital (Pozsony - Bratislava) and the Szenc district are the western-most representatives of Hungarians in Slovakia *(Figs.14., 15.)*. The most important settlements of the Hungarians of this region (Szenc, Magyarbél, Fél, Éberhárd), belong to the Pozsony - Bratislava agglomeration. Due to the favourable geographical location of these settlements, the immigration of Slovaks continues to increase, causing the decrease in the population percentage of Hungarians.

In the Dunaszerdahely district with its strong Hungarian character, significant numbers of Slovaks inhabit only the towns of Dunaszerdahely, Somorja and Nagymegyer. The most important villages in the district – all predominantly Hungarian – include Nagymagyar, Illésháza, Nagylég, Bős, Várkony, Ekecs, Nyárasd, Vásárút and Diósförgepatony.

The centre of the Galánta district, with 41-52% Hungarian inhabitants, is located at an important railway junction. A majority of the Hungarians living in the Galánta and Vágsellye districts work at the "Duslo" chemical works in Vágsellye and the machine-tool and food industry in Galánta and Diószeg. Most of the Hungarian villages in this region (called "Mátyusföld" - Land of Matthew of Csák, 13-14th cent.)

Table 13. The largest Hungarian communities in Slovakia (1991)

Settlements	Population
1. Komárom / Komárno	23,745
2. Pozsony / Bratislava	20,312
3. Dunaszerdahely / Dunajská Streda	19,347
4. Érsekújvár / Nové Zámky	13,350
5. Kassa / Košice	10,760
6. Rimaszombat / Rimavská Sobota	9,854
7. Párkány / Štúrovo	9,804
8. Gúta / Kolárovo	9,101
9. Somorja / Šamorín	8,561
10. Nagymegyer / Veľký Meder	8,043
11. Fülek / Fiľakovo	7,064
12. Galánta / Galanta	6,890
13. Királyhelmec / Kráľovský Chlmec	6,400
14. Nagykapos / Veľké Kapušany	6,007
15. Rozsnyó / Rožňava	5,826
16. Ipolyság / Šahy	5,562
17. Tornalja / Tornaľa	5,547
18. Vágsellye / Šaľá	5,413
19. Léva / Levice	5,165

Source: Final data of the Czechoslovakian census of 1991 (ethnicity).

are located between the Little Danube and the Pozsony–Érsekújvár railway line, such as Jóka, Nagyfödémes, Felsőszeli and Alsószeli.

In the Komárom district, the other area in Slovakia with a Hungarian majority, most Hungarians live in the towns of Komárom, Gúta and Ógyalla. Other centres in the network of settlements in this district are Naszvad, Marcelháza, Perbete, Bátorkeszi, Nemesócsa and Csallóközaranyos. The Komárom shipyard and the Ógyalla brewery are the two main industrial employers of the region.

Table 14. Towns in Slovakia with absolute Hungarian majority (1991)

Settlements	Percentage of the Hungarians
1. Nagymegyer / Veľký Meder	87.0
2. Dunaszerdahely / Dunajská Streda	83.3
3. Gúta / Kolárovo	82.7
4. Királyhelmec / Kráľovský Chlmec	80.4
5. Párkány / Štúrovo	73.5
6. Somorja / Šamorín	71.0
7. Tornalja / Tornaľa	67.8
8. Fülek / Fiľakovo	67.6
9. Ipolyság / Šahy	65.0
10. Nagykapos / Veľké Kapušany	63.8
11. Komárom / Komárno	63.6
12. Ógyalla / Hurbanovo	53.5
13. Zseliz / Želiezovce	53.5

Source: Final data of the Czechoslovakian census of 1991 (ethnicity).

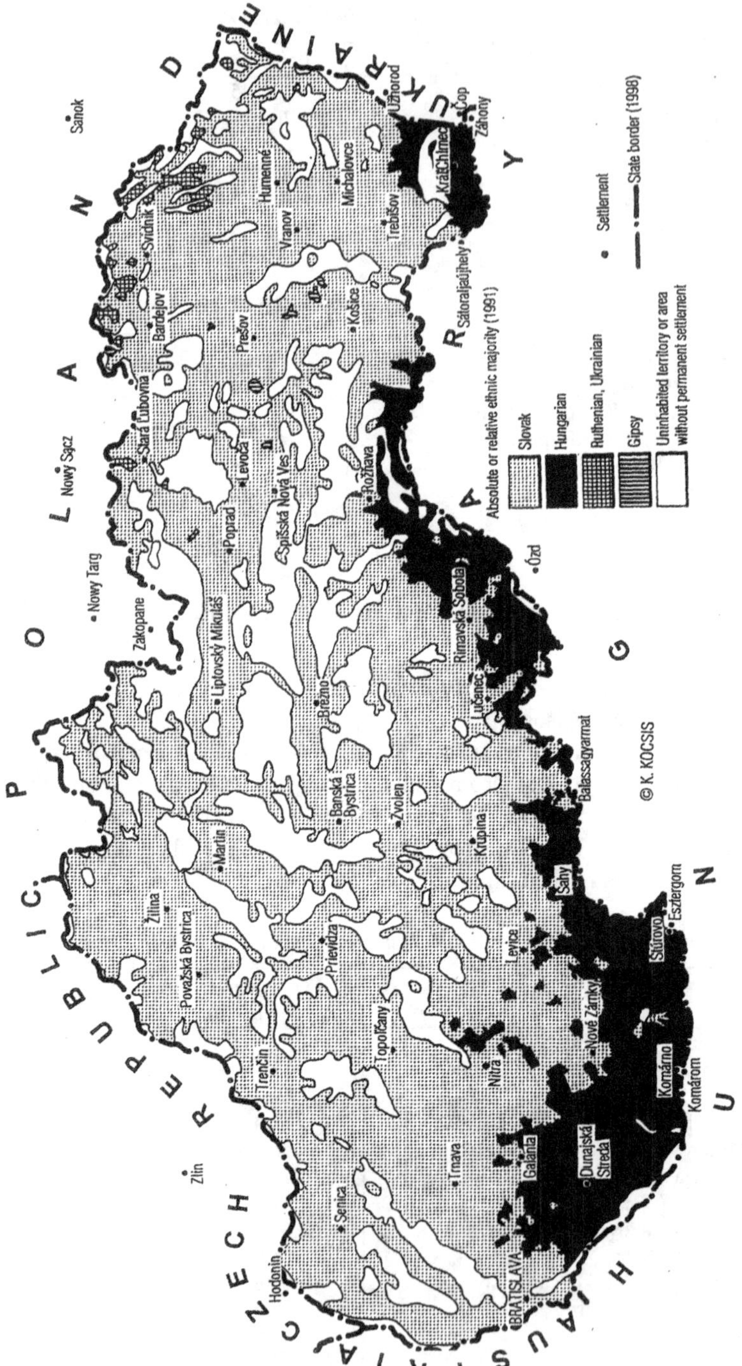

Figure 15. Ethnic map of Slovakia (1991)

The majority of the Hungarian population of the Érsekújvár district, which lies between the Vág and the Danube Rivers and extends along the Pozsony-Budapest international railway line, live in the proximity of the famous cellulose and paper-producing town of Párkány. Most Hungarians living in the vicinity of the half-Slovak and half-Hungarian Érsekújvár, an important railway junction and the centre of the electro-technical refrigerating machine industry, inhabit Tardoskedd, Udvard, Szimő and Zsitvabesenyő.

Nyitranagykér, located in the northern part of the Érsekújvár district, together with Nagycétény and Nyitracsehi close to the territory of the Nyitra district, form an important Hungarian enclave. The percentage of Hungarians in the population of Hungarian villages on the southern slopes of the Tribecs mountain range in Nyitragerencsér, Alsócsitár, Barslédec, Ghymes, Zsére, Kolon, Pográny, Alsóbodok is gradually decreasing because of development in the vicinity of Nyitra, Slovak immigration, and linguistic assimilation.

The Hungarian language border in the Léva district, enlarged since the incorporation of the Ipolyság and Zseliz districts, was driven back in the direction of the Ipoly as a consequence of evacuations preceding battles along the Garam river in 1945 and the ruthless post-war deportation of local Hungarians. In the district seat of Léva, known mostly for its textile industry, the percentage of Hungarians is 15.2% according to 1991 Czechoslovak census data. (In 1941 it was 87.2 %). In the immediate proximity of Léva, Hungarians inhabit only a few small villages (Zsemlér, Alsószecse, Felsőszecse, Várad, Vámosladány etc.). The Calvinist Hungarian population of Mohi was resettled elsewhere in the early 1980s due to the new nuclear power-plant (Mochovce) being constructed there. In the strongly mixed ethnic surroundings of Zseliz, the greatest number of Hungarians live in Nagyölved, Farnad, Nagysalló and Oroszka – the location of one of Slovakia's most important sugar factories. In the environs of Ipolyság, most Hungarians inhabit Palást and Ipolyvisk.

The shrinking and disconnected ethnic Hungarian territory on the right bank of the Ipoly river is part of the Nagykürtös district. In addition to the largest Hungarian community of Ipolynyék, we must also mention Lukanénye, Csáb, Ipolybalog, Bussó and Ipolyhídvég.

In the Losonc district, the northern part of the former Nógrád county, the most important Hungarian communities live mainly in the villages of Ragyolc, Gömörsid, Fülekpüspöki, Béna, Sőreg, Csákányháza etc. in an ethnic territory also containing Slovakian colonies. This is in the vicinity of the towns of Losonc and Fülek, known for its enamelled pots and furniture.

In Southern and Central Gömör, the districts of Rimaszombat and Nagyrőce were enlarged with the addition of the formerly almost entirely Hungarian, and later dismembered districts of Feled and Tornalja. The most important Hungarian settlements here are Rimaszombat, Tornalja towns and Rimaszécs, Feled, Ajnácskő, Várgede, Vámosbalog, Sajógömör.

Upstream along the Sajó, in the district of Rozsnyó we reach the northernmost area of the Carpathian Basin's ethnic Hungarian territory (at Krasznahorkaváralja). In the Sajó valley settlements of the Hungarian-inhabited borderland, especially in Rozsnyó and Pelsőc, the percentage of Hungarians is diminishing due to a large immigration of Slovaks. In contrast, the percentage of Hungarians is increasing in the villages of the Gömör-Torna (Slovak) Karst of peripheral location (Szilice, Szádalmás, Hárskút, Várhosszúrét etc).

In the vicinity of Kassa City, Hungarian communities can be found only in the territory of the former Szepsi district, not more than 10-15 kilometres from the Hungarian border (Torna, Szepsi, Szádudvarnok, Tornaújfalu, Debrőd, Jászó, Buzita, Jánok etc.). The Hungarians in this region who work in industry, make their living in the plants of Kassa – the East-Slovakian metropolis with over 235,000 inhabitants and at the centre of the historical Abaúj-Torna county, and in Szepsi and Nagyida, as well as at the cement works of Torna. The scattered Hungarian (partly Calvinist) population east of Kassa (between Magyarbőd and Eszkáros) declared themselves to be Slovaks at the time of the postwar censuses.

After crossing the Szalánci mountains (the northern, Slovakian side of the Tokaj-Eperjes Mountains), we reach the districts of Tőketerebes and Nagymihály, which include the former ethnic Hungarian districts of Nagykapos and Királyhelmec. The Hungarians in this area live in a relatively compact ethnic block, between the Ung-Bodrog rivers and the Ukrainian and Hungarian border. The unity of the almost thousand-year-old Hungarian ethnic area is disrupted only by the newly-settled Slovak population in the modest industrial centres of Nagykapos (34.5%), Királyhelmec (16.3%), Bodrogszerdahely (32.3%), Vaján (15.4%) – the location of one of Slovakia's largest thermal power plants, and Tiszacsernyő (30.8%) – the very important international railway border crossing. Most of the Hungarian rural population in parts of the historical counties of Zemplén and Ung (which are located in Slovakia) live in Lelesz, Bodrogszerdahely, Szomotor, Kisgéres, Nagytárkány, Battyán and Bély.

Chapter 3

THE HUNGARIANS OF TRANSCARPATHIA

Transcarpathia[1] is the name given to the present West-Ukrainian region in the North-east of the Carpathian Basin, bordered by Slovakia, Hungary and Rumania. The administrative name of Subcarpathia - Transcarpathia, refers to an area of 12,800 square kilometres, which gradually became commonly known after the Peace Treaty of Trianon (1920). On this territory belonging to the Ukraine, the 1989 census recorded 155,711 inhabitants of Hungarian ethnicity and 166,700 Hungarian native speakers. According to our calculations this number differs from the probable number of Hungarian speakers of 220,000[2]. The Hungarians of this region – far fewer in number than the Hungarians of Transylvania and Slovakia – represent 6.1% of Hungarian national minorities inhabiting the Carpathian Basin.

THE NATURAL ENVIRONMENT

Ninety-one percent of Transcarpathian Hungarians live on the north-eastern periphery of the Great Hungarian Plain (Alföld), the official name of which is the Transcarpathian Lowland. Apart from the peat of the drained Szernye marsh and the alluvial soil along the rivers, the plain is covered by meadow soil. Several young volcanic cones and elevations can be found near Beregszász, Mezőkaszony, Salánk and Nagyszőlős *(Fig.16.)*.

The overwhelmingly Hungarian-populated plain, characterised mainly by brown forest soil and beech groves and interspersed here and there with oak woods, plays a decisive part in the food supply of Transcarpathia. It is flanked by 700 -1100 meter high volcanic mountains called Pojána-Szinyák, Borló-Gyil, the Nagyszőlős and Avas mountain ranges. The rest of the region's Hungarian population (9 %) lives in the highlands not far from the Tisza River between Huszt and Kőrösmező.

---

[1] Transcarpathia (Ukr. Zakarpatye, Hung. Kárpátalja) or Transcarpathian Region of Ukraine between the 9th century and 1918 formed continously a part of Hungary, on the territory of Ung, Bereg, Ugocsa and Máramaros counties. Following the World War I., according to the Treaty of Trianon (June 4, 1920) this northeast Hungarian, historic region was annexed to the new created Czechoslovakia under the name: Subcarpathian Rus' (Podkarpatská Rus) or Ruthenia (Rusinsko). Transcarpathia returned to Hungary between 1938/39 and 1944 as Subcarpathia (Kárpátalja). Following the Soviet supremacy (1945 - 1991) this area became an administrative region (called "Zakarpatska oblast") of the independent Ukraine.

[2] Including the Greek Catholics and Gipsies of Hungarian native tongue.

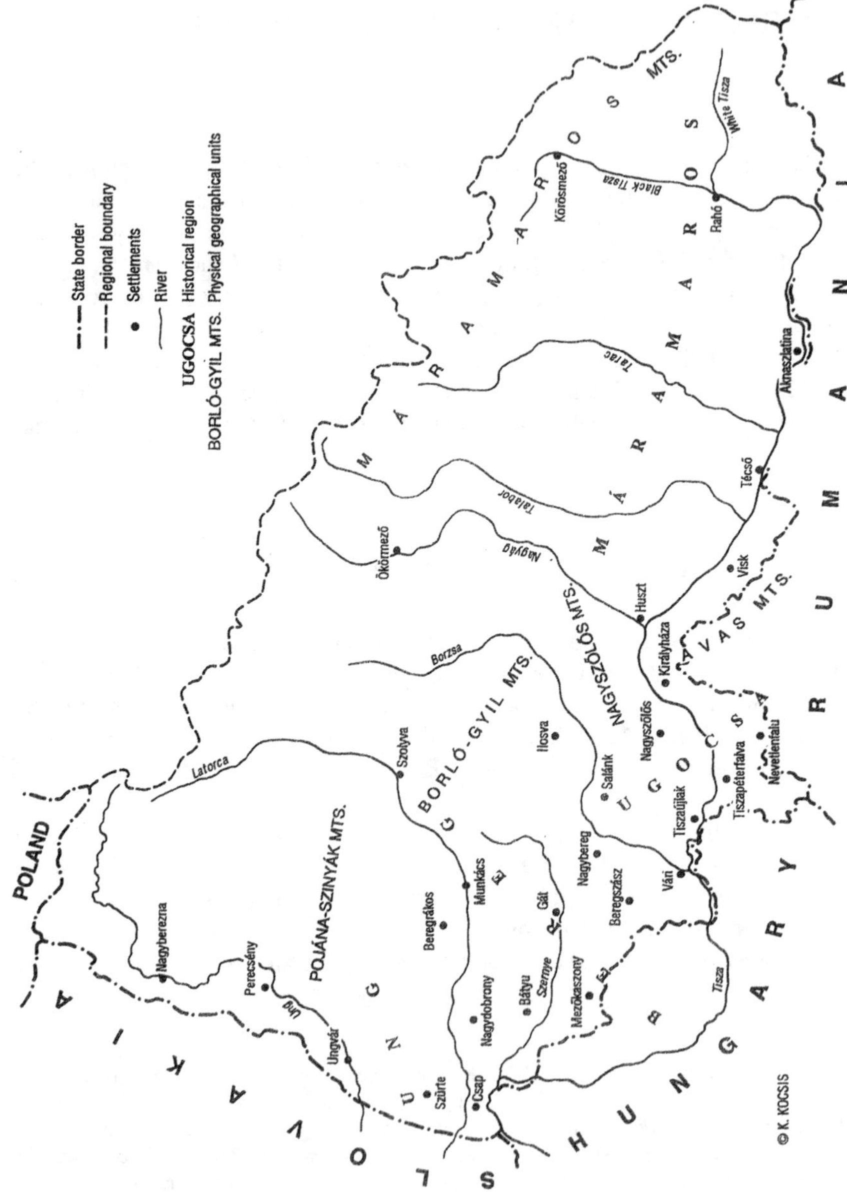

Figure 16. Important Hungarian geographical names in Transcarpathia

The most important river in the territory is the Tisza, made up of two branches, the Black Tisza and the White Tisza originating in the Máramaros Mountains and flowing 223 kilometres on Ukrainian territory. The still relatively rapid Tisza breaks through the volcanic mountain range at the "Huszt-Gate" and then slows down and builds up an alluvial deposit in the Ugocsa region. Its most important tributaries in the Máramaros region are the Tarac, Talabor and Nagyág.

ETHNIC PROCESSES DURING THE PAST FIVE HUNDRED YEARS

According to the taxation census of 1495, carried out on the territory of Ung, Bereg, Ugocsa and Máramaros counties (almost constituting present-day Transcarpathia), 75,685 people[3] are assumed to have lived in 21 towns and 592 villages[4], out of which 19 towns and 347 villages may have had a Hungarian ethnic majority[5]. If we postulate that in this area there was almost a tenfold difference between the population in towns and in villages[6], 69 % of the population were Hungarians, 16.8 % of them were Ruthenians, 8.4 % Slovaks and 7.5 % Rumanians *(Tab. 15.)*. The proportion of Hungarians reached 65 % in Ung County, 81 % in Bereg County and 92 % in Ugocsa. Hungarians represented a relative majority (37.6 %) in Máramaros as opposed to Rumanians (32.6 %) and Ruthenians (29.8 %). By the end of the 15th century, on the present-day territory of Transcarpathia, the area of ethnic Hungarian settlement extended up to the foothills of the mountains along the former defence strip (Hung. "gyepű") which was abandoned in the 13th century *(Fig. 17.)*. This Hungarian ethnic boundary linked Ungvár-Szered-Munkács-Beregszentmiklós-Nagyszőlős between the Ung and Tisza rivers. The Hungarian ethnic area was also extensive in the eastern part of Ugocsa and in Máramaros (almost uninhabited until the flourishing of salt mining), thus the Tisza section of the defence zone included the most important Hungarian settlements: the towns of Huszt, Visk, Técső and (now a part of Rumania) Hosszúmező and Máramarossziget. Most of the descendants of German and Flemish miners, artisans and viniculturists settled during the 13th and 14th centuries and assimilated with the Hungarians by the end of the 15th century[7]. A sizeable population with German names could be found only in Visk, Szászfalu and Beregszász.

---

[3] Kubinyi A. ibid. pp.157-158.

[4] Csánki D. ibid. pp.384-453., The Drugeth - Estate (1437) SSUArchive of the Convent of Lelesz 1400-172.Df. 234.235 (after Engel P.)

[5] The assumed distribution of the villages by ethnic majority could be the following: Hungarian 347, Ruthenian 137, Slovak 47, Rumanian 60.

[6] Szabó I. 1937 Ugocsa megye, MTA, Budapest, Bélay V. 1943 Máramaros megye társadalma és nemzetiségei (Society and Ethnic Groups of Máramaros County), Település és Népiségtörténeti értekezések 7., Budapest.

[7] Szabó I. 1937 ibid. 24., 25.p., Bélay V. 1943 ibid. 27.p.

Table 15. Ethnic structure of the population of historical Northeast Hungary (1495-1910)

Year	Total population		Hungarians		Ruthenians		Slovaks		Germans		Rumanians		Jews		Others	
	number	%	number	%	number	%	number	%	number	%	number	%	number	%	number	%
1495	75,685	100	51,900	69.0	12,600	16.6	5,300	7.0			5,680	7.5			205	0.3
1720		100		38.0		49.7		←		0.2		1.6				10.8
1787	234,377	100											1,887	0.8		
1840	443,827	100	136,833	31.0	180,088	40.6	32,771	7.4	9,691	2.2	61,527	13.9	22,882	5.2	35	0.0
1850	480,537	100	127,721	27.0	216,650	45.1	23,858	4.9	11,047	2.3	51,608	10.7	40,695	8.5	8,958	1.9
1857	469,744	100	172,146	37.0	184,830	39.3	41,959	8.9	12,346	2.6	58,463	12.4				
1869	571,259	100	165,673	29.0	257,177	45.0	37,919	6.6	23,970	4.2	72,366	12.7			14,154	2.5
1880	572,897	100	154,761	27.0	248,057	43.3	42,204	7.4	46,572	8.1	65,427	11.4			15,876	2.8
1890	658,444	100	185,034	28.0	276,546	42.0	38,937	5.9	80,862	12.3	74,008	11.2			3,057	0.5
1900	754,769	100	227,045	30.0	314,526	41.7	47,858	6.3	78,692	10.4	84,519	11.2			2,129	0.3
1910	848,160	100	270,442	32.0	331,186	39.0	55,487	6.5	93,289	11.0	94,608	11.2			3,148	0.4

Remarks: Historical Northeast Hungary = Territory of Ung, Bereg, Ugocsa and Máramaros Counties (1914). 1720: Ruthenians with Slovaks.

Sources: 1495: Estimation of Kocsis K. based on Csánki D. 1890 Magyarország történelmi földrajza a Hunyadiak korában, MTA Budapest and Kubinyi A. 1996 A Magyar Királyság népessége a 15. század végén — Történelmi Szemle XXXVIII. 1996. 2-3. pp.135-161., 1720: Acsády I. 1896 Magyarország népessége a Pragmatica Sanctio korában 1720 - 21. — Magyar Statisztikai Közlemények XII. /Új folyam/, Budapest 1787: Danyi D. - Dávid Z. 1960 Az első magyarországi népszámlálás (1784-1787), KSH, Budapest 1840: Fényes E. 1842 Magyarország statistikája I., Pest 1850: Hornyánsky, V. 1858 Geographisches Lexikon des Königreiches Ungarn, G. Heckenast, Pest 1857: Fényes Elek 1867 A Magyar Birodalom nemzetiségei és ezek száma vármegyék és járások szerint, Pest 1869: Keleti K. 1871 Hazánk és népe a közgazdaság és a társadalmi statistika szempontjából, Athenaeum, Pest 1880: A Magyar Korona országaiban az 1881. év elején végrehajtott népszámlálás ...Országos Magyar Királyi Statisztikai Hivatal, Budapest 1882 1890: Jekelfalussy József (szerk.) 1892 A Magyar Korona országainak helységnévtára, Országos M. Kir. Statisztikai Hivatal, Budapest, 1900: A Magyar Korona országainak 1900. évi népszámlálása 1. rész. 1902. A népesség általános leírása községenkint, Magyar Statisztikai Közlemények I., 1910: A Magyar Szent Korona országainak 1910. évi népszámlálása 1. rész. 1912 Magyar Statisztikai Közlemények 42.

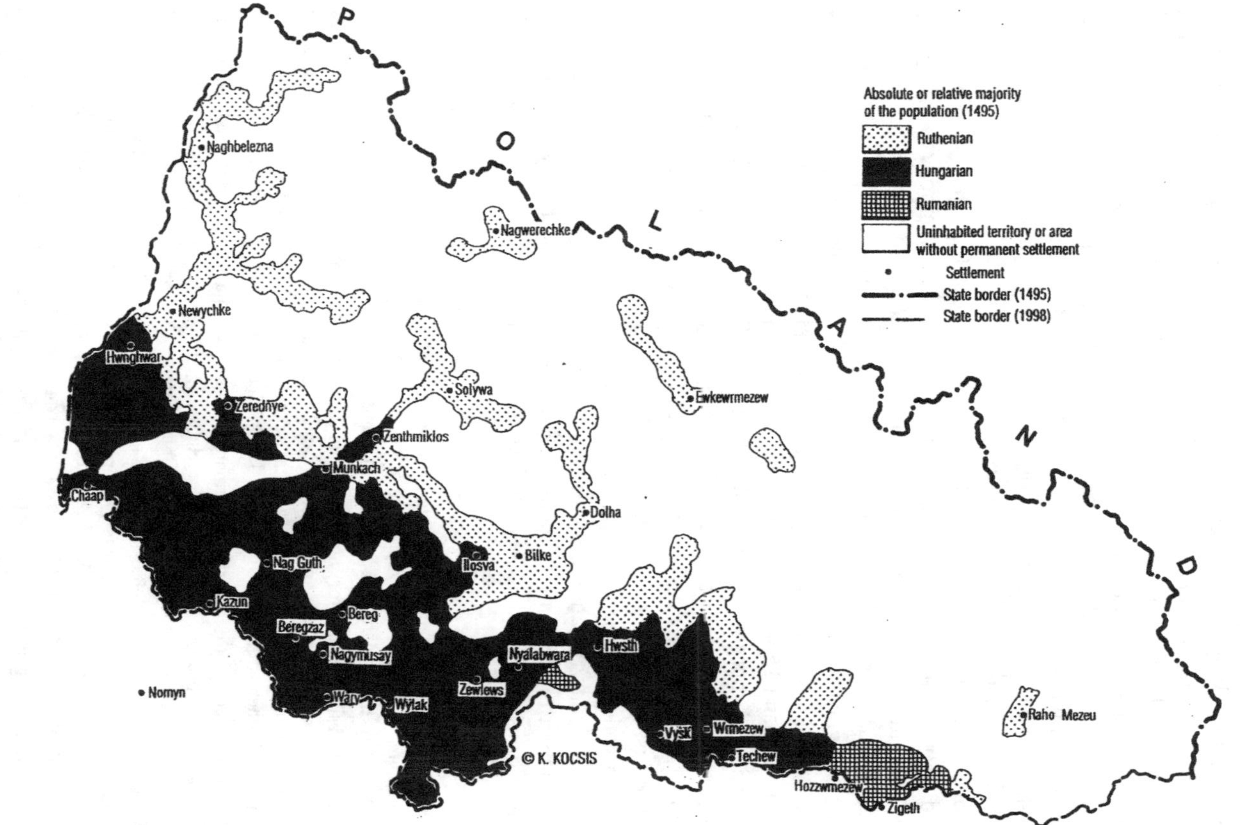

Figure 17. Ethnic map of the present-day territory cf Transcarpathia (late 15th century)
Source: Bélay V. 1943 Máramaros megye társadalma és nemzetiségei, Budapest, Csánki D. 1890 Magyarország történelmi földrajza a Hunyadiak korában, Budapest, Szabó I. 1937 Ugocsa megye, Budapest

Nearly 13,000 Ruthenians, who cannot be regarded as autochtonous[8] in Transcarpathia, formed the majority population in 137 villages at the end of the 15th century. The overwhelming number of these villages were to be found in the neighbourhood of the Hungarian ethnic area, i.e. on the southwestern slopes of the mountains and in the upper, mountainous reaches of the rivers Ung, Latorca, Borzsava, Nagyág, Talabor and Tarac. This was an uninhabited borderland area until the 13th century, when Ruthenians pursuing a pastoral way of life, began to penetrate this zone from Galicia, Volhynia and Podolia, led by their "magistrates" (Hung. kenézes)[9]. They gradually populated higher areas in the borderland zone. At the end of the 15th century, however, most of the mountainous regions of Máramaros, Bereg and Ung counties were still uninhabited woodland and alpine pastures.

Although the area in question had never fallen under Ottoman (Turkish) rule, being situated between the Transylvanian Principality (which symbolized Hungarian independence) and the rest of Hungary under Habsburg administration[10], it was often destroyed, being an area of military operations during the 16th and 17th centuries. Of these disasters the gravest were those caused by the Tartar invasions of 1565, 1594, 1661 and 1717, the Polish incursion of 1657, the campaign of the imperial Habsburg troops between 1684 and 1688 (the siege to the Munkács fortress) and the ravages of the Transylvanian and Habsburg armies crossing the region. These wars and the epidemics accompanying them struck almost exclusively at the Hungarian ethnic territory, i.e. the surroundings of the castles, fortresses and towns, the zones along transport routes and the valley of the Tisza River. As a result, there was a decline in the predominantly Hungarian population which dropped from 102 thousand to 73 thousand between 1598 and 1640[11]. In Ugocsa County located at the opening to the Tisza Valley (still with a 95 % Hungarian population in the mid-16th century[12]) , most seriously hit by warfare , the number of the portas[13] paying tax was 1,775 in 1565/74, 829 in 1638, and 491 in

---

[8] Sobolevskij 1894 Kak davno Russkie živut v Karpatah i za Karpatami (How long Russians live in the Carpathians and beyond), Živaja Starina, pp.524-528., Petrov, A. 1913 Materiali k istorii Ugorskoj Rusi (Materials to the history of Ruthenia in Hungary) VI., St.Petersburg, p.149.

[9] Kenéz ("Cnesius", contactor, magistrate): organizers of settlements, who instigated a massive move of Ruthenian serfs from the areas east of the Carpathians (then part of the Kingdom of Poland) to the previously uninhabited areas of royal estates, on behalf of the new landlords. See Bonkalo, A. 1922 Die ungarländischen Ruthenen, Ungarische Jahrbücher, Bd. I., Berlin - Leipzig, 226.p.

[10] In the 16th and 17th centuries Máramaros County was part of Transylvania, while Ung County belonged to the territory of Hungary under Habsburg rule. Bereg and Ugocsa counties were most frequently occupied by the troops of the Habsburg Empire, but between 1621-1629 and 1645-1648 they were part of the Transylvanian Principality.

[11] Bakács I. 1963 A török hódoltság korának népessége (The Population of Hungary during the Ottoman Period)— in: Kovacsics J. (Ed.) Magyarország történeti demográfiája (Historic Demography of Hungary), Budapest, 129.p., Bélay V. 1943 ibid. 112.p.

[12] Of those figuring in the 1567/74 tithe register of Ugocsa 1371 persons held Hungarian surnames, 61 Slavic, 24 German, 5 Rumanian, 6 Turkish family names and 308 names were ethnically ambiguous (Szabó I. 1937 ibid. 74.p.)

[13] Porta: royal tax-unit which in these years corresponded to a whole serf's tenement.

1663[14]. Parallel to the decline in the Hungarian population there was massive immigration and resettlement of the Ruthenians[15] from beyond the Carpathians, from the Regions of Galicia which then belonged to then to the Kingdom of Poland. They settled in predominantly mountainous areas in the counties of Máramaros, Bereg and Ung which had remained unaffected by the wars. In the 17th century Ruthenians appeared not only in wooded mountainous areas but in ever -increasing numbers in the devastated villages on the fringes of the Hungarian settlement area, and even in some towns (Ungvár, Munkács, Huszt[16]).

Following the failure of the war of independence (1703-1711) led by Prince F. Rákóczi II, the census of 1715 found 6,402 taxpayers (heads of households) on the present territory of Transcarpathia, 41.4 % of whom had Hungarian, and 52.8 % Slavic (Ruthenian) names[17]. At this time, the Hungarian ethnic border stretched northwest and northeast of Munkács, and along the foothills of the Polyána and Borló mountains. The area inhabited by Hungarians included the western third of the present Ilosva district, the whole of Ugocsa County and the Tisza valley up to Técső. The most populous communities of Transcarpathia and the Hungarian ethnic area in 1715 were Beregszász and Visk . However, Hungarian serfs from these areas of mountain foreland (primarily from the Tisza valley and the vicinity of Nagyszőlős and Munkács) who had survived the ravages of war, began to move in increasing numbers to the central regions of the Great Plain. This area had extremely rich soil, and had become depopulated during the Ottoman-Turkish rule and the wars of liberation (e.g. 1683-1699, 1703-1711). At the same time, in the villages of Ugocsa[18], West Máramaros and Central Bereg counties which were abandoned by the Hungarians, Ruthenians moved down from the mountain areas and started to appear while colonisation was also organised by landlords. The immigration of Ruthenians from Galicia and Bukovina to the uninhabited area of Máramaros began to accelerate as salt mining and timber felling in the Upper Tisza region developed (e.g. Rahó, Tiszabogdány and Körösmező). A new Ruthenian ethnographic group had also emerged here between the 17th and 19th centuries: the Hutzuls[19].

By the mid-18th century, as a result of large-scale migration, the Hungarian-Ruthenian ethnic boundary had retreated an average of 10-20 km to the Great Plain. Villages of Ugocsa located at the Tisza gate (where the river enters the plain from the Ruthenian Máramaros) became Hungarian-Ruthenian in ethnic composition. Nevertheless, the more important settlements of the Transcarpathian region (Ungvár, Munkács,

---

[14] Szabó I. 1937 ibid. 74., 92.p.

[15] The Ruthenians were mostly settled by the Hungarian noble families of Bilkei, Dolhai, Lipcsei, Homonnay, Rákóczi (See Bélay V. 1943 ibid. 91.p.).

[16] In 1614 there were 105 Hungarian households and 16 Ruthenian recorded in Huszt (Bélay V. 1943 ibid. 111.p.).

[17] Acsády I. 1896 ibid. pp.25-30., 72-74., 146-150. The ethnic distribution of the taxpayers of Ung, Bereg, Ugocsa and Máramaros counties (8,651 households) was the following: 49.7 % Slavs (Ruthenians and Slovaks), 38 % Hungarians, 1.6 % Rumanians (1715).

[18] Szabó I. 1937 ibid. pp.98-115.

[19] Bonkalo, A. 1922 ibid. 226.p.

Beregszász, Nagyszőlős, Huszt, Visk and Técső) still preserved a majority Hungarian population in 1773[20] *(Fig.18.)*.

In the 18th century Ruthenians moved into the uninhabited or destroyed Hungarian areas, and also German colonists: peasants, vine growers and artisans. After the unsuccessful War of Independence (1703-1711) led by Hungarian Prince F. Rákóczi II, some of his vast estates were granted to L.F. Schönborn (archbishop of Mainz, Germany), who encouraged the massive immigration of Germans from the vicinity of Bamberg and Würzburg. As a result of this colonisation several German villages appeared in the environs of Munkács (e.g. Felsőschönborn, Munkácsújfalu, Pósaháza, Németkucsova and Leányfalva) between 1732 and 1775. In the 1770s and 1780s the Imperial Treasury (Vienna) initiated the resettlement of Austrian lumbermen from Salzkammergut to Máramaros, who founded the settlements of Királymező and Németmokra.

As far as the rate of Hungarians and Ruthenians is concerned, the ethnic structure thus brought about had not changed significantly by the 1880 population census (the only exception now that the Huszts became overwhelmingly Ruthenian). During this period the ethnic-religious structure of the present territory of Transcarpathia was primarily modified by the ever growing influx of Jews (persons of Israelite religious affiliation and of mostly Yiddish native tongue) from the Russian Empire[21] and Galicia[22]. The proportion of the Israelite population was 4.5 % in 1840 and increased to 13 % by 1880[23]. In the changed situation following the Austro-Hungarian Compromise (1867), the assimilation of Jews in the Hungarian forming state accelerated. As a consequence, 25.7 % of the total population (i.e. 105 thousand people) declared themselves to be native Hungarian speakers and this number increased to 30.8 % (184 thousand) by 1910 *(Tab.16.)*. Such a considerable growth of Hungarians was due to the 30 thousand Jews who declared themselves to be Hungarian native speakers, and to the prevalence of Hungarian sympathy among Greek Catholics with ambiguous ethnic identity, i.e. a bilingual population (speaking both Ruthenian and Hungarian) living mainly in Ugocsa (e.g. Nagyszőlős, Királyháza, Tekeháza, Szőlősvégardó, Mátyfalva, Karácsfalva and Batár) as well as town dwellers of the region *(Fig.19.)*.In the two biggest towns of contemporary Transcarpathia (Ungvár and Munkács) with a 30-40 % Jewish population, the share of those declaring themselves to be Hungarian was close to 74 % in Ungvár and 60 % in Munkács, while in the present-day urban settlements of Beregszász, Nagyszőlős, Csap

---

[20] Lexicon locorum Regni Hungariae populosorum anno 1773 officiose confectum, Magyar Békeküldöttség, Budapest, 1920.

[21] The majority of the Russian Jews arrived from the heartland of the Ashkenazic Jews, called "Pale of Settlement" (e.g Russian provinces Volhynia, Podolia, Minsk, Kiev). The migration of Jews was motivated by economic and politic reasons (e.g. anti-Semitic pogroms). See Magocsi, P.R. 1993 Historical Atlas of East Central Europe, University of Washington Press, Seattle - London, 107.p.

[22] Between 1772 and 1918 a province of the Habsburg (Austrian) Empire or Austro-Hungarian Monarchy, which was between the 14th and 18th centuries the southern part of the Polish Kingdom around Lwów-Lviv-Lemberg,. In the medieval Poland was called Halicz Rus or Red Ruthenia.

[23] The number of the Jews of Ung, Bereg, Ugocsa and Máramaros counties increased from 1,887 persons (1787) to 40,695 by 1850 and to 78,424 by 1880.

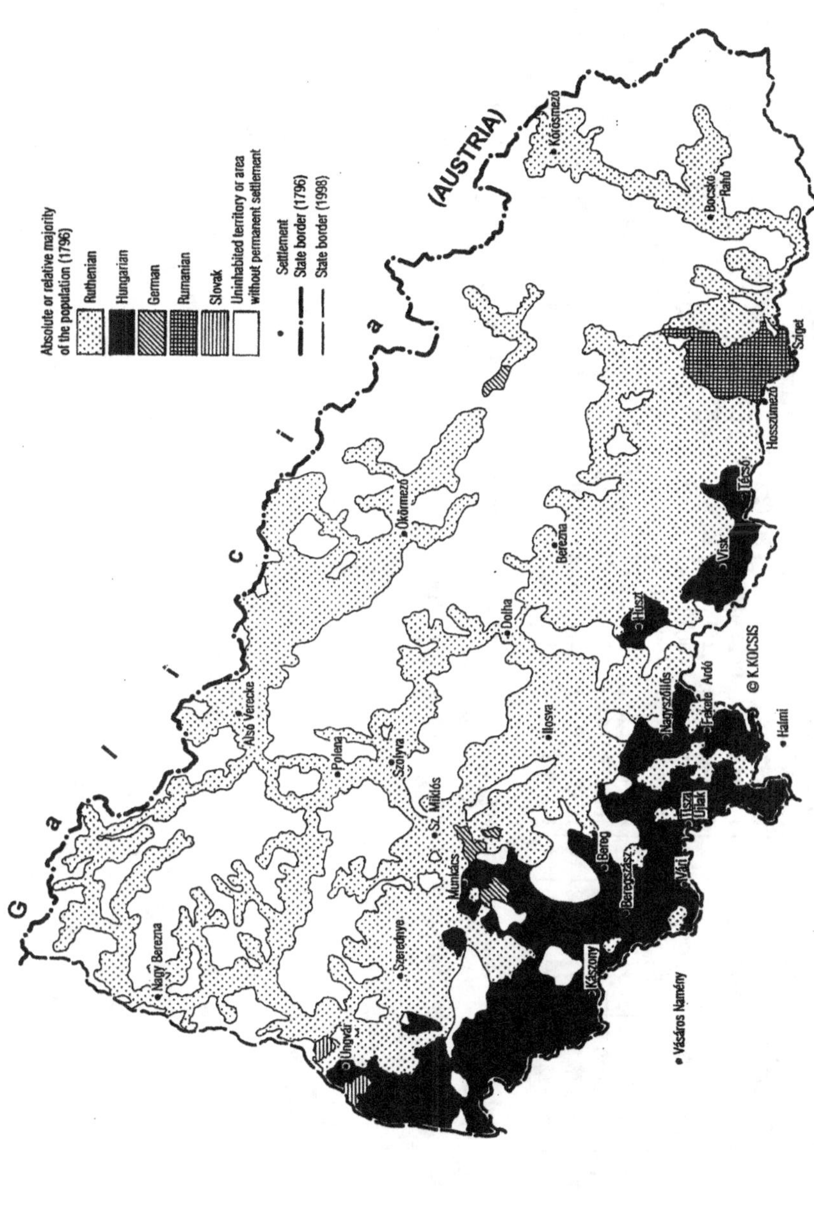

Figure 18. Ethnic map of the present-day territory of Transcarpathia (late 18th century)

Sources: Korabinszky, J. M. 1804 Atlas Regni Hungariae portatilis, Wien, 60p., Lexicon locorum Regni Hungariae populosorum anno 1773 officiose confectum, Magyar Békeküldöttség, Budapest, 1920, Vályi A. 1796 - 1799 Magyar országnak leírása I - III., Buda

Table 16. Ethnic structure of the population on the present territory of Transcarpathia (1880 - 1989)

Year	Total population		Ruthenians, Ukrainians		Russians		Hungarians		Germans		Ethnic Jews		Rumanians		Slovaks		Gipsies		Others	
	number	%	number	%	number	%	number	%	number	%	number	%	number	%	number	%	number	%	number	%
1880	408,971	100.0	244,742	59.8	..	..	105,343	25.7	31,745	7.8	..	..	16,713	4.1	8,611	2.1	..	..	1,817	0.5
1910	598,863	100.0	331,625	55.4	..	..	184,287	30.8	63,249	10.6	..	..	11,423	1.9	6,333	1.1	227	0.0	1,719	0.2
1921	612,442	100.0	372,523	60.8	..	..	111,052	18.1	..	..	80,132	13.1	..	..	19,284	3.1	..	..	29,451	4.8
1930	733,956	100.0	447,127	60.9	..	..	116,548	15.9	13,273	1.8	91,839	12.5	..	..	34,032	4.6	1,387	0.2	17,158	2.3
1941	854,772	100.0	502,329	58.9	..	..	233,840	27.3	13,251	1.5	78,727	9.2	15,602	1.8	6,853	0.8	1,204	0.1	1,643	0.2
1959	920,173	100.0	686,464	74.6	29,599	3.2	146,247	15.9	3,504	0.4	12,169	1.3	18,346	2.0	13,253	1.4	..	..	10,591	1.2
1970	1,056,799	100.0	808,131	76.5	35,189	3.3	151,949	14.4	4,230	0.4	10,857	1.0	23,454	2.2	10,294	1.0	..	..	12,695	1.2
1979	1,155,759	100.0	898,606	77.8	41,713	3.7	158,446	13.7	3,746	0.3	3,848	0.3	27,155	2.3	8,914	0.8	5,586	0.5	8,414	0.7
1979*	1,155,759	100.0	895,997	77.5	52,444	4.5	166,055	14.4	3,072	0.3	1,415	0.1	26,902	2.3	3,466	0.3	777	0.1	5,631	0.5
1989	1,245,618	100.0	976,749	78.4	49,458	4.0	155,711	12.5	3,478	0.3	2,639	0.2	29,485	2.4	7,845	0.6	12,131	1.0	8,638	0.7
1989*	1,245,618	100.0	972,827	78.1	62,510	5.0	166,700	13.4	2,576	0.2	663	0.1	28,964	2.3	2,555	0.2	2,491	0.2	6,332	0.5

Sources: 1880, 1910, 1941: Hungarian census data (mother/native tongue), 1921, 1930: Czechoslovakian census data (ethnicity), 1959, 1979, 1989: Soviet census data (ethnicity), 1979*, 1989*: Soviet census data (mother/native tongue).

Remarks: The data between 1880 and 1941 for the present territory of Transcarpathia were calculated by K.Kocsis. Slovaks include the Czechs in 1921, 1930.

and Técső it exceeded 75 % *(Tab.17.)*. For these reasons the proportion of Hungarians within the urban population had reached 68.7 % by 1910.

The Trianon Peace Treaty at the close of World War I (1920) annexed the territory of present-day Transcarpathia to the Republic of Czechoslovakia (together with the Hungarian ethnic area along the Csap-Beregszász-Királyháza-Nevetlenfalu-Halmi railway line, which provided transport links between Czechoslovakia and Rumania, and in the lowlands where it provided cereals for the mountain regions). Owing to this separation and the fact that the Hungarians became an oppressed national minority, the number of those registered as Hungarians fell from 184 thousand (1910) to 111 thousand (1921) and then to 115 thousand (1930). The reasons for this considerable drop (apart from approx. 18,600 Hungarians who escaped between 1918 and 1924[24]) was the fact that the Czechoslovakian authorities did not allow those who had voluntarily become Magyarized, Jews and Greek Catholics, to declare themselves to be Hungarian. They were instead registered as Jews (sometimes "Czechoslovaks") and Ruthenians. At the same time during the 1930 census 15,839 (2.2 %), predominantly Hungarian persons (who had not been granted Czechoslovakian citizenship) were recorded as "foreigners" so they did not figure in the ethnic statistics. Owing to this, 11-21% of people in several Hungarian villages (e.g. Csonkapapi, Mezőkaszony, Tiszacsoma, Nevetlenfalu and Akli) did not have Czechoslovakian citizenship (!), while this figure did not reach 1 % in Ruthenian villages. Naturally, the fall in the number of Hungarians can be attributed to their identification with the polyglot, mainly urban population mentioned above and people of the Ugocsa region of uncertain ethnic identity, with their descendants the Ruthenians, and (to a lesser extent) with the "Czechoslovaks". As a result the official proportion of ethnic Hungarians dropped between 1910 and 1930 in the territory of Transcarpathia from 30.8 % to 15.9 % (the corresponding change was 73.3 - 16.4 % for Ungvár, 59.3 - 18.2 % for Munkács and 96.4 - 51.3 % for Beregszász). Over the same period the number of settlements with a Hungarian majority population, according to present-day administrative divisions, diminished from 128 to 89. The shrinking Hungarian ethnic area lost the towns along the ethnic border (Ungvár, Munkács and Nagyszőlős), and by 1930 only Visk and Aknaszlatina retained their Hungarian majority. A uniform ethnic Hungarian belt of 20-30 km width along the border posed an irredentist danger, so Czechoslovakian land reform made an attempt to break it by means of Czech, Slovak and Ruthenian colonisation - mainly along the Csap-Királyháza railway which was strategically important, and where new colonies of settlements were founded in the neighbourhood of Hungarian villages (Tiszasalamon, Eszeny, Bátyú, Bótrágy, Beregsom, etc.). The most prominent group of settlements established for Czech colonists consisted of Nagybakos (Sloboda), Kisbakos (Slobodka) and Újbátyú (Dvorce), established on the former administrative areas of Nagylónya and Kislónya, which had remained in Hungary after annexation.

The statistical decline of Hungarians in Transcarpathia was halted by the re-annexation of the ethnic Hungarian area (together with the towns of Ungvár and

---

[24] Petrichevich-Horváth E. 1924 Jelentés az Országos Menekültügyi Hivatal négy évi működéséről (Report about the activity of the National Office for Refugees) , Budapest

Year	Total population		Ruth., Ukrain.		**Hungarians**		Germans		Others	
	number	%	number	%	**number**	%	number	%	number	%
Ungvár – Užhorod										
1880	14,783	100.0	2,418	16.4	**9,169**	**62.2**	933	6.3	2,263	15.1
1900	18,939	100.0	2,940	15.5	**12,594**	**66.5**	1,371	7.2	2,034	10.8
1910	21,630	100.0	2,411	11.1	**15,864**	**73.3**	1,426	6.6	1,929	9.0
1921	25,683	100.0	5,722	22.3	**8,224**	**32.0**	480	1.8	11,257	43.9
1930	35,628	100.0	10,648	29.9	**5,839**	**16.4**	911	2.5	18,230	51.2
1941	38,660	100.0	6,755	17.5	**27,987**	**72.4**	275	0.7	3,643	9.4
1979	89,037	100.0	57,920	65.0	**7,619**	**8.6**	96	0.1	23,402	26.3
1989	116,101	100.0	81,054	69.8	**9,179**	**7.9**	69	0.0	25,799	22.3
1989*	116,101	100.0	77,586	66.8	**11,784**	**10.1**	31	0.0	26,700	23.1
Munkács – Mukačeve										
1880	13,319	100.0	3,378	25.4	**6,177**	**46.4**	3,332	25.0	432	3.2
1900	19,521	100.0	3,956	20.3	**9,550**	**48.9**	5,783	30.0	232	0.8
1910	23,406	100.0	3,985	17.0	**13,880**	**59.3**	5,380	23.0	161	0.7
1921	26,932	100.0	8,194	30.4	**5,563**	**20.7**	1,700	6.3	11,475	42.6
1930	34,267	100.0	10,539	30.8	**6,227**	**18.2**	2,890	8.4	14,611	42.6
1941	39,702	100.0	8,138	20.5	**22,228**	**56.0**	2,133	5.4	7,203	18.1
1979	71,393	100.0	47,403	66.4	**6,883**	**9.6**		0.0	17,107	24.0
1989	83,308	100.0	58,489	70.2	**6,713**	**8.1**	815	1.0	17,291	20.7
1989*	83,308	100.0	56,385	67.7	**9,280**	**11.1**	556	0.7	17,087	20.5
Beregszász – Berehove										
1880	7,695	100.0	224	2.9	**7,295**	**94.8**	112	1.5	64	0.8
1900	10,810	100.0	120	1.1	**10,524**	**97.4**	82	0.8	84	0.7
1910	14,470	100.0	232	1.6	**13,953**	**96.4**	141	1.0	144	1.0
1921	15,376	100.0	1,668	11.0	**9,371**	**60.9**	100	0.7	4,237	27.4
1930	20,897	100.0	2,084	10.0	**10,719**	**51.3**	405	1.9	7,689	36.8
1941	21,540	100.0	922	4.3	**19,784**	**91.8**	62	0.3	772	3.6
1979	27,810	100.0	9,048	33.0	**15,759**	**56.7**			3,003	10.3
1989	29,221	100.0	10,226	35.0	**15,125**	**51.8**			3,870	13.2
1989*	29,221	100.0	9,842	34.0	**16,310**	**55.8**			3,069	10.2
Csap – Čop										
1880	1,187	100.0	2	0.2	**1,154**	**97.2**	11	0.9	20	1.7
1900	1,819	100.0	1	0.1	**1,781**	**97.9**	14	0.8	23	1.2
1910	2,318	100.0	4	0.2	**2,294**	**99.0**	11	0.5	9	0.3
1921	3,098	100.0	36	1.2	**2,208**	**71.3**	37	1.2	817	26.3
1930	3,572	100.0	106	3.0	**2,082**	**58.3**	19	0.5	1,365	38.2
1941	3,498	100.0	26	0.7	**3,416**	**97.7**	13	0.4	43	1.2
1979	7,503	100.0	2,416	32.0	**3,434**	**45.8**			1,653	22.2
1989	9,307	100.0	3,575	38.0	**3,679**	**39.5**			2,053	22.5
1989*	9,307	100.0	3,347	36.0	**4,040**	**43.4**			1,920	20.6
Tiszaújlak - Vilok										
1880	2,588	100.0	55	2.1	**2,236**	**86.0**	277	11.0	20	0.9
1900	3,008	100.0	15	0.5	**2,923**	**97.0**	70	2.3	0	0.0
1910	3,470	100.0	15	0.4	**3,411**	**98.0**	33	1.0	11	0.6
1921	2,968	100.0	605	20.4	**1,042**	**35.0**			1,321	44.6
1930	3,382	100.0	499	14.8	**1,571**	**46.0**	10	0.3	1,302	38.9
1941	3,429	100.0	13	0.4	**3,353**	**98.0**	6	0.2	57	1.4
1979	3,346	100.0	630	18.8	**2,574**	**77.0**			142	4.2
1989	3,404	100.0	711	20.9	**2,611**	76.7			82	2.4
1989*	3,404	100.0	690	20.3	**2,636**	77.4			78	2.3

'Sources: 1880, 1900, 1910, 1941: Hungarian census data (mother/native tongue), 1921, 1930: Czechoslovakian census data /ethnicity/, 1979, 1989: Soviet census data /ethnicity/.

settlements of present day Transcarpathia (1880-1989)

Year	Total population		Ruth., Ukrain.		Hungarians		Germans		Others	
	number	%	number	%	number	%	number	%	number	%
Nagyszõlõs - Vinohradiv										
1880	4,185	100.0	1,545	36.9	**2,450**	**58.5**	148	3.5	42	1.1
1900	5,750	100.0	1,320	23.0	**4,034**	**70.2**	378	6.6	18	0.2
1910	7,811	100.0	1,266	16.2	**5,943**	**76.1**	540	6.9	62	0.8
1921	9,248	100.0	3,930	42.5	**1,977**	**21.4**			3,341	36.1
1930	11,054	100.0	4,429	40.1	**2,630**	**23.8**	60	0.5	3,935	35.6
1941	13,331	100.0	4,000	30.0	**7,372**	**55.3**	66	0.5	1,893	14.2
1979	21,813	100.0	16,850	77.2	**3,042**	**13.9**			1,921	8.9
1989	25,046	100.0	19,669	78.5	**3,174**	**12.7**			2,203	8.8
1989*	25,046	100.0	19,388	77.4	**3,363**	**13.4**			2,295	9.2
Visk - Viškove										
1880	3,616	100.0	852	23.6	**2,558**	**70.7**	182	5.0	24	0.7
1900	4,443	100.0	745	16.8	**3,430**	**77.2**	256	5,8	12	0.2
1910	4,839	100.0	831	17.2	**3,871**	**80.0**	126	2,6	11	0.2
1921	4,700	100.0	1,511	32.1	**2,520**	**53.6**	203	4,3	466	10.0
1930	6,127	100.0	2,187	35.7	**3,257**	**53.2**	34	0,6	649	10.5
1941	7,647	100.0	2,910	38.1	**4,299**	**56.2**	10	0,1	428	5.6
1979	7,517	100.0	3,277	43.6	**3,967**	**52.8**			273	3.6
1989	7,844	100.0	3,632	46.3	**3,889**	**49.6**			323	4.1
1989*	7,844	100.0	3,588	45.7	**3,920**	**50.0**			336	4.3
Huszt - Hust										
1880	6,228	100.0	3,363	54.0	**1,452**	**23.3**	1,236	19.8	177	2.9
1900	8,716	100.0	4,161	47.7	**3,602**	**41.3**	942	10.8	11	0.2
1910	10,292	100.0	5,230	50.8	**3,505**	**34.1**	1,535	14.9	22	0.2
1921	11,835	100.0	6,738	56.9	**906**	**7.7**	409	3.5	3,782	31.9
1930	17,833	100.0	9,301	52.2	**1,383**	**7.8**	732	4.1	6,417	35.9
1941	21,118	100.0	10,503	49.7	**5,191**	**24.6**	418	2.0	5,006	23.7
1979	26,298	100.0	21,659	82.4	**2,029**	**7.7**			2,610	9.9
1989	30,716	100.0	26,023	84.7	**1,759**	**5.7**			2,934	9.6
1989*	30,716	100.0	26,434	86.1	**1,426**	**4.6**			2,856	9.3
Técsõ - Ťačiv										
1880	2,954	100.0	673	22.8	**1,932**	**65.4**	328	11.1	21	0.7
1900	4,550	100.0	1,216	26.7	**2,913**	**64.0**	367	8.1	54	1.2
1910	5,910	100.0	855	14.5	**4,482**	**75.8**	434	7.3	139	2.4
1921	5,399	100.0	1,851	34.3	**2,116**	**39.2**	20	0.4	1412	26.1
1930	7,417	100.0	3,066	41.3	**2,335**	**31.5**	36	0.5	1980	26.7
1941	10,731	100.0	3,487	32.5	**5,789**	**53.9**	48	0.4	1407	13.2
1979	8,921	100.0	5,459	61.2	**2,860**	**32.1**			602	6.7
1989	10,297	100.0	6,865	66.7	**2,640**	**25.6**			792	7.7
1989*	10,297	100.0	6,873	66.7	**2,646**	**25.7**			778	7.6
Aknaszlatina - Solotvina										
1880	3,642	100.0	50	1.4	**1,275**	**35.0**	674	19.0	1,643	44.6
1900	5,679	100.0	18	0.3	**2,587**	**46.0**	1,642	29.0	1,432	24.7
1910	6,190	100.0	12	0.2	**2,782**	**45.0**	1,836	30.0	1,560	24.8
1921	6,281	100.0	279	4.4	**2,198**	**35.0**	17	0.3	3,787	60.3
1930	7,478	100.0	455	6.1	**2,057**	**28.0**	17	0.2	4,949	65.7
1941	8,941	100.0	67	0.7	**4,638**	**52.0**	21	0.2	4,215	47.1
1979	8,487	100.0	954	11.0	**3,064**	**36.0**			4,469	53.0
1989	9,406	100.0	1,407	15.0	**2,723**	**28.9**			5,276	56.1
1989*	9,406	100.0	1,319	14.0	**2,771**	**29.5**			5,316	56.5

Remark: All data are calculated for the present administrative territory of settlements of present-day Transcarpathia (1880 – 1989).

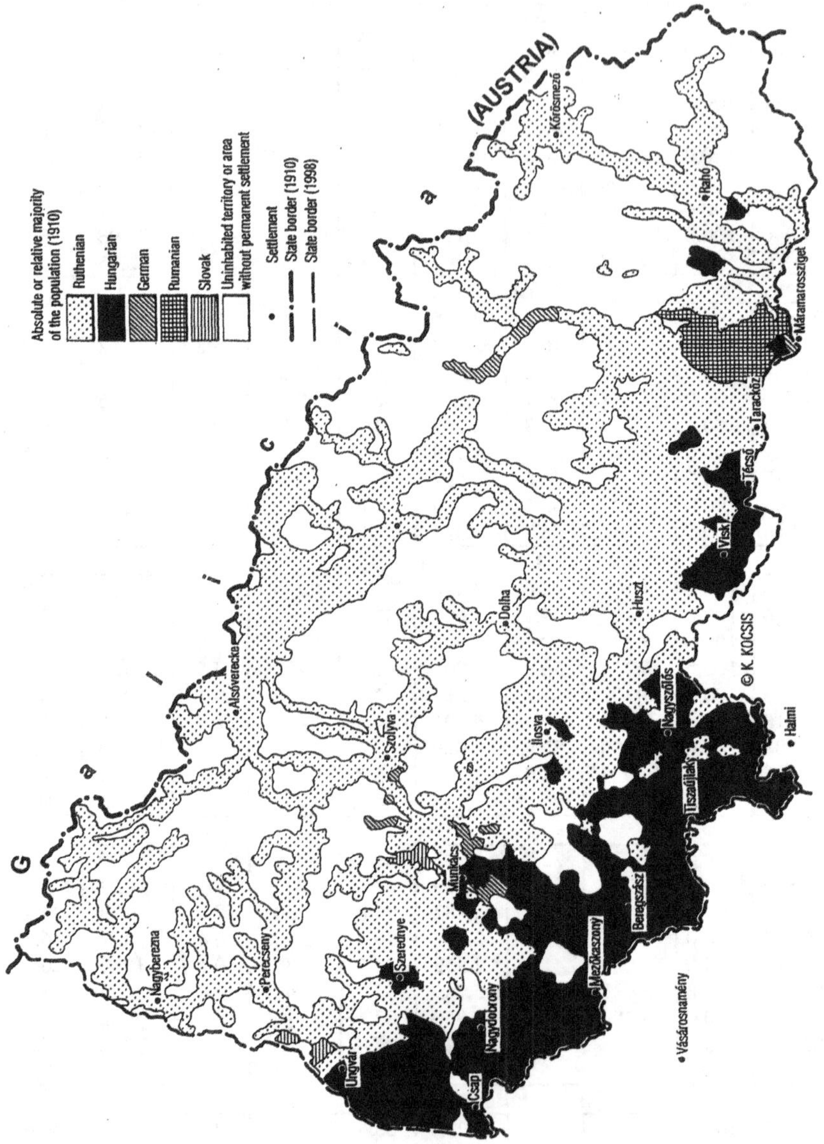

Figure 19. Ethnic map of the present-day territory of Transcarpathia (1910)
Source: Census 1910

Munkács)[25] following the first Vienna Accord (November 2, 1938), and the occupation of the rest of the region by Hungary, following the disintegration of Czechoslovakia and the proclamation of an independent Slovakia (March 15-18, 1939). At the 1941 census after the change of regime and with Hungarians in Transcarpathia becoming a state-forming nation again, from a total population of 851,694 27.4 % (i.e. 233 thousand persons) declared themselves to be native Hungarian speakers[26]. This doubling of the number and proportion of Hungarians can be attributed to the immigration of civil servants and military personnel from the "Trianon territory" of Hungary, and also to 34 % of Jews and 9 % of Greek Catholics identifying with Hungarians along with the majority of the Hungarian-Ruthenian population who were of uncertain ethnic affiliation. For the above reasons and due to the moving out of Czech colonists and civil servants, 103 settlements had regained their Hungarian majority by 1941. Of the towns "sensitive" to the change in power the proportion of Hungarian native speakers "suddenly" increased and was as follows: Ungvár: 76.6 %, Munkács: 63.5 %, Beregszász: 91.4 %, Nagyszőlős: 58.7 % and Técső: 56.9 %. As a consequence of the immigration of civil servants and military personnel and the presence of local Jews, a considerable number (20-40 %) of the population in the centres of the Ruthenian ethnic area (Szolyva, Perecseny, Nagyberezna, Huszt, Rahó and Kőrösmező) declared Hungarian to be their native language.

This favourable ethnic-demographic situation for the Hungarians lasted till the occupation of the country by the German Nazi army (March 19, 1944). To meet German demands, the Hungarian internal affairs administration soon started to organize the gathering of the Jewish population - in 1941 in Subcarpathia 115,908 persons of Jewish religious affiliation were deported to Germany. This meant a serious (16 %) loss for the population of native Hungarian speakers, since 37 thousand Jews were Hungarian - language speakers with a Hungarian identity. The most severe ethnic loss and demographic decline were suffered (based on 1941 census data) in Tiszaújlak (25.5 %), Beregszász (24.8 %), Munkács (20.6 5), Ungvár (20.2 %), Nagyszőlős (18.6), Mezőkaszony (17.2 %) and Csap (9.9 %). At the same time this created the conditions for the settlement of Russians and Ukrainians following the passage of the front.

Following the Soviet occupation of the territory of Transcarpathia in October 1944 Hungarian and German males liable to military service (aged between 18 and 50 years) were gathered in a concentration camp (Szolyva) and then deported to forced labour camps in the Ukraine and Russia. By December 17, 1944 14,990 Hungarians were deported, but according to a survey carried out on those liable to military service

---

[25] Rónai A. 1939 Új felvidéki határunk (Our new border in Upper Hungary), Földrajzi Közlemények LXVII. (1939). 3. pp.190-200.

[26] The Ruthenians were represented by 501,516 (58.9 %), the Yiddish-Hebrew native speakers by 78,655 (9.2 %), the Rumanians by 15,568 (1.8 %) and the Germans by 13,224 (1.6 %) persons 1941.

between July 1-7, 1945 about 30 thousand men were in unknown locations[27]. This source estimates that 4,953 Hungarians died in the forced labour camps. In parallel with the vengeance taken upon Hungarians who were regarded as enemies, Transcarpathia became a part of the Soviet Union in accordance with an agreement between Czechoslovakia and the Soviet Union of June 29, 1945. Prior to the change of power, along with the retreating Hungarian and German troops, a massive escape of Hungarians began into the territory of Trianon Hungary. According to the documents prepared for the Paris peace talks (1946) the number of these refugees amounted to 5,104. Russians and Ukranians almost immediately occupied those places previously inhabited by the deported Jews and the Hungarians and Germans who had escaped or been deported, especially the strategically important towns of Ungvár and Munkács. Within the framework of land reform Ruthenians moved from the mountains to settlements among the villages of the Hungarian ethnic block between 1944-1947.

The first Soviet census after World War II (1959) found that 146,247 people, 15.9 % out of the total Transcarpathian population of 920,000, were ethnic Hungarians[28]. The reason for a drop of nearly 100 thousand compared with 1941 (besides the above mentioned causes) was that the Hungarian Greek Catholics were regarded by the authorities as ethnic Ukrainians and of Orthodox religious affiliation[29]. Meanwhile, some Hungarians (about 10 thousand), intimidated by the 1944-45 wave of vengeance, declared themselves to be Slovaks[30] and "became" Ukrainians in the Hungarian-Ruthenian population of ambiguous ethnic roots. It should be mentioned, that among Hungarians there was some natural assimilation, especially in urban settlements due to ethnically mixed marriages and the feelings of remorse and an inferiority complex[31] which were created by the authorities. The Soviet authorities laid stress on liquidation of the Greek Catholic Church and on wasting of the Reformed (Calvinist) and Roman Catholic Churches which were the main supporters of local Hungarian ethnic identity. At the same time, owing to income disparity and ethnic discrimination regarding employment, there was massive emigration of skilled Hungarians from the relatively back-

---

[27] Dupka Gy. 1993 Egyetlen bűnük magyarságuk volt. Emlékkönyv a sztálinizmus kárpátaljai áldozatairól (Their only crime was to be Hungarian. White book on the victims of the Stalinism in Transcarpathia, 1944-1946), Patent - Intermix, Ungvár - Budapest, 286., 288.p.

[28] The number of Ukrainians were 686,464 (74.6 %), Russians 29,599 (3.2 %) and Jews 12,169 (1.3 %) in 1959.

[29] The Greek Catholic (Uniate) Church of Transcarpathia was supressed in 1949 and its (Ruthenian, Hungarian, Rumanian) congregations were forced into the Orthodox Church. See: Botlik J. 1997 Hármas kereszt alatt. Görög katolikusok Kárpátalján az ungvári uniótól napjainkig (Under triple cross. Greek Catholics in Subcarpathia from the Union of Ungvár /Užhorod till today, 1646-1997), Hatodik Síp Alapítvány - Új mandátum Könyvkiadó, Budapest, 335p.

[30] Since October 1944 thousands of terrified Hungarians (first of all Hungarians who could also speak Slovakian in Ungvár-Užhorod and in its environment) declared themselves to be ethnic Slovaks.

[31] Following 1944 the Soviet propaganda in Transcarpathia laid stress on the formation of an image of the "small, defeated" Hungarian nation in contrast with the image of the big, victorious Russian, Ukrainian nations.

ward border zone to Lviv (Lemberg), Kiev and the industrial Donets Basin. The number of Hungarians leaving Transcarpathia and settling within the borders of the Ukraine rose from 2,982 to 7,400 between 1959 and 1989, while the number of those scattered in the USSR outside the Ukraine increased from 5,509 to 8,309. Besides the natural assimilation already mentioned, and the internal Ukrainian-Soviet migration, accelerating emigration to Hungary, which had begun during the Soviet period, also contributed to a reduced growth rate in the number of Hungarians (1959: 146,247; 1989: 155 711) in spite of an 11.8 ‰ annual average birthrate (a total of 51,800)[32].

THE PRESENT TERRITORY OF HUNGARIAN SETTLEMENT IN TRANSCARPATHIA

According to the last Soviet census (1989), the number those declaring themselves to be native Hungarian speakers exceeded the number of ethnic Hungarians by 10,989, reaching 166, 700. This is due to the fact that, for various reasons, out of the Hungarian native speakers 7,973 persons declared themselves to be Gypsies (66 % of all Transcarpathian Gypsies) and 1,890 people as ethnic Slovaks.

At present, among the 598 settlements of Transcarpathia, there are officially only 78 with an ethnic Hungarian majority (in 1941 there were 103). This is due to the fact that both Greek Catholic, and many Roman Catholic Hungarian villages (e.g. Rafajnaújfalu, Nagybégány, Kisbégány and Kétgút) were registered as settlements with a Ukrainian majority in 1989. These Hungarian settlements can be found mostly in the Hungarian-Ukrainian border zone of 20 km width (the only exception is Visk between the Avas Mountains and the Tisza river) *(Fig. 20.)*. This ethnic block, where 61.3 % of the Hungarian population were living in 1989, primarily included the districts of Beregszász, Ungvár and Munkács (36.6 %, 16.4 % and 8.3 %, respectively). A further 28.1 % of Hungarians were urban-dwellers in an ethnically very mixed area along the ethnic border (Ungvár, Munkács, Nagyszőlős) and lived in the historical region of Ugocsa, while 10.6 % were scattered in mountain areas. As a consequence of socialist urbanisation which took place in the past few decades there was a massive influx of Ruthenians, Ukrainians and Russians into Ungvár and Munkács, which have doubled their populations, while the proportion of Hungarians has dropped to 7.9-8.1 % (ethnicity) and 10.1-11.1 % (native tongue). Among towns and "urban type settlements"[33] this was the period when Nagyszőlős, Técső and Aknaszlatina lost their Hungarian majority. As a re-

---

[32] See the data on the natural increase of the ethnic Hungarian district Beregszász-Berehove: Szabó L. 1993 Kárpátaljai demográfiai adatok (Demographic data of Subcarpathia), Intermix Kiadó, Ungvár-Budapest, pp.41-46.

[33] "Settlement of urban type" (Ukr. "selishch miskogo tipu", "smt.") is a special type of settlement in the post-Soviet republics and represents a transition between the towns and villages. In Transcarpathia can be found 8 urban, 562 rural settlements and 28 "smt".

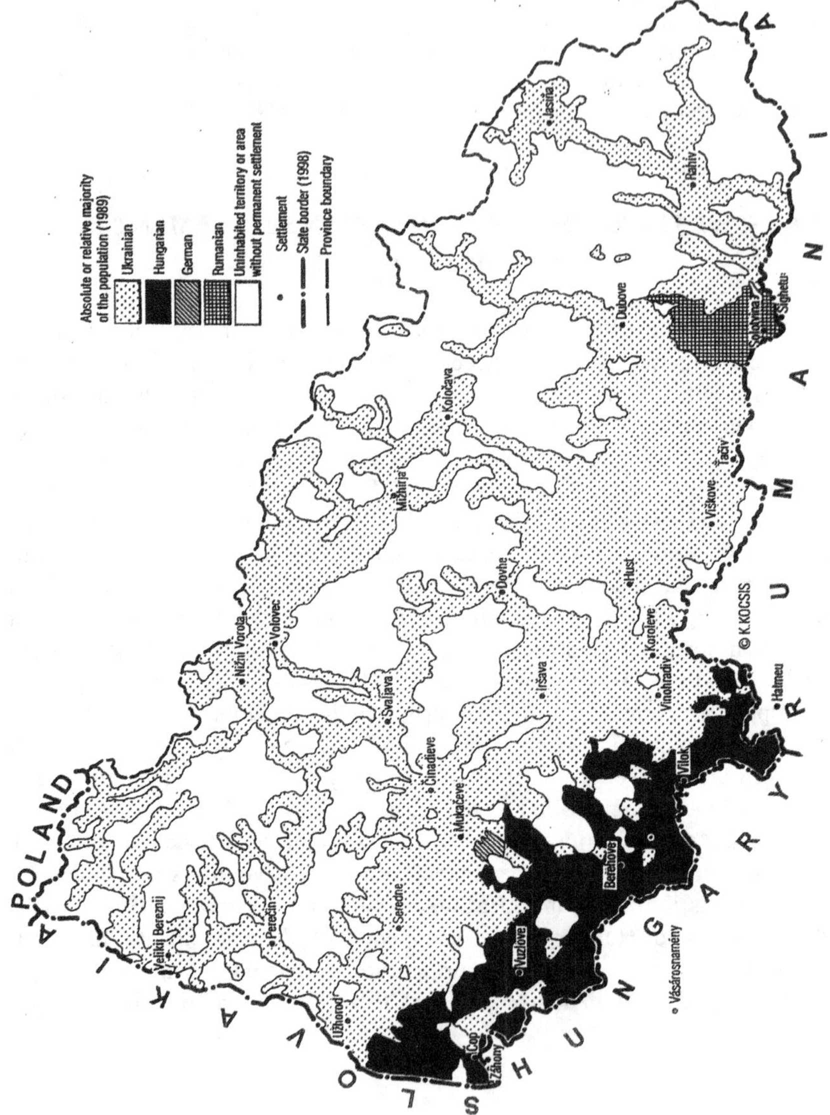

Figure 20. Ethnic map of Transcarpathia (1989)
Source: Census 1989

sult of this massive internal migration between villages and towns, which affected several hundred thousand Ruthenians and Ukrainians, the number of Hungarians in present-day towns dropped from 55.2 % (1941) to 11.6 % (1989), while that of Ruthenians and Ukrainians rose from 23.2 % to 74 %. The local Hungarian population is more "rural" (62.3 % of them live in villages), than the Ukrainians (61.6 %), the Russians (12.8 %), or the Gypsies (37.8 %). Accordingly, those registered as Hungarians live in settlements with 1,000-2,000 inhabitants (24 %) and 2,000-5,000 (23 %). The corresponding figures inside Hungary (1990) were 9 % in the former category and 13.7 % in the latter. At the same time, only one quarter of Hungarians lived in settlements with more than 10 thousand inhabitants and 5.6 % in towns over 100 thousand. This adherence of the Hungarians to the rural environment, as reflected in the statistics, might be partly attributed to their restricted migration into towns, or partly to a gradual assimilation of the people having moved there. As a result, in 1989 71.8 % of Hungarians lived in settlements where they formed an absolute majority. To maintain their ethnic awareness this may be positive, similar to the situation of Hungarians in Slovakia, where 46.8 % of them live in settlements where they constitute over 75 % of the population and only 16.1 % of them live in places where the Hungarian population makes up less than 25 %. As a consequence of history and the process of urbanisation, during the past decades the most populous ethnic Hungarian communities have become the towns of Beregszász (15,125), Ungvár (9,179) and Munkács (6,713) and the largest, "most Hungarian" village of Nagydobrony (5,250)[34] *(Tab.18., Fig.21.).*

In the Ungvár district, where a majority of the Hungarians live in the town of Ungvár – the capital of the Transcarpathian Region – the ethnic border has not changed much in the last few centuries. The Hungarian area of settlement continues to be located south of the Ungvár-Korláthelmec line. Nevertheless, in the town of Csap, along the Csap-Ungvár railway line, and in the villages of the Ungvár agglomeration, the percentage of the Hungarian population is falling rapidly due to increasing Ukrainian immigration. The largest Hungarian rural communities live in Nagydobrony, Eszeny, Kisdobrony, Tiszasalamon, Rát and Szürte.

One third of the Hungarians of the Beregszász district – the district with the longest border with Hungary – live in the district seat of Beregszász. The ethnic Hungarian unity of the district is disrupted only by some older (Kovászó, Nyárasgorond, Csikósgorond) and more recently founded (Badiv, Danilivka, Kaštanove, Zatišne, Velika-Bakta) Ruthenian enclaves. In addition to Beregszász, the largest number of Hungarians live in Vári situated on the right bank of the Tisza, in a former district seat of Mezőkaszony, next to the drained Szernye marsh in Gát, Makkosjánosi, Nagybereg, and Beregújfalu, in Nagymuzsaly and Beregdéda situated next to Beregszász and at the railway junction of Bátyú.

More than half of the Hungarians living in the neighbouring Munkács district, are residents of Munkács. The others live in the vicinity of Beregszász district's Hungarian villages (Dercen, Fornos, Izsnyéte, Csongor, Szernye, Barkaszó etc.). One single

---

[34] According to the native tongue the number of Hungarians were in Beregszász 16,310, in Ungvár 11,784, in Munkács 9,280 in 1989.

Table 18. The largest Hungarian communities in Transcarpathia (1989)

Settlements	Estimated data	Census data
1. Beregszász / Berehove	23,000	15,125
2. Ungvár / Užhorod	16,000	9,179
3. Munkács / Mukačeve	15,000	6,713
4. Nagyszőlős / Vinohradiv	7,600	3,174
5. Nagydobrony / Velika Dobroň	5,250	
6. Visk / Viškove	4,000	3,889
7. Aknaszlatina / Solotvina	3,800	2,723
8. Csap / Čop	3,750	3,679
9. Tiszaújlak / Vilok	3,200	2,611
10. Técső / Ťačiv	3,000	2,640
11. Vári / Vary	2,910	
12. Gát / Hat'	2,900	
13. Dercen / Drisina	2,710	
14. Salánk / Šalanki	2,700	
15. Mezőkaszony / Kosini	2,660	
16. Bátyú / Batove	2,350	1,977
17. Makkosjánosi / Ivanivka	2,310	
18. Nagybereg / Berehi	2,246	
19. Csongor / Čomanin	2,170	
20. Huszt / Hust	2,029	1,759
21. Barkaszó / Barkasove	2,010	
22. Nagymuzsaly / Mužijeve	2,000	

Source: Soviet census data 1989, Botlik J. - Dupka Gy. 1993, estimations by K.Kocsis.

village west of Munkács called Beregrákos – in Ruthenian surroundings – has been defying assimilation for centuries. For hundreds of years, it has been the guardian of the medieval Hungarian ethnic border.

In the Nagyszőlős district, in historical Ugocsa county where the Tisza River meets the plain, Hungarians have lived – mostly mixed – with the Ruthenian population for three centuries. Due to the century-old coexistence and, in many cases, the shared Greek Catholic or "Uniate" religion, the most significant deviation in the ethnic census statistics can be observed in the villages of this region. Today, most Hungarians can be found in the towns of Nagyszőlős, Tiszaújlak, Salánk, Nagypalád, Tiszapéterfalva, Csepe and Feketeardó.

Proceeding upstream along the Tisza, we reach the district of Huszt, situated in the former county of Máramaros. Here the majority of Hungarian town dwellers, dating back to the Middle Ages, are represented by the Hungarians of Visk. The Hungarian minority population of 2,092 in Huszt is also important.

A Hungarian community of 3,000 persons inhabits the seat of the neighbouring district, Técső. The famous salt-mining settlement of Aknaszlatina is located on the right bank of the Tisza, facing the town of Máramarossziget in Rumania. Its population includes approximately 3,800 Hungarians. A considerable Hungarian population lives in Bustyaháza, Kerekhegy, Taracköz and Királymező as well.

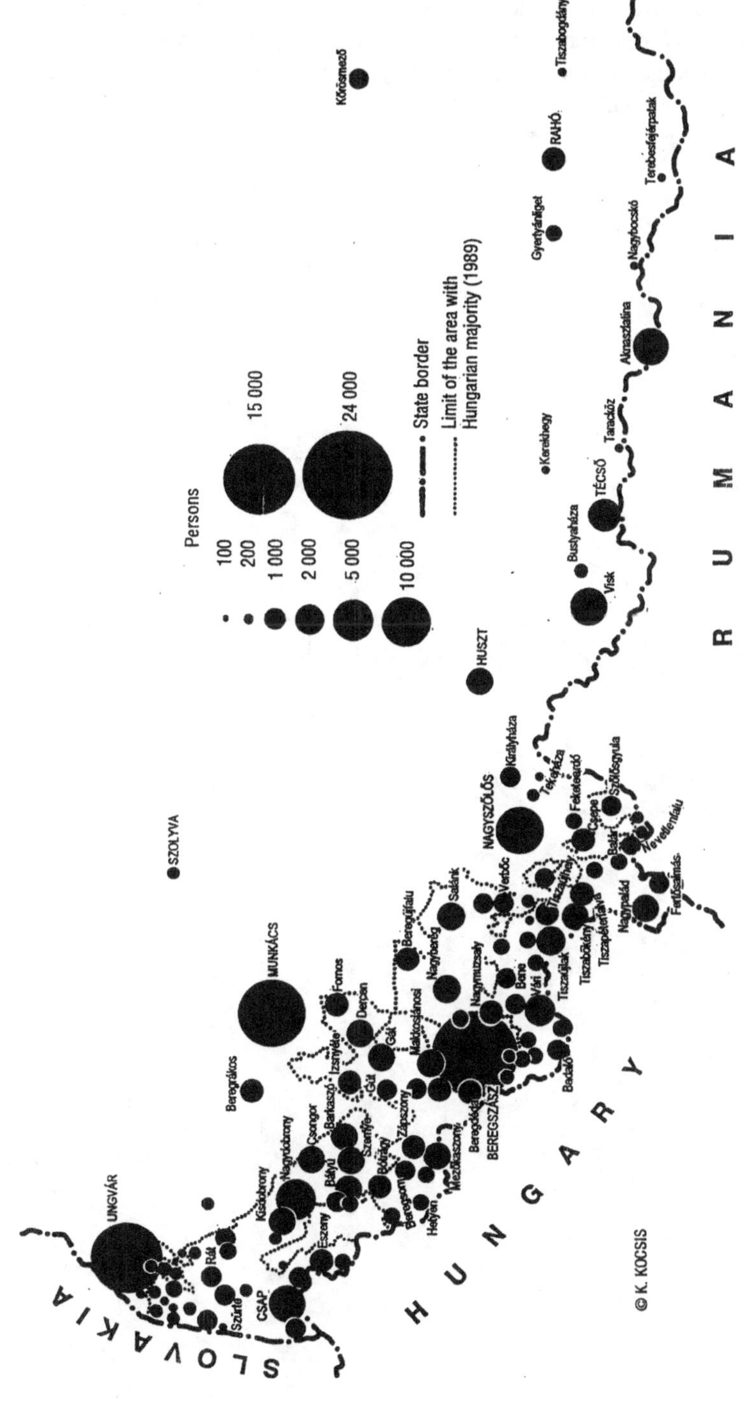

Figure 21. Hungarian communities in Transcarpathia (1989)
Source: Census 1989, Botlik, J. – Dupka, Gy. (1993), estimation of Kocsis K.

In the Rahó district, called the Ruthenian (or Hutzul) Switzerland, which is situated among the Carpathians near the sources of the Tisza, there are about 4000 to 5000 people of Hungarian ethnicity. The majority of them live in Rahó, Kőrösmező, Nagybocskó and Gyertyánliget.

Chapter 4

THE HUNGARIANS OF TRANSYLVANIA

The greatest number of Hungarians living outside the present-day borders of Hungary are to be found in Transylvania west of the Carpathians in Rumania. Here many ethnic groups of Central and South-eastern Europe (Hungarians, Rumanians, Gypsies, Germans, Ukrainians, Slovaks, Serbs, Czechs, Bulgarians etc.) also live in significant numbers. At the time of the last Rumanian census in 1992, the registered number of Hungarians in Rumania was 1,624,959 /ethnicity/ or 1,639,135 /mother tongue/. According to our estimates, however, the number of those people who claim Hungarian to be their native language was 2 million in 1986. The latter data indicates that close to 60 percent of Hungarians living outside the borders of Hungary in the Carpathian Basin and 13.3 percent of Hungarians in the world, are in Transylvania.

THE NATURAL ENVIRONMENT

According to our calculations, 51% of Hungarians in Transylvania live in hilly or submountainous areas, 28% inhabit lowlands and 21% live in the mountains. The lowlanders – living adjacent to the Hungarian border – dwell in the eastern part of the Great Hungarian Plain, called the Western or Tisza Plain in Rumania. The highlanders primarily include the inhabitants of the Székely Region, the Barcaság Basin, Hunyad, and Máramaros counties *(Fig. 22.)*. A majority of the Hungarian highlanders live in the Eastern Carpathians and the basins encircled by the mountain chains. The most important mountain ranges of the Carpathians also inhabited by Hungarians include the following: The sandstone range comprising the Nemere Mts. (Mt. Nemere 1649 m, Mt. Nagy Sándor 1640 m), the Háromszék Mts. (Mt. Lakóca 1777 m), the Brassó Mts. (Mt. Nagykő 1843 m, Mt. Csukás 1954 m), the Persány Mts. (Mt. Várhegy 1104 m), the Barót Mts. (Mt. Görgő 1017 m), the Bodok Mts. (Mt. Kömöge 1241 m), and the Csík Mts. (Mt. Tarhavas 1664 m, Mt. Sajhavasa 1553 m); also the limestone peaks of the Székely Region (Nagy-Hagymás 1792 m, Egyeskő 1608 m, Öcsémtető 1707 m, Nagy-Cohárd 1506 m, etc.), the mainly crystalline schist belt of the Máramaros, Radna, and Gyergyó Mts. (Mt. Siposkő 1567 m), the inner volcanic ring of the Avas, Kőhát, Gutin (famous for its non-ferrous metal mining), Lápos, and Cibles Mts., Kelemen Mts. and Görgény Mts. (Fancsaltető 1684 m, Mezőhavas 1776 m), and the Hargita (Madarasi-Hargita 1800 m, Mt. Kakukk 1558 m, Nagy-Csomád 1301 m). The most important basins inhabited also by Hungarians include the Máramaros, Gyergyó, Csík, Kászon, Háromszék and Barcaság basins.

Figure 22. Important Hungarian geographical names in Transylvania

The most noteworthy rivers of the Eastern Carpathians – as far as Hungarians are concerned – include the Tisza, Maros, Olt, Békás, Tatros, Feketeügy and Vargyas. Important lakes e.g. the Gyilkos-tó ("Lake Killer"), Szent Anna-tó ("Lake St. Ann's"), and Medve-tó ("Lake Bear") in Szováta can also be found in this region.

Outside the Eastern Carpathians, a considerable number of Hungarian highlanders inhabit the Torockó Mts. (Székelykő - Székelystone 1128 m, Torda and Túr Gorges), the northern base of the Bél Mts., the Belényes Basin and the Petrozsény Basin which is bordered by the Retyezát Mts., Vulkán Mts. and Páreng Mts.

A majority of Hungarians occupying the lowlands live on the Western Tisza Plain which is covered mostly with chernozem, meadow and alluvial soils. The richest agricultural land in Transylvania can be found in the Bánát region and the County of Arad. The most important subregions of the Western Plain are the Szatmár, Érmellék, Körösmenti, Arad and Temes lowlands. The most important rivers of the region as far as Hungarian settlements are concerned include, from north to south, the Szamos, Kraszna, Ér, Berettyó, Sebes - Rapid-Körös, Fekete - Black-Körös, Fehér - White-Körös, Maros, Béga and the Temes.

Outside the region of historical Transylvania, west of the limestone range, the Hungarian national minority inhabit the hilly regions and live mainly in the Szilágy hills whose streams include the tributaries of the Berettyó and Kraszna rivers. A majority, however, live in settlements located in the hills along the Szamos River between the Gyalu Mts. and the Gutin Mts., the chernozem covered southwestern part of the Mező-ség (Plain of Transylvania), the hills along the Küküllő rivers, and the sub-mountainous slopes of the Székely Region. The following larger rivers (and their tributaries) extend throughout the hilly regions: Szamos (Little and Big Szamos, Almás, Kapus, Nádas, Borsa, Füzes, Sajó), Maros (Kapus, Ludas, Aranyos, Nyárád, Görgény, Little Küküllő, Big Küküllő), and Olt (Big Homoród, Little Homoród, Hortobágy). The hilly regions of the Transylvanian Basin, shaped by mud flows and landslides and characterised by a mostly marly clay surface, are extremely rich in natural gas (Medgyes, Kiskapus, Nagysármás, Mezőzáh, Nyárádszereda, etc.), and salt deposits (Parajd, Marosújvár).

ETHNIC PROCESSES DURING THE PAST FIVE HUNDRED YEARS

During the 1495 assessment of taxes of the 2.9 million population of the Hungarian Kingdom, 454,000 people may have lived in the Transylvanian Voivodeship and 830,000 people in present-day Transylvania[1]. Of these, 101,000 lived in the autonomous Saxon Regions and 76,000 in the Székely Region. Of the population of the contemporary Transylvanian Voivodeship the number of Rumanians and Germans (Saxons) might be estimated at 100,000 each (22-22%) while Hungarians and Szeklers have already been reduced to about a quarter of million, i.e. 55% (*Tab. 19.*). Among the 5,321 present-day settlements ethnic majorities were distributed as follows: 1869 Hungarian, 1785 Rumanian, 359 German (Saxon), 167 Slavic, while 1,141 present-day settlements were uninhabited. Hungarians constituted the majority population in almost every town of the Banat, Körös-vidék and Máramaros regions, and in half of the major towns with more than 1000 inhabitants (e.g. in Kolozsvár, Gyulafehérvár, Torda, Dés). The largest towns, among wnich was Brassó the most populous one of Hungary, were still predominantly occupied by Saxons. Yet urban social structure was characterised at that time by a growing ethnic diversity, due to the migration from the villages to the towns which were epidemic ridden, and to the movement of Rumanians and Serbs into the southern areas which have been devastated by the plundering Ottoman (Turkish) army[2]. The previous ethnic homogeneity of the Hungarian and Saxon villages in the

---

[1] Kubinyi A. A Magyar Királyság népessége a 15. század végén (Population of the Kingdom of Hungary at the end of 15th century) — Történelmi Szemle XXXVIII. 1996. 2-3. p.159.

[2] Binder P. 1982 Közös múltunk. Románok, magyarok, németek és délszlávok feudalizmus kori falusi és városi együtteléséről (Our common past. About the rural and urban coexistence of Rumanians, Hungarians, Germans and Southern Slavs during the time of the feudalism), Bukarest, 11., 30.p.

*Table 19. Change in the ethnic structure of the population on the historical territory of Transylvania**
(1495-1910)

Year	Total population		Hungarians		Rumanians		Germans		Others	
	number	%	number	%	number	%	number	%	number	%
1495	454,000	100	251,000	55.2	100,000	22.0	100,000	22.0	3,000	0.7
1595	670,000	100	350,000	52.2	190,000	28.4	126,000	18.8	4,000	0.6
1720	806,221	100	300,000	37.2	400,000	49.6	100,000	12.4	6,221	0.8
1786	1,293,992	100	380,000	29.4	750,000	58.0	150,000	11.6	13,992	1.2
1832	1,859,681	100	544,000	29.2	1,113,000	59.8	200,000	10.8	2,681	0.1
1850	1,861,287	100	486,099	26.2	1,084,577	58.3	191,084	10.3	99,527	5.3
1869	2,152,805	100	620,000	28.8	1,242,800	57.7	213,000	9.9	77,005	3.6
1880	2,084,048	100	629,144	30.2	1,186,190	56.9	211,780	10.2	56,934	2.7
1890	2,067,467	100	663,631	32.1	1,132,619	54.8	217,132	10.5	54,085	2.6
1900	2,476,998	100	814,994	32.9	1,397,282	56.4	233,019	9.41	31,703	1.3
1910	2,678,367	100	918,217	34.3	1,472,021	55.0	234,085	8.74	54,044	2.0

Remark: The territory of Historical Transylvania this case: the medieval Voivodship of Transylvania.
Sources: 1495 - 1869: Estimations of K. Kocsis based on Acsády I. 1896 Magyarország népessége a Pragmatica Sanctio korában 1720 - 21. — Magyar Statisztikai Közlemények XII. /Új folyam/, Budapest, 58.p., Barta G. 1986 Az Erdélyi Fejedelemség első korszaka — in: Makkai L. - Mócsy A. (szerk.) Erdély története I. A kezdetektől 1606-ig, Akadémiai Kiadó, Budapest, 510.p., Barta G. 1989 Az Erdélyi Fejedelemség — in: Erdély rövid története, Akadémiai Kiadó, Budapest, 238.p., Bieltz, E. A. 1857 Handbuch der Landeskunde Siebenbürgens. Eine physikalisch-statistisch-topographische Beschreibung dieses Landes, Hermannstadt, 148.p., Jakó Zs. 1945 Adatok a dézsma fejedelemségkori adminisztrációjához, Kolozsvár, Kubinyi A. 1996 A Magyar Királyság népessége a 15. század végén, Történelmi Szemle XXXVIII. 2-3. p.159., Mályusz E. A magyarság és a nemzetiségek Mohács előtt - in: Magyar művelődéstörténet II. Budapest, p.123.p., Wagner, E. 1977 Historisch-statistisches Ortsnamenbuch für Siebenbürgen, Böhlau Verlag, Köln - Wien, 45.p.
1880 - 1910: Hungarian census data (mother tongue).

south had dissappeared for similar reasons. At this time Hungarians still dominated the lowlands and hills extending to the foothills in the western areas, in the Szilágy and Székely Regions and the Transylvanian Basin *(Fig. 23.).* Earlier ethnic uniformity in the Mezőség Region and the Maros valley which were inhabited by Hungarians, was however disturbed by the appearance of large numbers of pastoral Rumanians moving from the overpopulated mountains. At the end of the 15th century there was an ethnic expansion of Rumanians. This was not only as a result of the establishment of twin villages[3] but also as a result of Rumanians settling in former Hungarian (Catholic) villages which had become poor deserted following epidemics and feudal exploitation causing the

---

[3] On the outskirts of the following Hungarian rural settlements Rumanian twin villages were founded: e.g Bós-Boju, Bányabükk-Vâlcele, Detrehem-Tritenii, Zsuk-Jucu, Pata, Kara-Cara, Dezmér-Dezmir, Kályán-Căianu, Rőd-Rediu, Palatka-Pălatca, Méhes-Miheşu, (Makkai L. 1943a Erdély népei a középkorban (Peoples of Transylvania in the Middle Ages) — Deér J. - Gáldi L. (Eds.) 1943 Magyarok és románok (Hungarians and Rumanians) I., Budapest, 399-400.p.).

original population to escape or migrate to urban settlements[4]. Parallel to a slow decline in Hungarians as opposed to Rumanians (and Serbs in the Banat) there was a Hungarian expansion in Saxon mining towns[5] while the Hungarian majority in Kolozsvár which was lost following the Tartar invasion (1242) and Saxon immigration, was presumably re-established at the turn of the 15th and 16th centuries[6].

A mere 61% of Saxons in Transylvania, a total number of about 100,000, lived in areas with regional autonomy (King's Land-Königsboden, Barcaság-Bârsa-Burzenland, District of Beszterce). The rest of them inhabited 150 villages in the Hungarian counties (e.g. Lower and Upper Fehér, Küküllő, Torda, Kolozs, Doboka) and in some towns Saxons were mixed with Hungarians (Kolozsvár, Abrudbánya, Zalatna, Kőrösbánya, Torockó, Nagybánya, Felsőbánya etc.). At the same time the King's Land, belonging to the privileged territories directed by Universitas Saxorum, gradually lost its former Saxonian ethnic character, which can be attributed to the depopulation following Turkish incursions (e.g. 1420, 1438, 1479) and epidemics. Large-scale immigration of Rumanians into the areas where Saxons had been slaughtered or carried off was especially striking in the environs of Szászváros, Szászsebes, in the foreland of the Szeben Mountains and in the Olt[7]. As a result of this, the proportion of the Orthodox (Rumanian) population increased to 20 % in the King's Land[8] and to 13 % in Barcaság by the end of the 15th century[9].

The Orthodox Rumanians also estimated at 100,000 were still leading a mainly a pastoral way of life at that time, and by the end of the 15th century had established a centre to their ethnic territory migrating from the south to the north. This area stretched

---

[4] Szabó I. 1963 Magyarország népessége az 1330-as és az 1526-os évek között (Population of Hungary between 1330 and 1526) — in: Kovacsics J. (Ed.) Magyarország történeti demográfiája (Historic Demography of Hungary), Budapest, 65.p.

[5] Saxon mining towns becoming Magyarized from the 15th century: e.g. Torockó-Rimetea, Abrudbánya-Abrud, Zalatna-Zlatna, Aranyosbánya-Baia de Arieş, Nagybánya-Baia Mare, Felsőbánya-Baia Sprie, Kapnikbánya-Cavnic see Iczkovits E. 1939 Az erdélyi Fehér megye a középkorban (The Transylvanian Fehér-Alba County in the Middle Ages), Budapest and Maksai F. 1940 A középkori Szatmár megye (The Medieval Szatmár-Satu Mare County), Budapest.

[6] Makkai L. 1943 Társadalom és nemzetiség a középkori Kolozsváron (Society and Ethnicity in Medieval Kolozsvár-Cluj), Kolozsvár

[7] Wagner, E. 1978 Wüstungen in den Sieben Stühlen als Folge der Türkeneinfälle des 15. Jahrhunderts — Forschungen zur Volks- und Landeskunde (Bukarest) Bd.21. Nr.1. 41., 45.p.

[8]Niedermaier, P. 1986 Zur Bevölkerungsdichte und -bewegung im Mittelalterlichen Siebenbürgen — in: Forschungen zur Volks- und Landeskunde (Bukarest) Bd.29. Nr.1. 23.p., Wagner, E. 1978 ibid. 48.p.

[9]Graf, B. 1934 Die Kulturlandschaft des Burzenlandes, Verlag für Hochschulkunde, München

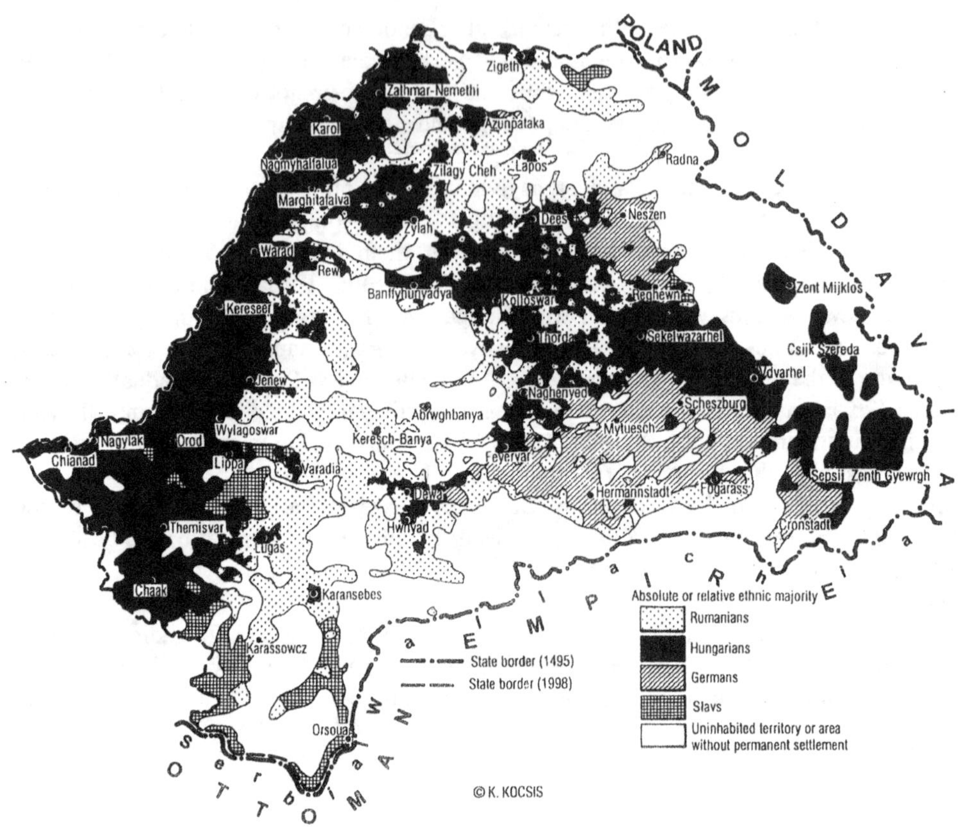

Figure 23. Ethnic map of the present-day territory of Transylvania (late 15th century)

Source: Csánki D. 1890 - 1913 Magyarország történelmi földrajza a Hunyadiak korában I - III., V., Budapest, Makkai L. 1943 Erdély népei a középkorban — Deér J. - Gáldi L. (szerk.) 1943 Magyarok és románok I., Budapest, pp.314-440., Makkai L. 1946 Histoire de Transylvanie, Les Presses Universitaires de France, Paris, 382p., Pâclişanu, Z. 1936 Un registru al quinquagesimei din 1461 - in: Albumul dedicat Fraţilor Alexandru şi Ion I. Lăpedatu, Bucureşti, pp.595 - 603., Pascu, Ş. 1971, 1979 Voievodatul Transilvaniei I-II, Editura Dacia, Cluj-Napoca, Prodan, D. 1967-68 Iobăgia în Transilvania în secolul al XVI-lea, I-III., Bucureşti, Suciu, C. 1967 - 1968 Dicţionar istoric al localităţilor din Transilvania, I - II., Editura Academiei R.S. România, Bucureşti, Wagner, E. 1977 Historisch-statistisches Ortsnamenbuch für Siebenbürgen, Böhlau Verlag, Köln - Wien, 526p.
Ugocsa-Ugocea: Szabó I. 1937 Ugocsa megye, Budapest, Szatmár-Satu Mare: Maksai F. 1940 A középkori Szatmár megye, Budapest, 240p., Máramaros-Maramureş: Bélay V. 1943 Máramaros megye társadalma és nemzetiségei. A megye betelepülésétől a VIII. század elejéig, Budapest, 224p., Bihar-Bihor: Jakó Zs. 1940 Bihar megye a török pusztítás előtt, Budapest, Győrffy I. 1915: Dél-Bihar népesedési és nemzetiségi viszonyai negyedfélszáz év óta — Földrajzi Közlemények 43. 6-7. pp.257-293., Arad-Zaránd: Márki S. 1892 Aradvármegye és Arad szabad királyi város története, Arad, 564p., Prodan, D. 1960 Domeniul catăţii Şiria la 1525 — Anuarul Institului de Istorie din Cluj III., pp.37-102., Csanád-Cenad: Borovszky S. 1896-97 Csanád megye története 1715-ig I-II. MTA, Budapest, Hunyad-Hunedoara: Pataki, I. 1973 Domeniul Hunedoara la începutul secolului al XVI-lea, Studiu şi documente 114., Editura Academiei R.S. Române, Bucureşti, 351p., Popa, R. 1988 Siedlungsverhältnisse und Ethnodemographie des Hatzeger Landes im 13-14. Jahrhundert — in: Forschungen zur Volks- und

from the Banat Mountains through the Bihar Mountains up to Máramaros[10]. There were no permanent settlements in the central, highly-elevated, expanding section of the ethnic territory of the Rumanians (with small villages and scattered farmsteads). This was because the population surplus had been absorbed by the depopulated Hungarian and Saxon villages in the Transylvanian Basin. As a consequence of their lifestyle, permanently-settled Rumanians in Transylvania at the end of the 15th century were village dwellers and they did not form an ethnic majority in any of the towns.

Other ethnic groups worth mentioning were present from about 1495 on the territory of present-day Transylvania : the indigenous but ethnically hardly separate Slavic population of the Banat; Ruthenians in the north (western margin of Máramaros, Kelemeni and Görgényi mountains); Bulgarians in the southern Saxonian areas (Rusciori, Cergău Mic), and Serbs in the Banat and in the Arad area. Both spontaneous and organised migration associated with the final occupation of Serbia by the Turks in 1459 (e.g. by Branković, Jakšić and Kinizsi) caused an influx of Serb immigrants, not only to South Banat, the Lippa Hills and the Maros-valley at Maroskapronca, but also to

◄————————————

Continuation of sources for *Fig. 23*
Landeskunde (Verlag der Akademie der Sozialistischen Republik Rumänien, Bukarest) Bd.31. Nr.2. pp.19-33., Szászföld-Districtele şi scaunele săseşti: Binder P. 1982 Közös múltunk. Románok, magyarok, németek és délszlávok feudalizmus kori falusi és városi együttéléséről., Bukarest, Binder, P. 1995 Ethnische Verschiebungen im mittelalterlichen Siebenbürgen — Zeitschrift für Siebenbürgische Landeskunde (Arbeitskreis für Siebenbürgische Landeskunde) Jg.18., H.2., pp.142-146., Graf, B. 1934 Die Kulturlandschaft des Burzenlandes. Ein geographischer Beitrag zur auslandsdeutschen Volks- und Kulturbodenforschung, Verlag für Hochschulkunde, München, 136p., Müller, G. 1912 Die ursprüngliche Rechtslage der Rumänen in siebenbürger Sachsenlande — Archiv des Vereins für Siebenbürgische Landeskunde 38. pp.85-314., Fehér-Alba: Iczkovits E. 1939 Az erdélyi Fehér megye a középkorban, Budapest, 88p., Kolozs-Torda-Doboka-Közép-és Belső-Szolnok-Kraszna / Cluj-Turda-Dobâca-Solnocul de mijloc şi din lăuntru-Crasna: Jakó Zs. 1944 A gyalui vártartomány urbáriumai, Erdélyi Tudományos Intézet CIII., 482p., Makkai L. 1942 Északerdély nemzetiségi viszonyainak kialakulása, Kolozsvár, 20p., Makkai L. 1942 Szolnok-Doboka megye magyarságának pusztulása a XVII. század elején, Kolozsvár, Makkai L. 1943 Társadalom és nemzetiség a középkori Kolozsváron, Kolozsvár, Petri M. 1901 - 1904 Szilágy vármegye monographiája I - VI., Budapest, Wagner, E. 1987 Register des Zehnten und des Schaffünfzigsten als Hilfsquellen zur historischen Demographie Siebenbürgens —in: Benda Kálmán et al. (Hrsg.) 1987 Forschungen über Siebenbürgen und seine Nachbarn I. Festschrift für Attila T. Szabó und Zsigmond Jakó, Dr. Rudolf Trofenik, München, pp.201-224.,

---

[10] At the end of the 15th century the Rumanian ethnic territory extended over the dominions around the following castles (mainly founded in the 13th century): Törcs-Bran, Talmács-Tălmaciu, Hunyad-Hunedoara, Déva, Sebes, Illyéd-Ilidia, Halmos-Almăj, Váradja-Vărădia, Solymos-Şoimoş, Világos-Şiria, Sólyomkő-Peştiş, Valkó-Valcău, Léta-Lita, Jára-Iara, Csicsó-Ciceu, Kővár-Chioar, Görgény-Gurghiu (Makkai L. 1943a, ibid. 353.p.)

the environs of Csák, Temesvár, Arad, Világos, and Lippa. Nevertheless, a Hungarian majority population is assumed to have existed in these areas around 1495[11].

Within this region the Hungarian population perished and their majority diminished, particularly in the flatlands of the Banat and in the Arad area - due both to the war[12] and epidemics of 1514-1552. They were replaced mainly by Serbs and, to a lesser extent by Rumanians, Gypsies and Turks. On the territory of the principality of Transylvania, which was a symbol of the survival of Hungarian statehood, the previous ethnic processes continued undisturbed till the end of the 16th century. In the towns of the Hungarian counties of Transylvania (especially in Kolozsvár, Torda, Gyulafehérvár and Déva) the Hungarian character of local society was strengthened by an influx of Hungarians who had escaped from the Great Hungarian Plain which was occupied by the Turks.

The Rumanian population became increasingly settled and changed from shepherding to farming. This was due to the relative demographic saturation of of their previous ethnic areas, and they not only occupied Hungarian and Saxon ethnic areas but settled in the earlier uninhabited parts of mountain regions[13]. At the end of the 16th century, historical Transylvania was assumed to have had a population of 670,000 with approx. 52% Hungarians, 28% Rumanians and 19% Saxons[14]. During the so-called fifteen year war, between 1599-1604, there were serious clashes between the Hapsburg (Austrian), Ottoman (Turkish) Empires, Transylvanian (Hungarian) and Wallachian (Rumanian) Principalities, and Giorgio Basta, a general of the Hapsburg Empire, and his ally the Wallachian voivode Mihai Viteazul („Michael the Brave"), imposed terror and organised subsequent massacres in Transylvania, a Hungarian principality striving for independence. Rumanians and Székely-Hungarians suffered less not only for political reasons, but because they occupied wooded mountain areas far from the routs of the campaigns. But the mainly Hungarian dwellers in the central parts of Transylvania (e.g. in the environs of Kolozsvár and Torda) were almost undefended. As a consequence of massacres, plague and famine, the population of (later called) Szolnok-Doboka county

---

[11] Makkai L. 1943a, ibid. 389.p., Makkai L. 1946 Histoire de Transylvanie, Les Presses Universitaires de France, Paris, Márki S. 1892 Aradvármegye és Arad szabad királyi város története (History of Arad County and Free Royal Town Arad), Arad, Borovszky S. 1896-97 Csanád megye története 1715-ig I-II. (History of Csanád County till 1715), MTA, Budapest

[12] Acts of war devastating and desolating the Banat and the vicinity of Arad: peasant uprising led by George Dózsa (1514), ravaging by Serb troops of Jovan Crni Nenad (1527), main Turkish campaigns of 1551, 1552, 1566.

[13] Barta G. 1986 Az Erdélyi Fejedelemség első korszaka (The First Period of the Principality Transylvania) — in: Makkai L. - Mócsy A. (Eds.) Erdély története (History of Transylvania) I. Akadémiai Kiadó, Budapest 493-494.p.

[14] Estimations of the population number of Transylvania around 1595 (350 thousand Hungarians, 190 thousand Rumanians, 130 thousand Saxons) based on the 1495 population and ethnic data using also the following sources: Barta G. 1986 ibid. 510.p., Barta G. 1989 Az Erdélyi Fejedelemség (The Principality of Transylvania) — in: Erdély rövid története (Short History of Transylvania), Akadémiai Kiadó, Budapest, 238.p., Jakó Zs. 1945 Adatok a dézsma fejedelemségkori adminisztrációjához (Data to the Administration of the Tithe during the Period of the Transylvanian Principality), Kolozsvár

with a Hungarian majority, dropped by 70% between 1553-1603 and that of Kolozsvár by 68% between 1590-1642[15]. The number Hungarians decreased by 85% and that of the Rumanians by 45% in Szolnok-Doboka over the same period. Based on the above data, and assuming Székely losses to have been similar to Rumanian ones, no more than 330,000 people might have lived on the territory of the now ruined Transylvania in 1604 *(Fig. 24.)*. During a relatively calm period until the mid-16th century a massive migration of Rumanians continued from the inner mountain areas (e.g. Kővár-Chioar Land, Bihar-Apuşeni Mts.), and from the Rumanian principalities (Wallachia, Moldavia), because of extreme social oppression and the uncertain political situation there. These large numbers of Rumanians, solving a shortage of labour in the area, were welcomed by Hungarian landowners and the leaders of Saxon settlements. By the mid-17th century the proportion of Rumanians probably exceeded one third of the population[16], and may have equalled the combined number of Hungarians and Székelys *(Fig. 25.)*.

Following an unsuccessful invasion of Poland by Prince George Rákóczi II between 1658-1660, certain regions of Transylvania were devastated by Turkish and Tartar troops and a subsequent plague decimated the population, again, predominantly its Hungarian part. Due to the annihilation, the kidnapping and fleeing of Hungarians, and the immigration of Rumanians into the territories of Kolozs, Doboka, Inner and Middle-Szolnok, and Kraszna counties, 177 out of 317 Hungarian villages changed to having a Rumanian majority population during the 17th century[17]. As a result, the Transylvanian Basin, which had been an area with Hungarian majority at the end of the medieval period, disintegrated, while the Saxon villages in the Beszterce district and in King's Land were ruined. Due to these events the number of Rumanians in Transylvania exceeded Hungarians in the second half of the 17th century. Wars between 1599 and 1711 had created a profound and irreversible shift in the ethnic composition of Transylvania in favour of the Rumanians who enjoyed a permanent replenishment of population from over the Carpathians, and these changes eventually proved decisive in shaping ethnic patterns well into the 20th century. According to the data on tax-payers of

---

[15]Makkai L. 1942 Szolnok-Doboka megye magyarságának pusztulása a XVII. század elején (The Destruction of the Hungarians of Szolnok-Doboka County in Early 17th Century), Kolozsvár, 31., 34.p., Bakács I. 1963 A török hódoltság korának népessége (The Population of Parts of Hungary under Ottoman Rule)— in: Kovacsics J. (ed.) Magyarország történeti demográfiája (Historic Demography of Hungary), Budapest, 136.p.

[16] According to V. Lupu, the Rumanian voivode of Moldavia, over one third of the population of Transylvania were already Rumanians at this time - Szilágyi S. 1890 Erdély és az északkeleti háború. Levelek és okiratok (Transylvania and the War in NW. Letters and Documents), I. kötet, Budapest, 246-247, 255-256.p.).

[17]Makkai L. 1942 Északerdély nemzetiségi viszonyainak kialakulása (The Formation of the Ethnic Structure of Northern-Transylvania), Kolozsvár, 18.p.

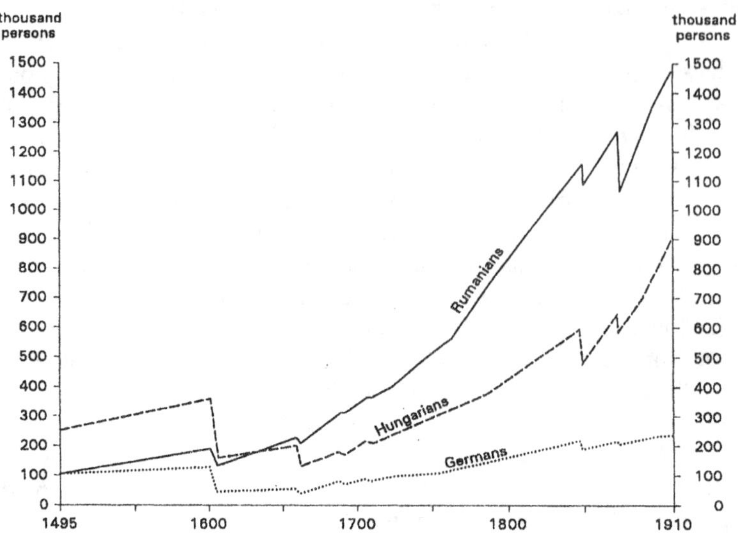

Figure 24. Change in the number of Hungarians, Rumanians and Germans on the historical territory of Transylvania (1495 - 1910)

1720 on the territory of historical Transylvania 806,000 people may have lived there[18], about half of them Rumanians[19].

Following the liberation of the Kőrös-vidék / Crişana region (1692) and of Banat (1718) from Ottoman (Turkish) occupation, large numbers of Rumanians from the mountain areas were attracted by the almost depopulated flatlands[20]. The Hapsburg administration settled predominantly Catholic Germans in the western, most fertile part of Banat, in the surroundings of strategically important towns like Temesv r and Arad, and in the mining areas of Oravicabánya, Dognácska, Szászka, Boksán, Resicabánya etc.[21]. As a result of this, a fairly uniform German ethnic area emerged west of the Lippa-Temesvár-Detta line, while to the east the Banat became essentially Rumanian. The ethnic composition of this region was made extremely colourful as a result of the

---

[18] Acsády I. 1896 Magyarország népessége a Pragmatica Sanctio korában 1720 - 21 (Population of Hungary 1720-21). — Magyar Statisztikai Közlemények XII. /Új folyam/, Budapest, 58.p.

[19] Also according to Prodan, D. this was the period when Rumanians attained their absolute ethnic majority in Transylvania - (1944 Teoria imigraţiei românilor din principatele române in Transilvania in veacul al XVIII-lea, Sibiu, 21.p.).

[20] Jakó Zs. 1943 Újkori román települések Erdélyben és a Partiumban (Rumanian Settlements in Transylvania and in Crişana during the 17-18th centuries) — in: Deér J. - Gáldi L. (eds.) 1943 Magyarok és románok (Hungarians and Rumanians)I., Budapest, 545-546.p.

[21] Buchmann K. 1936 A délmagyarországi telepítések története (The History of Colonization in Southern-Hungary) I. Bánát, Budapest, 130p., Feneşan, C. 1979 Kolonisation des Banater Berglandes im 18. Jahrhundert — Forschungen zur Volks- und Landeskunde (Bukarest) Bd.22. Nr.2. pp.43-50

108

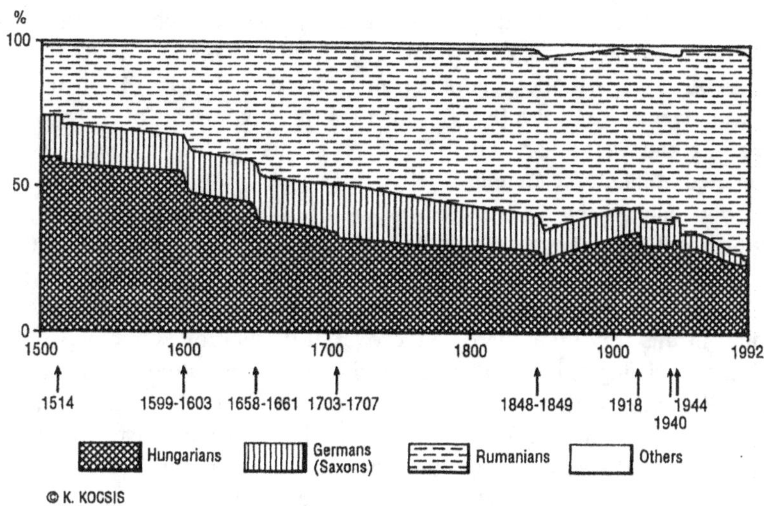

Figure 25. Change in the ethnic structure of population on the historical territory of Transylvania
(16th–20th century)

subsequent settlement of Serbs, Crashovans, Hungarians, Bulgarians, Slovaks and Czechs during the 18th century.

In the Bihar, Szilágy and Szatmár counties, apart from the Rumanian ethnic expansion which was to the detriment of Hungarians, important changes in ethnic composition were introduced in the 18th century by the settlement of Slovaks in the Réz Mountains and of Germans in the vicinity of Nagykároly. In the area of historical Transylvania, resettlement meant that the Rumanians came down from the mountain territories and migrated there from Wallachia and Moldavia. The Trans-Carpathian migration of Rumanians was not however exclusively one-way (into Transylvania); it depended on the socio-economic situation and was closely related to security considerations - it was often directed from Transylvania to Wallachia or Moldavia[22]. The positive balance of migration into Transylvania is witnessed by an increase well above average in the Rumanian population: their estimated number was 561,000 in 1720, 453,000 in 1733, 538,000 in 1750, 561,000 in 1762 and 729,000 in 1794[23]. Due

---

[22] Prodan, D. ibid. 21.p.

[23] Chirca, H. 1972 Intregire la conscripţia confesională din 1733 privind populaţia românească din Transilvania (Addenda to the census 1733 regarding to the Rumanian population of Transylvania) — in: Pascu, S. (Red.) Populaţie şi societate. Studii de demografie istorică, Vol. I., pp. 89-95., Togan, N. 1898 Românii din Transilvania la 1733. Conscripţia episcopului Ioan In. Klein de Sadu — Transilvania XXIX. (Sibiu), Bunea, A. 1901 Statistica Românilor în Transylvania în 1750 — Transilvania XXXII. (Sibiu) 1901, pp. 237-292., Nyárády R. K. 1987 Erdély népességének etnikai és vallási tagozódása a magyar államalapítástól a dualizmus koráig (Ethnic and religious structure of the population of Transylvania since the foundation of the Hungarian state till the time of Dualism) — in: A KSH

to the settlement of Orthodox Rumanians and Gypsies speaking Rumanian, on the territory of the 11 Saxon „seats" (administrative units), as well as 87,000 Lutheran Saxons, 66,000 (43%) Orthodox people (Rumanians and Gypsies) lived in 1765; their share had risen over 53 % by 1900[24]. By this time the Saxon seats of Szászváros, Szászsebes, Újegyház and Szerdahely which were devastated in the 16th and 17th centuries, had become predominantly Rumanian.

By the end of the 18th century as a result of migration, an ethnic pattern emerged which did not change essentially in the rural areas until the mid-20th century. During a hundred years following the 1770s the number of the Rumanian population rose at a lower rate, but in 1832 it surpassed one million in the historical area of Transylvania. In this way their share of the overall population was close to 60%, well exceeding that of Hungarians (29%). Several tens of thousands of Hungarians and Rumanians fell victim to the War of Independence of 1848-49 resulting in a drop of 190,000 between 1848 and 1850[25]. According to the Austrian census of 1850 out of a population of 1,861,000 living on the territory of historical Transylvania, 58.3% declared themselves to be Rumanian, 26.1 % Hungarian and 10.3% German.

Following the Austro-Hungarian Compromise (1867) when Transylvania was formally reannexed to Hungary and both socio-economic modernisation and capitalist transformation were taking place, the last cholera epidemic occurred in 1873 - even before there was any improvement in health conditions. As a result, the total population of Transylvania dropped by 3.2% between the 1869 and 1880 censuses[26]. At the time of the first Hungarian census in 1880, in answer to questions regarding native/mother tongue, it transpired that 21% of Hungarians, 17.1% of Germans and 3.4% of Rumanians lived in urban settlements. Hungarians formed the majority in 62% of towns[27]. At the turn of the century there was significant emigration to America, to Rumania and to the central parts of the country - primarily to Budapest, the capital. There was also some immigration of Jews from Ukrainian territories (Galicia Province) and Bukovina to Máramaros, to Northern Transylvania[28] and to the larger towns located along the periphery of the Great Hungarian Plain (e.g. Temesvár, Arad, Nagyvárad, Szatmárnémeti). Apart from the favourable rise in the birthrate among Hungarians between 1880 and 1910, the voluntary linguistic assimilation and Magyarization of the

---

Népességtudományi Kutató Intézetének történeti demográfiai füzetei 3., Budapest, pp.7-55., Ballmann, J. M. 1801 Statistische Landeskunde Siebenbürgens im Grundrisse, Hermannstadt, 120p., Lebrecht, M. 1804 Versuch einer Erdbeschreibung des Grossfürstentums Siebenbürgen, II. Auflage, Hermannstadt

[24] Müller, G. 1912 Die ursprüngliche Rechtslage der Rumänen in siebenbürger Sachsenlande — Archiv des Vereins für Siebenbürgische Landeskunde 38., 28.p.

[25] Bieltz, E.A. 1857. ibid.148.p.

[26] The cholera epidemics had reduced number of Rumanians by c 200,000 and that of Hungarians by c 60,000.

[27] Manuila, S. 1938 Aspects démographiques de la Transylvanie — La Transylvanie. Institut d'Istoire Nationale de Cluj, Académie Roumanie, Bucarest, 804.p.

[28] Growth of population of Jewish confession in historical Transylvania: 1850: 11,692; 1880: 29,993; 1910: 64,074.

Jews[29] greatly contributed to the growth of the Hungarian speaking population *(Figs. 26., 27.)*. An increase in the number of Hungarians was observed in urban settlements (e.g. in Temesvár, Arad, Brassó, Nagyszeben). On the Rumanian ethnic territory of South Transylvania, colonies mushroomed around heavy industrial works (Resicabánya, Boksán, Anina, Vajdahunyad, Kalán, Petrozsény etc.) where there were raw material deposits (coal and iron ore), and absorbed large masses of skilled workers, mainly Hungarians and Germans. As far as the Rumanian population is concerned, their Magyarization was negligible. Kovászna, Torda, Nagyszalonta, Bánffyhunyad, Marosvásárhely were towns where the proportion of Hungarians had dropped as a result of Rumanian immigration. Rumanian expansion was even stronger in Nagyszeben, Segesvár, Medgyes, at the expense of the Saxons.

At the time of the 1910 Hungarian census, of the nearly 5,3 million population living on the territory of present-day Transylvania, 54% declared Rumanian to be their mother tongue, 32% Hungarian and 11% German *(Tab. 20.)*. In comparison with the situation at the end of the 18th century the ethnic pattern had not essentially changed, only the partial Magyarization of Greek Catholics, Jews and Roman Catholic Germans created a more homogeneous ethnic Hungarian area of 20 to 30 km width along the present Hungarian-Rumanian state border (North-Bihar - Szatmár - Ugocsa), while in the Banat and in the southern part of Transylvania Hungarian language pockets, ethnic islands grew in number *(Fig. 28.)*. The ethnic territory of Germans (the Saxons and Swabians) was the least broken up by Rumanian villages in the environs of Beszterce, in remote parts of the Hortobágy Hills and in the Banat, between Temesvár and Nagyszentmiklós. In the Banat an extremely complex ethnic pattern survived (with Rumanians, Germans, Hungarians, Serbs, Gypsies, Czechs, Bulgarians, Crashovans and Slovaks) from colonisations of the 18th century. This relative ethnic stability characterised the ethnic territory of the Slovaks in the Réz Mts. and that of the Ruthenians in Máramaros. Nevertheless, there was an absolute or relative majority of those declaring themselves to be Hungarian in 30 of the 41 urban settlements of present-day Transylvania, those of the state-forming ethnic group. There was a Rumanian majority in 6 smaller towns (Karánsebes, Hátszeg, Szászváros, Szászsebes, Abrudbánya, Vízakna), while Germans dominated Nagyszeben, Medgyes, Segesvár, Szászrégen and Beszterce. Most of those people with Hungarian lingual affiliation (23 - 28,000) lived in Nagyvárad, Kolozsvár, Arad, Szatmárnémeti, Temesvár and Marosvásárhely in 1910. The largest Rumanian communities were in Brassó, Arad and Nagyszeben (9 - 12,000), the German ones (11 - 32,000) being Temesvár, Nagyszeben and Brassó. Among the 5,321 present-day settlements ethnic majorities were distributed as follows: 3,921 Rumanian, 1,026 Hungarian, 279 German, 81 Slavic, one Gypsy (Priszlop at Resinár in Szeben county); the areas of 13 present-day settlements were uninhabited.

---

[29] Of the Jewish population of Transylvania 55.6% in 1890, and 73.3% in 1910 declared their native tongue to be Hungarian (Jakabffy E. 1923 Erdély statisztikája – Statistics of Transylvania, Lugos, 7.p.)

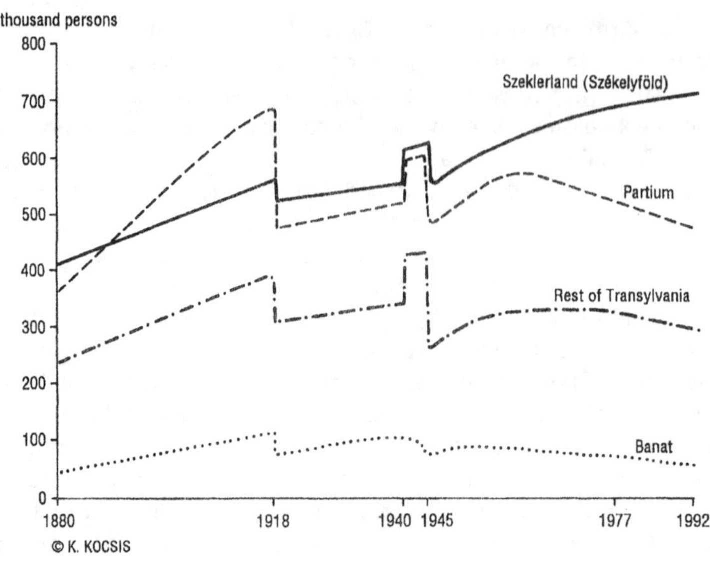

Figure 26. Change in the population number of ethnic Hungarians in major areas of Transylvania (1880–1992)

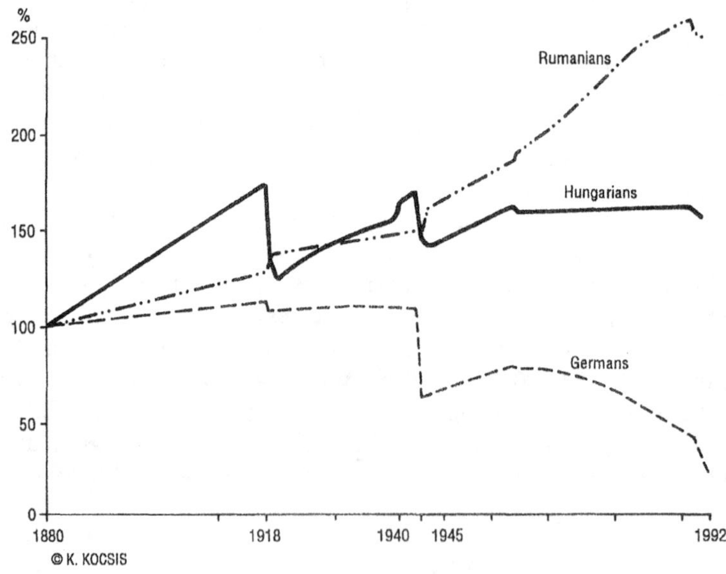

Figure 27. Change in the population number of the main ethnic groups on the present-day territory of Transylvania (1880–1992)

112

Table 20. Ethnic structure of the population on the present territory of Transylvania (1880–1992)

Year	Total population	Rumanians		Hungarians		Germans		Ethnic Jews		Gypsies		Others	
	number	number	%	number	%	number	%	number	%	number	%	number	%
1880	4,005,467	2,294,120	57.3	1,045,098	26.1	501,656	12.5	..	..	..	..	164,593	4.1
1900	4,872,366	2,685,122	55.1	1,438,296	29.5	582,034	12.0	..	..	..	..	166,914	3.4
1910	5,260,181	2,829,351	53.8	1,663,774	31.6	563,416	10.7	..	..	47,876	0.9	155,764	3,0
1920	5,114,124	2,930,120	57.3	1,305,753	25.5	539,427	10.5	181,340	3.5		0.0	157,484	3,2
1930	5,549,806	3,208,767	57.8	1,353,288	24.4	544,278	9,.1	178,810	3.2	109,156	2.0	155,507	2,8
1930	5,549,806	3,234,157	58.3	1,480,721	26.7	541,174	9.8	111,384	2.0	43,653	0.8	138,717	2,4
1941	5,912,413	3,304,063	55.9	1,744,179	29.5	535,359	9.0	..	0.0	..	0.0	328,812	5,6
1948	5,761,127	3,752,269	65.1	1,481,903	25.7	332,066	5.8	30,039	0.5	..	0.0	164,850	2,9
1956	6,218,427	4,041,156	65.0	1,558,254	25.1	367,857	5.9	43,749	0.7	78,278	1.3	129,133	2,0
1966	6,719,555	4,559,432	67.9	1,597,438	23.8	371,881	5.5	13,530	0.2	49,105	0.7	128,169	1,9
1977	7,500,229	5,203,846	69.4	1,691,048	22.5	347,896	4.6	7,830	0.1	123,028	1.6	126,581	1,8
1992	7,723,313	5,684,142	73.6	1,603,923	20.8	109,014	1.4	2,687	0.0	202,665	2.6	120,882	1,6
1992	7,723,313	5,815,425	75.3	1,619,735	21.0	91,386	1.2	324	0.0	84,718	1.1	111,725	1,4
1997	7,612,953	4,800,000	63.0	1,470,000	19.3	73,000	0.9	..	..	1,150,000	15.1	119,953	1.7

Sources: 1880, 1900, 1910: Hungarian census data, 1920, 1930, 1948, 1956, 1966, 1977, 1992: Rumanian census data, 1941: combined Hungarian and Rumanian census data, 1997: estimation of K.Kocsis. 1900, 1920 census data from Varga E.Á. 1992 Népszámlálások a jelenkori Erdély területén (Censuses on the present-day territory of Transylvania), Regio - MTA Történettudományi Intézet, Budapest, pp. 141-142.

Remarks: Present territory of Transylvania = historical Transylvania, Maramureş, Crişana, Rumanian Banat. Italic figures: mother / native tongue data, other figures: ethnic data. Rumanians with Aromunians and Macedorumanians; Hungarians with Székelys and Csángós; Germans with Saxons and Swabians.

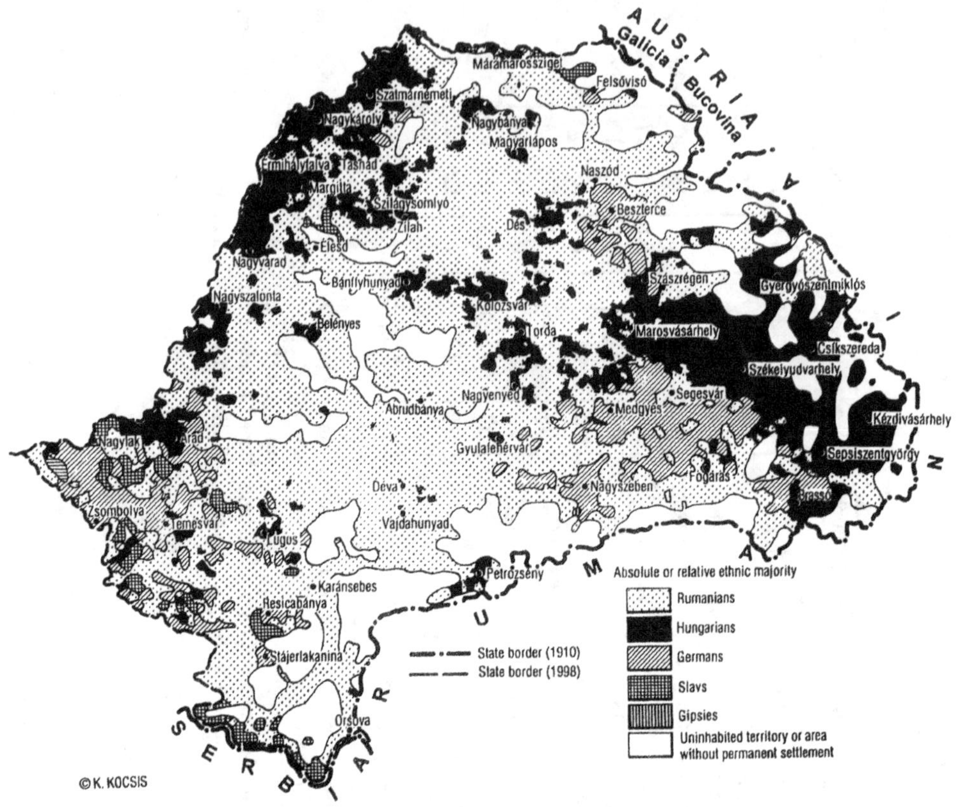

Figure 28. Ethnic map of the present-day territory of Transylvania (1910)
Source: Census 1910

At the end of World War I territories of Eastern Hungary were occupied by the Royal Rumanian Army. From this area of about 103,000 km² (Transylvania in the broader sense) was annexed to Rumania at the Peace Treaty of Trianon (4 June, 1920) by the victorious Entente Powers. Thus, according to the 1910 census data, nearly 2,5 million non-Rumanians (including 1,7 million Hungarians), 46% of the total population of Transylvania, were to become citizens of Rumania which suddenly turned into a multi-ethnic state. According to the figures of the National Office for Refugees in Budapest, between 1918 and 1924, following the Hungarian-Rumanian shift of power, 107,035 Hungarians fled Rumania to the new state territory of Hungary[30]. The number of Hungarians recorded in Rumanian statistics was further decreased firstly by the classification of Jews (mostly Hungarian speakers) into a separate ethnic category, and

---

[30] Petrichevich-Horváth E. 1924 Jelentés az Országos Menekültügyi Hivatal négy évi működéséről (Report about the activity of the National Office for Refugees) , Budapest

114

by the registration of already Magyarized Greek Catholics and Orthodox people as Rumanians, and of Roman Catholic Swabians of German origin in the Szatmár Region as Germans[31]. The decrease in the number and proportion of Hungarians between 1910 and 1930 for the above reasons was striking in the urban settlements of the western border region between Kőrös-vidék-Crişana and Máramaros, (e.g. Arad, Nagyvárad, Nagykároly, Szatmárnémeti, Máramarossziget), while there was a massive additional resettlement of Rumanians in Kolozsvár, Torda, Marosvásárhely, Zilah, Nagybánya, Déva, Petrozsény and Dés *(Tabs. 21., 22., Fig. 29.)*. As a consequence, a mere 37.9% of the urban population of Transylvania were registered as Hungarian in 1930. After the towns received 185,000 Rumanians between 1910 and 1930 they represented 35% of the total urban population. Outside of the towns, Rumanianization took place within the framework of land reform by establishing Rumanian colonies along the new Hungarian-Rumanian border, on the ethnic Hungarian territories of Szatmár and Bihar counties[32]. Economic reasons apart a policy of ethnic discrimination led to massive emigration of ethnic minorities; the distribution of emigrants from Rumania in 1927 was as follows: 30% Germans, 28% Jews, 12% Hungarians and 5% Rumanians[33].

The number of Germans between the two world wars stagnated, due to their low birthrate[34] and because of emigration. There was a sudden increase in Germans in the Szatmár region; they had previously declared themselves to be Hungarian. Among urban settlements, an absolute majority of Germans was retained only at Resicabánya (55.4% in 1930) and a relative one in Nagyszeben, Medgyes and Segesvár. Due to the expansion of Rumanians and Gypsies with a much higher birth rate, only two Saxon districts in Transylvania (Medgyes, Erzsébetváros) had a German majority population at that time. 68% of Transylvanian Jewry having previously undergone rapid Magyarization[35] and numbering 179,000 in 1930, lived mainly in the north, in the coun-

---

[31] See Varga E. Á. 1992 Népszámlálások a jelenkori Erdély területén (Censuses on the present territory of Transylvania), Regio - MTA Történettudományi Intézet, Budapest, 208p.

[32] Micula Nouă, Bercu Nou, Mireşul-Mesteacăn, Drăguşeni, Livada Mică-Colonia Livada Nouă, Principele Mihai-Traian, Locateşti-Dacia, Colonel Paulian, Gelu, Baba Novac, Lucăceni, Horea, Marna Nouă, Scărişoara Nouă, Mihai Bravu, Regina Maria-Avram Iancu etc.

[33] Braunias, K. 1927-28 Die Auswanderung aus Rumänien und die Minderheiten — Nation und Staat (Wien) 1. pp.296-298.

[34] Mean annual natural increase and vitality index by the main ethnic groups of Transylvania between 1931-1939: Rumanians 8.1 ‰, Hungarians 6.2 ‰, Germans 3.4 ‰ - (Manuila, S. 1941 Studii etnografice asupra populaţiei României. Cu o anexă despre evoluţia numerică a diferitelor grupe etnice din România în anii 1931-1939, Bucureşti, pp.95-103.) and Rumanians: 130.8, Hungarians: 130.4, Germans: 115.3 (Râmneantzu, P. 1946 The biological grounds and the vitality of the Transylvanian Rumanians, Centrul de Studii şi Cercetări Privitoare la Transilvania, Sibiu, 64.p.).

[35] In 1930 on the territory of present-day Transylvania the number of Jews (according to the religious affiliation) was 192,833, ethnic Jews numbered to 178,699, and 111,275 persons declared Yiddish their native tongue (Varga E. Á. 1992 ibid. pp.141-143.).

Table 21. Change in the number of ethnic Hungarians by major parts of Transylvania (1880–1992)

Year	Székely Region/ Szeklerland	Rest of Transylvania	Partium	Banat
1880	404,402	239,273	359,669	41,744
1910	536,968	370,383	645,809	104,885
1930	538,681	333,428	503,019	105,584
1948	577,679	296,899	507,114	100,211
1956	632,099	328,814	571,661	92,625
1977	701,958	353,291	549,036	86,763
1992	723,392	308,915	501,187	70,772

Sources:1880,1910: Hungarian census data (mother/native tongue), 1977, 1992: Rumanian census data (ethnicity), 1930, 1948, 1956: Rumanian census data (mother/native tongue)
Remark: Székely Region/Szeklerland = Maros/Mureş, Hargita/Harghita, Kovászna/Covasna counties; Rest of Transylvania = Beszterce-Naszód/Bistriţa-Nasăud, Kolozs/Cluj, Fehér/Alba, Szeben/Sibiu, Brassó/Braşov, Hunyad/Hunedoara counties; Partium = Máramaros/Maramureş, Szatmár/Satu Mare, Szilágy/Sălaj, Bihar/Bihor, Arad counties; Banat = Temes/Timiş, Krassó-Szörény/Caraş-Severin counties

ties Máramaros (34,000), Szatmár (24,000), Bihar (22,000), Kolozs (17,000), Szilágy (13,000) and Szamos (10 ,000).

During World War II ministers of foreign affairs in Germany and Italy decided to calm down the war-like tensions between their allies, Hungary and Rumania, dividing the territory of Transylvania between these two countries (Second Vienna Award, 30 August 1940). The northern half (43,104 km², with a 53.6% population of Hungarians (1941 Hungarian census data)[36] was reannexed to Hungary, while the southern part with a 68.5% population of Rumanian ethnic origin (1941 Rumanian census data) remained in Rumania. In this extremely tense situation, and for a variety of reasons (a sense of fear, being compelled to emigrate, being expelled), 219,927 Rumanians[37] left the northern area which was under Hungarian administration, between 1940-1943, while 190,132 Hungarians fled Southern Transylvania between 1938-[38]. As a result of a massive, enforced Hungarian-Rumanian population shift (1940-41), accelerated Rumanianization and a reduction in the Hungarian population of town in South

---

[36] The proportion of Hungarians in North Transylvania was 51.4% in 1910 (Thirring L. 1940 A visszacsatolt erdélyi és keletmagyarországi terület - The Reannexed Transylvanian and East-Hungarian Territory — Magyar Statisztikai Szemle 1940 / 7. 553.p.), and it dropped to 38.1% in 1930 (Die Bevölkerungszählung in Rumänien 1941, Publikationsstelle Wien, 1943, 20.p.), according to estimations by Manuila, S. the latter was 37.2% in 1940 (Spaţiul istoric şi etnic românesc III., Bucureşti, 1942, 17.p.).

[37] Universul (Bucureşti) 9.10.1943 and 9.01.1944, Schechtman, J.B. 1946 European Population Transfers 1939-45, New York - Oxford University Press, 430.p.

[38] Main data on Rumanian refugees according to the conscription of February 1944 — Magyar Statisztikai Szemle 1944 / 9-12. pp.394-410., Stark T. 1989 Magyarország második világháborús embervesztesége (Human Losses of Hungary during the War II), MTA Történettudományi Intézet, Budapest, 65.p.

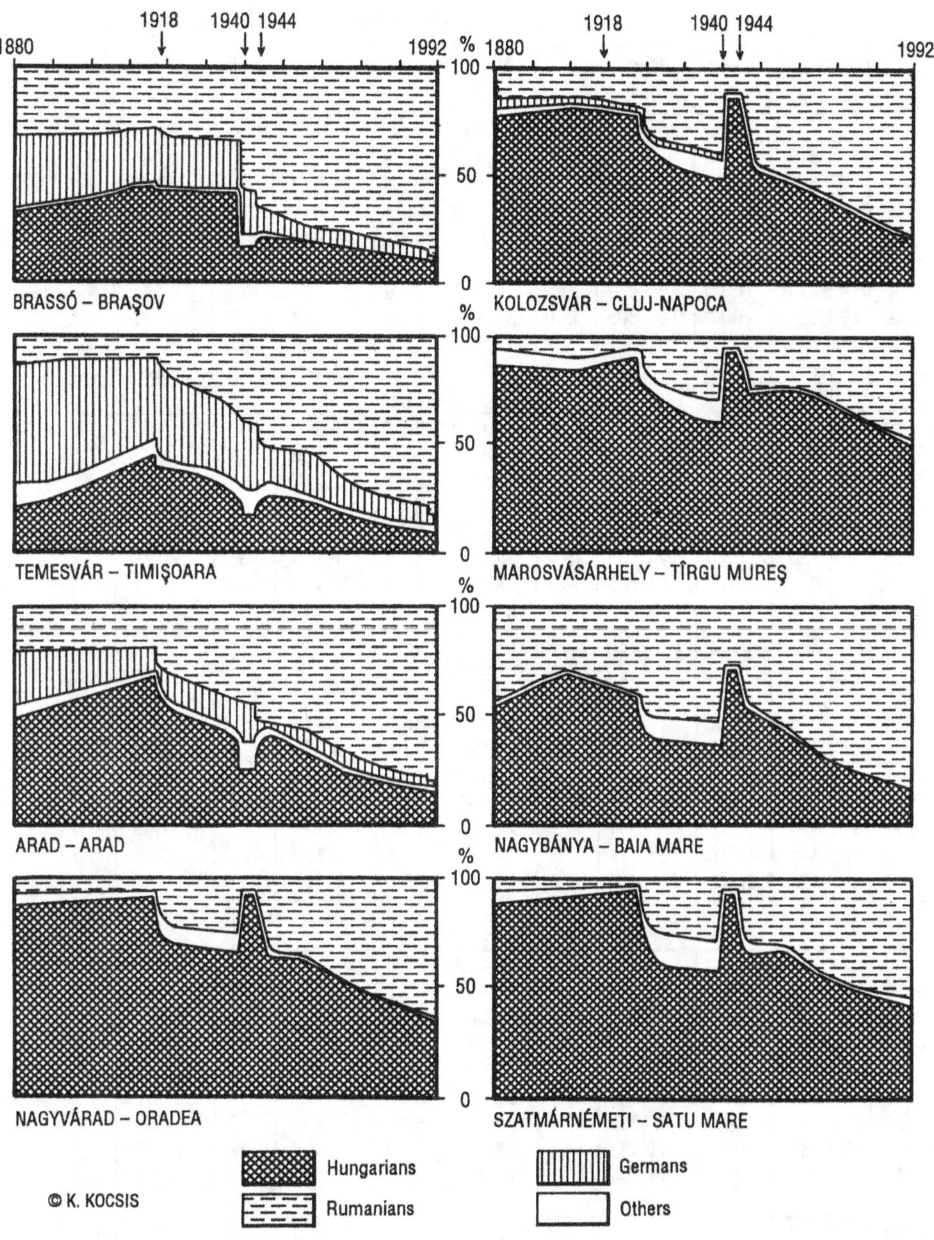

Figure 29. Change in the ethnic structure of population in selected municipalities of Transylvania (1880–1992)

Table 22. Change in the ethnic structure of selected

Year	Total population		Rumanians		**Hungarians**		Germans		Others	
	number	%	number	%	**number**	%	number	%	number	%
Temesvár - Timişoara										
1880	37,815	100.0	5,163	13.6	**7,749**	**20.5**	20,263	53.6	4,640	12.3
1910	72,555	100.0	7,566	10.4	**28,552**	**39.3**	31,644	43.6	4,793	6.7
1930	91,580	100.0	24,088	26.3	**32,513**	**35.5**	30,670	33.5	4,309	4.7
1941	110,840	100.0	44,349	40.0	**20,090**	**18.1**	30,940	27.9	15,461	14.0
1948	111,987	100.0	58,456	52.2	**30,630**	**27.3**	16,139	14.4	6,762	6.1
1956	142,257	100.0	76,173	53.5	**36,459**	**25.6**	25,494	17.9	4,131	3.0
1966	174,243	100.0	109,806	63.0	**33,502**	**19.2**	25,564	14.7	5,371	3.1
1977	269,353	100.0	191,742	71.2	**36,724**	**13.6**	28,429	10.6	12,458	4.6
1992	334,115	100.0	274,511	82.2	**31,798**	**9.5**	13,206	4.0	14,600	4.4
Kolozsvár - Cluj-Napoca										
1880	29,923	100.0	3,978	13.3	**23,490**	**78.5**	1,468	4.9	987	3.3
1910	62,733	100.0	8,886	14.2	**51,192**	**81.6**	1,678	2.7	977	1.5
1930	103,840	100.0	36,981	35.6	**55,351**	**53.3**	2,728	2.6	8,780	8.5
1941	114,984	100.0	11,524	10.0	**100,172**	**87.1**	1,841	1.6	1,447	1.3
1948	117,915	100.0	47,321	40.1	**67,977**	**57.6**	360	0.3	2,257	2.0
1956	154,723	100.0	74,623	48.2	**77,839**	**50.3**	1,115	0.7	1,146	0.8
1966	185,663	100.0	105,185	56.7	**78,520**	**42.3**	1,337	0.7	621	0.3
1977	262,858	100.0	173,003	65.8	**86,215**	**32.8**	1,480	0.6	2,160	0.8
1992	328,602	100.0	248,572	75.6	**74,892**	**22.8**	1,149	0.3	3,989	1.2
Brassó - Braşov										
1880	29,584	100.0	9,378	31.7	**9,822**	**33.2**	9,910	33.5	474	1.6
1910	41,056	100.0	11,786	28.7	**17,831**	**43.4**	10,841	26.4	598	1.5
1930	59,232	100.0	19,378	32.7	**24,977**	**42.2**	13,276	22.4	1,601	2.7
1941	84,557	100.0	49,463	58.5	**15,114**	**17.9**	16,210	19.2	3,770	4.4
1948	82,984	100.0	55,152	66.5	**17,697**	**21.3**	8,480	10.2	1,655	2.0
1956	123,834	100.0	88,651	71.6	**24,186**	**19.5**	10,349	8.3	648	0.6
1966	163,345	100.0	123,711	75.7	**28,638**	**17.5**	10,280	6.3	716	0.5
1977	256,475	100.0	210,019	81.9	**34,879**	**13.6**	9,718	3.8	1,859	0.7
1992	323,736	100.0	287,535	88.8	**31,574**	**9.7**	3,418	1.1	1,209	0.4
Nagyvárad - Oradea										
1880	34,231	100.0	2,143	6.2	**29,925**	**87.4**	1,223	3.6	940	2.8
1910	68,960	100.0	3,779	5.5	**62,985**	**91.3**	1,450	2.1	746	1.1
1930	88,830	100.0	21,790	24.5	**60,202**	**67.8**	1,165	1.3	5,673	6.4
1941	98,622	100.0	5,135	5.2	**90,828**	**92.1**	886	0.9	1,773	1.8
1948	82,282	100.0	26,998	32.8	**52,541**	**63.8**	165	0.2	2,578	3.2
1956	98,950	100.0	34,501	34.9	**62,804**	**63.5**	373	0.4	1,272	1.2
1966	122,534	100.0	55,785	45.5	**65,141**	**53.2**	499	0.4	1.109	0.9
1977	170,531	100.0	91,925	53.9	**75,125**	**44.0**	618	0.4	2,863	1.7
1992	222,741	100.0	144,244	64.8	**74,228**	**33.3**	959	0.4	3,310	1.5
Arad - Arad										
1880	44,320	100.0	9,440	21.3	**21,148**	**47.7**	10,770	24.3	2,962	6.7
1910	76,356	100.0	14,600	19.1	**48,409**	**63.4**	10,841	14.2	2,506	3.3
1930	86,181	100.0	30,381	36.2	**41,854**	**48.6**	11,059	12.8	2,887	2.4
1941	95,287	100.0	42,862	44.7	**27,344**	**28.5**	14,146	14.8	10,935	12.0
1948	87,291	100.0	45,819	52.5	**35,326**	**40.5**	2,234	2.5	3,912	4.5
1956	106,460	100.0	59,050	55.5	**37,633**	**35.3**	8,089	7.6	1,688	1.6
1966	126,000	100.0	81,005	64.3	**33,800**	**26.8**	9,456	7.5	1,739	1.4
1977	171,193	100.0	121,815	71.2	**34,728**	**20.3**	10,217	6.0	4,433	2.5
1992	190,114	100.0	151,438	79.7	**29,832**	**15.7**	4,142	2.2	4,702	2.5

Sources: 1880, 1910: Hungarian census data (mother/native tongue), 1930, 1948, 1956, 1966: Rumanian census data (mother/native tongue), 1941: Brassó, Temesvár, Arad = Rumanian census data (ethnic origin); other cities and towns = Hungarian census data (mother/native tongue), 1977, 1992: Rumanian census data (ethnicity).

cities and towns of Transylvania (1880 – 1992)

Year	Total population		Rumanians		**Hungarians**		Germans		Others	
	number	%	number	%	**number**	**%**	number	%	number	%
Marosvásárhely - Târgu Mureş										
1880	12,883	100.0	677	5.2	**11,363**	**88.2**	524	4.1	319	2.5
1910	25,517	100.0	1,717	6.7	**22,790**	**89.3**	606	2.4	404	1.6
1930	38,517	100.0	9,493	24.6	**25,359**	**65.8**	735	1.9	2,930	7.7
1941	44,946	100.0	1,725	3.8	**42,449**	**94.4**	436	1.0	336	0.8
1948	47,043	100.0	11,007	23.4	**34,943**	**74.3**	72	0.1	1,021	2.2
1956	65,194	100.0	14,315	21.9	**50,174**	**77.0**	45	0.1	660	1.0
1966	80,912	100.0	22,072	27.3	**58,208**	**71.9**	441	0.5	191	0.3
1977	130,076	100.0	45,639	35.1	**82,200**	**63.2**	773	0.6	1,464	1.1
1992	161,216	100.0	74,549	46.2	**83,249**	**51.6**	554	0.3	2,864	1.8
Nagybánya - Baia Mare										
1880	11,183	100.0	4,549	40.7	**6,266**	**56.0**	225	2.0	143	1.3
1910	16,465	100.0	5,546	33.7	**10,669**	**64.8**	191	1.2	59	0.3
1930	16,630	100.0	8,456	50.8	**6,515**	**39.2**	294	1.8	1,365	8.2
1941	25,841	100.0	6,415	24.8	**18,642**	**72.1**	127	0.5	657	2.6
1948	20,959	100.0	9,081	43.3	**11,257**	**53.7**	10	0.0	611	3.0
1956	35,920	100.0	18,768	52.2	**16,747**	**46.6**	96	0.3	309	0.9
1966	62,658	100.0	40,959	65.4	**21,265**	**33.9**	197	0.3	237	0.4
1977	100,985	100.0	73,877	73.2	**25,591**	**25.3**	440	0.4	1,077	1.1
1992	148,363	100.0	118,882	80.1	**25,940**	**17.5**	1,008	0.7	2,533	1.7
Szatmárnémeti - Satu Mare										
1880	19,708	100.0	982	5.0	**17,511**	**88.8**	758	3.8	457	2.4
1910	34,892	100.0	986	2.8	**33,094**	**94.8**	629	1.8	183	0.6
1930	51,495	100.0	13,941	27.1	**30,308**	**58.8**	669	1.3	6,577	12.8
1941	52,006	100.0	2,387	4.6	**47,914**	**92.1**	264	0.5	1,441	2.8
1948	46,519	100.0	13,571	29.2	**30,535**	**65.6**	83	0.2	2,330	5.0
1956	52,096	100.0	15,809	30.3	**35,192**	**67.5**	149	0.3	946	1.9
1966	68,246	100.0	29,345	43.0	**38,330**	**56.2**	284	0.4	287	0.4
1977	103,544	100.0	52,855	51.0	**48,861**	**47.2**	993	1.0	835	0.8
1992	130,584	100.0	71,502	54.8	**53,917**	**41.3**	3,681	2.8	1,484	1.1
Zilah – Zalău										
1880	5,961	100.0	358	6.0	**5,535**	**92.8**	–	–	68	1.2
1910	8,062	100.0	529	6.6	**7,477**	**92.7**	–	–	56	0.7
1930	8,340	100.0	2,058	24.7	**5,931**	**71.1**	–	–	351	4.2
1941	8,546	100.0	720	8.4	**7,749**	**90.7**	–	–	77	0.9
1948	11,652	100.0	4,982	42.7	**6,566**	**56.3**	–	–	104	1.0
1956	13,378	100.0	6,442	48.1	**6,875**	**51.4**	–	–	61	0.5
1966	14,380	100.0	7,580	52.7	**6,766**	**47.1**	13	0.1	21	0.1
1977	31,923	100.0	22,076	69.1	**9,665**	**30.3**	48	0.1	134	0.5
1992	67,977	100.0	53,547	78.8	**13,638**	**20.1**	92	0.1	700	1.0
Csíkszereda – Miercurea Ciuc										
1880	4,390	100.0	14	0.3	**4,297**	**97.9**	–	–	79	1.8
1910	6,831	100.0	44	0.6	**6,678**	**97.8**	–	–	109	1.6
1930	8,306	100.0	656	7.9	**7,395**	**89.0**	–	–	255	3.1
1941	8,870	100.0	45	0.5	**8,723**	**98.3**	–	–	102	1.2
1948	6,143	100.0	748	12.2	**5,280**	**85.9**	–	–	115	1.9
1956	11,996	100.0	668	5.5	**11,247**	**93.7**	–	–	81	0.8
1966	8,459	100.0	781	9.2	**7,652**	**90.5**	17	0.2	9	0.1
1977	30,936	100.0	4,894	15.8	**25,822**	**83.5**	87	0.3	133	0.4
1992	45,769	100.0	7,488	16.4	**37,972**	**83.0**	73	0.2	236	0.5

Remark: All data were calculated for the present administrative territory of the cities and towns excluding their "village components" (except in 1948 and 1977).

Transylvania was particularly striking between 1930 and 1941 in Torda (-30%), Brassó (-24%), Arad, Déva, Petrozsény (-20%), Temesvár and Nagyenyed (-17%). Meanwhile, in the Hungarian section of Transylvania, due to both the enforced Rumanian-Hungarian migrations, and the declaration of a majority of Jews and Szatmár County Swabians as having a Hungarian mother tongue, ethnic proportions similar to those of the 1910 census had been re-established in urban settlements (80-90% Hungarians). After Rumanian civil servants had fled and settled in Transylvania following 1918, a drop in the number in Rumanian population was observed in Kolozsvár (-25,000), Nagyvárad (-16,000), Szatmárnémeti (-12,000), Marosvásárhely (-8,000) and Nagykároly (-4,000). Because of the pressure exerted on the "hostile" minorities, large numbers of Hungarians fled rural areas of Rumania such as Szatmár and Bihar Counties, and villages of the southern regions of the Maros and Küküllő valleys (e.g. Piski, Alvinc, Tövis, Marosújvár, Felvinc, Aranyosgyéres, Radnót and Bonyha).

During World War II there was no massive extermination or deportation of Jews in South Transylvania, in contrast to Transnistria, Bessarabia and Moldavia. In Northern Transylvania, however, the overwhelming number of 151,000 Jews, predominantly Hungarian native speakers, were deported in May and June 1944[39]. Thus the Hungarian population was greatly reduced in Nagyvárad (-20,000), Kolozsvár (-16,000), Szatmárnémeti (-12,000) and Marosvásárhely (-5,000).

Following Rumania's siding with the Allied Powers towards the conclusion of World War II (23 August 1944), Northern Transylvania became undefendable and large masses of Hungarians began to escape, especially those who had settled there after 1940 and had compromised themselves politically; Saxons from the Beszterce region and Swabians from Szatmár County were evacuated. During the war, shifts of power were accompanied by bloody acts of vengeance committed both by Hungarians and Rumanians; these only had a local effect on demographic-ethnic patterns of population.

After Northern Transylvania was recovered by Rumania no official measures were taken to expatriate Germans. However, in order to achieve the social and national aims of Rumanian land reform which was adopted in 1945, the majority of Germans who remained in the country and were deprived of their land and property (mainly those in the Banat), were taken to labour camps. At least 70,000 of them were deported to the Soviet Union to do forced labour[40]. These migrations caused the number of Saxons to drop by 37% and Swabians by 39%.

---

[39] "Remember 40 years since the massacre of the Jews from Northern Transylvania under Horthyst occupation", 1985, Published by Federation of Jewish Communities in the S.R. of Romania, Bucureşti, 71p.

[40] Baier, H. 1994 Deportarea etnicilor din România în Uniunea Sovietică 1945 (Deportation of ethnic groups of Rumania into the USSR in 1945), Sibiu. Number of Transylvanian Saxons was put by Wagner, E. (1983, Die Bevölkerungsentwicklung in Siebenbürgen — in: Schuster, O. (Ed.) Epoche der Entscheidungen. Die siebenbürger Sachsen im 20. Jahrhundert, Böhlau Verlag, Köln - Wien, 87.p.) at 48 ,000.

About one third of Jews in North Transylvania survived World War II, similar to those of Moldavia and Bessarabia[41]. Since then the number of Transylvanian Jews has decreased to 2,687 (1992 census data) due to emigration to the State of Israel established in 1948. One third of Slovaks left their homeland (Nagylak, Réz Mts.) to make a home in settlements in South Slovakia from where Hungarians were expelled.

As a result of the deportation of Hungarian Jews and the exodus in autumn 1944, Hungarian speakers in Northern Transylvania diminished by c 238,000 between 1941 and 1948[42]. A massive population shift (of Hungarians, Jews, Germans and Rumanians), meant that by the time of the 1948 census Rumanians had achieved an absolute ethnic majority in Transylvanian urban settlements (50.2%) while the proportion of Hungarians was reduced to 39 % and that of Germans to 7.2 %[43].

Following the communist take-over in the 1950's, during the „heroic age" of Rumanian socialist industrialisation, a concentration of population, an increase in industrial jobs and urban population were the primary goals. Between 1948 and 1956 the urban population of Transylvania increased by over one million. In addition to fulfilling the socio-political aims of early East European socialist urbanisation, the Rumanian ethno-political aim was to turn cities and towns with a Hungarian character into ones with a Rumanian ethnic majority. The ethnic structure of urban settlements (with 49.9 % non-Rumanian native speakers), would undoubtedly have changed even without political interference, because the source of their population growth (the inhabitants of Transylvanian villages), had been two-thirds Rumanian for more than two centuries. Time would have determined where, when and to what extent the Rumanian majority in urban centres would prevail. It is a fact, that of the 2,1 million population that lived in present-day towns, the 1956 census found 58.1 % Rumanians, 30.3 % Hungarians and 7.4% Germans[44]. By this time on the present-day territory of Kolozsvár, the Hungarian cultural centre of the region, the number of the Rumanian population equalled that of Hungarians (47.9 %), while Nagybánya lost its Hungarian majority and became Rumanian (55.9%). It should be noted that in the period between the censuses of 1948 and 1956 there was an increase in the number and proportion of Germans in urban populations, since those who had returned from labour camps found themselves excluded from the land reform and deprived of their property. They had to look for jobs

---

[41] In 1947 33,476 Jews were recorded in urban settlements of North Transylvania and 11,230 persons in the rural ones (38.4 and 17.5% of the 1941 population) - (Remember ...1985, ibid.).

[42] According to census data the most dramatic drop in the number of persons who declared Hungarian to be their mother tongue was recorded in Nagyvárad (-33,000), Kolozsvár (-30,000) and Szatmárnémeti (-17,000) between 1941-1948.

[43] Source of the 1948 census data: Golopenţia, A. - Georgescu, D.C. Populaţia Republicii Populare Române la 25 ianuarie 1948, Extras din "Probleme economice", Nr. 2. Martie 1948, Bucureşti, pp.37-41.

[44] Az erdélyi települések népessége nemzetiség szerint (The Population of the Transylvanian Settlements according to the ethnicity, 1930-1992), 1996, Központi Statisztikai Hivatal, Budapest, 421p.

in cities, towns and industrial centres. As a result, half of the Transylvanian Germans became urban dwellers[45].

According to 1956 census data, 6,218,427 people lived on the present-day territory of Transylvanian counties. Of these 65 % (4,04 million) declared themselves to be Rumanian; 25.1 % (1,56 million) Hungarian; 5.9 % (368,000) German, and 1.3 % (78,000) Gypsies. Because of the massive migrations and losses during the war, the rural ethnic territory of Germans (whose numbers had diminished by 200,000 since 1941) vanished completely. An ethnic vacuum in this fertile region of the Banat and in the agriculturally less important area of the Saxon villages which were emerging in 1944-45, had been almost completely filled by Rumanians by 1956. There had been a massive settlement of Rumanians in the Barcaság Land, while 95 % of Saxons left the Beszterce region in 1944. Thus, no settlements with an absolute majority of Germans existed in these areas. In this area, in the environs of Szászrégen and Bátos, Hungarians moved into vacant villages. People of Swabian origin who had undergone Magyarization already in the 19th century and lived in the Szatmár region, overwhelmingly declared themselves to be Hungarian both regarding their nationality and native tongue, in contrast to the period between 1920 and 1940. At the same time, the Rumanian population returned to small colonies founded between 1920 and 1940 along the borderline, in the Szatmár - Bihar ethnic Hungarian territory, and new villages were also established.

In spite of a 7.8 % average natural increase in population, the inhabitants of the Transylvanian counties only grew by about 1.5 million, i.e. 24.2% in the period between the 1956 and 1992 censuses[46]. Owing to the high discrepancies among different ethnic groups regarding their birthrate and demographic trends, due to changes in ethnic identity (assimilation - dissimilation), the number of Gypsies increased by 159 %, the Ukrainians-Ruthenians by 59.7 %, the Rumanians by 40.7 % and Hungarians by 2.9 %, while there was a 93.9 % decrease in the number of Jews, 70.4 % in Germans, and a 16-23 % decrease in Slovaks, Bulgarians, Serbs and Croats-Crashovans during the 36 years studied. An average annual natural increase according to ethnic groups can only be estimated for this period (Rumanians: 8.6 ‰, Hungarians: 6.6 ‰, Germans: 3.3 ‰)[47]. Based on these figures, the number of Rumanians should have been 5,3 million (instead of the recorded 5,684,000), the Hungarians 1,928 million (as oppposed to 1,6 million) and Germans 412,000 (instead of 109,000) in 1956. Large changes in proportions were due to emigration from and immigration into Transylvania which affected more than one million people, causing a negative balance for ethnic minorities

---

[45] Proportion of urban dwellers within the main ethnic groups in 1956: Rumanians 30.4 %, Hungarians 41.1 %, Germans 42.4 % (24.2 % in 1948).

[46] Hungary's population increased by 5.2% and the population of Rumania Proper grew by 11.2% between 1956-1992. In this period a mean annual natural increase was 2,3 ‰ in Hungary and 11,2 ‰ in Rumania Proper.

[47] Our estimations, checked by migration components were based on differences between rates of natural increase by the main ethnic groups in the period 1931-1939 and the recorded Transylvanian average (7,8 ‰).

and a positive one for Rumanians. According to the statistics concerning place of birth and demographic trends, reliable estimates put the number of Rumanians who resettled from the regions over the Carpathians at about 800,000, while a quarter of a million people went to Wallachia and Moldavia between 1945 and 1992[48]. Of the latter, the number of Hungarians may have reached 60,000. An overwhelming number of immigrants from Moldavia and Wallachia were directed to South Transylvania, into the counties of the Brassó-Arad-Resicabánya triangle of heavy industry, where an increased demand for workers could not be satisfied. This was due to a traditionally low birthrate (which subsequently became a decline) and later, to a rise in the emigration of Germans. Later on, large numbers coming from Moldavia and Wallachia were used to accelerate the Rumanianization of certain municipalities in Northern Transylvania (Kolozsvár, Nagyvárad).

Aside from the massive influx of Rumanians, the rapid process of decline in the number of ethnic minorities in Transylvania was the result of their increased emigration. While there was an annual emigration between 1956 and 1975 of 2,000-3,000 Germans and a maximum 1,000 Hungarians within the framework of family unification, 389,000 people (215,000 Germans, 64,000 Hungarians, 6,000 Jews and 5,000 others) left Transylvania between 1975 and the 1992 census[49]. The annual number of German emigrants - according to the agreement concluded in 1978 between German chancellor H. Schmidt and Rumanian president N. Ceauşescu, was fixed at between 10 and 14,000 annually[50]. In the same period the number of Hungarians leaving the region rose from 1,058 in 1979 to 4,144 in 1986 and 11,728 in 1989, in parallel with the gradual deterioration of the economic and political situation. As a result of the exodus which started with the collapse of the Ceauşescu regime, 60,072 Germans, 23,888 Rumanians and 11,040 Hungarians abandoned Rumania in 1990 alone. Out of the 96,929 persons that had left the country, 83,512 (86.2 %) were from Transylvania. The influencing factors were the higher living standards abroad and a hope for a better future for their children, together with a shattered confidence in Rumania and an open burst of nationalism[51]. This wave of emigration has recently diminished and stabilised at a national rate of 20,000 annually[52].

---

[48] Varga E. Á. 1996 Limbă maternă, nationalitate, confesiune. Date statistice privind Transilvania în perioada 1880 - 1992 — in: Fizionomia etnică şi confesională fluctuantă a regiunii Carpato-Balcanice şi a Transilvaniei, Asociaţia Culturală Haáz Rezső, Odorheiu Secuiesc, 111.p.

[49] 503,553 persons emigrated from Romania between 1975-1992 (of them 235,744 were Germans, 171,770 Rumanians, 64,887 Hungarians, 21,006 Jews and 10,146 people of other ethnicities) (Anuarul Statistic al României 1993, 143.p.).

[50] Anuarul...1993, ibid. 143.p., Schreiber, W. 1993 Demographische Entwicklungen bei den Rumäniendeutschen — Südosteuropa Mitteilungen 33.Jg. Nr.3. 205.p.

[51] Schreiber, W. 1993 ibid. 209.p.

[52] Number of emigrants from Rumania. Germans: 1991: 15.567, 1992: 8.852, 1995: 2.906, Hungarians 1991: 7.494, 1992: 3.523, 1995: 3.608. (Anuarul Statistic al României 1996, 133.p.). Ratio of Transylvanians within Rumanian emigrants dropped between 1992-1994 from 76% to 64.4%.

Massive migrations in different directions which took place over the past four decades, especially the internal shifts caused by socialist urbanisation, that is, from rural to urban settlements, resulted in a population growth in Transylvanian cities and towns from 2,1 to 4,4 million, while the population of villages dropped from 4,1 to 3,3 million between 1956 and 1992. In rural areas, due to the exodus of Germans, all of the three present-day dominant ethnic groups (Rumanians, Hungarians and Gypsies) were able to increase their proportion[53]. However, in the centres of the settlement system and governmental power, focuses of Rumanianization, the number and proportion of Rumanians rose considerably (1956: 1,2 million, i.e. 58.1%; 1992: 3,3 million, 75.6% in urban settlements). During this period eight towns with a majority Hungarian population and one with a German majority (Zsombolya in 1990), turned into settlements with Rumanian majority. As a result of the accelerated population growth, dictated by party resolutions and implemented through the resettlement of people from Rumanian villages in Transylvania and Moldavia, Wallachia, the following formerly Hungarian towns turned into ones with a Rumanian population majority (over 50 %): Kolozsvár in 1957, Zilah in 1959, Balánbánya and Szászrégen in 1969, Nagyvárad in 1971, Bánffyhunyad in 1972, Szatmárnémeti in 1973 and Élesd in 1978. Relatively rapid and profound social changes took place in urban settlements of Transylvania. Groups of different social structure and behaviour, ethnic and religious affiliation were mixed together and later, a total ruralization of towns increased the danger of emerging ethnic conflicts in the largest of them. Similar transformations took place at the expense of ethnic minorities in the rapidly growing suburbs of big cities (e.g. Arad, Temesvár, Kolozsvár, Marosvásárhely and Brassó). But the local society of the rural areas beeing in unfavourable traffic situation could protect or even strengthen its original ethnic character due to the increasing emigration, aging and natural decrease of the population. Such Hungarian villages exist in most parts of the Székely Region, Küküllő Hills, Mezőség region, Szilágy and in more remote parts along the Hungarian-Rumanian border. At the same time, independent of natural and other demographic factors, a dissimilation of Swabians in Szatmár (previously almost completely Magyarized) and of many Hungarian speaking Gypsies, several settlements lost their former statistical majority. An ethnic group with the highest birthrate in Transylvania, the Gypsies (Romas) have been able to substantially increase their local proportion in their traditional ethnic territory: in Bihar, Szatmár, Szilágy, Kolozs, Maros, Szeben and Brassó counties and in villages of the Olt-Maros Interfluve abandoned by the Saxons. This resulted from a high natural increase, a strengthened awareness, and a gradual dissimilation from Rumanians and Hungarians. In certain regions of South Transylvania, however, a reverse ethnic process took place among the population of Gypsy native speakers: their massive return to the Rumanians[54].

---

[53] In the Transylvanian villages the proportion of Rumanians increased from 68.5 to 70.8%, that of Hungarians grew from 20.3 to 21.4%, and of Gypsies from 1.6 to 4%, while the proportion of Germans shrunk from 7.4 to 1.6% between 1956-1992.

[54] Some examples of re-Rumanization of Gypsies in the communes of Berény-Beriu, Tordos-Tordaş, Resinár-Răşinari, Nagycsűr-Şura Mare, Veresmart-Roşia, Bodola-Budila, Bölön-Belin etc.

For the five years since the 1992 census, the population number of Transylvania declined to 7,6 million by 1 January, 1997 mainly due to natural decrease[55]. Based on demographic trends and ethnic data of the 1992 census, 74.5 % of the population of Transylvania were officially Rumanians (5,670,000), 20.2 % of them Hungarians (1,540,000), and 2.7 % Gypsies (208,000). Our calculations based on the more likely number of Gypsies for 1992 (1,150,000), the ethnic composition of Transylvania at the beginning of 1997 was presumably as follows: 4,8 million Rumanians (63 %), 1,470,000 Hungarians (19.3 %), 1,150,000 Gypsies (15.1 %), 73,000 Germans (0.9 %) and 120,000 others (1.7 %).

THE PRESENT TERRITORY OF HUNGARIAN SETTLEMENT IN TRANSYLVANIA

According to the census carried out on 7 January 1992, the population of the Rumanian Banat, Kőrös-vidék - Crişana, Máramaros and the historical territory of Transylvania was found to be 7,759,466 (310,000 less than in the middle of 1989). Of these 5,7 million (73.6 %) declared themselves to be Rumanian, 1,6 million (20.7 %) Hungarian, 204,000 (2.6 %) Gypsy (Roma), and 109,000 (1.4 %) German. There were 50,000 Ukrainians, 28,000 Serbs, 19,000 Slovaks, 8,000 Bulgarians, 7,000 Croats, and 5,000 Czechs[56]. As a consequence of the above outlined migrations and demographic processes which took place during the 20th century, the ethnic picture of Transylvania has become simpler and less diverse at the expense of the national minorities and in favour of the Rumanians, and with the ethnic expansion of Gypsies, more colourful.

In 1992 ethnic Hungarians numbered 1,604,000 while 1,620,000 regard Hungarian as their mother tongue. They formed a population majority in Hargita and Kovászna counties and in four municipalities (Marosvásárhely, Csíkszereda, Székelyudvarhely, Sepsiszentgyörgy), as well as in 14 other Transylvanian towns (9 in the Székely Region) and in 795 villages *(Tabs. 23., 24., Figs. 30., 31.)*. 56 % were urban dwellers, while those living in settlements with a population of over 100,000 represented 20.4 %. Their proportion in middle-sized towns with 20,000 -100,000 inhabitants (20.6

---

[55] Our estimations as to January 1, 1997 are based on the results of the 1992 census, on the demographic data in the Statistical Yearbook of Rumania (1996), and a publication by V. Gheţău (Costul în oameni al tranziţiei — Adevărul, 7 februarie 1996, 3.p.). Since 1992, in Rumania in general and in Transylvania in particular the number of deaths has exceeded the number of births and the natural decrease reached -1,15 ‰ in Transylvania and -0,59 ‰ in the rest of Rumania.

[56] Census data were calculated by the author: Rumanians with Aromunians and Macedorumanians, Hungarians with Székelys and Csángós, Germans with Saxons and Swabians, Ukrainians with Ruthenians, Croats with Crashovans. On the territory of the Transylvanian counties the distribution of population according to mother tongue was as follows: 5,815,425 (75.3 %) Rumanians, 1,619,735 (21 %) Hungarians, 91,386 (1,2 %) Germans, 84,718 (1,1 %) Gypsies (Romas), 47,873 (0,6 %) Ukrainians, 31,684 Serbo-Croatians (0,4 %), 18,195 Slovaks, 7,302 Bulgarians, 3,934 Czechs.

Table 23. Change in the ethnic structure of population of selected counties of Transylvania (1910 – 1992)

Year	Total population		Rumanians		**Hungarians**		Germans		Others	
	number	%	number	%	**number**	%	number	%	number	%
SZATMÁR - SATU MARE county (megye - judeţ)										
1910	267,310	100.0	92,412	34.6	**167,980**	**62.8**	6,690	2.5	228	0.1
1956	337,351	100.0	173,122	51.3	**158,357**	**46.9**	3,355	1.0	2,517	0.8
1977	393,840	100.0	227,630	57.8	**152,738**	**38.8**	6,395	1.6	7,077	1.8
1992	400,789	100.0	234,541	58.5	**140,394**	**35.0**	14,351	3.6	11,503	2.9
MÁRAMAROS – MARAMUREŞ county (megye - judeţ)										
1910	299,764	100.0	189,643	64.6	**61,217**	**20.9**	28,215	9.6	20,689	4.9
1956	367,114	100.0	284,900	77.6	**51,944**	**14.1**	2,749	0.7	27,521	7.6
1977	492,860	100.0	394,350	80.0	**58,568**	**11.9**	3,495	0.7	36,447	7.4
1992	540,099	100.0	437,997	81.1	**54,906**	**10.2**	3,416	0.6	43,780	8.1
SZILÁGY - SĂLAJ county (megye - judeţ)										
1910	223,096	100.0	136,874	61.3	**67,348**	**30.2**	..	..	18.874	8.5
1956	271,989	100.0	200,391	73.7	**67,474**	**24.8**	..	..	4,124	1.5
1977	264,569	100.0	194,420	73.5	**64,017**	**24.2**	..	..	6,132	2.3
1992	266,797	100.0	192,552	72.2	**63,159**	**23.7**	146	0.1	10,940	4.1
BIHAR - BIHOR county (megye - judeţ)										
1910	475,847	100.0	242,299	51.0	**218,372**	**45.9**	3,407	0.7	11,769	2.4
1956	574,488	100.0	359,043	62.5	**204,657**	**35.6**	858	0.1	9,930	1.8
1977	633,094	100.0	409,770	64.7	**199,615**	**31.5**	1,417	0.2	22,292	3.6
1992	638,863	100.0	425,097	66.5	**181,706**	**28.4**	1,593	0.2	30,467	4.8
ARAD - ARAD county (megye - judeţ)										
1910	509,968	100.0	295,510	57.9	**130,892**	**25.7**	59,257	11.6	24,309	4.8
1956	488,612	100.0	339,772	71.4	**89,229**	**18.8**	42,711	9.0	16,900	0.8
1977	512,020	100.0	375,486	73.3	**74,098**	**14.5**	39,702	7.8	22,734	4.4
1992	487,617	100.0	392,600	80.5	**61,022**	**12.5**	9,392	1.9	24,603	5.1
TEMES - TIMIŞ county (megye - judeţ)										
1910	526,875	100.0	213,888	40.6	**91,390**	**17.3**	175,128	33.2	46,469	8.9
1956	568,881	100.0	327,295	57.5	**84,551**	**14.9**	116,674	20.5	40,361	7.1
1977	696,884	100.0	472,912	67.9	**77,525**	**11.1**	98,296	14.1	48,151	6.9
1992	700,033	100.0	561,200	80.2	**62,888**	**9.0**	26,722	3.8	49,223	7.0
KOLOZS - CLUJ county (megye - judeţ)										
1910	391,303	100.0	229,487	58.6	**151,723**	**38.8**	3,965	1.0	6,128	1.6
1956	580,344	100.0	407,401	70.2	**165,978**	**28.6**	1,435	0.2	5,530	1.0
1977	715,409	100.0	532,543	74.4	**171,431**	**24.0**	1,818	0.3	9,617	1.3
1992	736,301	100.0	571,275	77.6	**146,210**	**19.9**	1,407	0.2	17,409	2.4
MAROS - MUREŞ county (megye - judeţ)										
1910	365,076	100.0	144,317	39.5	**183,453**	**50.2**	27,177	7.4	10,129	2.9
1956	513,261	100.0	255,641	49.5	**234,698**	**45.4**	20,341	3.9	2,581	1.2
1977	605,380	100.0	297,205	49.1	**268,251**	**44.3**	18,807	3.1	21,117	3.5
1992	610,053	100.0	317,541	52.1	**252,685**	**41.4**	4,588	0.8	35,239	5.8
HARGITA - HARGHITA county (megye - judeţ)										
1910	241,184	100.0	15,061	6.2	**223,215**	**92.5**	1,969	0.8	939	0.5
1956	273,694	100.0	22,916	8.3	**248,310**	**90.4**	246	0.1	2,222	1.2
1977	326,310	100.0	44,794	13.7	**277,587**	**85.1**	281	0.1	3,648	1.1
1992	348,335	100.0	48,948	14.1	**295,243**	**84.8**	199	0.1	3,945	1.1

KOVÁSZNA - COVASNA county (megye - judeţ)									
1910	148,933	100.0	17,035	11.4	**130,300**	**87.5**	626	0.4	972	0.7
1956	172,509	100.0	30,330	17.7	**140,091**	**81.6**	472	0.3	1,616	0.4
1977	199,017	100.0	38,948	19.6	**156,120**	**78.4**	276	0.1	3,673	1.9
1992	233,256	100.0	54,586	23.4	**175,464**	**75.2**	252	0.1	2,954	1.3

BRASSÓ – BRAŞOV county (megye - judeţ)									
1910	241,160	100.0	132,094	54.8	**54,597**	**22.6**	48,362	20.0	6,107	2.6
1956	373,941	100.0	272,983	72.8	**59,885**	**16.0**	40,129	10.7	944	0.5
1977	582,863	100.0	457,570	78.5	**72,956**	**12.5**	38,623	6.6	13,714	2.4
1992	643,261	100.0	553,101	86.0	**63,612**	**9.9**	10,059	1.6	16,489	2.6

Sources: 1910: Hungarian census data (mother/native tongue), 1956: Rumanian census data (mother /native tongue), 1977, 1992: Rumanian census data (ethnicity).
Remarks: Census data of 1910 and 1956 for the present territories of the counties were calculated by K.Kocsis. Rumanians with Aromunians and Macedorumanians; Hungarians with Székelys and Csángós; Germans with Saxons and Swabians.

%) was similar to that of Rumanians, while Hungarians had above average representation in middle-sized and large villages with 1,000-5,000 people. 44 % of Hungarians lived in rural areas, mainly the Székely Region, Bihar and Szilágy; 56.9 % of Transylvanian Hungarians lived in settlements where they formed an absolute majority, 28 % of Hungarians were resident in settlements where their proportion was above 90 %, while 9.2 % of them are scattered and doomed to vanish and be assimilated (where their proportion is below 10 %). The most populous Hungarian communities - excluding Marosvásárhely - are to be found in towns (Kolozsvár, Nagyvárad, Szatmárnémeti), where the ratio of Hungarians has been reduced to a 23-41 % minority over the past 30-40 years *(Tab. 25., Fig. 32.)*. 45.2 % of Hungarians lived in the Székely Region, 31.2 % in the Kőrös-vidék – Crişana region, 4.4 % in the Banat and 19.2 % in other counties of historic Transylvania. They have been able to maintain a relative homogeneity in only the ethnic territories of the Székely Region and North Bihar. In Szatmár and Szilágy counties Hungarians live mixed with Rumanians, Germans, Gypsies, and in other regions they form ethnic pockets of various sizes, or are scattered.

Table 24. The largest Hungarian communities in Transylvania (1956, 1986 and 1992;
thousand persons)

1956		1986		1992
Kolozsvár / Cluj-Napoca	77,8	Kolozsvár / Cluj-Napoca	*120,9*	74,9
Nagyvárad / Oradea	62,8	Nagyvárad / Oradea	*111,3*	74,2
Marosvásárhely / Târgu Mureş	50,2	Marosvásárhely / Târgu Mureş	*96,5*	83,2
Arad / Arad	37,6	Szatmárnémeti /Satu Mare	*69,3*	53,9
Temesvár / Timişoara	36,5	Temesvár / Timişoara	*65,2*	31,8
Szatmárnémeti /Satu Mare	25,2	Brassó / Braşov	*58,7*	31,6
Brassó / Braşov	24,2	Arad / Arad	*54,0*	29,8
Nagybánya / Baia Mare	16,7	Sepsiszentgyörgy/Sfântu Gheorghe	*51,4*	50,0
Sepsiszentgyörgy/Sfântu Gheorghe	15,3	Nagybánya / Baia Mare	*43,7*	25,9
Székelyudvarhely / Odorheiu Sec.	13,6	Székelyudvarhely / Odorheiu Sec.	*35,6*	39,0
Nagyszalonta / Salonta	13,0	Csíkszereda / Miercurea Ciuc	*35,4*	38,0
Nagykároly / Carei	11,9	Kézdivásárhely/ Târgu Secuiesc	*21,0*	19,4
Csíkszereda / Miercurea Ciuc	11,2	Zilah / Zalău	*20,3*	13,6
Gyergyószentmiklós /Gheorgheni	11,1	Gyergyószentmiklós /Gheorgheni	*19,3*	18,9
Szászrégen / Reghin	10,0	Nagykároly / Carei	*19,2*	13,8

Sources: 1956: Rumanian census data (mother/native tongue), *1986: estimation* of Kocsis, K. (Hungarian native speaker, see Kocsis, K. 1990), 1992: Rumanian census data (ethnicity).

Table 25. Towns in Transylvania with absolute Hungarian majority (1992)

Settlements	*Percentage of the Hungarians*
1. Szentegyházas / Vlăhiţa	99.1
2. Székelyudvarhely / Odorheiu Secuiesc	97.6
3. Székelykeresztúr / Cristuru Secuiesc	95.5
4. Barót / Baraolt	94.5
5. Tusnádfürdõ / Băile Tuşnad	93.0
6. Kézdivásárhely / Târgu Secuiesc	91.2
7. Szováta / Sovata	88.9
8. Gyergyószentmiklós / Gheorgheni	88.7
9. Érmihályfalva / Valea lui Mihai	85.0
10. Csíkszereda / Miercurea Ciuc	83.0
11. Borszék / Borsec	79.8
12. Sepsiszentgyörgy / Sfântu Gheorghe	74.4
13. Kovászna / Covasna	66.4
14. Szilágycseh / Cehu Silvaniei	61.3
15. Nagyszalonta / Salonta	61.1
16. Nagykároly / Carei	53.4
17. Marosvásárhely / Târgu Mureş	51.6

Source: Final data of the Rumanian census of 1992 (ethnicity).

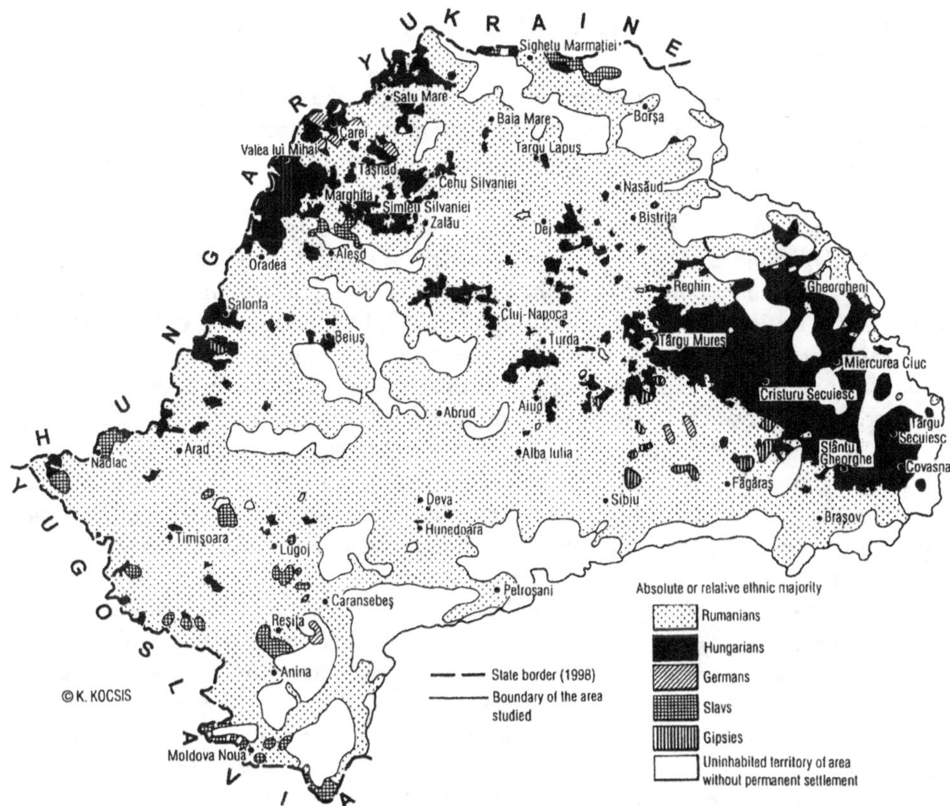

Figure 30. Ethnic map of Transylvania (1992)
Source: Census 1992

THE HUNGARIAN ETHNIC TERRITORY OF THE SZÉKELY REGION[57]

More than one third of Hungarians in Transylvania live in the Székely Region. The survival of this almost compact Hungarian ethnic block is due partly to its autonomous status between the 13th century and 1876, and to the mountainous surroundings which offered protection to its inhabitants during the great catastrophies and invasions of the 17th century.

84,000 Hungarians live in Marosvásárhely, the ever expanding capital of Maros county. The Rumanian population in the city and its suburban communities is growing rapidly due to settlers mainly from Mezőség region and the region of the Küküllő rivers. As a result, their percentage is over 46 in the county seat. Despite the changes in the ethnic structure in urban areas, the borders of the Hungarian rural ethnic territory next to the Maros and Nyárád rivers extend along the Balavásár–Lukafalva–Mezőbánd–Szabéd–Mezőcsávás–Beresztelke–Magyarpéterlaka–Nyárádremete lines. The most important centres of this Székely area – apart from Marosvásárhely – are Szováta, Erdőszentgyörgy, Nyárádszereda and Szászrégen, the town with a current Hungarian population of one-third. Although the Hungarian majority populated villages located to the north of Szászrégen in the Maros Valley and among the Rumanians of the Görgény district, they do not belong strictly to the Székely region, but they can be considered part of the compact ethnic Hungarian population of this area both ethnically and geographically (Marosfelfalu, Marosvécs, Holtmaros, Magyaró, Görgényüvegcsûr, Alsóbölkény, etc.). Travelling along the upper Maros – passing through a few villages with Hungarian minority populations (Palotailva, Gödemesterháza, etc.) – one reaches the Gyergyó Basin at Maroshévíz whose population is one-third Hungarian. In the Gyergyó region, the century-old Gyergyóremete-Ditró-Hágótőalja line continues to be the Hungarian-Rumanian ethnic border. The most important Hungarian settlements north of this border include the resort of Borszék with an 80 % Hungarian majority population, and Galócás, Salamás, Gyergyótölgyes and Gyergyóholló, all with Hungarian minority communities. The economic centre of the basin is Gyergyó-szentmiklós with a population of 18,888 Hungarians and 2,169 Rumanians.

---

[57] Székely Region (Hungarian: Székelyföld; German: Szekerland; Rumanian: Pamîntul Secuilor; Latin: Terra Siculorum). An area populated – since the 12th century – almost exclusively by Székely-Hungarians in the centre of present-day Rumania, bordered by the Eastern Carpathians. The clan division of this privilegized borderland was followed – in the 14-15th century – by the establishment of special territorial administrative units (Hungarian: "szék"), namely Marosszék, Csíkszék, Kászonszék, Udvarhelyszék, Sepsiszék, Kézdiszék and Orbaiszék. Due to the devastation of war, the mass immigration of the Rumanians and the shattering of the Hungarian ethnic territory in the Northwest and Central Transylvania during the 16th and 17th centuries, the direct ethnic-territorial connection between the Hungarian ethnic block of the Great Hungarian Plain and the Székely Region ceased. Since then the Székely ethnic block has become completely encircled by Rumanians. The special status of this region came to an end after the administrative reorganization of Hungary in 1876. The entire Székely ethnic block was formally united within the framework of an autonomous province of Rumania ("Hungarian Autonomous Province") only for a short period, between 1952 and 1960.

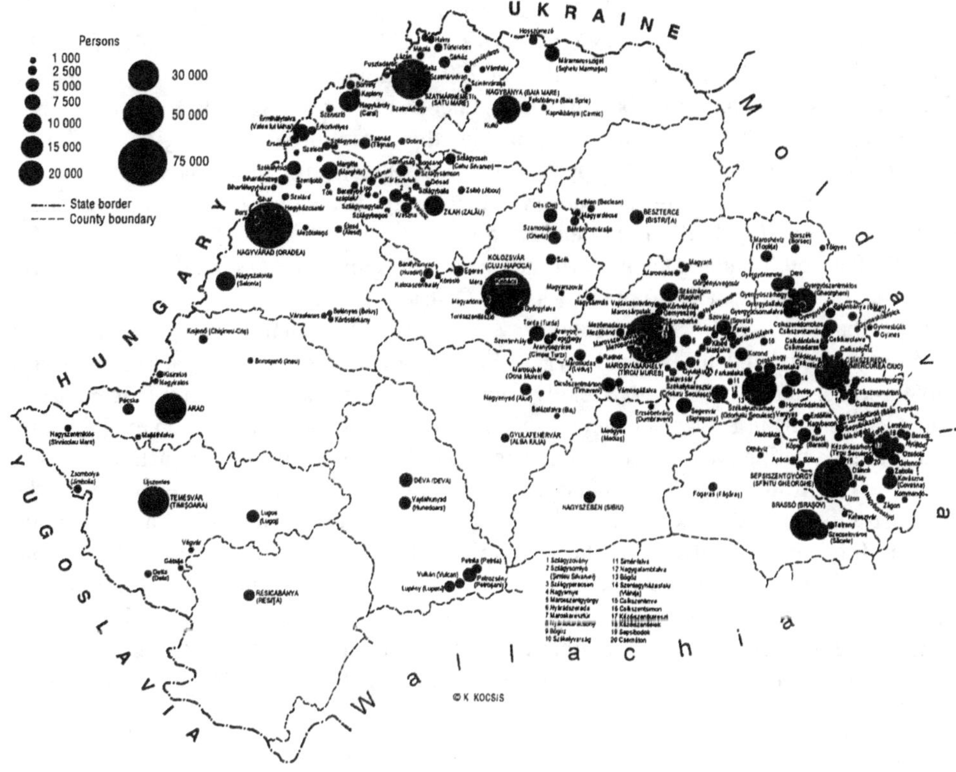

Figure 32. Hungarian communities in Transylvania (1992)
Source: Census 1992

The route into the neighbouring Székely Basin of Csík leads through two Rumanian majority populated villages (Vasláb, Marosfő). Csíkszereda, the seat of the former Csík cunty and the present Hargita county, lies at the intersection of the road from Segesvár to Moldavia and the road along the River Olt. In 1948 the total population of Csíkszereda was only 6,000, whereas today there are already 45,769 inhabitants. Today, over 16% of the city or 7,488 people are Rumanian due to its central location and the immigration of Rumanians from Moldavia. Among the other larger settlements in Csík, it is worth mentioning two other towns, copper-producing Balánbánya with a 30% Hungarian, 70% Rumanian population, and the spa town of Tusnádfürdő with its two thousand Hungarian inhabitants (the smallest Transylvanian town). A few other villages are also important (Csíkszentdomokos, Csíkszépvíz, Mádéfalva, Csíkszentkirály, Csíkszenttamás etc.). Kászonaltíz is the most important settlement in the former Kászonszék district located in the basin between Csíkszék and Háromszék.

131

The former county of Udvarhely, was disbanded as a unit approximately four decades ago, and is now in the southwestern part of Hargita county. Székelyudvarhely, near to the size of Csíkszereda with 39,959 inhabitants and with 97.6 % ethnic Hungarians, is the capital of this most homogeneous part of the Székely Region. Outside of Székelyudvarhely, most of the jobs in this less urbanised region which is characterised by small settlements are provided by the agro-industry in Székelykeresztúr, the iron-ore industry, metallurgy in Szentegyházas, the ceramic industry of Korond and salt mining and refining in Parajd.

The southernmost territory of the Székely Region is Kovászna county, formerly known as the region of Háromszék ('Three Districts') composed of the subregions of Sepsi, Orbai and Kézdi. Sepsiszentgyörgy, with 67,220, inhabitants is the capital of Kovászna county and the second largest Székely town. Today, Hungarians comprise only three-quarters of this south Székely county seat. There is a significant percentage of ethnic Rumanians in Kovászna, Bereck, Kézdimartonos, Zabola and Zágon explained by their presence dating back to the middle ages up to the period of modern history.

The following Hungarian villages in the Olt valley were never under the administration of any Székely district and do not currently belong to Kovászna county, yet they form an integral part of the Hungarian ethnic territory of the Székely Region: Apáca, Örményes, Alsórákos (with its basalt and limestone quarries) and Olthévíz (famous for its construction material industry). Based on the above, the Hungarian-Rumanian ethnic border in the southern Székely Region extends along the Újszékely-Székelyderzs-Homoródjánosfalva-Olthévíz-Apáca-Árapatak-Kökös-Zágon-Kommandó line.

HUNGARIAN ETHNIC ENCLAVES IN HISTORICAL TRANSYLVANIA

The regions with the most ancient Hungarian settlements in Transylvania are the Mezőség region and the area surrounding the Szamos rivers. The devastation of previous centuries hit these territories especially hard. Today, Hungarians inhabit only a few ethnic enclaves and numerous scattered communities. The most ethnic Hungarian settlements in the valley of the Big Szamos are Magyarnemegye, Várkudu, Bethlen, Felőr, Magyardécse, Árpástó, and Retteg, and those near the lower part of the Little Szamos include Dés, Désakna, Szamosújvár, Kérő, Bonchida, Válaszút and Kendilóna. In the Mezőség Region, located between the Maros and Szamos Rivers, Hungarian settlements include Mezőbodon, Mezőkeszü, Vajdakamarás, Visa, Szék, Zselyk, Vice, Ördöngösfüzes, Bálványosváralja, Szentmáté and Cegőtelke.

The largest Hungarian community of Transylvania with 75-120 thousand people live in Kolozsvár with a total population of 328,602, where the Little Szamos, Nádas creek and numerous national and international roads meet. The villages of the region of Kalotaszeg (Körösfő, Kalotaszentkirály, Magyarvalkó, Jákótelke, Bogártelke, Magyarvista, Méra etc.), one of the most important as regards Hungarian folk culture, are located west of Kolozsvár City – considered to be the cultural capital of Hungarians of Transylvania – and near the upper part of the Nádas creek and the Sebes Körös. The ethnic Hungarian profile of the Kalotaszeg region's centre, Bánffyhunyad, has changed significantly due to the settlement of Rumanian highlanders from a broader periphery.

Some Hungarian villages in the Erdőfelek Hills (Györgyfalva, Tordaszent-lászló, Magyarléta, Magyarfenes, Szászlóna) provide a link between the Hungarians of the Kalotaszeg and Torda regions. In the former Székely district of Aranyosszék[58] and its surroundings, the percentage of Hungarians declined primarily in Székelykocsárd, Hadrév, Felvinc, Aranyosegerbegy and Szentmihály as a result of the increased settlement of Rumanians and the urbanisation of the Torda region and Maros valley. The highland villages, on the other hand, were able to preserve their Hungarian majorities (Torockó, Torockószentgyörgy, Kövend, Bágyon, Kercsed, etc.).

Some of the most important factors in migration were the roads, railways and employment as well as commuting opportunities which reshaped or left untouched the ethnic composition of the Maros and Küküllő regions. Rumanians became a majority in settlements which formerly had a Hungarian majority along the nationally and regionally important roads and in the industrial centres, for example, Radnót, Marosludas, Marosugra, Marosújvár, Nagyenyed and Dicsőszentmárton. The former Hungarian character of small, deserted villages whose young populations emigrated, has remained or even intensified in certain places (Magyarbece, Magyarlapád, Nagymedvés, Magyarózd, Istvánháza, Csávás, etc.). A majority of cthnic Hungarians in the territory between the Little Küküllő and Olt inhabit larger industrial centres (Medgyes, Segesvár, Kiskapus, Nagyszeben) or remote villages (Halmágy, Kóbor, Dombos, Nagymoha, Sárpatak, Bürkös, etc.) and Vízakna.

In Hunyad county, the Hungarians mostly inhabit towns in the Zsil valley (Petrozsény, Lupény, Vulkán, Petrilla), Vajdahunyad, Déva, Kalán and Piski. The few hundred descendants of the medieval Hungarians and the Székely-Hungarians from Bukovina who settled in this region at the turn of the century live mainly in Bácsi, Hosdát, Gyalár, Haró, Nagyrápolt, Lozsád, Csernakeresztúr and Rákosd – in the last three villages as the absolute majority of the local population.

Brassó, the largest city in Transylvania with a population of 323,736, is the main traditional urban centre of the Székelys – aside from Marosvásárhely. For this reason, growth of the Hungarian population of the city has been uninterrupted since the Second World War (31,574 in 1992). Four Csángó-Hungarian[59] – Rumanian villages of

---

[58] Aranyosszék ("Golden District"). A small Székely-Hungarian ethnographical, untill 1876 an administrative region including 22 settlements in West-Central Transylvania, between the towns of Torda and Nagyenyed. It was founded by the Hungarian King Stephen V with Székelys from Kézdiszék (today north of Covasna county) on the territory of the deserted royal estate of Torda, between 1264 and 1271. The historical seat of the Aranyosszék district was Felvinc (Rumanian: Unirea).

[59] Csángó (Rumanian: Ceangău; German: Tschango): general name of the persons separated from the Székely-Hungarians, emigrated from the Székely Region. The Csángó Hungarian ethno-graphical group primarily includes Roman Catholic Hungarians in Moldavia, but also the Hungarians in the Upper-Tatros /Trotuş Valley around Gyímes /Ghimeş and the Hungarians in the Barcaság /Bîrsa /Burzenland region, west of Brassó City, the last two situated in the Eastern Carpathians. The number of the Csángós of Hungarian ethnic identity in Moldavia is decreasing due to intensive, forced Rumani-

the city's suburbs (Bácsfalu, Türkös, Csernátfalu, Hosszúfalu) were united under the name of Szecseleváros, where the percentage of Hungarians has dropped to 27.2 due to an influx of Rumanians who settled there after the establishment of the electrical industry.

HUNGARIANS IN THE PARTIUM REGION[60] (ARAD, BIHAR, SZILÁGY, SZATMÁR AND MÁRAMAROS COUNTIES)

The majority of the Hungarian national minority in the Partium region, estimated to be approximately 700,000 primarily inhabit cities along the main traffic routes on the periphery of the Great Hungarian Plain, approximately 40 kilometres from the Hungarian-Rumanian border. More than half of the ethnic Hungarians of the overwhelmingly Rumanian Máramaros county live as a 17-31 % minority in Nagybánya, the county seat, famous for its non-ferrous metal processing plants. Hungarians also comprise a similar proportion (20-30 %) in the other towns of the county (Felsőbánya, Kapnikbánya, Máramarossziget, Szinérváralja), with the exception of Borsa, Magyarlápos and Felsővisó. Important Hungarian communities can be found in some villages located near the periphery (Rónaszék, Aknasugatag, Hosszúmező, Kistécső, Domonkos, Erzsébetbánya, Magyarberkesz, Koltó, Katalin, Monó, Szamosardó etc.).

Due to the attractions of Kolozsvár, Nagyvárad, Szatmárnémeti and Nagybánya, the Szilágyság region was not the destination of large numbers of immigrants, also because of unfavourable local potentials for economic development. In fact, this county in Transylvania became one of those with the largest number of people leaving it. This situation led to the relative stability of the ethnic structure in villages. The large degree of migration within the Szilágyság region led to a decline in the percentage of the Hungarian population in towns especially Zilah, Szilágysomlyó or Szilágycseh. Hungarians became a minority in the first two of the above-mentioned towns. The largest Hungarian communities of the county live in Zilah (13,638), Szilágysomlyó (4,886), Kraszna (3,936), Sarmaság (3,829), Szilágycseh (3,774), Szilágynagyfalu (2,404) and Szilágyperecsen (2,259).

---

zation (1930: 20,964; 1992: 6,514). The number of Roman Catholics in Moldavia exceeded the 184,000 in 1992 (untill the end of the 19th century they were predominantly Hungarian speaking). Similarly to the predominantly English speaking and Roman Catholic Irish in Ireland, only some of the Csángós, from among the Moldavian Roman Catholics of ethnic Hungarian origin can be counted as Hungarian native speakers (c. 50,000). They live mostly around the towns of Bákó /Bacău and Roman, in the Szeret /Siret river valley.

[60]Partium (Hungarian: "Részek", English: "Parts"). As a geographical collective term this included the territories of the Principality of Transylvania outside – mostly west – of historic Transylvania (Máramaros, Kővárvidék, Közép-Szolnok, Kraszna, Bihar, Zaránd and Szörény counties) in the 16th and 17th centuries. Nowadays it is often used by Hungarians to represent the former Hungarian territories annexed to Rumania in 1920 – apart from historic Transylvania and Banat: the present-day Rumanian counties of Arad, Bihar, Szilágy, Szatmár and Máramaros or the former Rumanian provinces of Crişana and Maramureş.

Following the land reform, the Rumanian colonies established between the two world wars (Decebal, Traian, Dacia, Paulian, Lucăceni, Aliza, Gelu, Baba Novac, Crişeni, Horea, Scărişoara Nouă, etc.) and the villages with a population of Swabian origin (e.g. Béltek, Mezőfény, Mezőterem, Csanálos, Nagymajtény) disrupted the previous homogeneity of Szatmár county's Hungarian ethnic territory along the Rumanian-Hungarian border. In 1941 there was a 92-95 % majority Hungarian population in the new county seat of Szatmárnémeti and the old county seat of Nagykároly. This dropped according to Rumanian statistics, to 41-53 % by 1992, despite the significant rise in the birthrate. In addition to the above-mentioned towns, a significant number of Hungarians can be found in Tasnád, Mezőpetri, Szaniszló, Kaplony, Börvely, Erdőd, Béltek, Bogdánd, Hadad, Szatmárhegy, Lázári, Batiz, Sárköz, Halmi, Kökényesd, Túrterebes and Avasújváros.

The third largest Hungarian community in Transylvania with 74,228 people is in Nagyvárad, the seat of Bihar county, where Hungarians currently number 33.3 %, according to the 1992 Rumanian census. The compact ethnic Hungarian population of Bihar is located north of the county's capital and west of the Fugyivásárhely–Szalárd–Szentjobb–Micske–Margitta line. Among the notable local centres in this area, Margitta, Érmihályfalva, Székelyhíd, Bihardiószeg and Bihar are worth mentioning. Important medieval language enclaves continue to preserve Hungarian culture in the upper regions of the Berettyó and Sebes/Rapid Körös rivers (Berettyószéplak, Bályok, Mezőtelegd, Pusztaújlak, Pósalaka, Örvénd, Mezőtelki, Élesd, Rév etc.). In Southern Bihar, the majority Hungarian populated territories have shrunk over the last three centuries to the environs of Nagyszalonta, Tenke and Belényes (Árpád, Erdőgyarak, Mezőbaj, Bélfenyér, Gyanta, Köröstárkány, Kisnyégerfalva, Várasfenes, Körösjánosfalva, Belényessonkolyos, and Belényesújlak). Of the above-listed settlements, Tenke, Körösjánosfalva and Belényessonkolyos have already lost their Hungarian majority – due to an influx of Rumanians as well as natural assimilation.

More than half of the Hungarians of Arad county live in the county seat. Arad has 29,832 Hungarians and the rest live primarily in the environs of Arad and Kisjenő. Among these, the largest Hungarian population can be found in Magyarpécska (now united with the mainly Rumanian and Gypsy inhabited Ópécska), Kisjenő, Kisiratos, Nagyiratos, Borosjenő, Pankota, Nagyzerénd, Simonyifalva, Ágya, Zimándújfalu and Kispereg.

HUNGARIAN ETHNIC ENCLAVES IN THE BÁNÁT

The total number of Hungarians living in the rural ethnic enclaves and urban diaspora of the Bánát is estimated to be approximately 90,000 (1992 census data: 70,772 ethnic Hungarians). This number has stagnated due to the movement of Hungarians (mainly Székelys) from other Transylvanian territories to Temesvár, Resica and other industrial centres – thereby evening out the natural decrease of the population and assimilation. Due to this, as well as to the increasing regional concentration of

Hungarians in the Bánát, 45% of Hungarians in this region claim to be from Temesvár City. In addition to inhabiting this city of 334,115 people, important numbers and percentages of ethnic Hungarians live only in around 30 settlements, for example, Pusztakeresztúr, Porgány, Nagyszentmiklós and Majláthfalva in the northwest, Nagybodófalva, Szapáryfalva, Igazfalva, Nőrincse, Vásáros and Kisszécsény in the northeast, and Dézsánfalva, Omor, Detta, Gátalja, Végvár, Ötvösd, Józsefszállás, Torontálkeresztes and Magyarszentmárton in the south. In the Temesvár agglomeration, the percentage of Hungarians has drastically decreased in the formerly majority Hungarian populated settlements of Győröd, Újmosnica, Magyarmedves and Újszentes due to considerable immigration of Rumanians and the natural decrease of local Hungarians.

Chapter 5

THE HUNGARIANS OF VOJVODINA

The southernmost area of Hungarian settlement in the Carpathian Basin can be found in Vojvodina[1]. At the time of the last Yugoslav census in 1991, 339,491 people declared themselves to be ethnic Hungarian in Vojvodina. This Hungarian minority makes up 2.6% of Hungarians living in the Carpathian Basin and 12.5 % of Hungarians living outside the borders of Hungary. Due to an exceptionally adverse history, the Hungarians inhabiting the broad area of the Danube and Tisza river valleys preserve Hungarian culture in compact ethnic blocks of varying size as well as in ethnic enclaves.

THE NATURAL ENVIRONMENT

The Vojvodina Hungarians inhabit the southern part of the Great Hungarian Plain, referred to in Yugoslavia as the Pannonian Plain *(Fig. 33.)*. This flatland territory — with the exception of the alluvial soil of the river regions, the brown forest soil of the Fruška Gora (Pétervaradi) Mountains, and the meadow soils and the ameliorated peats of the Bánát — is covered to a great extent with chernozem. Having some of Europe's best agricultural land and most favourable climates, the quantity and quality of wheat and corn yields are outstanding in this region. As a result, Vojvodina plays a determining role in Serbia's food supply. Extensions of the monotonous flatlands include the Fruška Gora (Pétervaradi) Mountains (538 metres) famous for their vineyards, the Versec Mountains (640 meters), the loess plateau of Bácska (Telecska) and the Titel Plateau (128 metres) and the Deliblát sand hills (250 metres). There has been a long tradition of controlling rivers in Bácska and Bánát, for example, by draining the Versec-Alibunár marshland. The enormous canal projects of the last few decades, including the construction of the navigable Danube-Tisza-Danube canal between Bezdán-Óbecse-Palánka, aimed to provide uninterrupted irrigation of the extremely important Vojvodina agricultural land. The major rivers of the lowland regions inhabited by Hungarians are the tributaries of the Danube - the Száva, Temes and Tisza all of which flow directly

---

[1] Vojvodina ("Voivodship", Hungarian: Vajdaság). Province in Federal Republic of Yugoslavia, and in Serbia, north of the Sava and Danube rivers. Territory: 21,506 square kilometres, population number: 2 millions, capital: Újvidék /180,000 inhabitants/. Between the 10th century and 1918 a part of South Hungary, since then a part of Yugoslavia, between 1945 and 1989 as an autonomous province of Serbia. Its only historical precedent was the province "Serbian Voivodship and Bánát of Temesvár" created, separated from Hungary (1849), repealed (1860) by Habsburg absolutism as part of its revenge for the Hungarian War of Independence of 1848-1849.

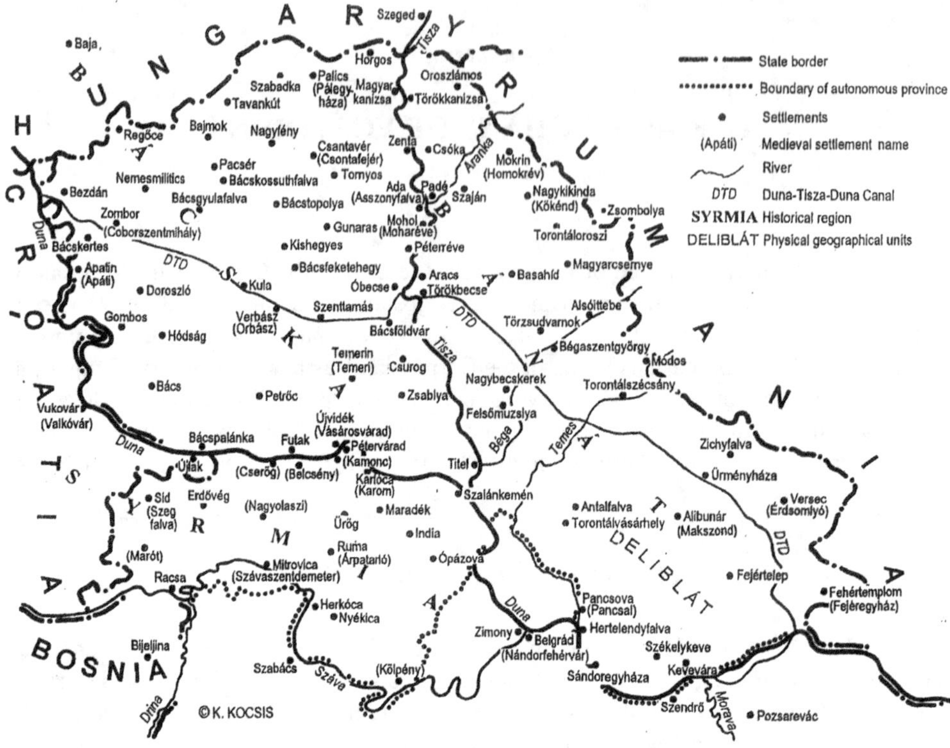

Figure 33. Important Hungarian geographical names in Vojvodina

into the Danube. The most important still waters for Hungarians include the Palics and Ludas Lakes near Szabadka and the Fehér /White/ Lake near Nagybecskerek.

ETHNIC PROCESSES DURING THE PAST FIVE HUNDRED YEARS

During medieval times the southern Hungarian ethnic area also became increasingly homogeneous and larger *(Fig. 34.)*. Ethnic processes favourable to the Hungarians, slowed down from the late 14th century, when a continuous, never-ending stream of Serbs fled to southern Hungary (mostly to Syrmia-Szerémség and South Bánát), following catastrophic defeats suffered at the hands of the Ottoman-Turks (e.g. 1389 battle in Kosovo Polje). Serb immigration escalated after 1459 (the fall of the Serbian capital Smederevo), and the Ottoman conquest of Serbia. As a result of this, the majority of the population in the southern Hungarian territories, primarily Syrmia region, which became a permanent seat of operations and was abandoned by the local

138

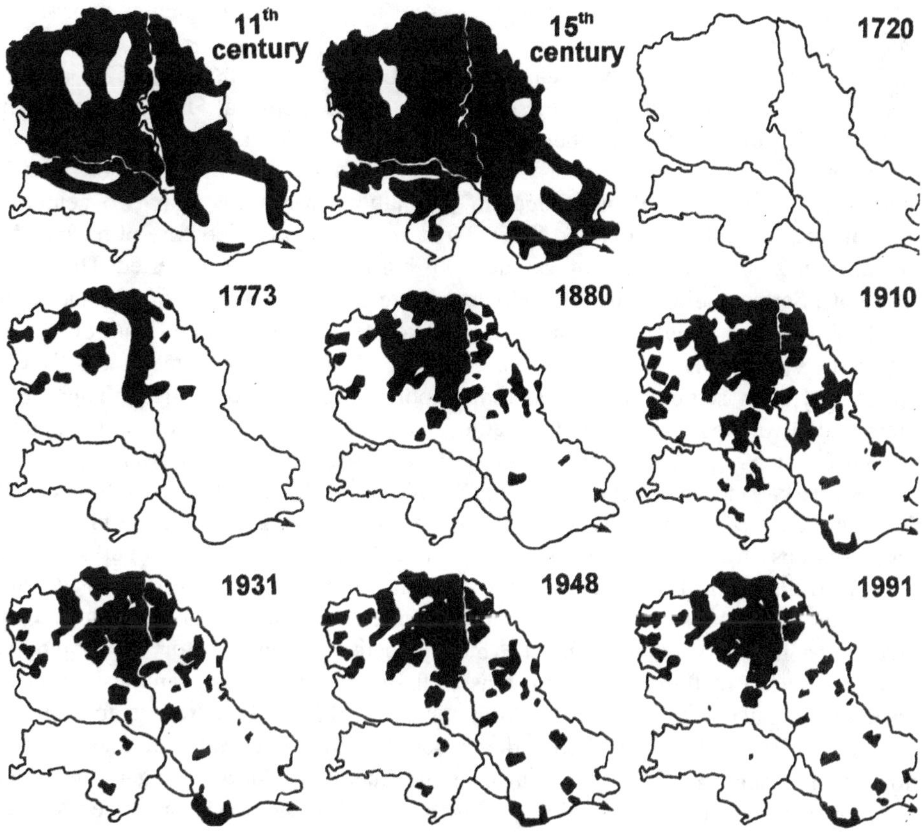

Figure 34. Change in the ethnic territory of Hungarians on the present-day territory of Vojvodina
(11th–20th century)

Catholic Hungarian population, counted as orthodox Serbs. Not only the Turkish devastation, but serious Hungarian ethnic-demographical losses and the casualties during the Peasant War of G. Dózsa contributed to the immigration of Serbian refugees (1514)[2]. In the second half of the 15th century the most important centres of the Hungarian settlement network on the territory of present-day Vojvodina were in the Bácska region: Szabadka, Tavankút, Coborszentmihály (today Zombor), Apáti (today Apatin), Bodrog (today Monostorszeg), Bács, Pest (today Bácspalánka), Futak, Vásárosvárad (today Újvidék), Titel, Becse, Zenta, in the Bánát region: Kanizsa, Basahida, Aracs, Becskerek, Pancsal (today Pancsova), Keve (today Kevevára), Érdsomlyó (today Ver-

---

[2] Popović, D. J. 1957 Srbi u Vojvodini (Serbs in Vojvodina) I. Matica Srpska, Novi Sad, 104.p.

sec), and in the Syrmia-Szerémség region: Csörög (today Čerević), Bánmonostor (today Banoštor), Pétervárad and Karom (today Karlóca)[3].

The total defeat of the Hungarian Royal Army at Mohács in 1526, and the events which followed, resulted in the dissolution of the medieval Hungarian state and its ethnic structure. Because of the permanent Ottoman (Turkish) occupation and the devastation by Serbian troops under J. Crni (Nenad) in 1527, the majority of southern Hungarian territories lost their Hungarian populations for more than two centuries, Syrmia in 1526, Bácska in 1541 and West Bánát in 1551. On the territory of present-day Vojvodina next to the ruins of about 600 burnt down and deserted Hungarian settlements, Serbian colonies developed which were suited to the state of war and to the way of life (military service, semi-nomadic stock-breeding) of the immigrant Serbs. At the same time, Muslims (Turks, Bosnians), Serbian soldiers and in some places Greeks, Gypsies and Jews settled in the restored, important towns and castles[4]. This ethnic pattern had developed by the late 16th century and was characterised by Serbian ethnic dominance which remained unchanged untill the collapse of Ottoman power.

Bácska and the greater part of Syrmia were liberated from Ottoman rule following the peace treaty of Karlóca (1699). Important changes had taken place in the ethnic-religious structure of the population since 1688. The Muslims (Turks and the Muslimized Slavs and Hungarians) fled to Bosnia from Hungarian territories liberated by the Christian troops. Later, the Catholic Shokats and Bunjevats from Bosnia and Hercegovina fled to southern Hungary, mostly to the present territory of Vojvodina. Following the fall of Belgrade (1690) tens of thousands of Serbian families, under the leadership of patriarch Arsenije III Crnojević (1633-1706), took refuge in Hungary, where the Austrian Emperor Leopold I assured them wide political and religious autonomy in exchange for fighting against the enemies (Turks, Hungarians) of the Habsburg Imperial Court. The majority of them settled in the newly organized Military Border along the Maros, Tisza, Danube and Száva rivers.

Following the defeat of the anti-Habsburg Hungarian War of Independence (1703 - 1711) lead by F. Rákóczi and the reannexing of Bánát in the peace-treaty of Požarevac (1718), a census of the taxpaying population was organised in Hungary (1720). Of the 3,111 taxpaying households in Bácska 97.6 % were Serbian and Croatian, 1.9 % Hungarian and 0.5 % German[5]. At the same time in Bánát and Syrmia the Hungarians were almost totally absent. In these border regions during the first half of the 18th century the Imperial Court, primarily the Imperial War Council in Vienna, prevented the return of Hungarians, who were regarded as politically 'unreliable'. During this period — for economic and political reasons — tens of thousands of Catholics, mostly from southern Germany, were settled in the war-stricken, almost deserted and

---

[3] Csánki D. 1890-1913 Magyarország történelmi földrajza a Hunyadiak korában (Historic Geography of Hungary in 15th century) I-V., Budapest

[4] Nyigri I. 1941 A visszatért Délvidék nemzetiségi képe (Ethnic Patterns in the Returned Southern Region) - in: A visszatért Délvidék, Halász, Budapest, pp. 298-299., Popović, D. J. 1957 ibid.

[5] Acsády I. 1896 Magyarország népessége a Pragmatica Sanctio korában 1720-21 (Population of Hungary 1720-21). Magyar Statisztikai Közlemények XII. Budapest, 288p.

agriculturally uncultivated Bácska and Bánát. The majority of the economically very 'useful' and politically reliable German population were settled in west-southwest Bácska and South Bánát.

The mass return of Hungarians to historical southern Hungary was only allowed after the accession of Maria Theresia to the throne (1740). The first important Hungarian colonies were established in the non-military part of Bácska during the gradual dismantling of the Military Border of Tisza - Maros which lost its military importance (1741-1750): Nemesmilitics, Bezdán, Kula, Bácstopolya etc. The majority of Serbs from the old Military Border of Tisza who were used to military service and to independence from the Hungarian authorities, migrated to the south-east corner of Bácska, to the Military District of Sajkás and to the west of Bánát, to the autonomous Serbian District of Nagykikinda. Between 1750 and 1770 the Hungarians returned from the Jász and Kun districts, from Csongrád county and Transdanubia (Dunántúl) to the deserted regions of Bácska, partly taking the place of the Serbs in Doroszló, Bácstopolya, Bajsa, Ada, Mohol, Magyarkanizsa, Zenta, Szabadka, Bajmok, Csantavér, Péterréve, Bácsföldvár etc[6]. Due to this Hungarian migration the population number of Szabadka increased 5-fold, to 10,000 between 1720-1771. In this period the Hungarian ethnic block of the Szabadka - Tisza Region was formed between the German ethnic area in W-Bácska and the Serbian districts of Sajkás and Nagykikinda. During the reign of Maria Theresia mass German immigration supported by the state continued and was accompanied by the immigration of the Slovaks, Ruthenians and Rumanians. The characteristic ethnic-religious character and diversity of the territory of present-day Vojvodina was formed in the second half of the 18th century.

The mass return of Hungarians to the present Serbian part of the Bánát region was due to the expansion of the tobacco-growing from Szeged area, famous in the 18th century. Thousands of Hungarian tobacco growers settled on the large estates of Bánát between 1773 and 1810 in the areas between the Serbian District of Nagykikinda and the Military Border of Bánát: e.g. Magyarmajdány, Törökkanizsa, Csóka, Oroszlámos, Szaján[7].

The colonization policy during the reign of Joseph II (1780-1790) was characterised by predominantly German immigration, but at that time the settlement of Protestants, for example Calvinist Hungarians, was also made possible (e.g. in Bácsfeketehegy, Bácskossuthfalva, Pacsér, Piros). Later, between 1840-1847 the settlement of Hungarians in the Bánát area increased with the immigration of Hungarian tobacco gardeners from Csongrád and Csanád counties from Magyarszentmihály, Tamásfalva, Ürményháza etc.

The proclamation of a Serbian Vojvodina — independent from the Hungarian Kingdom — was made in Karlóca on May 13, 1848. During the time of the Hungarian

---

[6] Bodor A. 1914 Délmagyarországi telepítések története és hatása a mai közállapotokra (History of the Colonizations in South Hungary and their Effects on the Present Situation), Stephanum, Budapest, 14.p.

[7] Banner J. 1925 Szegedi telepítések Délmagyarországon (Colonizations from the Szeged region in South Hungary), Földrajzi Közlemények, LIII, pp. 75-79

War of Independence (1848 - 1849), Serbian troops burnt down the majority of Hungarian and some German settlements, and expelled their populations (e.g. Temerin, Bácsföldvár, Zenta, Magyarkanizsa, Versec, Fehértemplom) following battles between the Hungarian Army and local and foreign Serbian troops. A significant number of Hungarian refugees from Bácska fled to Szabadka. As a result of this migration, the Austrian census of 1850 in Szabadka recorded nearly 30,000 (about 61 % of the total population of 48,823) Hungarians. Later, the Hungarian refugees returned to their original settlements in Bácska, where the number of Hungarians grew steadily due to the increasing north-south migration, motivated by economic and demographic considerations.

The first Hungarian census enquiring into linguistic (mother tongue) affiliation was carried out at the end of 1880 following the Austro-Hungarian Compromise (1867). At that time, of the 1.2 million inhabitants living on the territory of present-day Vojvodina, 35.5 % was Serbian, 24.4 % German, 22.6 % Hungarian and 6.2 % Croatian according to their mother tongue *(Tab. 26.)*[8]. According to this census data, outside the Hungarian ethnic block of the Szabadka - Tisza Region, where 56 % of the Hungarians of the region concentrated, Hungarians represented the majority of the population in 27 settlements (Bácska 7, Bánát 19, Syrmia 1).

After 1880, as a result of growing economic development, sanitary conditions primarily in the German and Hungarian settlements improved rapidly. As a consequence, mortality gradually decreased and the natality grew significantly among the Hungarians of the Great Hungarian Plain. Between 1901 and 1910 the natural increase in settlements with a Hungarian majority - excluding Szabadka - on the territory of present-day Vojvodina, was 14.1 % (Germans: 13.6%, Serbs: 10.9%). This Hungarian population growth caused many social problems (division of the land, impoverishment, unemployment etc) mainly on the Great Hungarian Plain. It was alleviated by the partial division of government estates and by establishing colonies. But this government-organized settlement policy — between 1883 and 1899 — was small scale, and affected not only ethnic Hungarians, but also Germans, Slovaks and Bulgarians and did not result in any major change in the ethnic structure of the region. During this period some of the Hungarians from Bukovina settled along the Danube (Székelykeve, Sándoregyháza, Hertelendyfalva). At the turn of the century, the number of ethnic Hungarians increased significantly not only in the bigger towns (Újvidék, Szabadka, Nagybecskerek, Pancsova, Versec etc), but on the farms of the large estates (e.g. the Csekonits, Karátsonyi, Pejacsevich and Kotek families) and in certain industrial centres (Beočin, Vrdnik) *(Tab. 27.)*. Mainly as a result of the mass exodus of the population from the Hungarian ethnic block, the number of Hungarians in south-east

---

[8] Data of the 1880 census — as in the case of the censuses of 1890, 1900 and 1910 — are calculated on the present territory of Vojvodina including the data of the present-day Kelebia, Tompa and Csikéria settlements of Hungary which belonged to Szabadka City till the peace-treaty of Trianon (1920). In the calculation of persons in the so-called 'beszélni nem tud / can not speak' statistical category, they were was proportionally divided between the linguistic-ethnic groups. Those in the Serbo-Croatian linguistic category were divided on the basis of their religious affiliation between the Orthodox Serbs and Catholic Croats.

Table 26. Ethnic structure of the population of the present territory of Vojvodina (1880–1991)

Year	Total population	Serbs		Hungarians		Germans		Croats		Montenegrins		Slovaks		Rumanians		Ruthenians, Ukrainians		Others	
	number	number	%	number	%	number	%	number	%	number	%	number	%	number	%	numb.	%	number	%
1880	1,172,729	416,116	35.5	265,287	22.6	285,920	24.4	72,486	6.2	..	..	43,318	3.7	69,668	5.9	9,299	0.8	10,635	0.9
1890	1,331,143	45,7873	34.4	324,430	24.4	321,563	24.2	80,404	6.0	..	..	49,834	3.7	73,492	5.5	11,022	0.8	12,525	1.0
1900	1,432,748	483,176	33.7	378,634	26.4	336,430	23.5	80,901	5.6	..	..	53,832	3.8	74,718	5.2	12,663	0.9	12,394	0.9
1910	1,512,983	510,754	33.8	425,672	28.1	324,017	21.4	91,016	6.0	..	..	56,690	3.7	75,318	5.0	13,497	0.9	16,019	1.1
1921	1,528,238	533,466	34.9	363,450	23.8	335,902	22.0	129,788	8.5	..	..	59,540	3.9	67,675	4.4	13,644	0.9	24,773	1.6
1931	1,624,158	613,910	37.8	376,176	23.2	328,631	20.2	132,517	8.2	..	..	..	..	..	..	..	..	172,924	10.6
1941	1,636,367	577,067	35.3	465,920	28.5	318,259	19.4	105,810	6.5	..	..	..	..	..	..	..	..	169,311	10.3
1948	1,640,757	827,633	50.4	428,554	26.1	28,869	1.8	132,980	8.1	30,531	1.9	69,622	4.2	57,899	3.5	22,077	1.3	42,592	2.7
1953	1,701,384	867,210	51.0	435,210	25.6	..	..	127,040	7.5	30,532	1.8	71,191	4.2	57,219	3.4	23,040	1.3	89,942	5.2
1961	1,854,965	1,017,713	54.9	442,560	23.9	..	..	145,341	7.8	34,782	1.9	73,830	4.0	57,259	3.1	..	..	83,480	4.4
1971	1,952,533	1,089,132	55.8	423,866	21.7	7,243	0.4	138,561	7.1	36,416	1.9	72,795	3.7	52,987	2.7	25,115	1.3	106,418	5.4
1981	2,034,772	1,107,375	54.4	385,356	18.9	3,808	0.2	119,157	5.9	43,304	2.1	69,549	3.4	47,289	2.3	24,306	1.2	234,628	11.6
1991	2,013,889	1,143,723	56.8	339,491	16.9	3,873	0.2	98,025	4.9	44,838	2.2	63,545	3.2	38,809	1.9	22,217	1.1	259,368	12.8
1996	2,213,000	1,422,000	64.3	285,000	12.9	3,000	0.1	62,000	2.8	46,000	2.1	60,000	2.3	34,000	1.5	21,000	0.9	280,000	13.1

Sources: 1880, 1890, 1900, 1910, 1941: Hungarian census data (mother/native tongue), 1921, 1931: Yugoslav census data (mother /native tongue), 1948, 1953, 1961, 1971, 1981, 1991: Yugoslav census data (ethnicity), 1941: combined Hungarian (in Bácska 1941) and Yugoslav (in Banat and Syrmia/ Szerémség/ Srem 1931) census data. *1996: estimation of K. Kocsis based on "Census of Refugees...., Belgrade, 1996.*

Remarks: Data between 1880 and 1910 include the settlements of Tompa, Kelebia, Csikéria of the present-day Republic Hungary at that time belonging to the administrative area of Szabadka/Subotica City. The Croats include the Bunyevats, Shokats and Dalmatinian ethnic groups and the "Serbs of Roman Catholic religious affiliation" in 1890.

Year	Total population		Serbs		**Hungarians**		Germans		Others	
	number	%	number	%	**number**	%	number	%	number	%
Újvidék - Novi Sad										
1880	21,325	100.0	8,676	40.7	**5,702**	**26.7**	5,332	25.0	1,615	7.6
1910	33,590	100.0	11,594	34.5	**13,343**	**39.7**	5,918	17.6	2,735	8.1
1931	56,585	100.0	20,679	36.5	**17,000**	**30.0**	8,500	15.0	10,406	18.5
1941	61,731	100.0	17,531	28.4	**31,130**	**50.4**	7,662	12.4	5,408	8.8
1948	69,439	100.0	35,340	50.9	**20,523**	**29.5**	1,297	1.9	12,279	17.7
1961	102,469	100.0	61,326	59.8	**23,812**	**23.2**	..	..	17,331	17.0
1971	141,375	100.0	88,659	62.7	**22,998**	**16.3**	608	0.4	29,110	20.6
1981	170,020	100.0	103,878	61.1	**19,262**	**11.3**	313	0.2	46,567	27.4
1991	179,626	100.0	114,966	64.0	**15,778**	**8.8**	319	0.2	48,563	27.0
Szabadka - Subotica										
1880	62,556	100.0	2,904	4.6	**31,592**	**50.5**	1,828	2.9	26,232	42.0
1910	94,610	100.0	3,514	3.7	**55,587**	**58.8**	1,913	2.0	33,596	35.5
1931	100,058	100.0	9,200	9.2	**41,401**	**41.4**	2,865	2.9	46,592	46.5
1941	102,736	100.0	4,627	4.5	**61,581**	**59.9**	1,787	1.7	34,741	33.9
1948	112,194	100.0	11,617	10.4	**51,716**	**46.1**	480	0.4	48,381	43.1
1961	75,036	100.0	9,437	12.6	**37,529**	**50.0**	..	..	28,070	37.4
1971	88,813	100.0	11,728	13.2	**43,068**	**48.5**	218	0.2	33,799	38.1
1981	100,516	100.0	13,959	13.9	**44,065**	**43.8**	97	0.1	42,395	42.2
1991	100,386	100.0	15,734	15.7	**39,749**	**39.6**	138	0.1	44,765	44.6
Zombor - Sombor										
1880	24,693	100.0	11,062	44.8	**5,318**	**21.5**	2,799	11.3	5,514	22.4
1910	30,593	100.0	11,881	38.8	**10,078**	**32.9**	2,181	7.1	6,453	21.2
1931	32,334	100.0	13,700	42.4	**5,852**	**18.1**	3,400	10.5	9,382	29.0
1941	32,111	100.0	11,807	36.8	**11,502**	**35.8**	2,255	7.0	6,547	20.4
1948	33,613	100.0	16,107	47.9	**7,296**	**21.7**	595	1.8	9,615	28.6
1961	37,760	100.0	19,629	52.0	**7,474**	**19.8**	..	..	10,657	28.2
1971	44,100	100.0	23,339	52.9	**7,115**	**16.1**	277	0.6	13,369	30.4
1981	48,454	100.0	24,195	49.9	**5,857**	**12.1**	163	0.3	18,239	37.7
1991	48,993	100.0	25,903	52.9	**4,736**	**9.7**	201	0.4	18,153	37.0
Temerin - Temerin										
1880	7,865	100.0	7	0.1	**6,765**	**86.0**	1078	13.7	15	0.2
1910	9,768	100.0	30	0.3	**9,499**	**97.3**	231	2.4	8	0.1
1931	11,290	100.0	1,430	12.6	**8,718**	**77.2**	1,038	9.2	104	1.0
1941	11,035	100.0	37	0.3	**10,067**	**91.2**	892	8.1	39	0.4
1948	11,438	100.0	1,820	15.9	**9,478**	**82.9**	45	0.4	95	0.9
1961	12,705	100.0	2,571	20.2	**9,927**	**78.1**	..	..	207	1.7
1971	13,584	100.0	3,271	24.1	**9,945**	**73.2**	29	0.2	339	2.5
1981	14,875	100.0	4,197	28.2	**9,781**	**65.8**	24	0.2	873	5.9
1991	16,971	100.0	6,002	35.4	**9,495**	**55.9**	22	0.1	1,452	8.6
Bácstopolya - Bačka Topola										
1880	9,500	100.0	9	0.1	**9,244**	**97.3**	204	2.1	43	0.5
1910	12,471	100.0	17	0.1	**12,339**	**98.9**	63	0.5	52	0.5
1931	15,059	100.0	1,620	10.8	**12,839**	**85.3**	134	0.9	466	3.0
1941	14,124	100.0	362	2.6	**13,420**	**95.0**	140	1.0	202	1.4
1948	13,924	100.0	1,185	8.5	**12,706**	**91.3**	23	0.2	10	0.0
1961	15,079	100.0	1,453	9.6	**12,969**	**86.0**	..	..	657	4.4
1971	15,989	100.0	1,837	11.5	**13,112**	**82.0**	32	0.2	1,008	6.3
1981	17,027	100.0	2,548	15.0	**12,617**	**74.1**	0	0	1,862	10.9
1991	16,704	100.0	3,087	18.5	**11,176**	**66.9**	5	0.0	2,436	14.6

Sources: 1880, 1910, 1941: Hungarian census data (mother/native tongue), 1921, 1931: Yugoslav census data (mother /native tongue), 1948 — 1991: Yugoslav census data (ethnicity).

cities and towns of Vojvodina (1880 – 1991)

Year	Total population		Serbs		**Hungarians**		Germans		Others	
	number	%	number	%	**number**	%	number	%	number	%
Magyarkanizsa - Kanjiža										
1880	13,069	100.0	460	3.5	**12,481**	**95.5**	86	0.7	42	0.3
1910	17,018	100.0	329	1.9	**16,655**	**97.9**	28	0.2	6	0.0
1931	19,108	100.0	1,900	9.9	**16,696**	**87.4**	117	0.6	395	2.1
1941	19,336	100.0	314	1.6	**18,849**	**97.5**	31	0.2	142	0.7
1948	11,611	100.0	1,128	9.7	**10,149**	**87.4**	45	0.4	289	2.5
1961	10,722	100.0	728	6.8	**9,797**	**91.4**	..	..	197	1.8
1971	11,240	100.0	783	7.0	**10,177**	**90.5**	4	0.0	276	2.5
1981	11,759	100.0	736	6.3	**10,466**	**89.0**	0	0	557	4.7
1991	11,541	100.0	769	6.7	**10,183**	**88.2**	7	0.1	582	5.0
Zenta – Senta										
1880	21,200	100.0	1,963	9.3	**18,706**	**88.2**	467	2.2	64	0.3
1910	29,666	100.0	2,020	6.8	**27,221**	**91.8**	177	0.6	248	0.8
1931	31,969	100.0	4,300	13.4	**25,924**	**81.1**	412	1.3	1,333	4.2
1941	32,147	100.0	2,076	6.5	**29,463**	**91.7**	148	0.5	460	1.3
1948	25,277	100.0	3,536	14.0	**20,898**	**82.7**	32	0.1	811	3.2
1961	25,062	100.0	3,371	13.4	**20,980**	**83.7**	..	..	711	2.9
1971	24,723	100.0	3,071	12.4	**20,548**	**83.1**	30	0.1	1,074	4.4
1981	23,690	100.0	2,781	11.7	**18,863**	**79.6**	19	0.1	2,027	8.6
1991	22,827	100.0	2,485	10.9	**17,888**	**78.4**	11	0.0	2,443	10.7
Óbecse - Bečej										
1880	15,040	100.0	5,337	35.5	**9,101**	**60.5**	504	3.4	98	0.6
1910	19,372	100.0	6,582	34.0	**12,488**	**64.5**	193	1.0	109	0.5
1931	20,519	100.0	7,050	34.4	**12,459**	**60.7**	318	1.5	692	3.4
1941	21,200	100.0	6,113	28.8	**14,576**	**68.8**	201	1.0	310	1.4
1948	23,551	100.0	7,921	33.6	**14,701**	**62.4**	412	1.7	517	2.3
1961	24,963	100.0	8,448	33.8	**15,537**	**62.2**	..	..	978	4.0
1971	26,722	100.0	9,171	34.3	**15,815**	**59.2**	56	0.2	1,680	6.3
1981	27,102	100.0	8,938	33.0	**14,772**	**54.5**	0	0	3,392	12.5
1991	26,634	100.0	9,477	35.6	**13,464**	**50.6**	37	0.1	3,656	13.7
Törökbecse - Novi Bečej										
1880	12,983	100.0	7,103	54.7	**5,473**	**42.2**	307	2.4	100	0.7
1910	16,810	100.0	8,847	52.6	**7,586**	**45.1**	219	1.3	158	1.0
1921	16,400	100.0	8,814	53.7	**6,919**	**42.2**	219	1.3	448	2.8
1931	16,338	100.0	9,100	55.7	**6,432**	**39.4**	220	1.3	586	3.6
1948	15,644	100.0	9,125	58.3	**6,346**	**40.6**	18	0.1	155	1.0
1961	16,378	100.0	9,392	57.3	**6,601**	**40.3**	..	..	385	2.4
1971	16,075	100.0	9,356	58.2	**6,074**	**37.8**	21	0.1	624	3.9
1981	16,091	100.0	9,089	56.5	**5,422**	**33.7**	0	0	1,580	9.8
1991	15,404	100.0	8,659	56.2	**4,657**	**30.2**	13	0.1	2,075	13.5
Nagybecskerek - Zrenjanin										
1880	19,529	100.0	8,166	41.8	**3,777**	**19.3**	6,596	33.8	990	5.1
1910	29,414	100.0	8,955	30.4	**12,395**	**42.1**	6,930	23.6	1,134	3.9
1921	30,815	100.0	10,452	33.9	**10,675**	**34.6**	7,964	25.8	1,724	5.7
1931	36,315	100.0	13,000	35.8	**12,249**	**33.7**	8,234	22.7	2,832	7.8
1948	38,591	100.0	19,179	49.7	**15,583**	**40.4**	792	2.1	3,037	7.8
1961	55,578	100.0	33,459	60.2	**18,083**	**32.5**	..	..	4,036	7.3
1971	71,474	100.0	45,308	63.4	**18,521**	**25.9**	359	0.5	7,286	10.2
1981	81,327	100.0	49,839	61.3	**17,085**	**21.0**	0	0	14,403	17.7
1991	81,316	100.0	52,094	64.1	**14,312**	**17.6**	237	0.3	14,673	18.0

Remark: All data were calculated for the present administrative territory of the cities and towns excluding Szabadka (1880-1948), Zenta, Bácstopolya and Magyarkanizsa (1880-1941).

Bácska increased by 66.3 % between 1880 and 1910, by 82.3 % in Central and South Bánát, and by 130 % in Syrmia. The present Hungarian ethnic enclaves of Syrmia (Satrinca, Maradék, Herkóca, Nyékica etc) were formed following Hungarian emigration from Bácska (e.g. Kishegyes, Temerin, Mohol and Kula).

Emigration may have played an important role in the change of the population. Between 1899 and 1913 about 150,000 people migrated from the present area of Vojvodina (mostly from the Bánát). 53 % out of them counted as German, 18 % as Serbian and 10 % as Hungarian[9].

The rapid growth of native Hungarian speakers was also contributed to by natural assimilation, a change in language use and ethnic identity, and voluntary 'Magyarization'. The effect of these processes was especially noticeable among Germans, Bunjevats, Jews and Serbs living in towns, first of all in Újvidék, Nagybecskerek, Zombor, Szabadka, Pancsova and Versec.

The last Hungarian census was carried out in the whole area of the present-day Vojvodina in 1910. At that time 28.1 % of the 1.5 million inhabitants of the region declared themselves to be Hungarian, 33.8 % Serbian, 21.4 % German and 6 % Croatian, Bunjevats and Shokats native speakers. At this census the Hungarian ethnic territory was at its largest since the middle of the 16th century. Outside their ethnic block along the Tisza river, Hungarians represented an absolute or relative majority of the local population in the area of 53 present-day settlements, also in Újvidék and Nagybecskerek *(Fig. 35.)*. In 1910 the largest Hungarian communities were concentrated in the triangle of Újvidék - Szabadka - Magyarkanizsa.

At the end of the First World War, following the liberation of Serbia and Montenegro, until November 14, 1918, the Serbian troops supported by the Entente occupied the southern Hungarian territories till the line of Barcs-Pécs-Baja-Szeged-Arad. This military action was seen as occupation by 60.8 % of the population (Hungarians, Germans, Bunjevats) of the later Yugoslav parts of Baranya, Bácska and Bánát and as liberation by the Serbs (28 %). This Serbian minority announced the annexation of Bácska, Bánát and Baranya to Serbia on November 25, 1918 behind the front line in Újvidék, to legitimise the presence of the Serbian Royal Army. The Serbian authorities immediately started to liquidate Hungarian state authority there and to ruin the local Hungarians both politically and economically. Power was given to the local Serbian minority while the majority of Hungarian public employees were dismissed or forced to retire, and schools were nationalised by Serbia (August 20, 1920). On February 25, 1919 Serbia started to expropriate the majority of large landed estates of over 500 cadastral acres — a little later, of over 100 cadastral acres — predominantly in Hungarian and German hands. This measure called 'agrarian reform' served both ethnic and social aims: to ruin the class of large Hungarian landowners, indirectly to ruin Hungarian peasants and workers, and to satisfy Serbian — generally South Slavian — claims for land. 48.6 % out of the large private estates selected for expropriation were

---

[9] Maletić, M. (Ed.) 1968 Vojvodina. Znamenitosti i lepote (Places of interests), Književne Novine, Beograd, 104.p.

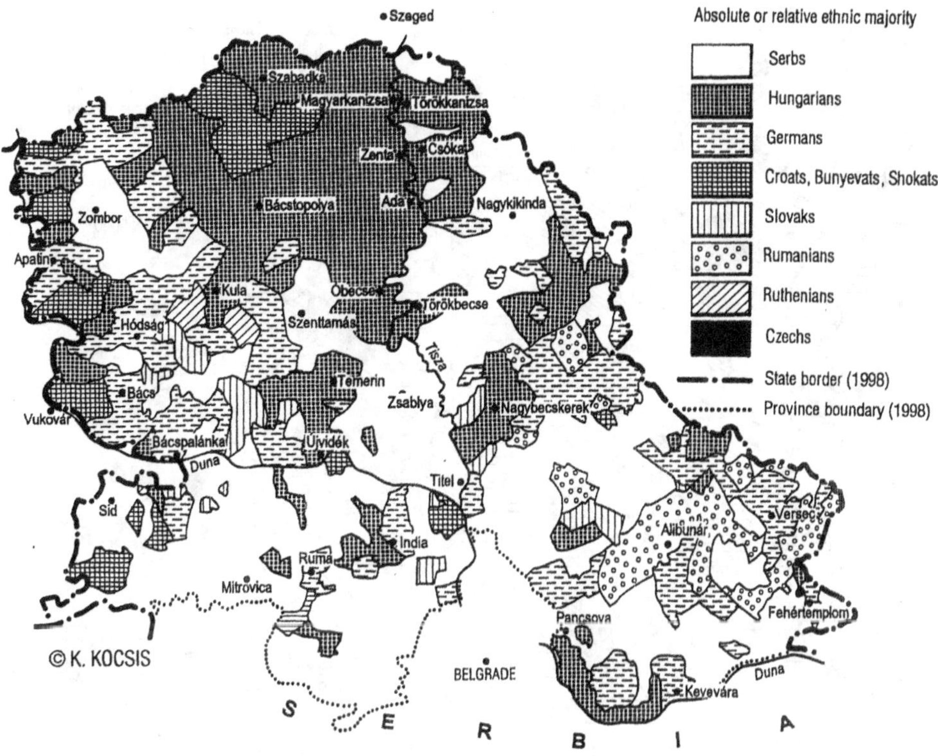

Figure 35. Ethnic map of the present-day territory of Vojvodina (1910)
Source: Census 1910

Hungarian, 36.3 % German, Jewish or Italian[10]. In spite of the fact that early in 1919 from 57,631 landless peasants of Bácska 41.4 % were Hungarian and 18.2 % were German, these ethnic groups, considered as enemies, were almost totally omitted from the redistribution of land. This included the farms of expropriated estates, and according to our calculations, 14,345 Hungarian and 1,239 German workers and farmhands were expelled to make room for Serbian colonists and volunteers (dobrovoljci) *(Fig. 36.)*. The peace-treaty of Trianon (June 4, 1920) took place under these circumstances, and 8,558 km² from the Hungarian Bács-Bodrog County were annexed to the Kingdom of Serbs-Croats and Slovenes, and 9,324 km² from Bánát (e.g. Torontál and Temes counties).

The first census of the new South Slavian state was carried out on January 31, 1921. According to the data, 363,450 (23.8 %) of the 1.5 million inhabitants of present-day Vojvodina were registered as Hungarian, 34.9% as Orthodox and 8.5 % as Catholic

---

[10] Kecić, D. 1972 Revolucionarni radnički pokret u Vojvodini (Revolutionary workers movement in Vojvodina) 1917-1921, Institut za Izučavanje Istorije Vojvodine, Novi Sad

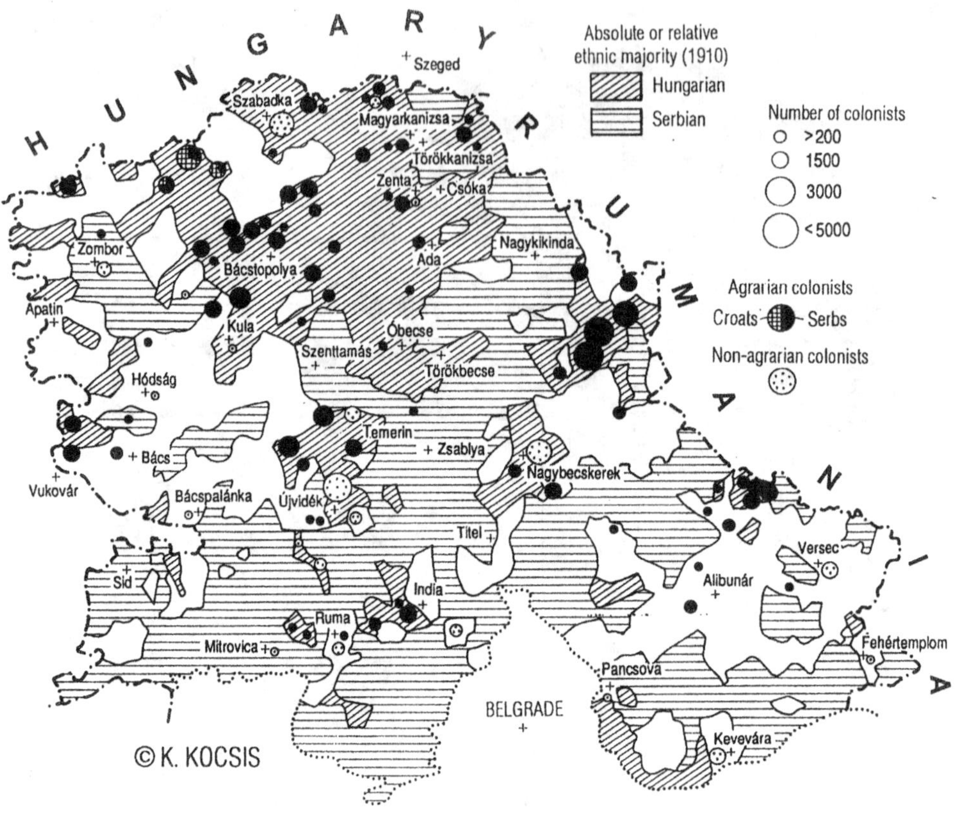

Figure 36. Serbian (Yugoslav) colonization in Vojvodina (1918 – 1941)

Serbo-Croatian native speakers[11]. Due to the Hungarian-Serbian take-over in 1918, the statistically registered number of the Hungarians had extraordinarily decreased by the census of 1921. At this time — according to our calculations — out of the persons who declared themselves in 1910 as Hungarian native speakers in the new, anti-Hungarian situation, about 52,000 inhabitants declared themselves or were registered without asking on the base of the 'surname analysis order of Svetozar Pribičević'[12] as non-

---

[11] From the official census data of 1921 relating to Horgos (today in Kanjiža Commune), we have subtracted 7551 Hungarian inhabitants of the present-day settlements of Röszke, Ásotthalom and Mórahalom in Hungary which were under Serbian occupation as a part of Horgos until 1923 (see Magyar Statisztikai Közlemények Vol. 83., 1932). The Serbo-Croatian linguistic category was divided on the basis of religious affiliation into Serbs and Croats.

[12] According to this Serbian order it was not allowed for persons with a surname of linguistically non-completely Hungarian origin to declare themselves as ethnic Hungarian, e.g. at the census or at school registration (Kirilovič, D. 1937 Asimilacioni uspesi madjara u Bačkoj, Banatu i

Hungarians (12,330 as German, 32,620 as 'Catholic Serbo-Croatian' and 6,850 as other non-Hungarian). As a result of these events according to the census the number of ethnic Hungarians was drastically reduced, primarily in Szabadka and Zombor, towns of the new border region *(Fig. 37.)*. Similar to the above mentioned 'dissimilation', local Hungarians suffered heavy losses due to the escape, expulsion or repatriation of about 33,000 Hungarian employees, intellectuals and landowners[13].

In the period between the censuses of 1921 and 1931 Yugoslav (Serbian) agrarian reform[14] developed completely, which, in accordance with the Great-Serbian ethnic policy, aimed to increase the number of southern Slavs (first of all Serbs), to break up the Hungarian ethnic block of the Tisza region and to destroy the majority of Hungarian ethnic enclaves.

According to our calculations, 48,000 foreign Slavs (45,000 Serbs, 3,000 optant Bunjevats) were settled on the estates of 468,989 cadastral acres in Vojvodina beside the local Slavs. This land was expropriated mostly within 50 km of the border area on Hungarian ethnic territory between 1918 and 1931 *(Fig.36.)*. We estimate that about 16,200 Serbs (military, civil servants, craftsmen, tradesmen etc) were settled in place of the escaped or expelled urban Hungarians during this period. At the same time landless Hungarians (24,000 in 1919) migrated in increasing numbers to the seat of the Dunavska Banovina (Danubian Banate), to Újvidék and to the capital, Belgrade. In the period between 1921 and 1929, 14,442 Hungarians migrated from Yugoslavia to America or Australia (about 10,000 from Vojvodina)[15].

In 1929 the Kingdom of Serbs, Croats and Slovenes was transformed into Yugoslavia openly controlled by the Serbs. The second Yugoslav census was carried out in 1931, in the year of the proclamation of the new constitution, which both disclaimed the presence and prohibited the organisation of national-ethnic minorities. At that time 376,176 people were registered as Hungarians on the territory of present-day Vojvodina. Due to the intensive overseas emigration of Hungarians, their number increased only gradually in the period 1921-1931, in spite of the fact that their natural increase was

---

Baranji. Prilog pitanju demadjarizacije Vojvodine (Assimilatory results of Hungarians in Bácska, Bánát and Baranya. Contributions to the question of Magyarization in Vojvodina), Novi Sad, 41p., Nyigri I. 1941 ibid. 378.p.).

[13] Hollós I. 1932 A régi magyar államterület népességének fejlődése 1910-1930 között (The Development of the Population of the Old Hungarian State Territory between 1910 and 1930), Magyar Statisztikai Szemle, pp. 891-914.

[14] Jojkić, V. 1931 Nacionalizacija Bačke i Banata (Nationalisation of Bácska and Banat), Novi Sad, Nyigri I. 1941 ibid., Gaćeša, N.L. 1968 Agrarna reforma i kolonizacija u Bačkoj (Agrarian reform and colonization in Bácska) 1918-1941, Matica Srpska, Novi Sad, 285p., 1972 Agrarna reforma i kolonizacija u Banatu (Agrarian reform and colonization in Banat) 1918-1941, Matica Srpska, Novi Sad,420p, 1975 Agrarna reforma i kolonizacija u Sremu (Agrarian reform and colonization in Syrmia) 1918-1941, Matica Srpska, Novi Sad, 341p., Mesaroš Š. 1981 Položaj madjara u Vojvodini (Situation of the Hungarians in Vojvodina) 1918-1929. Filozofska Fakulteta, Univerzitet u Novom Sadu, Novi Sad.

[15] Nyigri I. 1941 ibid.

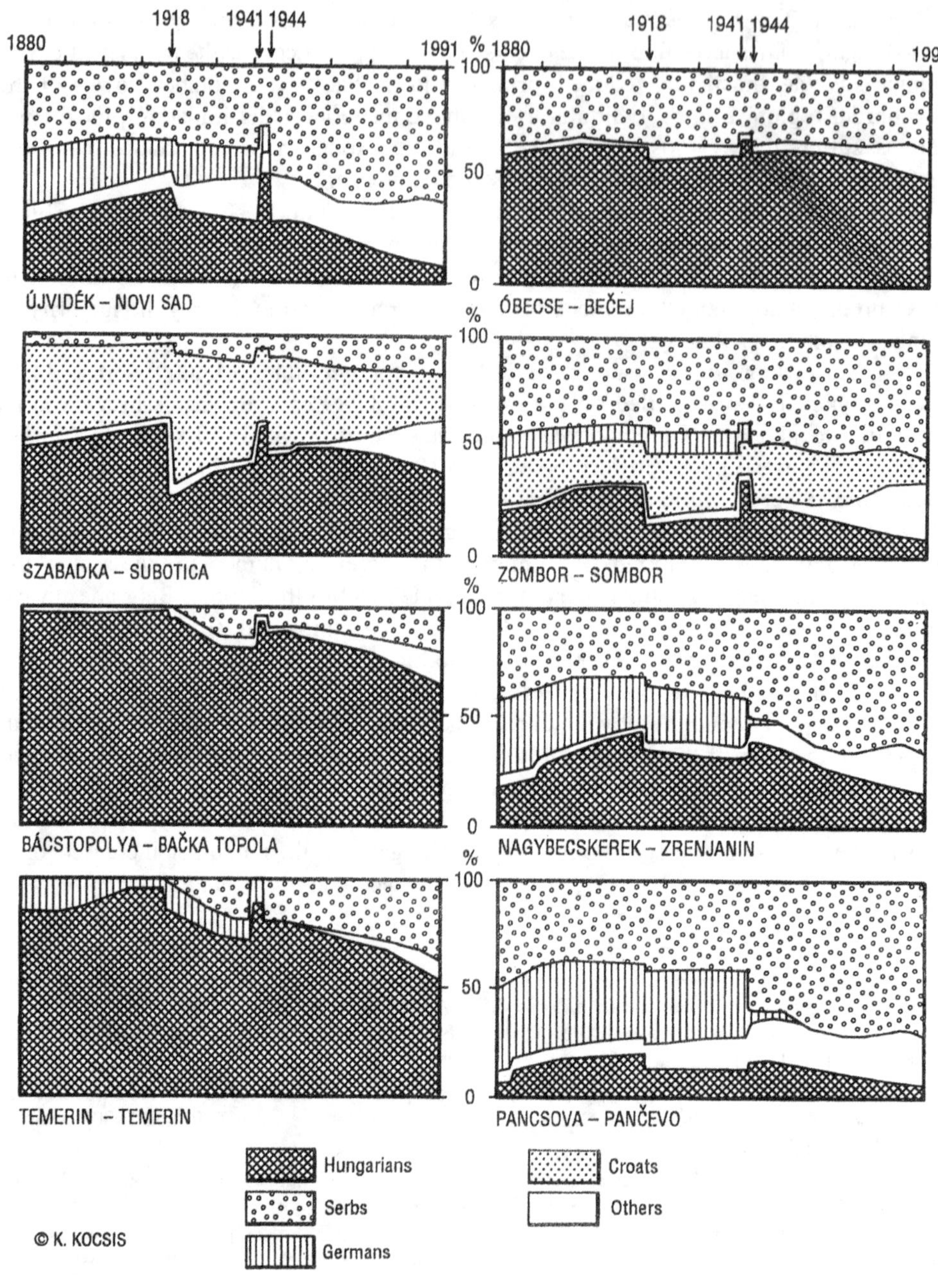

Figure 37. Change in the ethnic structure of population in selected cities and towns of the present-day Vojvodina (1880–1991)

150

considerable (1921-1931: 7,5%,[16]). The ratio of the Hungarians in the total population decreased to 23.2 %, the share of the Serbs — due to the immigration of about 64,000 Serbs — increased to 37.8 %. Serbian colonization significantly transformed not only the demographical-ethnical structure of the province, but the ethnic patterns of certain districts of Hungarian (or German) character. Between 1910 and 1931 the population of 53 present-day settlements (in Bácska 26, in Bánát 21, in Syrmia 6) changed from a Hungarian to a Serbian ethnic majority.

Following the coup overthrowing the Cvetković government (March 27, 1941) Hitler ordered the occupation of Yugoslavia with its very unstable internal situation. On April 6, 1941 German and Italian troops started to invade the country. This formally ended with the capitulation of the Yugoslav Army (April 17, 1941). Meanwhile, on April 10, 1941 the Independent State of Croatia (NDH) was proclaimed. This meant the dissolution of Yugoslavia. On the day (April 11, 1941) that the Germans occupied Syrmia and Bánát, Hungarian troops announced the recapture of SE-Baranya and Bácska with a relative majority population of ethnic Hungarians which had been occupied by Serbian troops in October and November, 1918. Military administration was introduced in the returned territories together with pacification. The internment and deportation of the Serbs[17] who had immigrated after December 31, 1918 also started on the basis of a Hungarian government decree of April 28, 1941. The Hungarian authorities treated the German and Croatian minorities considerately because of Hungarian international relations, but they had their revenge on the Serbs for the humiliation of local Hungarians between 1918 and 1941. Parallel to the emigration and displacement of Serbian colonists and state employees, the Hungarian state policy served to reinforce the local Hungarians *(Fig. 38.)*. Between May 11 and June 20 1941, 13,200 Bukovinian, 161 Moldavian and 481 Hungarian veteran ('Knight' - vitéz) families (2,325 persons) were settled in the evacuated settlements of the former Serbian colonists[18], who had settled there

---

[16] Jojkić, V. 1931 ibid.

[17] In May 1941 10,459, in June 12,000 immigrated Serbs, Jews and political unreliable persons were interned mostly in the camps in Újvidék, Bácstopolya, Bajsa and in some others along the Danube. In the period of 1941-1944 24,921 Balkanian Serbs escaped or were trasported back by the Hungarian authorities from Bácska to Serbia (Milošević, S.D. 1981 Izbeglice i preseljenici na teritoriji okupirane Jugoslavije 1941-1945, Beograd, 276.p., A.Sajti E. 1987 Délvidék (South Hungary) 1941-1944, Kossuth Kiadó, pp.40-44.).

[18] Hungarians from Rumanian Bukovina were settled in the greatest number in Novi Žednik (Hadžićevo, Bácsjózseffalva, 860 persons), Višnjevac (Radivojevićevo, Istenes-Istenvárára, 683), Novo Selo (Bajmočka Rata, Hadikújfalu, 1,264), Rastina (Hadikfalva, 733), Karadjordjevo (Andrásfalva, 927), Bački Sokolac (Bácsandrásszállás, 643), Njegoševo (Istenáldás, 613), Lipar (Sokolac-Emušić, Istensegíts, 1,341), Stepanovićevo (Horthyvára, 1,324), Temerin-Staro Djurdjevo (Hadikföldje, 652) and in Sirig (Hadiknépe, 796 persons) (see Merk Zs. 1995 A bukovinai székelyek Bácskába telepítése az egyházi források tükrében, 1941-1944 (The settlement of the Székely-Hungarians of Bukovina in Bácska in the mirror of the church sources, 1941-1944) —in: Bárth J. (Ed.) Dunáninnen - Tiszáninnen, Kecskemét, pp.57-66.). The "Vitéz- knight" families were settled in Vajska and in Bač-Mali Bač (Vitézfalu). Besides these, the Hungarian government resettled 395 Hungarian families (1,552 persons) in April 1941 from the eastern part of the Independent State of Croatia (NDH) (e.g. Bijeljina, Brčko, Vučijak, Gunja) to Bácska in Stepanovićevo (Horthyvára), Veternik (Hadikliget) and in Sirig (Hadi-

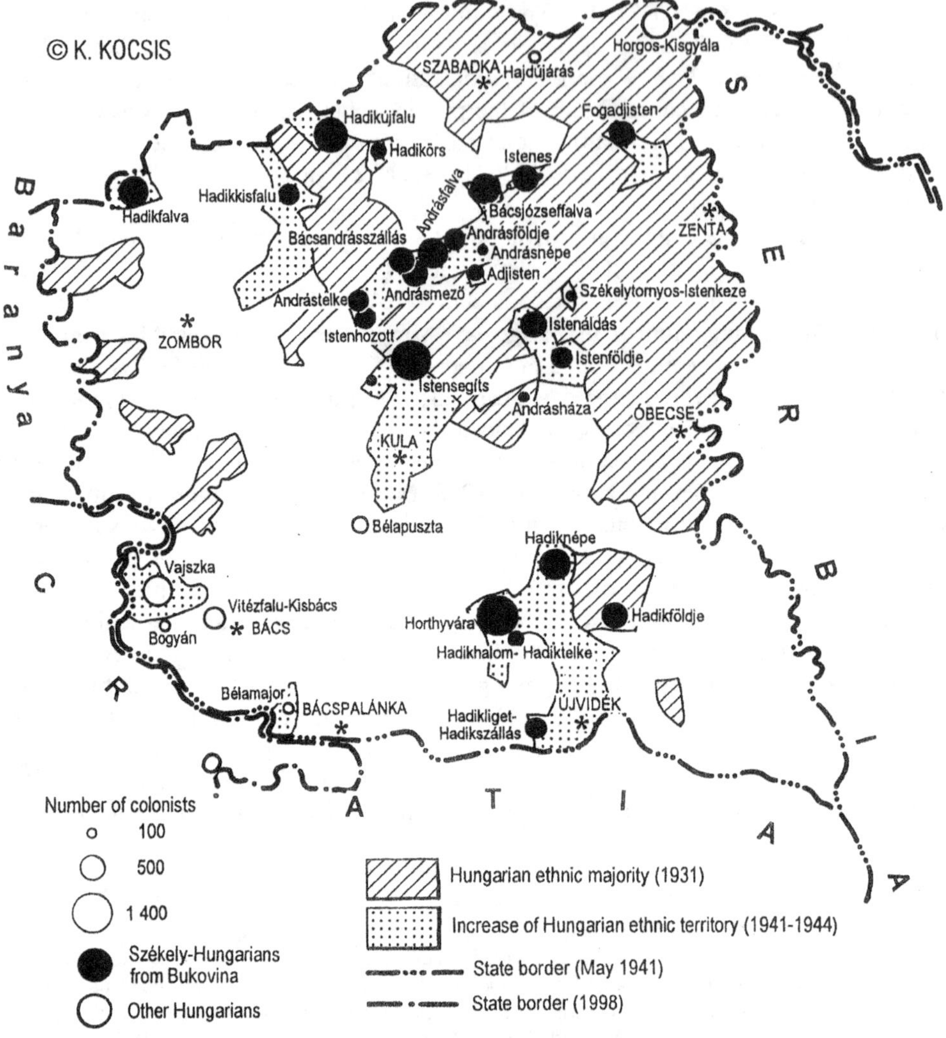

Figure 38. Hungarian colonization in Bácska (1941-1944)

between 1918 and 1931 on the large Hungarian and German estates, following the expulsion of local (mostly Hungarian) farmers and workers.

knépe) (Faluhelyi F. 1943 Baranya, Bácska, Bánát nemzetiségi képe (Ethnic Pattern of Baranya, Bácska and Bánát region), Délvidéki Szemle 1943/8. (aug.) p.342., Albert G. 1983 Emelt fővel (With head erect), Szépirodalmi Könyvkiadó, Budapest, 511p., A.Sajti E. 1987 ibid.).

In addition to the agrarian colonization, the number of Hungarians in Bácska and Baranya increased with the settlement of about 20,000 people (state employees, military personnel, land-owners, craftsmen etc) from the territory of 'Trianon-Hungary'. Due to these events, at the time of the 1941 census — held in the returned southern areas between 11 and 25 October — 45.4 % or 47.2 % of the 789,705 inhabitants of Bácska declared themselves to be Hungarian native speakers or ethnic Hungarians. The proportion of Hungarians in Northeast Bácska reached 74.7 % (in 1931 60.8 %, in 1991 57.4 %) while the area north of the Bajmok-Kula-Bácsföldvár line, excluding the small Bunjevats ethnic area south of Szabadka, became an almost homogeneous ethnic Hungarian area. The number and the ratio of local Hungarians increased in every town, but their ethnic expansion in Szabadka, Újvidék and Zombor was the most remarkable — compared with Yugoslav statistics from 1921 and 1931. Újvidék, the current provincial seat of Vojvodina, was statistically recorded as a city populated by a Hungarian majority of 50.4 % in 1941.

Following the Hungarian recapture of Bácska, Serb-Yugoslav partisans began subversive activity against the Hungarian state. It became more and more intensive after mid-December 1941. Their armed activity was concentrated in the Serbian ethnic block of SE-Bácska, in the historical Sajkás District (e.g. Csurog, Zsablya, Mozsor), where the Hungarian Army, gendarmerie and counterintelligence avenged their losses with increasing brutality. Due to these raids in January 1942 the Serbian population was collectively called to account in many places, such as Óbecse, Szenttamás and Újvidék , 2,550 Serbs, 743 Jews and 47 other people also fell victim[19].

Following the German occupation of Hungary (March 19, 1944), between April and August 16,034 people of Jews were deported to Germany. According to our estimation there were about 10,000 Hungarian native speakers among them. Later in September and October 1944 the escape of Hungarian state employees and colonists and the evacuation of about 60,000 - 70,000 Germans from Bácska started[20].

In October 1944 Soviet, Yugoslavian and Bulgarian troops took the majority of the present-day territory of Vojvodina and under Tito's orders military rule was introduced. Internment of local Germans (about 140,000 persons) and Hungarian men of military age began in 41 concentration camps. Immediately after the take-over, in the first weeks according to different sources[21] and to our calculations based on the analysis of the censuses of 1931, 1941 and 1948, about 16,800 Hungarians fell victim to a Serbian vendetta in Bácska (in Vojvodina it was about 20,000) *(Fig. 39.)*.

During this time, within the framework of the second Yugoslavian agrarian reform, 389,256 hectares of German estates were confiscated, which was 58.2 % of all the

---

[19] A.Sajti E. 1987 ibid. 159.p.

[20] Mirnić,J.1974 Nemci u drugom svetskom ratu (Germans during the World War II),Novi Sad, pp.324-332.

[21] Cseres T. 1993 Vérbosszú Bácskában (Vendetta in Bácska), Magvető, Budapest, 276 p., Matuska M. 1991 A megtorlás napjai (The days of revenge), Montázs Könyvkiadó, Budapest, 376p.

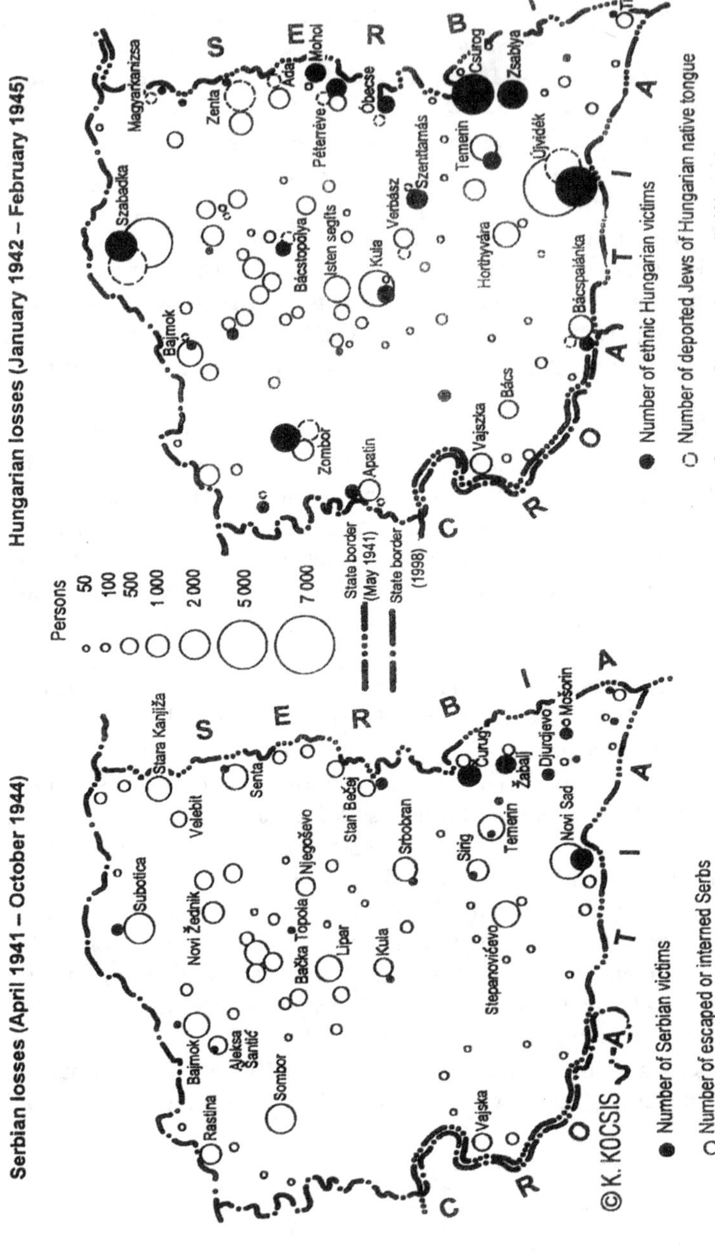

Figure 39. Serbian and Hungarian losses in Bácska (1941 – 1945)

land distributed in Vojvodina[22]. Only 9.9 % of the land redistributed among private individuals was given to Hungarians, while 84 % was given to Serbians (or other 'Yugoslavs'). Between September 1945 and July 1947 225,696 people[23] mostly from the Krajinas in Croatia and Bosnia (162,447 Serbs, 40,176 Montenegrins, 12,000 Macedonians, 7,134 Croats, 2,091 Slovenes etc.) took the unique historical opportunity and settled in the areas of the Germans who had fled or been deported.

According to the first census of the second Yugoslavia (1948) 60.4 % of the 1,640,757 inhabitants of Vojvodina were Serbs, Montenegrins and Croats, due to the vast population movements between 1944 and 1947. With these events, the former ethnic aims of the Serbs were realised and the two-hundred-year-old ethnic balance between the Serbs, Hungarians and Germans of Vojvodina came to an end with the Serbs in an absolute majority in the province, as in the days of the Ottoman-Turkish occupation. In spite of the heavy losses, 428,554 persons declared themselves to be ethnic Hungarian in 1948. According to our calculations based on the censuses of 1931, 1941 and 1948, about 30,800 of these may have been of German origin. They declared themselves Hungarian rather than German, due to the relatively better political situation of the Hungarians, their knowledge of Hungarian and their sympathy with the Hungarians in their misfortune.

During the last half century, in the period between the censuses of 1948 and 1991, the demographical- ethnic geographical situation of the Vojvodina Hungarians was influenced by many objective factors (e.g. natural increase, migration) and subjective factors (e.g. statistical methods of the censuses, state policy towards minorities, mixed marriages, change in ethnic identity, natural assimilation). The birthrate of the local Hungarians between 1948 and 1991 (according to the data of Mirnics K.[24]) together with our estimations for 1948-1953 was 4 %, that is 17,191 persons. The low increase in number was a result of their decreasing fertility (1953: 19.5 ‰, 1991: 11.4 ‰) and their increasing mortality (1953: 11.2 ‰, 1989: 18.0 ‰). This unfavourable demographical trend was connected with the distortion of their age structure, their gradual ageing. The old age index of the Hungarians in Vojvodina increased between 1961 and 1991 from 63.9 to 155.2 ! Similar ageing was noticeable only among the Rumanians, Croats and Slovaks (176.7, 150.0 and 136.4). On the other hand, the demographical situation of the state forming ethnic groups (Serbs, Montenegrins) and the 'Yugoslavs', who did not declare their ethnic affiliation, was relatively favourable[25]. The demographic situation of the Hungarians was very grave in the small ethnic enclaves of the

---

[22] Gaćeša, N.L. 1984 Agrarna reforma i kolonizacija u Jugoslaviji (Agrarian reform and colonization in Yugoslavia) 1945-1948. 1984 Matica Srpska, Novi Sad, 404p.

[23] Gaćeša, N.L. 1984 ibid.

[24] Mirnics K. 1993 Kissebségi sors (Minority destiny), Fórum Könyvkiadó, Novi Sad - Újvidék, 139p.

[25] The old age index (number of the persons over 60 years to 100 persons under 14 years) of other ethnic groups of Vojvodina in 1991: 'Yugoslavs' 32.5, Montenegrins 56.8, Serbs 91.7. Natural increase or decrease of different ethnic groups of Vojvodina in 1989: 'Yugoslavs' +11.3 ‰, Montenegrins +4.2 ‰, Serbs -1.1 ‰, Croats -4.9 ‰, Slovaks -6.4 ‰, *Hungarians -6.6 ‰*, Rumanians -8.0 ‰.

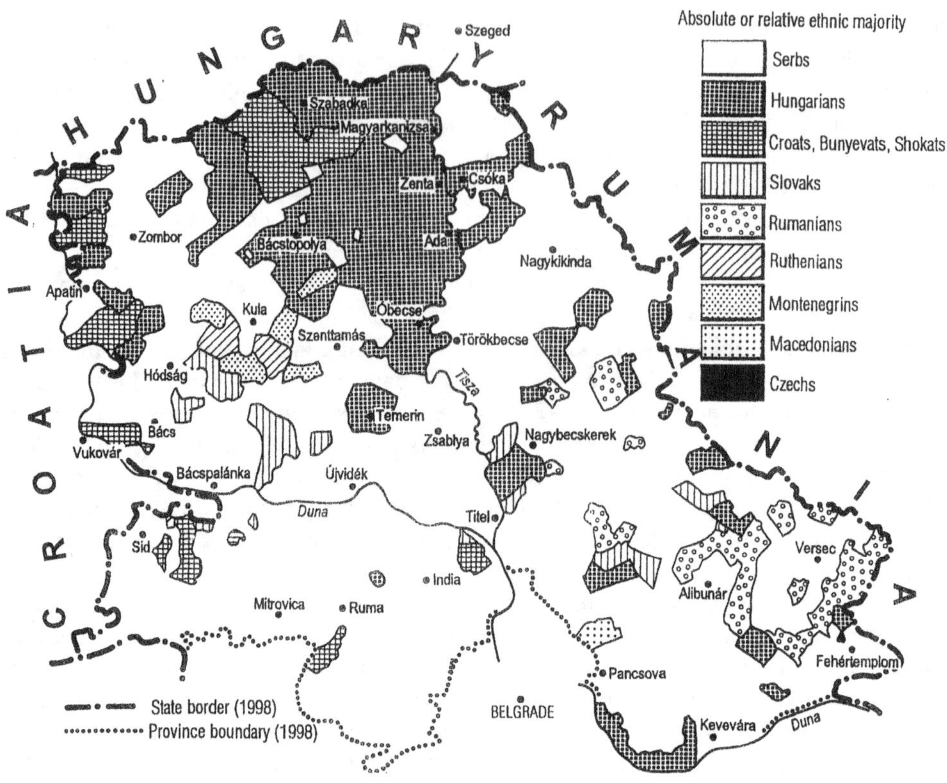

Figure 40. Ethnic map of Vojvodina (1991)

Bánát and Syrmia (Rábé, Magyarmajdány, Torontáltorda, Alsóittebe, Ürményháza, Sándoregyháza, Satrinca etc.). They were in a very unfavourable situation regarding transport, with poor living conditions, and were badly affected by the rural exodus and in having certain villages with a Calvinist religious character (e.g. Pacsér, Bácskossuth-falva).

It was partly the unfavourable migration processes which resulted in only 339,491 ethnic Hungarians being registered at the census of 1991 instead of 445,745 Hungarians — calculated on the basis of the natural increase between 1948 and 1991. During the Yugoslavian socialist urbanisation, in the 'heroic age' of communist, social and economic modernisation, tens of thousands of Hungarians were indirectly forced to migrate from the ethnically closed rural societies to the ethnically and linguistically mainly foreign urban environment. The accelerated migration of the population from the Hungarian ethnic enclaves was directed not only towards the big industrial centres, towns of Serbian character and western countries, but towards the towns of Northeast Bácska in Hungary, too. Due to this internal migration, the share of those Vojvodina Hungarians who lived in the Tisza Region increased from 52.1 % to 59.6 % between

1948 and 1991. The Hungarians of the province suffered much heavier losses due to the international migration, compared to internal population movements. According to our calculations based on natural movement of population and assimilation, Hungarian migration losses between 1948 and 1991 were 69,193 people, 25,228 of whom left in the 80s. The negative migration balance between 1948 and 1961 was mainly due to the emigration of the majority of people of German origin who had declared themselves to be Hungarians in 1948. The first big emigration wave took place between 1965 and 1970. It was considered at that time to be a temporary phenomenon, related to the possibility of foreign employment in western countries and due to the Yugoslavian economic crisis. In these years 16,627 Hungarians — 27.5 % of Vojvodina's 'Guest workers' — were employed abroad[26]. Hungarian migrant workers ("Guest workers") left in the greatest numbers from the communes of Szabadka (2,677), Újvidék (1,419), Bácstopolya (950), Zombor (909) and Ada (906), and left in the greatest ratio from the ethnic enclaves in the Bánát.

During the last decades subjective factors influencing ethnic identity played a very important role in the statistical change in number of ethnic Hungarians. Yugoslavian ethnic policy — seemingly 'exemplary' from the outside — filled the Hungarians with the feeling of having no future and being rootless as a minority group. This was exacerbated by the Yugoslavs discrediting the Hungarian nation which was at that time under Soviet control and a member of the Warsaw Pact. Special attention was paid to the reorganisation and 'internationalisation' of the Hungarian education system and stress was laid on the importance of the Serbian language. Due to this policy, the ratio of Hungarian school children studying in Serbo-Croat increased between the school years 1959/1960 and 1989/1990 from 13.1 % to 20 %[27].

With mixed marriages becoming more and more common natural assimilation increased with a change in the mother tongue and ethnic identity. The ratio of ethnically homogeneous marriages decreased from 82.2 % to 73.6 % between 1956 and 1988. This resulted in the growing assimilation of children of mixed families. Due to state propaganda glorifying Yugoslavia and disparaging the culture and language of national minorities and thanks to mixed marriages the number of the population with an uncertain or absent ethnic identity continued to increase. While at the 1961 census only 0.3 % of the province's population did not want to (or could not) declare their ethnic affiliation, this percentage increased to 9.8 by 1991. Of these, primarily the fairly young, slightly religious minority population, with a very uncertain ethnic identity declared themselves to be 'Yugoslavs'. In 1991, 71.2 % of the so-called 'Yugoslav' population with an undeclared ethnicity were younger than 40 years old.

---

[26] Bukurov, B. 1977 Kolonizacija Bačke za vreme drugog svetskog rata (Colonization of Bácska during the World War II), Glasnik Srpskog Geografskog Društva LI. 1.pp.55-63.

[27] Mirnics K. 1993 ibid.

THE PRESENT TERRITORY OF HUNGARIAN SETTLEMENT IN VOJVODINA

At the time of the last Yugoslavian census (March 31, 1991) — carried out in a turbulent political atmosphere — only 339,491 inhabitants in Vojvodina decided to be open about their Hungarian ethnicity. 174,295 of inhabitants 'without ethnic affiliation' (197,718) declared themselves to be 'Yugoslavs'. In so far as we divide this 'Yugoslav' population proportionately between the ethnic groups, the estimated number of Vojvodina Hungarians would have been 376,000 in 1991.

The majority of Hungarians in Vojvodina (202,000 people) live in their ethnic block along the Tisza River, where they represent 56.5 % of the local population *(Fig. 40.)*. Only seven of the communes had an absolute Hungarian majority in 1991 (Magyarkanizsa, Zenta, Ada, Bácstopolya, Kishegyes, Csóka and Óbecse). Hungarians were in a relative majority in the Szabadka community with 42.7 %, and represented a strong minority in the communities of Temerin (38.7 %) and Törökkanizsa (33.8 %). In keeping with historical events and the unique geographical environment of this region, Hungarians primarily inhabit small towns (26.4 %) and large villages (19.5 %). Thus, the biggest Hungarian community in Vojvodina — and also Serbia — (officially 39,749 but 49,000 according to our estimates) inhabit the city of Szabadka, but more than ten thousand Hungarians live in Zenta, Újvidék, Nagybecskerek, Óbecse, Bácstopolya, Magyar-

Table 28. The largest Hungarian communities in Vojvodina (1991)

Settlements	Population
1. Szabadka / Subotica	39,749
2. Zenta / Senta	17,888
3. Újvidék / Novi Sad	15,778
4. Nagybecskerek / Zrenjanin	14,312
5. Óbecse / Bečej	13,464
6. Bácstopolya / Bačka Topola	11,176
7. Magyarkanizsa / Kanjiža	10,183
8. Ada / Ada	10,010
9. Temerin / Temerin	9,495
10. Csantavér / Čantavir	7,619
11. Horgos / Horgoš	6,022
12. Péterréve / Bačko Petrovo Selo	5,975
13. Nagykikinda / Kikinda	5,932
14. Ómoravica / Stara Moravica	5,546
15. Kishegyes / Mali Idjoš	5,356
16. Mohol / Mol	4,787
17. Zombor / Sombor	4,736
18. Törökbecse / Novi Bečej	4,657
19. Palics / Palić	4,562
20. Szenttamás / Srbobran	4,397
21. Pancsova / Pančevo	4,052

Source: Final data of the Yugoslav census of 1991 (ethnicity).

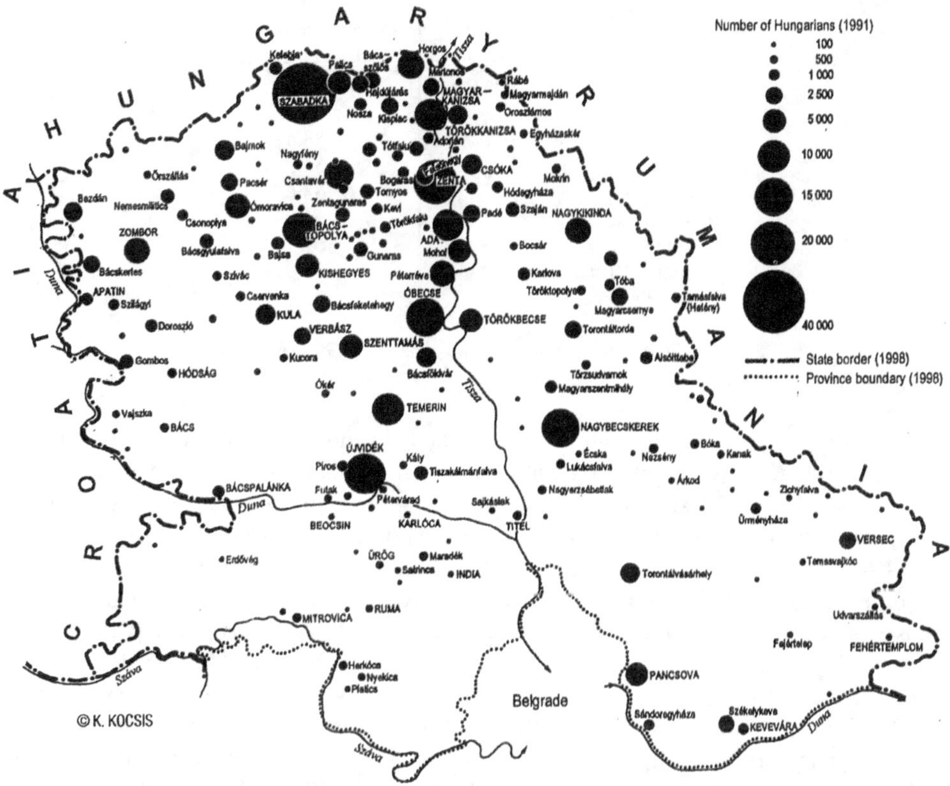

Figure 41. Hungarian communities in Vojvodina (1991)
Source: Census 1991

kanizsa and Ada *(Tab. 28., Fig. 41.).* Besides the Tisza Region, Hungarians represent the majority of the population in only 30 settlements (in Bánát 20, in Syrmia 2, in South and West Bácska 8) *(Tab. 29.).* The fact that 43.4 % of Hungarians live in settlements where they are in the minority (in addition to other previously mentioned demographic characteristics) has had a negative influence on the change in the population of Hungarians in Vojvodina, their sense of identity and their exposure to linguistic assimilation.

Recently, the demographic situation and the ethnic identity of Hungarians in Vojvodina have been influenced by many factors. The emigration of about 25,000 - 30,000 Hungarians[28], escaping from the sometimes ethnically discriminative recruiting policy during the war in Croatia and Bosnia is a threatening phenomenon. Thousands of Hungarians also left Vojvodina due to the economic crisis, poverty, soured relations and the tense atmosphere between the Serbs — particularly Serbian refugees (242,340 per-

---

[28] Mirnics K. 1993 ibid.

Table 29. Towns in Vojvodina with absolute Hungarian majority (1991)

Settlements	Percentage of the Hungarians
1. Magyarkanizsa / Kanjiža	88.2
2. Ada /Ada	82.9
3. Zenta / Senta	78.4
4. Bácstopolya / Bačka Topola	66.9
5. Mohol / Mol	63.6
6. Palics / Palić	61.9
7. Csóka / Čoka	61.1
8. Temerin / Temerin	55.9
9. Óbecse / Bečej	50.6

Source: Final data of the Yugoslav census of 1991 (ethnicity).

sons in 1996)[29] from Croatia and Bosnia — and the minorities (Hungarians, Croats, Bunjevats etc). 75% of former Croatian and Bosnian Serbs looking for a new homeland settled in southwest Bácska and in the Syrmia region between 1991 and 1996. They mainly went to the settlements of their relatives who had colonised Vojvodina between 1945-1948 and to the villages of Croats who had emigrated, fled or been expelled (e.g. Szond, Herkóca, Kukujevci, Gibarac, Novi Slankamen) and of course to the bigger towns which offered favourable living conditions (e.g. 24,487 Serbs in Újvidék, 6 - 8 Thousand in Ruma, Zombor, Pancsova, India and Mitrovica) *(Fig. 42.)*. In the Hungarian ethnic area of the Tisza Region, Serbian refugees were settled in limited numbers (5,891 persons) or were accepted by the local authorities. At the same time Serbs in significant numbers found new homes in towns of Hungarian character and with good transport (e.g. Szabadka 6,401, Temerin 3,444, Óbecse 1,471, Palics 1,359 and Bácstopolya 1,200). Due to this Serbian settlement and the partial emigration and natural decrease of local Hungarians the ratio of the ethnic Hungarians fell below 50 % e.g. in Óbecse, Bácsföldvár, Nemesmilitics and in Palics by 1996. Moreover, in Temerin, Bajmok and Törzsudvarnok the number of Serbs now exceeds that of Hungarians. The recent large-scale immigration of Serbian refugees and the increasing emigration of Croats and Hungarians resulted an important change in the ethnic structure of the population of Vojvodina. According to our estimation the proportion of Serbs reached the 64.3 % (56.8 % in 1991) and of Hungarians fell to 12,9 % (16.9 % in 1991) in 1996 *(Tab. 26.)*.

---

[29] Census of Refugees and Other War-Affected Person in the Federal Republic of Yugoslavia, UNHCR - UN High Commision for Refugees - Commisioner for Refugees of the republic of Serbia, Belgrade, 1996

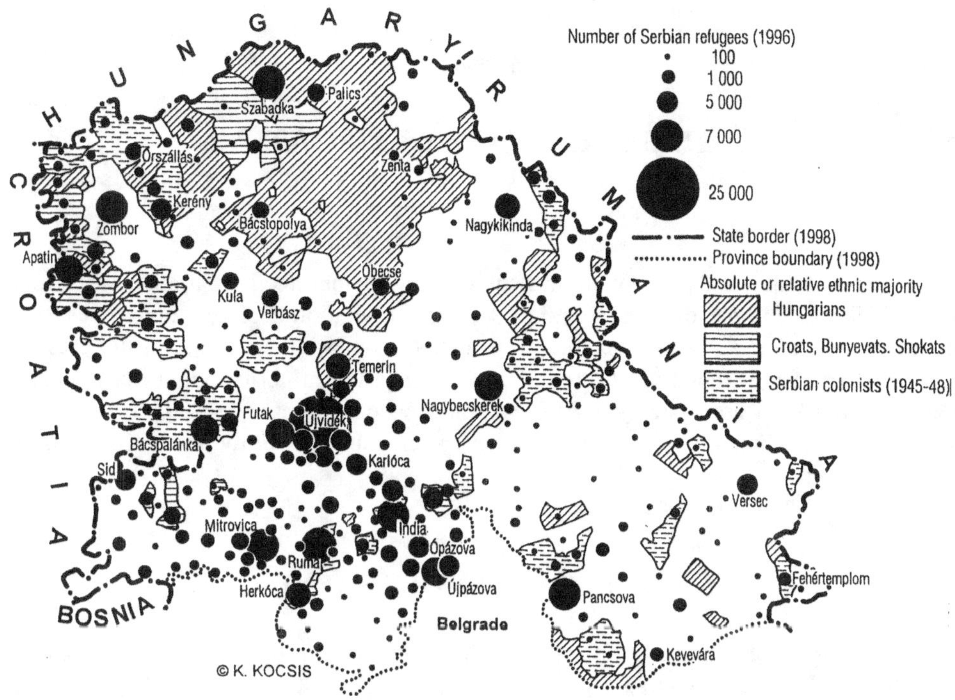

Figure 42. Serbian refugees in Vojvodina (1996)
Source: Census of Refugees and other War-affected Persons in the Federal Republic of Yugoslavia
UNHCR - UN High Commissioner for Refugees - Commissioner for Refugees of the Republic of
Serbia, Belgrade, 1996

Chapter 6

THE HUNGARIANS OF CROATIA

According to the Yugoslav census carried out before the Croatian war broke out in 1991, 22,355 persons, i.e. 0.5 % of the total population declared themselves to be ethnic Hungarian, and 19,687 persons were native Hungarian speakers, in the present-day territory of the Republic of Croatia. This Hungarian minority populace, predominantly scattered in areas struck by the war and occupied between 1991-1997, represented 0.2 % of Hungarians in the Carpathian Basin and 0.8 % of the Hungarian minorities of that region.

THE NATURAL ENVIRONMENT

The autochthonous ethnic Hungarians of Croatia (70.4 %) inhabit the south-western periphery of the Great Hungarian Plain (Nagyalföld): the Danubian Plain of Baranya[1], the Plain of Lower Dráva, the Plain of Valkó (Vuka) and the West-Syrmian loess plateau *(Fig. 43.)*. Diluvial gravel, clay, sandy terraces, and loess platforms emerge above the alluvia of the above-mentioned flatlands. Loess plateaus were terrain especially favourable for the formation of very fertile soils, such as chernozems, along the southern foothills of Hills of Bán (Báni-hegység, Baranyahát, Bansko Brdo)[2] and in the surroundings of Vukovár. The highest elevations of the flatland inhabited by Hungarians are the Hills of Bán (243 m) and the Ridge of Erdőd, the latter can be found at the confluence of the Danube and Dráva rivers (Dályahegy, Čvorkovo brdo, 189 m). The marshy areas along the Danube and the Valkó (Vuka), e.g. Kopácsi-rét (meadow) are refuges which provided security during the destruction of war in the past thousand years. They ensured the survival of the autochthonous Hungarian population several times. The ever-shrinking scattered communities of Hungarians which mainly emerged as a result of migrations in the 19th century (12 % of the Hungarians in Croatia, i.e. 2,690 people)

---

[1] Baranya: historical Hungarian county and region in the southeastern part of Transdanubia cut by a state border since the Trianon Peace Treaty (1920). For the sake of simplicity in this chapter, Baranya means the present-day Croatian territory to be found between the Danube, Dráva and the Hungarian border. It should be mentined that during medieval times Baranya County extended to areas south of the Dráva, to the environs of the present-day Eszék, Valpó and Našice.

[2] Bognar A. 1991 Changes in Ethnic Composition in Baranya, Geographical Papers 8., Institute of Geography, University of Zagreb, 303.p.

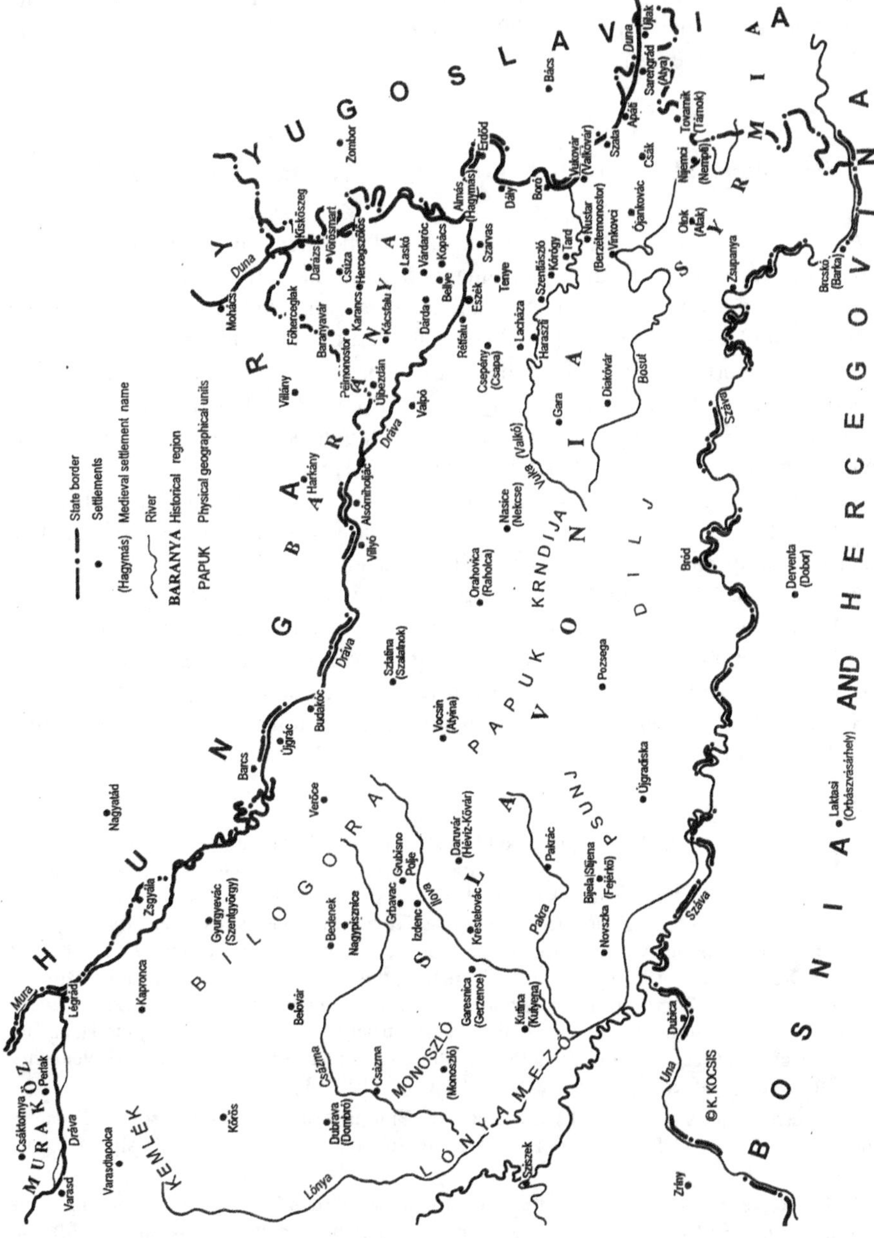

Figure 43. Important Hungarian geographical names in Croatia

163

live in the Belovár and Daruvár basins of Western Slavonia[3] enclosed by the Psunj (984 m), Papuk (953 m), Monoszló (Moslavačka Gora, 489 m) and Kalnik Mountains (643 m) built of crystalline schists and granite, and by Mt. Bilogora (294 m) constituting Pliocene limestone and marl with foothills covered by loessy clay. The most important rivers in these areas are the Császma, Ilova and Pakra.

ETHNIC PROCESSES DURING THE PAST FIVE HUNDRED YEARS

At the end of the 15th century Baranya, and the areas along the Danube and Dráva rivers in present-day Croatia were inhabited predominantly by Hungarians. Slavonian-Croatian and Hungarian settlement areas were separated by marshes and the woodlands of Karašica, Vučica, Vuka and Bosut rivers extending beyond the Dráva river. The most important medieval towns of the Hungarian ethnic area were Baranyavár, Danóc, Karancs, Laskó and Csemény (north of the Dráva), and Villyó, Szeglak, Verőfény, Szombathely, Valpó, Eszék, Drávaszád, Hagymás, Erdőd, Boró, Valkóvár, Berzétemonostor, Szata, Atya and Újlak[4] (south of the river). The basically Hungarian character of the above territory along the Danube and Dráva rivers is evidenced by the tax inventories of the estates at Kórógy, Eszék and Baranyavár of 1469[5]. At that time the number of family names of Hungarian, Slav and uncertain origin in Baranyavár - Karancs was 53.3 %, 5.3 % and 41.4 %, respectively, while it was 52.8 %, 7.5 % and 39.7 % in Eszék. From the second half of the 15th century the ethnic character of the Hungarian settlement area started to change, owing to the northward migration of Croats and Serbs moving there who had escaped from the Turks. Fundamental ethnic changes occurred in present-day eastern Croatia as a result of migrations following the crushing defeats by the Turks (e.g. Mohács 1526, Gara-Gorjani 1537), and the Turkish occupa-

---

[3] Slavonia: In the Middle Ages, as a southwestern principality (Hung. "Tótország", Country of Slavones) it comprised the counties of Zágráb, Varasd, Kőrös, Dubica, Szana and Orbász along the Száva River. Its Roman Catholic inhabitants called themselves Slavones (Slovenes) until the 17th century. Later, under Turkish rule, simultaneously with a massive northward escape of the Croatian population, the name Croatia became a reference to the (formerly Slavonian) area between the Kapela Ranges and the Dráva river, not occupied by the Turks. In this way Slavonia as a region gradually turned into an area east of Zágráb (Zagreb) situated between the Dráva, Danube and Száva rivers, repopulated by Croats and Serbs. It was also called as "Austrian Mesopotamia" during the Hapsburg times, in the 18th century. (See: Szabó P. Z. 1945 Horvátország és mai részei a magyar történelemben - in: Földrajzi Zsebkönyv 1945, Magyar Földrajzi Társaság, pp. 210-233.)

[4]The current names of the listed settlements are: Branjin Vrh, Topolje-Duboševica, Karanac, Lug, Čeminac and Viljevo, Zelčin, Topolina-Bizovac, Lug Subotički, Valpovo, Osijek, Aljmaš, Erdut, Borovo, Vukovar, Nuštar, Sotin, Šarengrad, Ilok.

[5] 1469 Regestrum super taxam ordinariam et extraordinariam in pertinentiis Korogh, Ezeek et Baronyawar nec non Hagmas et Drazad impositam, primo et principaliter in Baranywar. Magyar Országos Levéltár (Hungarian National Archive) Dl. 32.365 (See: Mažuran, I. 1980 Porezni popis grada i vlastelinstva Osijek i njegove okolice 1469. Godine (Tax census of the town and estate Eszék and of its environs in 1469), Starina Kn. 58 / 1980., JAZU, Zegreb, pp.125-165.)

tion of present-day Baranya and Slavonia between 1526-1552. There was a massive flight of Catholic Croats-Slavones to the north, from the occupied areas, situated east of the Sziszek-Császma-Verőce line, and an organised resettlement of people from the Slavonian estates of the Zrínyi, Batthyány, Erdődy, and Nádasdy families to Western Hungary (mainly to present-day Burgenland)[6]. The overwhelming majority of those Catholic Slavones-Croats staying in their former place of residence (e.g. three-quarters of them in the Pozsega Basin)[7], especially noblemen and town dwellers who stayed for economic and social reasons, became converted to the Islamic faith. In the first half of the 16th century there were heavy losses (killing, flight), and conversion to Islam (especially in towns[8]) among the Hungarians living along the Belgrád-Eszék-Baranyavár-Buda military route. In remote areas lying closer to the rivers (Danube, Dráva), in the marshland of Vuka-Palacsa and in the vicinity of Kórógy, however, Hungarians survived and were converted to Protestantism (Reformed Church) from the second half of the 16th century. According to the tax inventory carried out by the Turks in 1554, of the 1,131 taxpayers in present-day Croatian Baranya 69.9 % bore Hungarian and 9.2 % Slavic family names and 20.9 % of them were of uncertain ethnic origin[9]. At that time 47 of the villages in the region were Hungarian, and 1 (Gragoróca) had a Slavic majority. The most populous Hungarian communities were Laskó, Újfalu (today Darázs), Hercegszőlős and Vörösmart near the marshes along the Danube. In Baranyavár and Karancs, which lay along the military route between Eszék and Mohács, and which were earlier considered to be the flourishing towns of the region, the number of taxpayers dropped from 67 to 10 and from 139 to 43 between 1469 and 1554. Following the voluntary migration and resettlements by the Turks during the 16th century, the share of the Slavic population (Serbs, Vlachs-Iflaks) gradually expanded. According to a census from 1591, in present-day Croatian Baranya 36 settlements were considered Hungarian, 8 settlements had a Slavic majority and 3 settlements were ethnically mixed[10].

On the territories south of the Dráva, Orthodox Vlach-Serbs leading a pastoral-military way of life were settled from Bosnia in place of the Slavones-Croats and Hun-

---

[6] Pavičić, S. 1953 Podrijetlo hrvatskih i srpskih naselja i govora u Slavoniji (Origin of the Croatian and Serbian settlements and of dialects in Slavonia), Djela JAZU 47., Zagreb, 204.p.

[7] Karger, A. 1963 Die Entwicklung der Siedlungen im Westlichen Slawonien, Kölner Geographische Arbeiten 15., Franz Steiner Verlag, Wiesbaden, 46.p.

[8] This was chiefly due to similar conversions in Újlak, one of the most flourishing towns of medieval Hungary, where 386 Muslim and 18 Christian households were recorded in 1572. (See: Popović, D. 1957 Srbi u Vojvodini (Serbs in Vojvodina) I-III. Matica Srpska, Novi Sad, 261.p.)

[9] Káldy-Nagy Gy. 1960 Baranya megye XVI. századi török adóösszeírásai (Turkish tax-censuses of Baranya County in 16th century), Magyar Nyelvtudományi Társaság, Budapest. This inventory did not contain data about the Hungarian settlements of Kopács, Bellye, Várdaróc and Csamafalva.

[10] Bognár A. 1991 Changes in ethnic composition in Baranya, Geographical Papers 8. (Zagreb), 311.p.

garians[11] who had fled. In Slavonia there was a massive resettlement of Serbs as border guards. The target areas were the entrances to the Pozsega Basin and the Papuk, Krndija and Dilj mountains, an area between the Ilova River (a Christian-Moslem front line) and the mountains of Papuk and Psunj, which at that time was called Little Wallachia (Mala Vlaška)[12]. With the movement of the Moslem population (e.g. Bosnians, Turks), and the conversion of the majority of Hungarians and Croats to Islam ("renegades"), most of the Slavonian towns counted as Moslem in the 16th century[13]. According to the number of houses, the largest towns of the region in 1620 were Eszék, Pozsega (1,000-1,000), Verőce (400), Pakrác (350), Orahovica, Velika (200-200) and Valkóvár-Vukovár (100)[14]. Of these Eszék, a bridgehead of strategic importance, was overwhelmingly Hungarian even in 1663 (though most of the people converted to Islam)[15].

The present-day territory of Eastern Croatia was liberated from Ottoman-Turkish occupation between 1684 and 1688, as a consequence of which the local Muslims (not only the Turks but also the "renegades", i.e. the Islamized Slavs and Hungarians) fled to Bosnia[16]. Almost immediately Catholic Croats entered the liberated Slavonia. From 1690 onwards, there was a massive influx of Orthodox Serbs (led by patriarch Arsenija Crnojević III.), Roman Catholic Shokatses[17] (from the environs of Srebrenica) and Bunevatses following the recapture of Serbia and Bosnia by the Turks and the retreat of Hapsburg troops. Between 1686 and 1696 the population of the freed territories which had grown by tens of thousands, and which had been the base of operations suffered severely from brutality of the Hapsburg troops. They passed through demanding food and shelter, which raised taxes, causing many people to emigrate[18]. As a consequence of the destruction at the end of the 17th century, the number of villages with a Hungarian ethnic majority decreased from 36 to 14 between 1591 and 1696. At the 1696 census 5 ethnic Serb and 4 Croat-Shokats villages were recorded. At that time 57 % of the registered 449 families lived in Hungarian villages, while 23.8 % of them

---

[11] Serbs increasingly moved into the place of Hungarians who had fled from the following settlements: Ilok, Šarengrad, Vukovar, Borovo, Dalj, Erdut, Aljmaš, Osijek, Bobota, Tenja stb. (Popović, D. 1957 ibid. 110.p.)

[12] Karger, A. 1963 ibid. 64.p. From these environs of Daruvár and Pakrác, being the borderland between the Hapsburg and Ottoman Empires, parallel with the recurring destruction between 1587 and 1600, the Hapsburg troops made Serbs move to the Austrian side of the border, and settled them in the vicinity of Kapronca

[13] Karger, A. 1963 ibid. 70.p.

[14] Smičiklas, T. 1891-92 Spomenici o Slavoniji u XVII. vijeku (Rememberances about Slavonia in 17th century) (1640-1702), Zagreb, 4.p.

[15] Karácson I. 1904 Evlia Cselebi török világutazó magyarországi utazásai (Travels of Turkish world traveller, Evlia Chelebi in Hungary) 1660-1664, MTA, Budapest, 179.p.

[16] As a result the population number of e.g. Pozsega, site of a former sanjak, had dropped from 15,000 down to 220 by 1702. (See: Karger, A. 1963 ibid. 28.p.)

[17] Shokatses chiefly moved to Izsép, Dályok, Hercegmárok and Baranyavár (on the territory of Baranya) and to Újlak, Tárnok and Szata in the Croatian Syrmia (Szerémség, Srijem).

[18] Taba I. 1941 Baranya megye népessége a XVII. század végén (Population of Baranya County at the end of 17th century), Pécs, 9.p.

resided in Serb villages and 19.2 % were inhabitants of smaller Croat settlements[19]. The former medieval Hungarian settlement area south of the Danube and Dráva rivers had completely broken up and became ethnically Serb, especially in the areas of Eszék and Valkóvár. In 1697 only 66 Hungarian families belonged to the Reformed Church at Szentlászló, Kaporna[20] and Kórógy[21] in the Vuka marshland. The Islamized Hungarian population disappeared almost totally from the towns giving way to a new wave of Serb and Shokats refugees, or to Germans who settled down immediately after the liberation (i.e. at the Eszék fortress). At the turn of the 17th and 18th centuries, spontaneous and organized resettlement was disturbed by an anti-Hapsburg war of independence led by Prince F. Rákóczi II (1703 - 1711). Serbs fought on the side of the Austrian emperor, causing serious damage,[22] so in a punishing campaign by the Rákóczi troops (1704) not only Serb villages in Bácska but those in Baranya were burnt down and their inhabitants driven away. Following the Szatmár Peace Treaty (1711) the Serbs returned and the resettlement of Bosnian Catholics (e.g. Shokatses) proceeded under the auspices of the Franciscan Order. The large estate owners of Baranya and Slavonia (e.g. those with a centre in Bellye belonging to the Savoy family, in Dárda to the Veteranis, later an Eszterházy estate, in Erdőd to the Pálffy family, in Valkóvár to the Eltz family, in Újlak to the Odeschalchis, later Pejačević) and the imperial chamber, continued their policy of resettling Catholic Germans and Croats on depopulated territories or those which were inhabited by a sparse pastoral-military Serb population, i.e. areas to be turned into fertile cropland. As a result of these migrations the autochthonous Hungarians gradually became an ethnic minority in the first half of the 18th century, among Croats and Serbs. While in 1720, of the 580 registered heads of households on the territory of present-day Croatian Baranya 53.4 % bore a Hungarian family name[23], in 1752, of the 1,717 households only 29.7 % could be considered Hungarian[24]. In the period between 1720 and 1752 the number of Croats increased from 24.9 % to 31.6 %, that of Serbs rose from 20.3 % to 25.9 %, and the number of Germans increased from 1.4 % to 12.8 %. Germans mainly from Wurttemberg, Baden, Hessen, and Bavaria settled in Pélmonostor, Dárda, Baranyabán, Baranyaszentistván and Keskend (in the Baranya region), or moved to Eszék-Újváros, Új-Vukóvár, Vinkovci and the surrounding villages (in Slavonia). Ruthenians settled on the estate belonging to the archbishop of Kalocsa (Petrovci, Miklusevci) in the environs of Vukóvár in 1765[25]. As a result of the above settlements the area situated north of the present-day towns of Donji Miholjac - Vinkovci - Šid, which

---

[19] Taba I. 1941 ibid. pp.22-27.

[20] Presumably together with Haraszti and Lacháza.

[21] Popović, D. 1957 ibid. II. 52.p.

[22] E.g. Sacking and burning down of town Pécs by the Serbs on February 1 and 2. 1704.

[23] Acsády I. 1896 ibid. pp.16-19. By 1720 the Hungarian ethnic area, similar to the present situation retreated to the area between the Hills of Bán and the Danube. At that time most of the Hungarian households were recorded at Kopács (39), Karancs (38), Várdaróc (33), Laskó (31), Hercegszőlős (26) and Vörösmart (25).

[24] Bognár A. 1991 ibid. 312.p.

[25] Popović, D. 1957 ibid. II. 53.p.

used to be Hungarian during the Middle Ages, acquired a mosaic-like ethnic pattern (with Croats, Serbs, Hungarians and Germans as the main ethnic components) similar to Vojvodina in Serbia. The ethnic spatial pattern formed by the end of the 18th century in the present-day area of Eastern Croatia did not change significantly until the second half of the 19th century. In Baranya Croats retained their relative majority over Hungarians between the mid-18th and early 19th centuries and gained an absolute majority in the counties of Pozsega, Verőce and in the military border districts of Croatia (53.1 - 50,9 %) by the first half of the 19th century[26]. By 1840, 1,605,730 people lived in the area of the the counties and border zones south of the Dráva (later Croatia-Slavonia) and the Hungarian Coast of the Adriatic Sea (the towns of Fiume-Rijeka, Buccari-Bakar and their environs); 67 % of them were Croats and 31.4 % Serbs. At that time Germans numbered 13,226, Hungarians 5,151, Slovaks 3,558 and Jews 1,559[27]. At that time the most populous town of Croatia was Eszék, a bridgehead on the Dráva and a market centre of this fertile agricultural region, an overwhelmingly German-Croatian settlement with 12,562 inhabitants. The Croatian capital, Zágráb (12,231) was second to it. 36,706 people lived on the territory of present-day Baranya in Croatia; 34.1 % were Hungarians, 28.9 % Croats, 22.4 % Germans and 13.3 % Serbs *(Tab. 30.)*. The largest villages (with 2,000-1,900 inhabitants) of the time in Croatia were Dárda (with a German-Hungarian-Serbian mixed population), the German and Serbian village of Baranyabán and the Hungarian village Vörösmart. The largest Hungarian communities (with 1,900 - 1,100 persons) in Baranya were Vörösmart, Karancs, Kopács and Laskó. In the first half of the 19th century Hungarian colonists from the Bácska and Transdanubia were added sporadically (in Ójankovác, Csák, Antunovác) to the autochthonous Hungarians of Slavonia who survived the devastations of the 16th and 17th centuries[28].

The economic boom which gradually emerged after the abolition of serfdom (1848), the Austro-Hungarian Compromise (1867) and the Hungaro-Croatian Compromise (1868) and, subsequently the dissolution of the Croato-Slavonian Military Border districts[29] between 1871 and 1881, accelerated the mobility of the population and this resulted in considerable changes in the ethnic pattern with certain typical areas of immigration. During the last decades of the 19th century and at the turn of the century, there was a massive emigration of Slovaks and Ruthenians from Upper Hungary, of Germans

---

[26] In 1840, according to Fényes E. 1842 ibid.

[27] Fényes E. 1842 ibid.

[28] See Ruh Gy. 1941 Magyarok Horvátországban (Hungarians in Croatia), Szociográfiai Értekezések Tára 4., Magyar Szociográfiai Intézet, Budapest.

[29] A gradual abolition of the southern Military Border districts of the Hapsburg Empire (after 1867 Austro-Hungarian Monarchy) was motivated by an outdated military system. It was uneconomic in character and was losing its function in foreign affairs (which resulted in an extremely weakened Ottoman Empire as a neighbour and the elimination of the "Turkish menace", occupation of Bosnia-Herzegovina by the Monarchy in 1878 and the emergence of Serbia as an independent state). From the Hungarian side the measure was favoured by the supporters of (Austro-Hungarian) dualism in order to get rid of a military border zone inhabited by Serbs, Croats, Rumanians and Germans under the auspices of the Viennese Ministry of Defense as a potential internal source of danger in the event of political change.

Table 30. Ethnic structure of the population of Croatian Baranya (1840 - 1992)

Year	Total population	Croats	Serbs	**Hungarians**	Germans	Yugo-slavs	Others
1840	36,706	10,600	4,900	**12,500**	8,230		476
1880	45,329	10,574	5,425	**14,230**	13,156		1,944
1890	48,885	10,701	6,276	**17,184**	14,304		420
1900	48,758	10,614	5,873	**17,325**	14,321		625
1910	51,616	9,912	6,267	**20,381**	14,269		787
1921	49,452	9,434	6,170	**16,638**	16,253		957
1931	52,846	10,893	10,434	**13,973**	15,751		1,795
1941	51,781	8,492	7,813	**18,648**	14,238		2,590
1948	54,190	19,328	11,465	**17,025**	4,500		1,872
1953	50,866	17,984	11,607	**16,012**	3,228	263	1,772
1961	56,087	23,514	13,698	**15,303**		115	3,457
1971	56,322	23,283	15,614	**13,473**	773	1,046	2,133
1981	53,409	19,136	12,857	**9,920**	410	8,397	2,689
1991	54,265	22,740	13,851	**8,956**	433	4,265	4,020
1992	39,482	7,689	23,458	**6,926**		490	919

Year	Total popul. %	Croats %	Serbs %	**Hung. %**	Germ. %	Yug. %	Other %
1840	100.0	28.9	13.3	**34.1**	22.4	0	1.3
1880	100.0	23.3	12.0	**31.4**	29.0	0	4.3
1890	100.0	21.9	12.8	**35.2**	29.0	0	1.1
1900	100.0	21.8	12.0	**35.5**	29.0	0	1.7
1910	100.0	19.2	12.1	**39.5**	28.0	0	1.2
1921	100.0	19.1	12.5	**33.6**	33.0	0	1.8
1931	100.0	20.6	19.7	**26.4**	30.0	0	3.3
1941	100.0	16.4	15.1	**36.0**	27.0	0	5.5
1948	100.0	35.7	21.2	**31.4**	8.3	0	3.4
1953	100.0	35.4	22.8	**31.5**	6.3	0.5	3.5
1961	100.0	41.9	24.4	**27.3**	0	0.2	6.2
1971	100.0	41.3	27.7	**23.9**	1.4	1.9	3.8
1981	100.0	35.8	24.1	**18.6**	0.8	16	4.7
1991	100.0	41.9	25.5	**16.5**	0.8	7.9	7.4
1992	100.0	19.5	59.4	**17.5**	0	1.2	2.4

Sources: 1840: Fényes E. 1851 Magyarország geographiai szótára I-II., Pest, 1880 - 1910, 1941: Hungarian census data (mother/native tongue), 1921, 1931: Yugoslav census data (mother /native tongue), 1948 - 1991: Yugoslav census data (ethnicity), 1992: Serbian local census (Ćurčić, S. - Kicošev, S. 1993 Development of the population of Baranya, Beli Manastir - Novi Sad)
Remarks: The Croats include the Bunyevats, Shokats and Dalmatinian ethnic groups and the "Serbs of Roman Catholic religious affiliation" in 1890.

(Swabians) from South Hungary to America, and Szeklers of Transylvania to the neighbouring Rumania. The ever-increasing Hungarian population surplus of Bácska and Transdanubia (entrepreneurial smallholders and landless people) moved to Slavonia in great numbers, and purchased still neglected land and property from the former military personnel who were unable or unwilling to cultivate the land[30]. The massive immigration of peasants, servants working on the large estates, industrial workers and civil servants also added to the number of Hungarians. At the beginning the spontaneous agrarian immigration of Hungarians from Bácska and Transdanubia was restricted to the environs of the Dráva and the Danube, e.g. to the Verőce, Szlatina and Vukovár districts, but then it extended to Belovár-Körös and Pozsega counties. This voluntary economic migration which spread Hungarians over the Croatian and Serbian settlement area of Slavonia was in four main directions[31]: 1. From Somogy, Tolna, Zala and Vas counties to Belovár-Körös County (to the basin between Bilogora, Monoszló mountains (Moslavačka Gora) and Ilova river; 2. From the Transdanubian region to Pozsega County (the districts of Daruvár and Pakrác); 3. From Somogy, Győr and Baranya counties to Verőce County (the districts of Verőce, Szlatina, Alsómiholjác, Nasice, Diakóvár and Eszék); 4. From the Bácska region mainly to the Vukovár district of Syrmia (Szerém) County. As a result of this intensified immigration, the number of Hungarians rose from 15,360 to 66,045 in the eastern part of present-day Croatia between 1840 and 1910, and grew from 4,951 to 45,664 in East Slavonia[32]. The number of native Hungarian speakers was 105, 948 on the territory of the contemporary Croatian-Slavonian Kingdom[33], and 121,408 in the area of present-day Croatia in 1910 *(Tab. 31.)*. There was an explosive population boom (a 14 - 16-fold increase) among urban Hungarians (Eszék, Vukovár, Vinkovci) and in rural areas caused by migration and the high natural increase[34] *(Tab. 32., Fig. 44.)*. At the same time, the number of autochthonous Hungarians (e.g. those in Kórógy, Szentlászló, Haraszti, Lacháza) rose by a "mere" 66 % between 1840 and 1910. Such an intense growth of the Hungarian population and

---

[30] Margitai J. 1918 A horvát-és szlavón magyarok sorsa, nemzeti védelme és a magyar-horvát testvériség (Destiny, defence of the Hungarians in Croatia-Slavonia and the Hungarian-Croatian fraternity), Budapest, pp.21-22.

[31] Margitai J. 1918 ibid., pp.21-22., Ruh Gy. 1941ibid. 10.p. In the choice of a new place of residence, when purchasing a new small holding, a natural environment similar to one's homeland was one of the criteria also taken into account.

[32] Eastern part of Croatia: territory of the Republic of Croatia situated east of the Szlatina-Okučani line. East Slavonia:see 'Eastern part of Croatia' without Baranya.

[33] Croato-Slavonian Kingdom: as part of the Hungarian Holy Crown between 1868 and 1918 it comprised counties situated between the Adriatic coast and Dráva River. A considerable difference from the present-day territory of Croatia is that it included Syrmia in present-day Serbia, but it failed to contain Baranya, Muraköz (Medjimurje), Istria, Fiume (Rijeka) and Dalmatia.

[34] During the period between 1906 and 1910 on the territory of Croatia-Slavonia the average annual natural increase of Hungarians was 17.4 ‰, that of Croats 12.7 ‰, of Serbs 13.5 ‰. (Ruh Gy. 1941 ibid. 7.p.)

170

Table 31. Ethnic structure of the population on the present territory of Croatia (1900-1991)

Year	Total population	Croats	Serbs	Hungarians	Italians	Germans	Slovenes	Muslims	Czechs	Slovaks	Ruthenians, Ukrainians	Yugoslavs	Others
1900	3,160,406	2,159,888	548,302	**101,617**	140,365	115,948	28,485		31,484	7,660	2,075		24,582
1910	3,460,201	2,371,634	575,922	**121,408**	155,749	119,587	28,179		31,479	9,807	5,596		40,840
1921	3,447,594	2,374,752	584,058	**81,835**	210,336	99,808	32,023		42,444		3,883		18,455
1931	3,785,455	2,641,144	636,518	**69,671**	230,000	99,670	37,143	3,565	37,366	7,172	4,242		18,964
1948	3,753,524	2,972,994	545,568	**51,297**	74,359	10,143	37,798	1,180	28,903	10,111	6,375		14,796
1953	3,936,019	3,113,236	591,534	**47,480**	32,517	11,122	42,064		35,503			15,954	46,609
1961	4,159,690	3,339,866	624,935	**42,329**	21,101		38,973	3,111	23,390	8,129	62	15,750	42,044
1971	4,426,221	3,513,647	626,789	**35,488**	17,433	2,791	32,497	18,457	19,001	6,482	6,521	84,118	62,997
1981	4,601,469	3,454,661	531,502	**25,439**	11,661	2,175	26,136	23,740	15,061	6,533	5,836	379,057	119,668
1991	4,784,265	3,736,356	581,663	**22,355**	21,303	2,635	22,376	43,469	13,086	5,606	5,747	106,041	223,628

Year	Total popula. %	Croats %	Serbs %	Hung. %	Ital. %	Germ. %	Sloven. %	Musl. %	Czech%	Slovaks %	Ruth. %	Yugosl. %	Oth. %
1900	100.0	68.3	17.3	**3.2**	4.4	3.7	0.9		1.0	0.2	0.1		0.9
1910	100.0	68.5	16.6	**3.5**	4.5	3.5	0.8						2.6
1921	100.0	68.9	16.9	**2.4**	6.1	2.9	0.9		1.2		0.1		0.6
1931	100.0	69.8	16.8	**1.8**	6.1	2.6	1.0	0.1					1.8
1948	100.0	79.2	14.5	**1.4**	2.0	0.3	1.0	0.0					1.6
1953	100.0	79.1	15.0	**1.2**	0.8	0.3	1.1		0.9			0.4	1.2
1961	100.0	80.3	15.0	**1.0**	0.5		0.9	0.1	0.6	0.2		0.4	1.0
1971	100.0	79.4	14.2	**0.8**	0.4	0.1	0.7	0.4	0.4	0.2	0.1	1.9	1.4
1981	100.0	75.1	11.5	**0.5**	0.2	0.1	0.6	0.5	0.3	0.1	0.1	8.2	2.8
1991	100.0	78.1	12.2	**0.5**	0.4	0.1	0.5	0.9	0.3	0.1	0.1	2.2	4.6

Sources: Stanovništvo prema vjeroispovjedi (1880-1890) i narodnosti (1880-1991) po naseljima (manuscript), Državni Zavod za Statistiku, Zagreb, 1995
1900, 1910: Hungarian-Croatian, Austrian census data (mother/native tongue, language affiliation), 1921, 1931: Yugoslav census data (mother/native tongue), 1948-1991: Yugoslav census data (ethnicity).

Table 32. Change in the number of Hungarians in different parts of East Croatia (1881 - 1991)

Year	Baranya	Kórógy & environs	Eszék, Vukovár, Vinkovci	East-Slavonian diasporas	West-Slavonian diasporas
1880	14,230	2,800	2,517	13,148	10,088
1890	17,184	2,950	3,223	23,846	..
1900	17,325	3,109	4,431	30,971	27,242
1910	20,381	3,321	6,670	35,673	29,950
1921	16,638	3,370	3,878	23,842	22,738
1931	13,973	3,188	4,959	21,990	17,371
1941	18,648	3,100	4,860	21,992	..
1948	17,025	3,061	3,320	12,885	11,984
1953	16,012	2,991	3,213	11,295	10,507
1961	15,303	2,775	3,699	8,470	8,423
1971	13,473	2,374	3,286	6,153	6,271
1981	9,920	1,640	2,424	4,185	3,836
1991	8,956	1,445	2,298	3,196	2,747
1991	8,791	1,438	1,924	2,466	1,422

Sources: Calculations of K. Kocsis based on Stanovništvo prema vjeroispovjedi (1880-1890) i narodnosti (1880-1991) po naseljima (manuscript), Državni Zavod za Statistiku, Zagreb, 1995
Remarks: Italic figures: mother/native tongue data. Kórógy & environs = Kórógy, Szentlászló, Haraszti and Lacháza (Slavonian autochtonous Hungarian villages). East-Slavonian diaspores= Hungarians east of the line of Szlatina-Okučani, excluding "Kórógy & environs" and the towns Eszék, Vukovár and Vinkovci. West-Slavonian diaspores= Hungarians in the former communes Verőce, Daruvár, Pakrác, Novszka, Grubisno Polje, Garesnica, Kutina, Belovár and Csázma.

the rule of K. Khuen-Héderváry, the Croatian Ban[35] between 1883 and 1903 and hated by the Croats, provoked bitter and nationalistic resistance from the Croatian authorities, and of the local Croats and Serbs on the territory of the Croato-Slavonian Kingdom which belonged to the Hungarian Holy Crown. This frequently led to violent clashes between them and the newcomer Hungarians. The chauvinist representatives of south Slavic separatism considered the growing Hungarian peasantry who were buying up more and more land, as agents of "violent Magyarization" and used all means to prevent them from asserting their cultural and linguistic rights, and to render their living conditions as difficult as possible[36].

---

[35] Ban= governor / viceroy of Croatia. The activities of K. Khuen-Héderváry as Croatian Ban were focused on a struggle against the national aspirations of Croats, and for the assertion of Hungarian political and economic influence, not ruling out autocratic rule and violence. In the course of his activities he successfully applied the method "divide et impera" in playing off Serbs against Croats.

[36] See: Makkai B. 1994 Református magyar iskola és szeretetház (Calvinist Hungarian school and rest-home) Vukovár (1904-1919) - in: Arday L. (Ed.) Fejezetek a horvátországi magyarok történetéből, Teleki László Alapítvány, Budapest, pp.73-84., Makkai B. - Makkai Várkonyi I. 1994 A "Szlavóniai Magyar Újság" és a horvátországi magyarság (The newspaper „Szlavóniai Magyar Újság" and the Hungarians in Croatia) (1908-1918) - in: Arday L. (Ed.) Fejezetek a horvátországi magyarok történetéből, Teleki László Alapítvány, Budapest, pp.85-108.

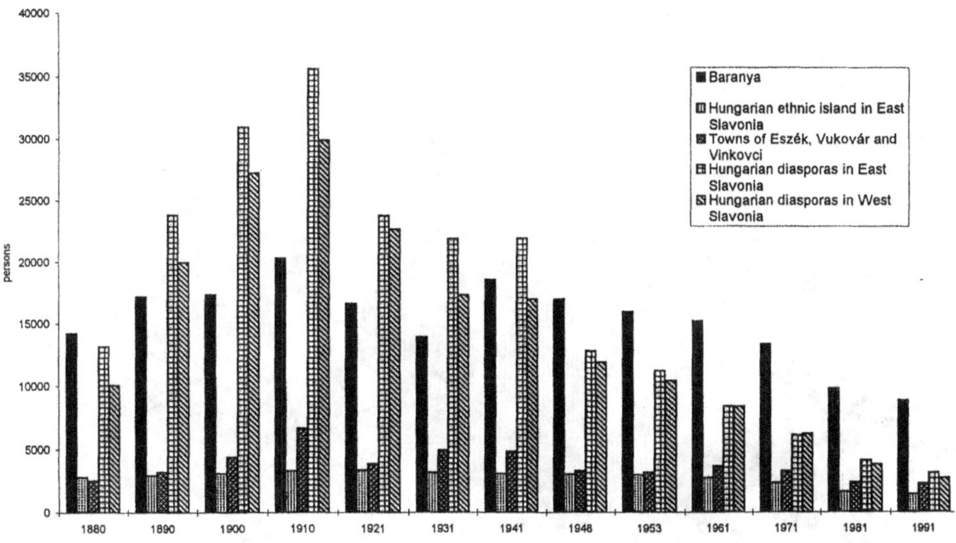

Figure 44. Change in the number of Hungarians in different parts of Croatia (1880 - 1991)

According to the data of the 1910 census, ethnic Hungarians were gathering ground – not only in the autochthonous settlements around Kórógy – but in the following areas located south of the Dráva River: the surroundings of Vukovár and Eszék, the Alsómiholjác-Szlatina-Našice triangle, the environs of Verőce, the area of Belovár-Grubišno Polje, and the Daruvár-Pakrác-Garešnica triangle[37] *(Fig. 45.).* In 1910 there was an absolute or relative Hungarian ethnic majority in 137 settlements out of the 6770 in present-day Croatia. Of these 112 were found south of the Dráva River. The most populous Hungarian communities were found in urban centres such as in the Hungarian port of Fiume on the Adriatic Coast (6,493), in the dynamically developing capital of Croatia, Zágráb (4,028), in the market centre of Eszék in the East Slavonian Hungarian ethnic settlement area in Baranya (3,729) and in the most important industrial town and railway junction of the Száva Region, Bród (2,538).

In Baranya, north of the Dráva, which belonged to the Hungarian Kingdom, there was a shift in the ethnic structure in favour of the Germans in the first half of the

---

[37] The most important settlements of the aullochthonous (immigrated) Hungarian population in 1910: in the surroundings of Vukovár: Lipovača, Marinci, Stari Jankovci, Srijemske Laze, Grabovo, Čakovci, Opatovac, Ivanci; in the surroundings of Eszék: Antunovac, Čepin, Orlovnjak, Palača, Šodolovci, Ludvinci, Dályhegy, Erdőd; Alsómiholjác-Szlatina-Našice triangle: Alsómiholjác, Viljevo, Martinci, Humljani, Slana Voda, Szlatina, Zdenci, Senkovac; in the surroundings of Verőce: Budakovac, Malo Gaćište, Sokolac, Detkovac, Novi Gradac, Terezino Polje, Rezovac; in the surroundings of Belovár-Grubišno Polje: Galovac, Mala Pisanica, Bedenik, Velika Pisanica, Lasovac, Grbavac, Grubišno Polje; Daruvár-Pakrác-Garešnica triangle: Pašijan, Popovac, Brekinjska, Gaj, Toranj, Lipik, Pakrác, Daruvár, Dežanovac, Imsovci, Kreštelovac, Sokolovac, Trojeglava, Babina Gora, Govedje Polje.

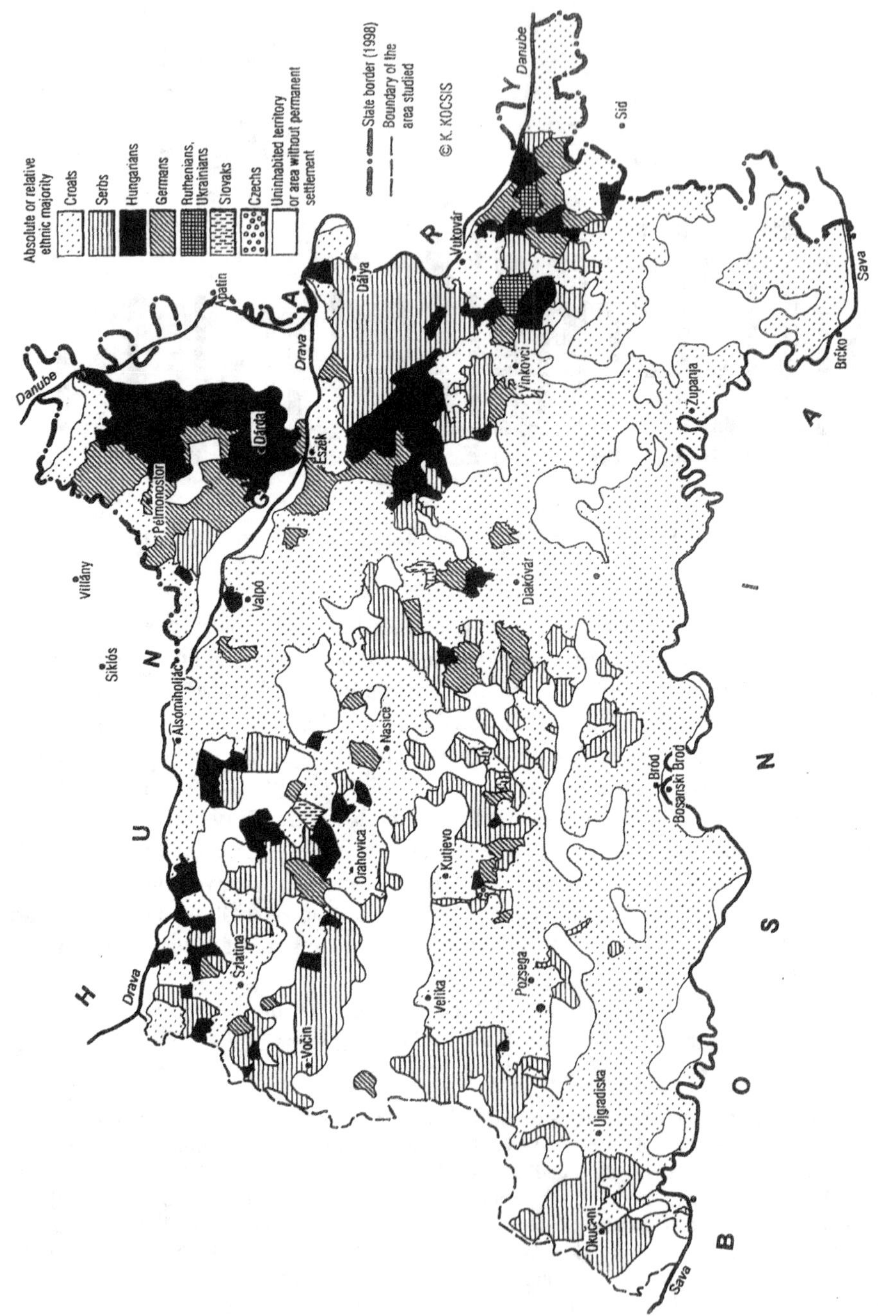

Figure 45. Ethnic map of the present-day territory of East Croatia (1910)
Source: Census 1910

19th century, while in the second half of the century the Hungarians dominated to the detriment of Croats and Shokatses. In the period between 1840 and 1880 the population of Croats and Shokatses with a low birthrate (one child per family) rose by a mere 13.7 % while the Germans expanded by 68.3 % during the same period. Their expansion was already spectacular in the 18th century, especially in villages mixed with Serbs (e.g. Kácsfalu, Dárda, Baranyabán). In the era between 1880 and 1910 the Hungarians gained ground due to the natural assimilation of Croats and Germans and an influx of Hungarians from the Bácska region *(Fig. 46.)*. By the end of this period (1910), a great number of Shokatses in Kiskőszeg, Darázs, and Izsép, and Germans in Vörösmart, Kiskőszeg, Dárda, Pélmonostor and Karancs declared themselves to belong to the state-forming nation, i.e. Hungarians. As a result, out of 51,616 inhabitants in the region of Croatian Baranya, 39.5 % declared themselves to be Hungarian together with 28 % Germans, 19.2 % Croats-Shokatses, and 12.1 % Serbs. Of the villages of Baranya there were 14 with a Hungarian ethnic majority, 10 German, 9 Croat-Shokats and 1 Serb[38]. Of the villages in Baranya in 1910 the largest Hungarian communities were found at Vörösmart (2,072), Kiskőszeg (1,854) and Laskó (1,806) .

In Muraköz (Medjimurje) between the Mura and Dráva rivers, which belonged to Zala County in Hungary, and was traditionally inhabited almost exclusively by Croats, the number of those declaring themselves to be Hungarian – mainly owing to the partial Magyarization of Croats living in Csáktornya and Perlak and a gradual settlement of Hungarians – rose to 6,766 by 1910[39].

North of the Dráva, but as part of the Croato-Slavonian County of Belovár-Körös, in some settlements in Gola (e.g. Zsgyála) an inverse process to the overall trend of Magyarization had been taking place for half a century, namely the Croatization of Hungarians[40]. A similar process was under way in Légrád located nearby but part of Zala County. This settlement had had a Hungarian population from the Middle Ages until the 19th century, but following the regulation of the Dráva river homes were transferred to the right side of the river (the Croatian settlement area). In a new geographical setting and owing to closer ties with the Croats, the settlement underwent Croatization (the number of Hungarians was 80 % in 1715 and it decreased to 32.4 % by 1910).

At the end of the First World War the Serbian Army, supported by the troops of the Entente, regained control of the territory of Serbia and Montenegro. Then (between

---

[38] Of the settlements of Baranya which have become separated since 1910 (small villages, manors, colonies groups of farmsteads etc.) 14 (e.g. Tikveš, Sokolovac, Mirkovac, Jasenovac, Sudaraž, Uglješ) had a Hungarian ethnic majority, while in a further three (Kneževo, Novi Čeminac, Širine) the majority was formed by Germans.

[39] The number of Hungarians living in Muraköz increased from 2,343 to 6,766 between 1880 and 1910, in Csáktornya the respective figures were 828 and 2,433 during the same period.

[40] On the territory of Gola a mere 34.3 % of the local population could speak Hungarian in 1910 (1900= 40%) and only 7.6 % declared themselves Hungarian native speakers (1900=29,7%). In the case of Zsgyála and Légrád see: Arday L. 1994 Az északnyugat-horvátországi szórványokról (About the Hungarian diasporas in NW-Croatia) - in: Arday L. (Ed.) Fejezetek a horvátországi magyarok történetéből, Teleki László Alapítvány, Budapest, pp.176-183.

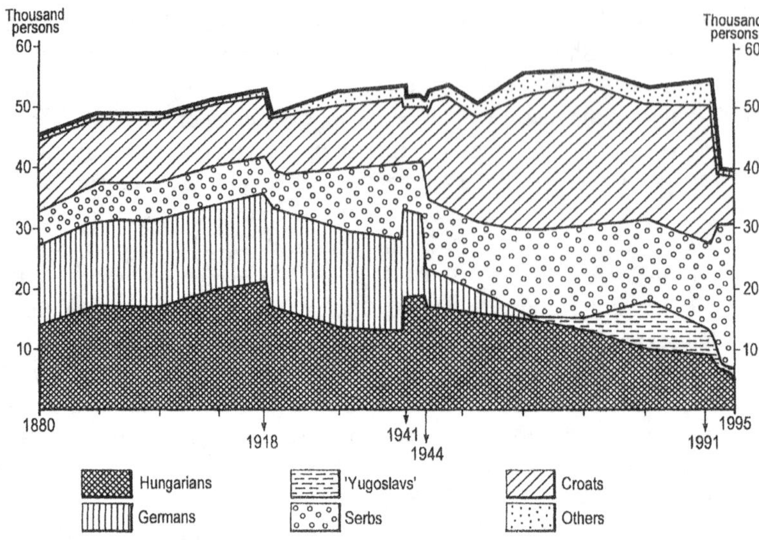

Figure 46. Change in the ethnic structure of the Croatian Baranya (1880 – 1992)

November 7 and 14, 1918) it occupied Syrmia, Slavonia and South Hungary (up to the Barcs-Pécs-Szeged-Arad line), and by December 25, 1918 they had taken Muraköz.

Alarmed by the advance of Italian troops towards Slovenian and Croatian ethnic territory, and by Serb territorial claims (Simović-Antonijević line[41]), the State of Slovenes-Croats-Serbs (formed on the territory of the Austro-Hungarian Monarchy on October 29, 1918) eventually joined Serbia thus finishing the war on the victorious side. This led to the founding of the Kingdom of Serbs-Croats-Slovenes (SHS) on December 1, 1918, the boundaries of which were drawn up between September 1919 and November 1920. Of the areas belonging to present-day Croatia and which had been part of Hungary until 1918, the Muraköz (Medjimurje) was ceded from Hungary in the Trianon Peace Treaty (1920) owing to its predominantly Croatian population, and Baranya owing to its vicinity near Eszék and Shokats-Croatian villages[42]. On the territory of present-day Croatian Baranya during the Serb occupation and at the time of annexation, 67.5 % of the population were Hungarian and German, and 31.3 % of them Croats and Serbs.

The authorities of the occupying Serbs – in Baranya as in Bácska and Bánát – immediately started to eliminate traces of Hungarian statehood and to ruin local Hungarians politically and economically. Most Hungarian civil servants were dismissed, forced to retire or expelled. Hungarian schools, cultural institutions and financial intitu-

---

[41] Simović-Antonijević line: the western border of the territories claimed by Serbia in Croatia in October, 1918 — in case of the possible Croatian rejection of unification with Serbia: Vitrovitica-Novska-Una river-Knin-Šibenik. See: Čović, B. /Ed./ 1991 Izvori velikosrpske agresije (Sources of the Great-Serbian aggression), Zagreb, 380p.

[42] Darázs, Hercegmárok, Izsép, Dályok, Baranyavár, Benge, Lőcs, Petárda, Torjánc.

tions were closed down. On February 25, 1919 an order was issued on the expropriation of the majority of large estates (predominantly in Hungarian and German ownership) i.e. of holdings over 500 cadastral holds (and not much later, of over 100). This measure, called "land reform", pursued national aims (it was a step to crush the Hungarian and German large landowners, and indirectly the peasants and working class of the same nationalities). It was also directed at social targets (to meet demands for land of the southern Slavs, primarily the Serbs). Hungarians found themselves almost totally excluded from the land reform; at the same time Hungarian workers, hired labourers, servants and tenants were chased away to provide room for Serbian and Croatian colonists, dobrovoljats and optants[43].

The political situation led to massive migrations in opposite directions as reflected in the first Yugoslavian census (1921). On the present-day territory of Croatia the number of Croats and Serbs[44] had risen to 68.8 % and 16.9 %, respectively, while that of Hungarians had dropped to 2.3% (81,835). Due to flight, expulsions and the dissimilation of previously Magyarized people (e.g. some of the Germans), there was an increasing assimilation of the descendants of autochthonous Hungarians on the territory of the present-day Croatia, and 32.6 % fewer Hungarians were registered in 1921 than in 1910. In this period the town of Bród lost 78.9 % of its Hungarian inhabitants, Zágráb 70.1 % and Eszék 38.8%. Both West Slavonia[45] and East Slavonia[46] suffered considerable losses (-24.5 % and -33.2 %, respectively). In the ceded Baranya the number of Hungarians fell by 18.4 %, (a loss of nearly 3,800 persons) which, apart from migration losses[47] was due to the return in the statistics of 1,500 formerly Magyarized Germans[48]. The number and ratio of Hungarians in Baranya decreased to below 14,000 or 26.4 % owing to their low birthrate, intensified emigration, the dissimilation of the earlier Magyarized Shokatses[49] and Serbian statistical manipulations based on surname analysis[50].

---

[43] Dobrovoljats: Serbian volunteer of the First World War who gained military distinction. Optant: Croats and Serbs having chosen the option of being resettled from Hungary to the Kingdom of Serbs-Croats-Slovenes.

[44] Between the two world wars the Yugoslavian statistics did not distinguish between Serbs and Croats but recorded a unified "Serbo-Croatian" native tongue. An approximate division could be made on the basis of religious affiliation, i.e. Roman Catholic of "Serbo-Croatian" native tongue =Croat; Orthodox of "Serbo-Croatian" native tongue=Serb.

[45] West-Slavonia includes Verőce, Daruvár, Pakrác, Novszka, Grubisnopolje, Garesnica, Kutina, Belovár and Császma districts.

[46] It should be noted that in spite of the change in 1918, the autochthonous Hungarian villages of East Slavonia (e.g. Szentlászló, Haraszti, Lacháza) were able to further increase their population between 1910 and 1921.

[47] Ca. 200-300 Hungarians fled from the following settlements by 1921: Dárda, Kiskőszeg, Izsép, Laskó, Vörösmart.

[48] Re-Germanization (1910-1921): Vörösmart, Kiskőszeg, Bellye, Karancs.

[49] In 1931 c. 500, earlier Magyarized Shokatses declared themselves to be Catholic "Serbo-Croatians" at Darázs, Hercegmárok and Dályok.

[50] 'Surname analysis order of Svetozar Pribičević': According to this it was not allowed for the persons with surname of linguistically non-completely Hungarian origin to declare themselves - e.g.

Parallel to the decrease in the number of Hungarians was that the new state-forming nation of Serbs had increased sharply (1921-1931: +69.1 %). This might be attributed to the resettlement of the afore-mentioned volunteers (dobrovoljats) and optants within the framework of land reform[51]. Besides the colonies established in the environs of Dárda, Kácsfalu and Bolmány, several hundred Serbs moved to Főherceglak, Pélmonostor, Karancs, Kő and Hercegszőlős which formerly had a Hungarian-German ethnic majority.

Hungarians left without a job and expelled from Slavonia in the course of the land reform emigrated to Hungary, Germany, France and America, or mved to nearby big towns. Having lost their roots and contracted mixed marriages, they soon gave up their Hungarian identity. As a result of this migration the number of Hungarians increased by 83.2 % in Zágráb and by 15-16 % in Eszék and Vinkovci between 1921 and 1931, while there was a -23.6 % and -7.8% loss in West and East Slavonia, respectively. Owing to the severe demographic loss, by the 1931 Yugoslavian census only 69,671 persons, or 1.8 % of the total population was considered Hungarian on the present-day territory of Croatia. Areas from which Hungarians had fled or emigrated were also occupied by Serbs in Slavonia, who established several colonies on the former estates confiscated estates (e.g. Eltz, Khuen-Belasi, Pejačević) in the environs of Eszék, Vukovár, Alsómiholjác, Szlatina and Verőce[52].

On March 27, 1941, following the coup d'état against the pro-German Cvetković government which had joined the three-power pact, Hitler gave the order to overrun Yugoslavia, then under Serbian hegemony, with the involvement of neighbouring countries. The military operations by the German and Italian forces against an unstable Yugoslavia[53] (with its extremely mixed ethnic structure) started on April 6, and the

---

at the census or at the registration at school - as ethnic Hungarian (Nyigri I. 1941 1941 A visszatért Délvidék nemzetiségi képe (Ethnic Patterns in the Returned Southern Region) - in: A visszatért Délvidék, Halász, Budapest, 378.p.).

[51] Serbs from Montenegro, Hercegovina and Hungary were predominantly settled in Southwest Baranya (e.g. to the Bellye estate) where, after expelling the Hungarian inhabitants of the confiscated land, 7 colonies were formed or repopulated on 2,141 cadastral holds (Novo Nevesinje, Majiške Medje, Novi Bolman, Zornice, Novi Jagodnjak,Uglješ, Švajcarnica). See: Nyigri I. 1941 ibid. 385.p., Šimončić-Bobetko, Z. 1986 Agrarna reforma i kolonizacija na području Baranje u medjuratnom razdoblju (Agrarian reform and colonization in Baranya in the interwar period) (1919-1941 godine) - in: Tri stoleća Belja, JAZU, Osijek, Bognár A. 1971-72 Stanovništvo Baranje (Population of Baranya), Geografski Glasnik 33-34., Zagreb

[52] Serbs from the Croatian areas of Lika, Bosnia-Herzegovina and Montenegro and from Hungary, living in the vicinity of Eszék and Vukovár, were settled in colonies with a former Hungarian population: e.g. Antunovac Tenjski, Ovčara-Čepin, Divoš, Paulin Dvor, Šodolovci, Lanka-Petrova Slatina, Križevci-Karadžićevo, Ada, Mlaka Antinska, Palača, Silaš, Lipovača, Ludvinci, Djeletovci, Ivanci. See Gaćeša, N. I. 1975 Agrarna reforma i kolonizacija u Sremu (Agrarian reform and colonization in Syrmia) 1919-1941, Novi Sad, 227.p.

[53] The multi-ethnic S-H-S Kingdom was a centralized, militarist, Greater Serbian state, which subdued the national and autonomous movements of the frustrated Croats and Slovenes, of the Muslimans persecuted for religious reasons, of Macedons, of non-Slavic Albanians and Hungarians. There was particularly bitter antagonism between the Serbs and Croats, the most populous rival ethnic

war officially ended with the capitulation of the latter on April 17. In the meantime the Independent Croatian State (NDH) was proclaimed on 10 April which meant the disintegration of Yugoslavia. The next day, Hungarian troops occupied the Baranya and Bácska regions which had virtually turned into a "no man's land" (they were annexed by Serbs in 1918 when they had had a relative Hungarian ethnic majority). In these areas, this time ceded by Hungary, provisional military rule was introduced and the pacification of the territories began: according to a governmental order issued on April 28, 1941, Serbs who had settled after December 31, 1918 and had not escaped were interned and expelled; as a result, their number fell by 2,600 persons compared with 1931. The number of Hungarians (in a minority position and having regained the status of a state-forming nation) was 18,648, that is 36 %, within the total population - due to the assimilation of some Germans and Croats (1,600 and 500 persons, respectively) [54]. In Muraköz the reappearance of Hungarian civil servants and military personnel, and the "statistical change of identity" of many Croats in the urban centres led to a rise in the number of Hungarians to 6,334, i.e. 6.1%. On the right bank of the Dráva, in Légrád (ceded to Hungary in 1941) there was a halt in the Croatization process of Hungarians, and 44.6 % of the 2,624 total population declared themselves to be native Hungarian speakers and 91.4 % of them to be ethnic Hungarians in a new political situation which was favourable to Hungarians.

The Hungarian authorities treated the Croatian minority politely (mainly for foreign political reasons). However, to secure a railway connection with Italy they occupied Muraköz[55] with a Croat ethnic majority, and this became a source of tension in Hungaro-Croatian inter-state relations between 1941 and 1945. That is why the position of the Slavonian Hungarians living in scattered settlements did not improve, but remained politically and culturally depressed, and they were forced to flee in great numbers from territories of the partisan war[56].

On the territory of the Independent Croatian State which included historical Croatia-Slavonia, Bosnia-Hercegovina and a large part of Dalmatia, the Croatian Ustasha troops took their revenge on the 1.8 million Serbs (who accounted for 32 % of the total population of the country) for the oppression and humiliation suffered by the Croats between the two world wars. Inhabitants of Serbian colonies formed after 1919 i.e. 105,000 persons[57] were expelled between April and June 1941. Of the Serbs re-

---

groups and only a rather delayed attempt was made to appease them (formation of the autonomous Croatian Banate, August 1939).

[54] According to the 1941 census, most Hungarians moved to Pélmonostor, Hercegszőlős, Baranyavár, Főherceglak, Bellye and Bolmány. Germans declared themselves to be Hungarian native speakers in great numbers in Vörösmart, Kácsfalu, Dárda, Bellye and Kiskőszeg, Croats-Shokatses in Darázs, Hercegmárok, Kiskőszeg.

[55] The ratio of the Croats within the total population of Muraköz was 92.8 % in 1941 and 97.2 % in 1931.

[56] Due to the partisan war and to deportations the number of Hungarians in the districts of Pozsega, Nasice, and Szlatina decreased by 62.7 % between 1931 and 1948.

[57] Serbian colonists were expelled predominantly from the Verőce, Szlatina, Alsómiholjác, Eszék, Vukovár, Vinkovci and Pozsega districts. See: Kurdulija, S. 1994 Atlas ustaškog genocida nad

maining in Slavonia, 33,089 persons were killed in concentration camps and in the partisan war, while the number of casualties in Croatian Krajina (Lika, Kordun, Banija) was 55,547[58].

This ethnic pattern changed profoundly as a consequence of the change in military power from German-Croatian-Hungarian rule to the Soviet-Yugoslav regime, as the front line moved over the territory (October 1944 - April 1945). About 52 % of Germans living in present-day Yugoslavia escaped from the approaching Red Army and the Yugoslav (Serbian) partisan troops as some German armed forces (in the units of Wehrmacht, SS or as refugees having been evacuated[59]). The remaining Germans, deprived of their property, were taken to detention camps[60], and to some Hungarian villages in Baranya (e.g. Hercegszőlős, Laskó and Várdaróc)[61]. As in the Bácska region in the first months following the change of power, internment, killing and the decimation of the local Hungarian population began[62].

10,323 Croats and 3,858 Serbs moved to the territory of Baranya, in place of expelled Germans between 1945 and 1948; 8,204 of them were settled there by the Croatian Ministry of Agriculture between 1946 and 1948.[63] Most of these Croats had come from overpopulated Zagorje, Muraköz-Medjimurje, Slavonia and Dalmatia and found their new homes in Baranyabán, Laskafalu, Albertfalu, Pélmonostor, Dárda and Baranyaszentistván, while the majority of Serbian colonists of Slavonian origin went to Pélmonostor, Kácsfalu and Főherceglak.

Although Hungarians in the Baranya region had suffered a loss of 2,400 people due to war and migration, and 200 people through assimilation, their number only dropped to 17 thousand because 1,000 Germans[64] declared themselves Hungarian in 1948 to avoid expulsion. Of the 39 settlements in Baranya 12 had a Hungarian ethnic majority, 17 of them were predominantly Croatian and 9 were prevailingly Serbian. The village of Hercegszőlős, which had been Hungarian for the past millennium, suddenly

---

Srbima (Atlas of the Ustasha genocide against the Serbs) 1941-1945, Privredne Vesti "Europublic", D.O.O. - Istorijski Institut SANU, Beograd, 64.p.

[58] Kurdulija, S. 1994 ibid., 82.p.

[59]Pauli, S. 1977 Berichte aus der Geschichte des Südostens... unter besonderer Berücksichtigung der Schicksale der Donauschwaben und Siebenbürger Sachsen von der Ansiedlung bis zur Vertreibung 1944/45, Langen, 259.p.

[60] The most important detention camps established for Germans in Slavonia were in Tenje, Valpovo, Velika Pisanica. See: Bohmann, A. 1969 Menschen und Grenzen Bd.2. Bevölkerung und Nationalitäten in Südosteuropa, Verlag Wissenschaft und Politik, Köln, 274.p.

[61] Of the deported civilian Germans on the present-day territory of Croatian Baranya 2,761 persons died, accounting for 19,4 % of their number according to the 1941 census (Gesamterhebung zur Klärung des Schicksals der deutschen Bevölkerung in der Vertreibungsgebieten, Bd.III. 1965, München, pp.575-580.).

[62] Matuska M. 1991 A megtorlás napjai (The days of vendetta), Magyar Szó - Fórum, Újvidék-Novi Sad, pp.349-355.

[63] Maticka, M. 1986 Agrarna reforma i kolonizacija u Baranji (Agrarian reform and colonization in Baranya) 1945-48. godine - in: "Tri stoljeća Belje", JAZU, Osijek

[64] Vörösmart, Karancs, Baranyabán, Bellye, Pélmonostor, Kiskőszeg.

achieved a relative German majority in 1948 due to the provisional detention of 1,500 Germans expelled from surrounding settlements. Due to the migrations mentioned above, Baranya, with a two thirds share of Hungarians and Germans in its population until 1944, now had 56.9 % Croats and Serbs. Hungarians numbered 31.4 %, and Germans 8.3 %. In Slavonia the Serb colonists (those chased away by the Croatian Ustashas in 1941) returned, while due to the land reform 20,000 Croats moved to Eszék, 5,000 of them to Vinkovci and 4,000 to Vukovár, occupying vacancies caused by the escape and expulsion of local Germans. Owing to massive colonization and severe German and Hungarian losses, of the 690,000 population who inhabited the territory of present-day East Croatia in 1948, the ratio of Croats grew to 70.3 % (1931=54.5 %), while that of the Germans fell to 1.1 % (1931=11 %), and the Hungarians to 5.3 % (1931= 7.1 %). The number of Hungarians in Croatia decreased by 26.4 % between 1931 and 1948 and dropped to 51,297 by the end of the period. After living in a diaspora under intense Serbo-Croat lingual and political pressure, the Hungarians in Slavonia had suffered an even higher demographic loss (-31 % in East Slavonia and -41,4 % in West Slavonia).

For the past half century, in the period between the 1948 and 1991 censuses, the demographic and ethnic geographical pattern of Hungarians in Croatia has been determined by several external factors influenced by geographic features of their settlement area (e.g. natural change, migration) and internal factors (statistical methods of registration, national policy of the state, mixed marriages, changes in the identity of the population, and natural assimilation). In the course of Yugoslavian socialist urbanization predominantly young people released from agricultural work in economically retarded, unviable villages in Hungarian ethnic areas, headed in large numbers for new ethnic and lingual urban environments, seeking employment. At the same time there was a migration of Hungarians from the Slavonian diaspora not only to large industrial towns in Croatia but also abroad, causing serious losses to local Hungarian communities. With the opportunity for work beyond the borders and the emergence of an economic crisis within Yugoslavia the first wave of emigration, then seen as temporary, took place between 1965 and 1970.

During the past decades, up till 1991, there has been an accelerating fall in the number of Hungarians in Croatia recorded by the censuses. A particularly important factor was played by subjective considerations, including ethnic identity. Disguised by the ideology of proletarian internationalism, but in fact dictated by a national policy to make the country "Yugoslavian-Serbian-Croatian", emphasis was placed on developing an inferiority complex among Hungarians stemming from their minority situation, emphasising their rootlessness, and lack of opportunity. There was also great emphasis put on the reorganisation of the remains of the Hungarian school system, its "internationalization". Factors promoting natural assimilation were a change of language, a loss of national identity and mixed marriages in ever increasing numbers, especially in the Slavonian diaspora of Hungarians. Assimilation was made easier by the internal migration of the rural population looking for job opportunities and going to towns with a Croatian ethnic majority (mainly to Zágráb, Eszék, Vukovár and Vinkovci).

As a result of successful state propaganda glorifying everything Yugoslavian, suppressing minority cultures and languages and supported by mixed marriages, the ratio of people with an uncertain ethnic identity increased, especially among the younger generation. At the time of the 1961 population census a mere 0.4 % of Croatia's population were not able or willing to declare their ethnic affiliation, this ratio had increased to 8.8 % by 1981. After 1971 there was an opportunity for those with an uncertain ethnic identity, maybe as a result of coming from an ethnically mixed family, to declare themselves "Yugoslav". In the atmosphere of the 1991 census heated by nationalistic emotions a mere 2.2 % of the population of Croatia declared themselves "Yugoslav" in contrast with 8.2 % in 1981.

For the above reasons the ratio of an ageing population declaring themselves to be ethnically Hungarian decreased to 22,355 persons, i.e. by 56.4 % between 1948 and 1991. Naturally, this fall affected Hungarian communities in different geographical settings. The loss was minimal (-30.8 %) in towns which were getting a continuous supply of immigrants from the villages. At the same time the diaspora in West and East Slavonia suffered a greater loss (-77,1 % and -75,2 %, respectively). During this period the rate of decline was about half among the autochthonous Hungarians of Baranya and Slavonian Kórógy and its environs (-47,4 % and -52,8%). Of the villages in Baranya with a traditional Hungarian majority, Bellye and Hercegszőlős became a focus of Croatian and Serbian resettlement and, as a result of development programs and assimilation Bellye had a Croatian majority by 1961, Hercegszőlős a Serbian majority by 1981, and Karancs a Serbian majority by 1971. In Slavonia, Lacháza kept its Hungarian majority until 1971, while Grbavac and Budakóc became Croatian in 1981. A general remark is also valid for the processes of the 19th century, that Croatization gained ground most rapidly among Roman Catholic Hungarians, while Calvinists were more resistant and the strongest adherents to their Hungarian identity both in Slavonia and Baranya[65].

THE PRESENT TERRITORY OF HUNGARIAN SETTLEMENT IN CROATIA

A presentation of the situation in the territory of Hungarian settlement in Croatia between 1991 and 1998, which is overwhelmingly under Serbian control and affected by the civil war, seems to be a futile attempt owing to the present chaotic circumstances. According to the population census of March 31, 1991, immediately before the outbreak of the Serbian-Croatian war, the ethnic geographical characteristics of the Hungarians in Croatia were the following: 22,355 people (0.47 %) declared themselves to be Hungarian and there were19,684 (0.4 %) native Hungarian speakers on the territory of the present-day Republic of Croatia. Of those of Hungarian ethnicity 40 % (8,956) live in Baranya, 6.5 % (1,445) were residents of the Slavonian autochthonous Hungarian "ethnic island" of Kórógy, Szentlászló, Haraszti, Lacháza, while10.3 % (2,298) of them were town dwellers of Eszék, Vukovár and Vinkovci, and 26.6 % (5,943) were found in the

---

[65] This statement is true also in the case of Lutheran Hungarians in Légrád on the right bank of the Dráva river.

Figure 47. Ethnic map of East Croatia (1991)
Source: Census 1991

183

Slavonian diaspora. Only 10 villages in Baranya[66] and 5 villages in Slavonia[67] were able to keep their absolute or relative Hungarian ethnic majority *(Fig. 47.)*. The demographic future and ethnic survival of Hungarians in Croatia was already in question in the decades before the war. Apart from their catastrophic ageing[68] – a mere 22.6 % of them (5,058 persons) lived in settlements where they numbered more than 50 % of the local population. At the same time, 54.8 % of them were struggling to retain their ethnic identity (rather hopelessly), where they did not even number 10 %. As a result of the Croatization of the younger Hungarian generations who have moved from rural areas into the towns, only 35.8 % of those declaring themselves to be Hungarian live in urban settlements. The number of Roman Catholics, most liable to become Croats, reached 72.4 %, while the number of Calvinists who are considered the most ardent supporters of national identity was 24.9 %. Calvinists prevailed in the Hungarian villages of Kórógy, Kopács, Várdaróc, Laskó and Csúza. Apart from the village of Vörösmart these settlements also had the most populous communities (500-900 persons) of Hungarians in Croatia.

The above-outlined ethnic spatial structure was eradicated by the Serbian-Croatian war which broke out in the spring of 1991. Following the ominous events[69] during the summer of 1991, the Yugoslav National Army (JNA), the local Serbian armed forces and paramilitary troops from Serbia occupied Baranya, the Serb ethnic areas of East Slavonia, and the Hungarian village of Kórógy between July 3 and September 3, 1991. On November 17, after nearly six months siege Vukovár fell[70], becoming a symbol of Croatian national defence.

On November 24 after five months' siege, the second most important settlement of Slavonian Hungarians, Szentlászló, was also taken by the Serbs. Thus, on the territory of East Croatia an area of 2,500 square km which was home to 99 thousand Croats, 69 thousand Serbs and 14 thousand Hungarians (almost the whole Hungarian settlement territory in Croatia) fell under the occupation of Serbian-Yugoslavian military forces, which subsequently became a "demilitarized area". But part of the "Republic of Serbian Krayina" came under the control of UNPROFOR and, later, UNTAES between April 10, 1992 and January 15, 1998. Approximately 68 % of Croats (about 16,000 persons) and 23-42 % of Hungarians (c. 2,000 to 5,000 persons) in Baranya, (together

---

[66] Absolute Hungarian majority (1991): Vörösmart, Nagybodolya, Csúza, Sepse, Laskó, Várdaróc, Kopács, Újbezdán. Relative Hungarian majority (1991): Kiskőszeg, Kő.

[67] Absolute Hungarian majority (1991): Kórógy, relative Hungarian majority (1991): Szentlászló, Haraszti, Csák, Krestelovác.

[68] The ageing index (number of elderly per 100 children) within the Hungarian community of Croatia as a total: 269.4 (!). Within the total population of the country: 90.1, in Hungary: 92.2 (1991). At that time 29.8 % of Hungarians in Croatia were older than 60, while the same figure was 17.4 % for the whole of Croatia.

[69] Proclamation of an independent Serbian Krajina (February 28, 1991), a bloody Serbian-Croatian clash at Borovo Selo (May 2, 1991), a plebiscite on the independency of Croatia (May 19, 1991), proclamation of the independence of Croatia (June 26, 1991).

[70] See Crkvenčić, I. - Klemenčić, M. 1993 Aggression against Croatia, Central Bureau of Statistics, Zagreb, pp.54-57.

with those declaring themselves Yugoslav in 1991) fled to Hungary or behind the Croatian front line from the atrocities and destruction caused by Serbian paramilitary troops until March 1992 *(Fig. 48.)*. Uncertainties concerning the number of refugees from Baranya stem from the fact that at the 1991 Yugoslav population census only 8,956 people dared to admit their Hungarian ethnicity; according to our estimations their number might have been c. 12,000. Croats and Hungarians were driven away in the greatest numbers from settlements of key importance and from the places of fiercest fighting (e.g. Bellye, Dárda and Pélmonostor). Due to the peripheral location of Hungarian settlements near the Danube, their ethnic composition had not changed considerably up to March 1992, with a few exceptions (e.g. Bellye, Kiskőszeg), i.e. no sizeable Serb population had settled here. The peripheral position, considered unfavourable during peace times, in the normal functioning of the economy, had proven to be "favourable" in saving the ethnic character of the villages. Naturally, this was corroborated by the Serbs striving to liquidate Croats not Hungarians who otherwise took a neutral position in most cases. After the occupation of the Croatian Baranya by the Serbs, 5,737 Serbs[71] who had escaped from Slavonia which was under Croatian control stayed until March

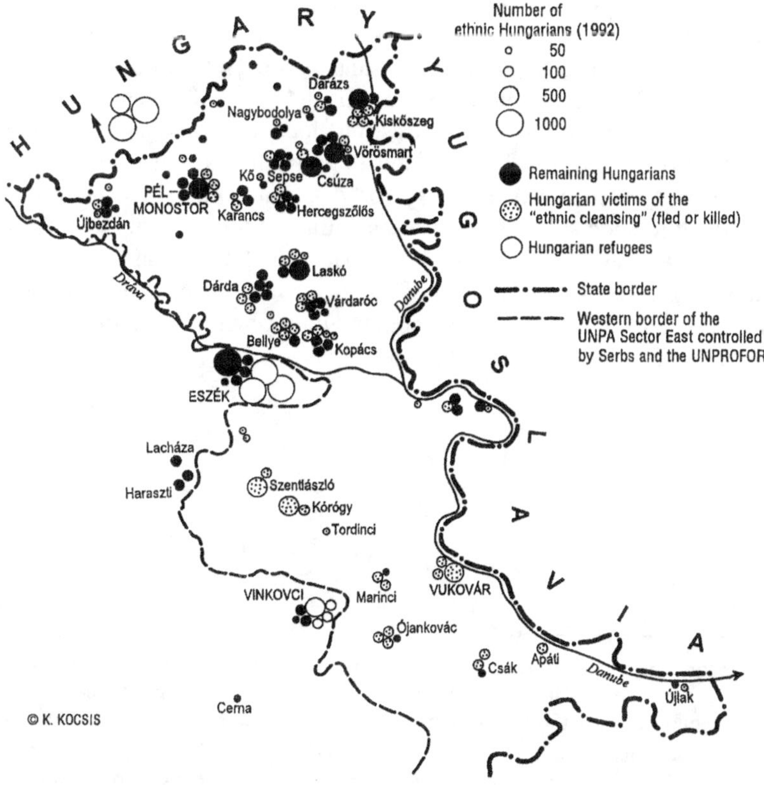

Figure 48. Hungarians and the War of 1991 in East Croatia

1992 in houses vacated by the Croats who had fled, and had originally appeared there as colonists in 1946-48 and were considered the main enemies (Pélmonostor, Dárda, Bellye, Baranyabán, Keskend, Laskafalu etc.). The autochthonous Croatian-Shokats villages in a peripheral position (e.g. Izsép, Dályok, Hercegmárok, Darázs, Lőcs) were hardly affected by the Serb colonization of 1991-92, and they managed to retain their Croatian ethnic majority. According to the Serb population census carried out between January 27 and March 5, 1992 the population of Baranya was 39,482, 59.4 % of them Serbs, 19.5 % Croats, 17.5 % Hungarians and 1.2 % "Yugoslavs". Owing to their massive emigration there was a considerable drop in the number of Hungarians, but because of an even greater exodus of Croats, Hungarians increased their proportion in Kopács, Várdaróc and Vörösmart. Compared with 1991, the number of villages with a Hungarian ethnic majority remained unchanged (10), that of the Serbs rose to 30, while that of the Croats dropped to 10. This situation remained more or less unchanged until May and August1995, when the Croatian Army took back the vicinity of the West Slavonian Okučani and the Knin Krajina (North Dalmatia, Lika, Kordun, Banija), from where more than 200,000 Serbs[72] fled towards Serbia and Bosnia. Some of them settled in Baranya, East Slavonia and in West Syrmia. 16,000 of these Serbs had returned to their original place of residence by the beginning of 1998, while of those who had taken provisional shelter in Yugoslavia 19,500 people went back to Krajina. Of the roughly 100,000 (mainly Croat) refugees (of 1991) from the territories of Baranya and Slavonia, which eventually reintegrated into Croatia on January 15, 1998, 15,000 have returned to their original place of residence since the summer of 1997[73]. The return of Hungarians has been a very slow process due to the disastrous local economic situation (e.g. ruined and looted property, a lack of job opportunities and schools), also due to many cases where Serbs have moved into their houses or flats, and other bureaucratic problems which are difficult to understand. In the present situation there is only a slight hope that maximum efforts will be made (both by the Croatian authorities and the affected Hungarian population) to restore the Hungarian ethnic spatial pattern which existed before the war, and to regenerate the Hungarian communities which proved their loyalty to the independent Croatia even by fighting in the war.

---

[72] According to the General Staff of the Army of Serbian Krayina the number of Serbs in North Dalmatia, Lika, Kordun, Baniya and in West Slavonia (only Okučani region) was 274,000 in June 1993. See Republika Srpska Krajina (specijalni prilog), Vojska (Beograd), Br.11. mart, 1994.

[73] Source of data concerning refugees: Displaced persons and refugees in Republic of Croatia, Report of the Office of Displaced Persons and Refugees, Government of the Republic of Croatia, Zagreb, 11 May 1998.

Chapter 7

THE HUNGARIANS OF THE TRANSMURA REGION

The southwestern area of Hungarian minority settlement in the Carpathian Basin is the Transmura Region[1] of Slovenia. At the time of the last census in 1991, 7,637 people in this territory declared themselves to be ethnic Hungarians and 8,174 to be Hungarian native speakers. This Hungarian minority makes up 0.06 % of Hungarians living in the Carpathian Basin and 0.3 % of Hungarians living outside the borders of Hungary.

THE NATURAL ENVIRONMENT

For over eight centuries the native Hungarian population of the Transmura Region in Slovenia has occupied the Lendva Basin, at the southern foot of the Lendva Hills (334 m) with vineyards covering about 500 hectares and the hills along the Kerka and Kebele: Vasi-hegyhát - Goričko (200 - 300 m) *(Fig. 49.)*. The most important rivers of the narrow Hungarian-inhabited borderland are the Mura, the Lendva, the Kebele, the Kerka streams.

ETHNIC PROCESSES DURING THE PAST FIVE HUNDRED YEARS

The Transmura Region is one of the borderland areas in the Carpathian Basin where the ethnic situation can be considered stable during the past one thousand years. At the end of the 15th century, when the Hungarian-Wend (Slovene) ethnic border was approaching to its present-day location, towns and market towns of the region either had a Hungarian ethnic majority (Alsólendva, Dobrónak), or had a sizeable Hungarian population (Muraszombat, Felsőlendva). Starting in the 13th century, landowners of the region (e.g. the Hoholds, known later as the Bánffy family, encouraged the resettlement

---

[1] Transmura Region (Hungarian: Muravidék, Murántúl, Vendvidék, Slovenian: Prekmurje). Northeast borderland of Slovenia north of the Mura river, between Austria, Hungary and Croatia. This region includes the present-day settlements of Muraszombat /Murska Sobota and Alsólendva /Lendava with an area of 947 square kilometres and 89,855 inhabitants (1991). Between the 10th century and 1919, then 1941 and 1945 as a part of Hungary; in the period 1919 - 1941 and 1945 - 1991 a region of Yugoslavia. Since then it belongs to the Republic of Slovenia.

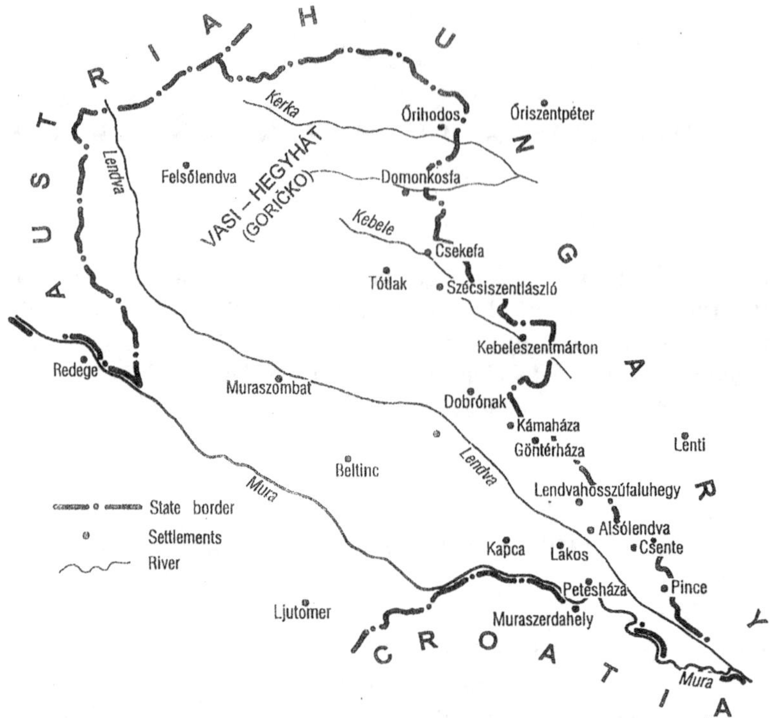

Figure 49. Important Hungarian geographical names in the Transmura Region

of the Slovenian and Wend population[2] to the uninhabited, wooded borderland (Hung. "gyepű") situated in the neighbourhood of the Alsó-Őrség (Lower Border Guard District). Thus, the settlement area had stabilized by the end of the 15th century. The Hungarian-Slovene ethnic boundary was not much modified either by the warfare of the 16th and 17th centuries, nor by the occasional Turkish devastation. This is corroborated by the analysis of the census carried out in 1720, following the failure of the War of Independence (1711) led by F. Rákóczi II. At that time in the present-day Transmura Region, with its scarce population owing to the military campaigns, most tax-paying Hungarian households were registered in Dobrónak (52), Alsólendva (44) and Muraszombat, the latter with 22 Wend, 19 Hungarian and 5 German taxpaying households[3].

---

[2] See map of M. Kos 1970 Agrarna kolonozacija Slovenske zemlje (Agrarian colonization of the Slovenian Lands) -in: Zgodovina agrarnih panog, I. Agrarno gospdarstvo, Gospodarska in družbena zgodovina Slovencev, SAZU, Ljubljana

[3] Acsády I. 1896 ibid. pp.152-160., 168-173.

The Hungarian-Slovene ethnic border in the Land of the Wends[4] remained relatively stable during the 18th and 19th centuries. Of the 73,800 population recorded at the time of the 1880 census, in the Transmura Region (the present-day Alsólendva and Muraszombat communities), 76.9 % was Slovene, while 17.8 % (13,159 persons) declared themselves to be native Hungarian speakers *(Tab. 33.)*. Of the 176 present-day settlements of the region 29 had a Hungarian majority. Most Hungarians lived on "ethnically mixed territory" (EMT, according to official Slovene categorization) adjoining the Hungarian state border, where their proportion reached 86.2 % in 1880. During the period between 1880 and 1910, the Hungarian language symbolised social self-assertion and personal economic success, therefore 23 % of the 90,132-strong population of the Transmura Region declared themselves to be Hungarian in 1910. This Magyarisation was especially striking in important settlements (e.g. Muraszombat 1880: 13,4 %, 1910: 46,9 %, Alsólendva 1880: 73 %, 1910: 87 %), and in villages with a Slovene population also speaking Hungarian (e.g. Kebeleszentmárton, Bántornya, Rátkalak). These villages, together with Kisfalu were becoming Hungarian, while Alsójánosfa, Mezővár and Szárazhegy were becoming Slovene. Thus, the number of villages with a Hungarian majority rose from 29 to 30 in this period *(Fig. 50.)*.

Following World War I and the withdrawal of the Hungarian Red Army on August 12, 1919, the Army of the Kingdom of Serbs-Croats-Slovenes (SHS) occupied the Transmura Region. This was then annexed by the Peace Treaty of Trianon (in spite of the protest of the local Wend-Slovene population[5]) to the new SHS Kingdom. This change of power involved the dismissal and expulsion of Hungarian civil servants and officials in charge of keeping public order, and even prior to that, the withdrawal of Hungarian military personnel, and the registration of about 4,000 Wends (who declared themselves to be Hungarian at the turn of the century) as Slovenes. Accordingly, in the 1921 Yugoslav census, the number of Hungarians was 14,065 and their proportion had decreased by 15.2 %. Between the two world wars there was an effort to Slovenise the Wend population who had shown their sympathy towards the Hungarian State and Hungarians quite openly. Another trend was the break up (and eventual elimination) of the Hungarian ethnic character of the borderland. Demographic aims were to be achieved through the settlement of Slovene civil servants in this area, and by the Slovene agricultural colonisation who had escaped from areas occupied by the Italians (Isonzo-Soča valley, and the vicinities of Gorizia and Istria). At this time the following Slovene colonies were established (mainly on land confiscated from the Hungarian aristocrats /e.g. from the Eszterházys): Petesháza (1921-1924), Benica (1922), Lendvahosszúfalu (1922-

---

[4] Land of the Wends (Hungarian: Vendvidék, historical "Tótság"). This is the historical name of the region SW of Vas and Zala counties of the Kingdom of Hungary, in the neighbourhood of Styria, between the Rába and Mura rivers. It nearly corresponds to the present name of "Transmura Region". It was named by the local Slovene population (the"Wends") whose ethnic development under Hungarian supremacy differed from the Slovens living between the Adriatic and the Mura rivers which was under German-Austrian rule until the middle of the 20th century. See Kossits J. 1828 A Magyar országi Vendus Tótokról (About the Wend-Slavs of Hungary), Tudományos Gyűjtemény V.pp.3-50. and Sever, B. 1991 Das Pomurje von A bis Z, Pomurska založba, Murska Sobota, 164.p.).

[5] Fall E. 1941 Jugoszlávia összeomlása (The collapse of Yugoslavia), Budapest, pp.61-62.

Table 33. Ethnic structure of the population on the present territory of Transmura Region (1880–1991)

Year	Total population		Slovenes		**Hungarians**		Croats		Others	
	number	%	Number	%	number	%	number	%	number	%
1880	*73,800*	*100*	*56,725*	*76.9*	*13,159*	*17.8*	*254*	*0.3*	*3,662*	*5.0*
1910	*90,132*	*100*	*66,205*	*73.5*	*20,737*	*23.0*	*163*	*0.2*	*3,027*	*3.3*
1921	*92,295*	*100*	*74,199*	*80.4*	*14,065*	*15.2*	*791*	*0.9*	*3,240*	*3.5*
1931	*90,717*	*100*	*80,469*	*88.7*	*7,607*	*8.4*	*566*	*0,6*	*2,075*	*2.3*
1941	*82,400*	*100*	*62,759*	*76.2*	*16,852*	*20.5*	*353*	*0.4*	*2,436*	*2.9*
1948	94,914	100	83,685	88.2	10,246	10.8	574	0.6	409	0.4
1953	93,888	100	80,615	85.9	10,581	11.3	841	0.9	1,851	1.9
1961	90,186	100	78,861	87.4	9,899	11.0	807	0.9	619	0.7
1971	90,772	100			9,064	10.0				
1981	91,016	100	79,112	86.9	8,617	9.5	1,516	1.7	1,771	1.9
1991	89,887	100	77,546	86.3	7,637	8.5	1,511	1.7	3,193	3.5
1991	*89,887*	*100*	*76,280*	*84.9*	*8,174*	*9.1*	*1,865*	*2.1*	*3,568*	*3.9*

Sources: 1880, 1910, 1941: Hungarian census data, 1921, 1931, 1948-1991: Yugoslav census data.
Remarks: Italic figures: mother / native tongue data.

1934), Pincemajor, Zalagyertyános, Lendvahídvég (1925), and Kámaháza (1931)[6]. In the interwar period the population of the underdeveloped Transmura Region with its low-fertility land, was separated by a rigid state border from the (Hungarian) Transdanubian region where they had previously found work. An increasing number emigrated to Germany, France and overseas, looking for work[7]. Many landless Hungarians in the surroundings of Alsólendva were excluded from the Yugoslav land reform and were indirectly forced to emigrate.

During World War II, following the occupation of Yugoslavia by the Germans, and its subsequent disintegration, the Transmura Region returned to Hungary and between April 16, 1941 and April 3, 1945 again formed part of the Hungarian counties of Vas and Zala. The new change of regime involved migration in the opposite direction of Hungarian and Yugoslav (Slovene) civil servants and military personnel. Due both to this and to the "Hungarophil" behaviour of the local Slovenes-Wends at the 1941 census, of the 82,400 population of the Transmura Region 20.4 % (16,852 people) declared themselves to be Hungarian and 77.2 % Wend native-speakers. Owing to the presence of Slovene colonists of the Interwar period, the proportion of Hungarians (82 %) on ethnically mixed territory (EMT) did not reach the level of 1910 (90.4 %). In the two largest centres of the region (Muraszombat and Alsólendva) the proportion of Hungarian native speakers was 39.8 % and 93.8 %, respectively *(Tab. 34.)*. A striking phenomenon of this census was that nearly three quarters of the Slovene-Wend population,

---

[6] Krajevni leksikon Slovenije IV. knjiga, Podravje in Pomurje, Državna Založba Slovenije, Ljubljana, 1980, 94., 101., 109., 110., 111.p., Sever, B. 1991 ibid. 71.p.

[7] Nyigri I. (Ed.) 1941 A visszatért Délvidék nemzetiségi képe (Ethnic Patterns in the Returned Southern Region), Halász Irodalmi és Könyvkiadóvállalat, Budapest, 537p.

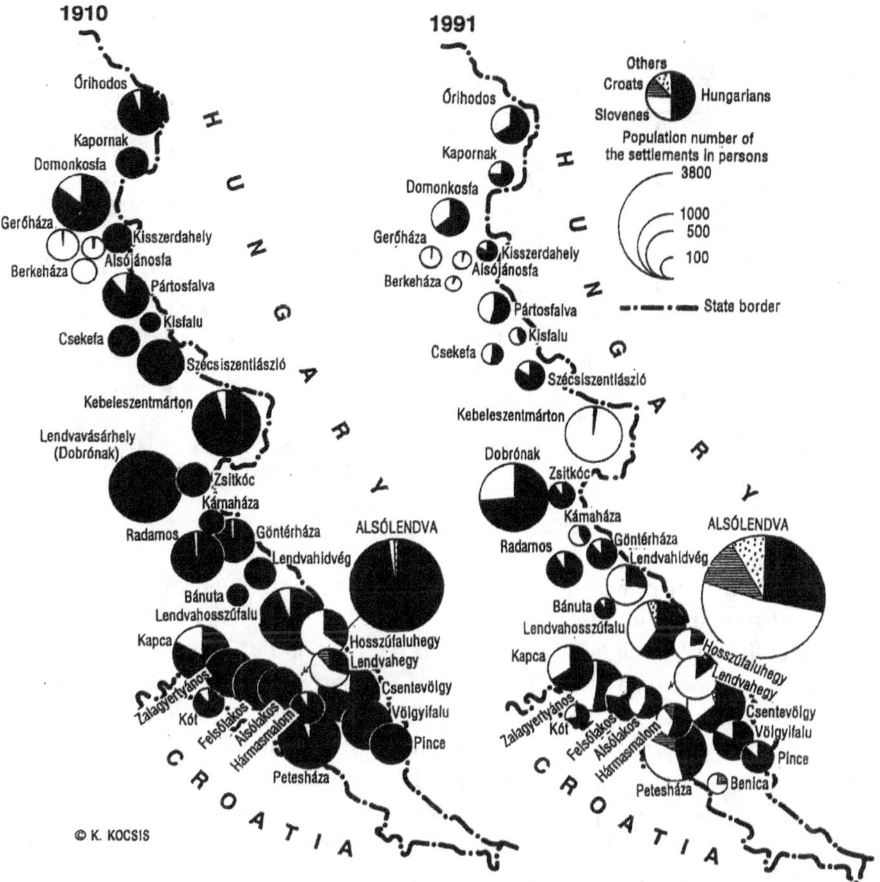

Figure 50. Ethnic map of the present-day Slovenian-Hungarian borderland (1910, 1991)

in an expression of solidarity with the Hungarian state, declared themselves to be ethnic Hungarians. As a consequence, in 1941, 77.6 % of the total population of the Transmura Region declared themselves to be ethnic Hungarians and 21.2 % ethnic Wends (Slovene), despite the fact that only 43.8 % of the total population could speak Hungarian and 80.1 % Wend (Slovene). The 23.9 % of bi-lingual speakers within the Transmura Region (in this case Hungarian and Wend) sometimes caused considerable fluctuation in statistics. During the years of World War II, apart from the war losses, the number of Slovenes declined somewhat owing to the internment of 668 indigenous Slovene colonists in Sárvár in June 1942. Meanwhile, Hungarian native speakers decreased due to the deportation of Magyarized Jews from Muraszombat and Alsólendva (366 persons in 1941)[8].

---

[8] Sever, B. 1991 ibid.. 71.p.

Table 34. Ethnic structure of the population of Alsólendva - Lendava (1880–1991)

Year	Total population		Slovenes		**Hungarians**		Croats		Others	
	number	%	number	%	**number**	%	number	%	number	%
1880	*1,879*	*100*	*336*	*17.9*	*1,372*	*73.0*	*56*	*3.0*	*115*	*6.1*
1900	*2,361*	*100*	*352*	*14.9*	*1.975*	*83.7*	*16*	*0.7*	*18*	*0.7*
1910	*2,729*	*100*	*283*	*10.4*	*2,375*	*87.0*	*51*	*1.9*	*20*	*0.7*
1921	*3,027*	*100*	*840*	*27.8*	*1,526*	*50.4*	*252*	*8.3*	*409*	*13.5*
1941	*2,160*	*100*	*350*	*16.2*	*1,750*	*81.0*	*24*	*1.1*	*36*	*1.7*
1948	2,402	100	1.375	57.2	**883**	**36.8**	130	5.4	14	0.6
1961	2,561	100	1,353	52.8	**850**	**33.2**	274	10.7	84	3.3
1971	3,044	100	1,617	53.1	**943**	**31.0**	270	8.9	214	7.0
1981	3,669	100	1,840	50.1	**1,018**	**27.7**	468	12.8	343	9.4
1991	3,807	100	1,952	51.3	**1,062**	**27.9**	482	12.7	311	8.1
1991	*3,807*	*100*	*1,776*	*46.7*	*1,221*	*32.1*	*555*	*14.6*	*255*	*6.6*

Sources: 1880, 1910, 1941: Hungarian census data, 1921, 1931, 1948-1991: Yugoslav census data.
Remarks: Including Lendvahegy and Hármasmalom between 1880-1948. Italic figures: mother / native tongue data.

The change of power in April 1945 led to the migration of various layers of public administration (military personnel, civil servants, etc.), this time in the opposite direction. The Slovenes who had been interned returned and were joined by newcomers. These changes together with the intimidation of Hungarians by deportation meant that at the 1948 Yugoslav census a mere 10.8 % (10,246 persons) of the region's population decided to declare themselves to be Hungarian. On the ethnically mixed territory of the borderland, owing to the massive settlement of Slovenes (1941: 2,338 persons, i.e. 15.7 %; 1948: 5,712, 34.9 %), the proportion of ethnic Hungarians decreased to 61.4 %. The ethnic structure of Alsólendva, a district seat and a centre of Slovenian oil mining changed profoundly: within its present administrative area the proportion of Hungarians fell to 37.3 % in 1948 (1941: 93.8 % Hung.). Owing to Kámaháza, Pártosfalu and Kisfalu becoming overwhelmingly Slovene, the number of villages with a Hungarian majority population dropped to 22. Socialist industrialisation, urbanisation and change in lifestyle accelerated the mobility of the population, although unlike other socialist countries, most agricultural land remained in private ownership. The Hungarian population of the Transmura Region suffered from a declining natural increase, and with a sense of identity shattered by Yugoslav propaganda, began to leave its ethnically mixed settlement areas in increasing numbers, and, looking for job opportunities, became dispersed over the Transmura Region with its Slovene majority, or migrated to more distant areas of Slovenia (Muraszombat, Maribor, Celje, Ljubljana, etc.). During the period between 1948-1991 the number of ethnic Hungarians living in the Transmura Region outside ethnically mixed territories had risen from 333 to 1,066, while that of the scattered Hungarians living west of the Mura River, in the inner areas of Slovenia had grown from 195 to 971. During the 1960s, 1970s and 1980s, with the possibility to work in and emigrate to the countries of western Europe, the number of Hungarians fell further. Since the 1974 constitution the political situation of local Hungarians has improved significantly, but due to a natural decrease, ageing, emigration, the ongoing process of assimilation and loss of linguistic and ethnic identity, the Hungarians of the Transmura Region lost a quarter of their population between 1948 and 1991.

THE PRESENT TERRITORY OF HUNGARIAN SETTLEMENT IN THE TRANSMURA REGION

According to the last Yugoslav census (1991) the number of ethnic Hungarians and Hungarian native speakers in Slovenia was 8,503 and 9,240, respectively. The corresponding figures for the Transmura Region were 7,637 and 8,174 (8.5 % and 9.1 %). The 23 villages with a Hungarian ethnic majority and 24 with a majority of native Hungarian speakers are to be found in the ethnically mixed territory of the Hungarian-Slovene borderland (EMT) between Őrihodos and Pince. Here, ethnic Hungarians make up 50.3 %, and Hungarian native speakers form 52.5 % of the total population, which is the lowest ever figure. 80.8 % of the Hungarians of Slovenia and 89.9 % of those of the Transmura Region live in this zone.

Hungarians represent a highly rural segment of the population in the Transmura Region, similar to the population as a whole (78.1 % of Hungarians live in villages, while 79.5 % of the total population lived in villages in 1991). In 1991, 80.8 % of younger Hungarians with higher qualifications who settled west of the Mura River in past decades were urban dwellers (in Ljubljana, Maribor, Celje, etc.). Reflecting physical geographical features of their area of settlement, 49.5 % of Hungarians live in tiny villages with less than 500 inhabitants, while 24.1 % of them inhabit small villages with a population of between 500-999, offering the most unfavourable conditions as regards local infrastructure and non-agricultural job opportunities. At the same time, this settlement pattern, which is characterised by an outflow of population, is responsible for maintaining a predominance of villages with an absolute Hungarian majority: 71.9 % of Hungarians live in such settlements. Ethnic (and native tongue) data testify that the largest Hungarian communities in the Transmura Region are Alsólendva 1,062 (1,221), Dobrónak 774 (783), Csentevölgy 498 (530), Lendvahosszúfalu 454 (473) and Petesháza 404 (422).

Chapter 8

THE HUNGARIANS OF BURGENLAND (ŐRVIDÉK)

The most popular Hungarian name for Burgenland, the easternmost and also the youngest province of Austria, which is used by the Hungarians of that region, is Őrvidék ('border-guard region') – not to be confused with the name of the region of Upper (Felső-) Őrség. At the end of the First World War, this West Hungarian Transdanubian territory was referred to as "Vierburgenland" (the region of four counties), including the German names of towns there: Pozsony, Moson, Sopron and Vas counties as Pressburg, Wieselburg, Ödenburg and Eisenburg. After the Czech troops occupied Pozsony City in January 1919, only the name of "Dreiburgenland" (the region of three counties) was used. In 1921 it finally became part of Austria under the name of Burgenland. The name is appropriate, for numerous places of the historical Hungarian border-fortress chain (Fraknó, Kabold, Lánzsér, Léka, Borostyánkő, Szalónak, Némétújvár, etc.) can be found in the 166 kilometre-long territory, which narrows to a width of 5 kilometres near Sopron.

The number of the Hungarian descendants of the medieval defenders of the former western Hungarian borderland, who mainly inhabit the Upper (Felső-) Őrség region and Felsőpulya, numbered 6,763 according to the 1991 Austrian "Every-day language" ("Umgangssprache") census data.

THE NATURAL ENVIRONMENT

The physical geography of the province is open towards the East (Hungary) and relatively closed towards the West (the inner part of Austria). The Hungarians of the Upper (Felső-) Őrség region inhabit an area next to the Pinka and Szék Streams which flow through the South Burgenland Hill and the Terrace Land while the inhabitants of Felsőpulya live in the Felsőpulya Basin surrounded by the Kőszeg, Lanzsér and Sopron Mountains *(Fig. 51.)*. The remaining Hungarians live mostly in Kismarton – with a population in 1991 of 10,349 – this is the capital of Burgenland at the southern foot of the Lajta Mountains, and in the Fertőzug region, located between the Hungarian border and Lake Fertő (Neusiedler See).

The important rivers of the region are the Lajta, Vulka, Csáva, Répce, Gyöngyös, Pinka, Strém, Lapincs and Rába. Its internationally renowned still waters include Lake Fertő, the third largest lake in Europe. The 35 kilometre-long lake gathers waters from Northern Burgenland. The pebble basin of Lake Fertő, a great tourist attraction and also referred to as the Lake of the Viennese, dates back to the Ice Age and is covered by close to one-hundred small lakes – most of them part of a nature conservation area.

As a result of settlement policies initiated by landowners to replenish the population on the estates within this borderland region, and owing to losses during warfare between kings Friedrich IV of Austria and Matthias Corvinus of Hungary, the Hungarian population formed a minority in the present-day territory of Burgenland by the end of the 15th century. Boundaries of a subsequent German ethnic area had already been formed by this time *(Fig. 52.)*. Apart from the much depleted Hungarian ethnic area (Fertőzug, patches in the Kismarton and Felsőpulya basins, in the Pinka Valley and

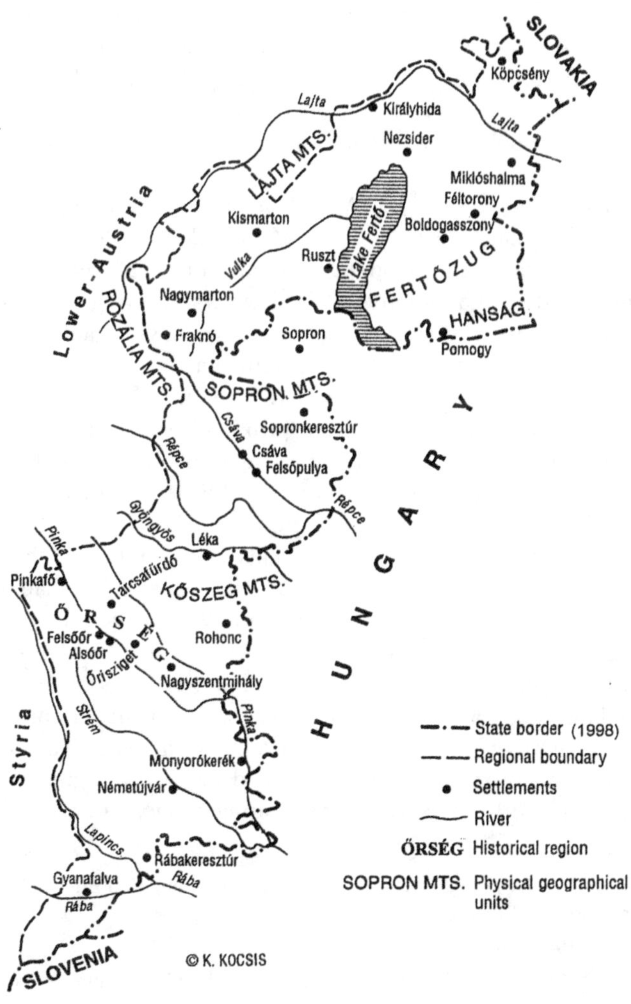

Figure 51. Important Hungarian geographical names in Burgenland

Németújvár), Burgenland was inhabited entirely by German speaking people. The biggest Hungarian ethnic pocket in the environs of Felsőőr was connected with the Hungarian ethnic block of West Pannonia through a corridor stretching along the Pinka Valley[1].

During the 16th and 17th centuries, as a consequence both of the Turkish campaigns (1529, 1532, 1664, 1683) and internal warfare, the Hungarian population which inhabited areas along military roads, river valleys and basins disappeared almost completely from the territory of Burgenland, except for the surroundings of Felsőőr and Felsőpulya. The survival of the Hungarians within these two ethnic pockets was ensured by the collective rights of nobility, which prevented the moving of foreigners into villages possessing such privileges or removing their collective land or property.[2]

A planned settlement of Croatian refugees into depopulated villages started in 1533, immediately after the siege of Kőszeg, and lasted for one and a half centuries, primarily targeting the following estates: Vörösvár, Szalónak, Rohonc, Kismarton. The Croatian newcomers naturally moved not only to abandoned villages but also created new settlements in unpopulated woodland areas, e.g. Újhegy, Őridobra, Pónic, Horváthásos, Lipóc, Borosd.[3]

After the Turkish wars and the War of Independence led by F. Rákóczi II, a re-population of the devastated areas (firstly in Moson County) took place almost exclusively by resettling German colonists in the first half of the 18th century. In some places, Hungarians were settled on the initiative of landowners, too (e.g. Felsőpulya, 1747). In the 1773 census, the present-day area of Burgenland was a Germanised region with both large and small Croatian ethnic blocks, and only ten settlements had a Hungarian-speaking majority. In the second half of the 18th century, due to the boom in cereal growing , its the geographical position (the proximity of the Danube as a means of transport), and the closeness to the market at Vienna, manors on the big estates of Moson County and primarily in the Fertőzug, were established in great numbers, specialising in cattle breeding, cereal and sugarbeet growing. The inhabitants of these manors were recruited from among the landless Hungarians living on the neighbouring Kapuvár estate and in the Csallóköz[4] region. The mushrooming of manors inhabited by Hungarians (they numbered 7 in 1784, 14 in 1869 and 38 in 1930) turned the formerly homogeneous German area between Lake Fertő and Moson-Danube into an ethnically varied one. At the same time, the abolition of the collective privileges of the nobility in 1848 created a grave ethnic situation for the descendants of the medieval border guards (Felső Őrség, Felsőpulya) who lived in the central and southern areas of Burgenland. The abolition of collective land property rights which had earlier strengthened the collective sense of identity and preserved the original Hungarian ethnic pattern, now allowed the

---

[1] Kovács M. 1942 A Felsőőri magyar népsziget (The Hungarian Ethnic Pocket of Oberwart), Település és Népiségtörténeti Értekezések 6., Budapest.

[2] Kovács M. 1942. ibidem

[3] Breu, J. 1934 Die Kroatensiedlung im südostdeutschen Grenzraum, Wien

[4] Csallóköz (Slovak: Žitný ostrov). Island in present-day South Slovakia, between the Danube and the Little Danube.

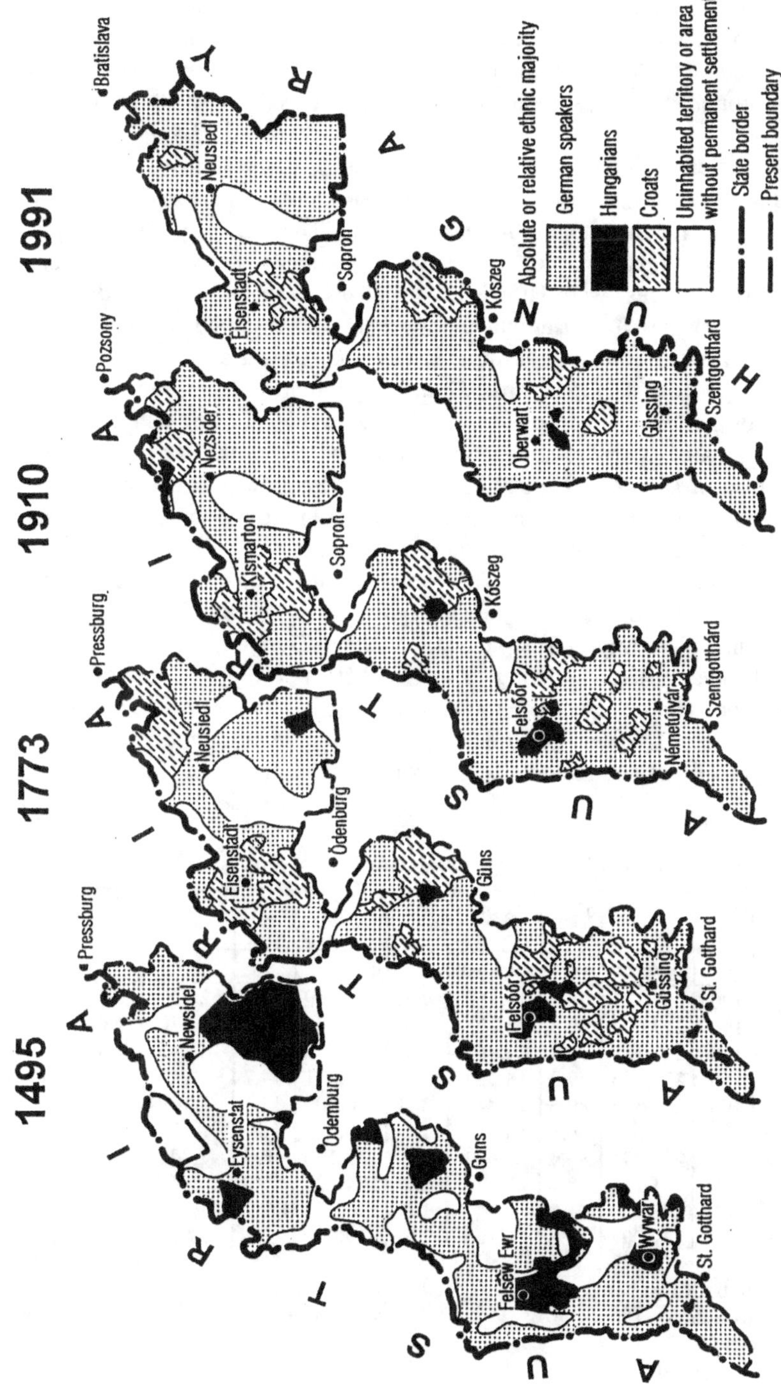

Figure 52. Ethnic map of the present-day territory of Burgenland (late 15th century, 1773, 1910, 1991)

resettlement of Germans in the Hungarian ethnic pockets. Germans came from surrounding villages to these areas which were centres of transport and markets (Felső- őr, Felsőpulya). In some villages of mixed population this accelerated Hungarian assimilation (whose proportion in Vasjobbágyi, for example, was 57 % in 1828, 16 % in 1880 and 8 % in 1920).

During the period following the Austro-Hungarian Compromise (1867), an event which curbed the process of Germanization, the first population census which also inquired about people's native language took place in 1880. The census of a total population of 266 thousand was taken on the territory of Burgenland; 78.8 % of them were Germans, 4.2 % (11,162 persons) were Hungarians and 16.1 % were Croats *(Tab. 35.)*. Due to the high esteem of the Hungarian statehood, there was a greater emigration of local Germans. There was also a natural assimilation of non-Hungarians between 1880 and 1910, thus the proportion of Hungarians within the population increased from 4..2 % to 9 %, while that of the Germans dropped from 78.8 % to 74.4 %. The ethnic pattern of the rural areas, compared with the state one hundred years before, did not change significantly, apart from a slow Germanization of ethnic Croatian pockets in the surroundings of Némétújvár, and the appearance of several manors in Moson County. The Hungarian-German ethnic border remained unchanged.

Similar to the present-day situation, an overwhelming majority of Hungarians living on Austrian territory lived not in Burgenland but in areas beyond the Lajta River, predominantly in Vienna. The imperial capital attracted the Hungarian aristocrats and their servants (also Hungarian) and, owing to the market opportunities, thousands of Hungarian craftsmen too. The number of Hungarians living in Vienna was 15 thousand in the 1840s, 30 thousand in 1890 and 45 thousand in 1910. Hungarian citizens of various ethnicities living in Vienna and its vicinity numbered 232 thousand in 1910.

Table 35. Ethnic structure of the population on the present territory of Burgenland (1880–1991)

Year	Total population		"Germans"		**Hungarians**		Croats		Others	
	number	%	number	%	**number**	%	number	%	number	%
1880	265,772	100	209,322	78.8	**11,162**	**4.2**	42,789	16.1	2,499	0.9
1910	291,800	100	217,072	74.4	**26,225**	**9.0**	43,633	15.0	4,870	1.6
1920	294,849	100	221,185	75.0	**24,867**	**8.4**	44,753	15.2	4,044	1.4
1923	286,179	100	226,995	79.3	**15,254**	**5.3**	42,011	14.7	1,919	0.7
1934	299,447	100	241,326	80.6	**10,442**	**3.5**	40,500	13.5	7,179	2.4
1951	276,136	100	239,687	86.8	**5,251**	**1.9**	30,599	11.1	599	0.2
1961	271,001	100	235,491	86.9	**5,642**	**2.1**	28,126	10.4	1,742	0.6
1971	272,119	100	241,254	88.7	**5,673**	**2.1**	24,526	9.0	666	0.2
1981	269,771	100	245,369	91.0	**4,147**	**1.5**	18,762	7.0	1,493	0.5
1991	270,880	100	239,097	88.3	**6,763**	**2.8**	19,460	8.1	5,560	0.8

Sources: 1880, 1910, 1920: Hungarian census data (mother/native tongue), 1923, 1934: Austrian census data (language affiliation), 1951, 1961, 1971, 1981, 1991: Austrian census data (every-day language /"Umgangssprache").
Remark: *"Germans": German (native) speakers.*

Following World War I, lost by Austria and Hungary, the Peace Treaty of Saint-Germain-en-Laye (September 10, 1919) gave the western part of Hungary with its predominantly German-speaking population to Austria. As a result of vehement Hungarian protest however, 'only' present-day Burgenland was ceded to Austria, following the plebiscite in Sopron and Pinka Valley which achieved favourable results for Hungary. Owing to the change of power, the Hungarian population of the province which had lived in language pockets since the 16th century, was forced into a political minority after having been a state forming nation. Although the new state boundary did not hinder the maintenance of former economic, social and cultural contacts, the social strata which had the closest ties with the Hungarian state and nation or were not indigenous (civil servants, military personnel, police, railwaymen, teachers, workers, etc.) moved to the actual territory of Hungary in large numbers. Owing to this large-scale resettlement the number of native Hungarian speakers decreased by more than 10 thousand, i.e. by 39 %. This especially affected ethnic Hungarians who were scattered, while the native population of villages in Őrség had only decreased by a few hundred. The number of workers and farm labourers, who formed the lowest social strata among Hungarians in Burgenland, dropped drastically owing to their repatriation. This process continued through the 1920s owing to the mechanisation of farming on the big estates and the attraction of well-paying industrial work, particularly in Vienna.

Even so, this latter migration and Hungarian political emigration could not counterbalance the rapid decline in the number of Hungarians living in Austria and Vienna following the disintegration of the Monarchy, and as a consequence of massive repatriation and emigration (Vienna; 1910: 45 thousand; 1923: 10,922; 1934: 4,844 Hungarians). Emigration and statistical manipulation (e.g. the registration of 6,507, overwhelmingly Hungarian-speaking Gypsies into a separate language category independent of their own declaration) showed that the number of Hungarians in Burgenland had fallen to the level of half a century before, according to the 1934 population census. By that time their most important settlement, Felsőőr (which acquired the status of a town in 1938) had lost its earlier absolute Hungarian majority owing to the ever intensifying immigration of Catholic German-speaking people (predominantly civil servants, merchants and craftsmen) *(Tab. 36.).*

Following the German occupation of Austria (March 12-13, 1938), the Hungarians of Burgenland found themselves in a very different situation. The German administration abolished Burgenland as a province and its territory was divided between Styria and the Lower Danube imperial provinces (Steiermark, Niederdonau Reichsgaus). Parallel to the closure of Hungarian church schools, the use of the Hungarian language was restricted to family life by Nazi propaganda and national policy. The previous self-esteem of Hungarians, including aristocrats with great economic power, vanished. They started to feel the disadvantages of their minority status. A significant transformation in their thinking occurred among the younger generation, who in an increasingly fascist climate felt their Hungarian origins to be shameful, particularly at school and in the army.[5]

After World War II, in spite of Burgenland being under Soviet occupation, the frontier was sealed and border crossing points eliminated during the Hungarian communist Rákosi regime. In this way the ethnic groups of West Transdanubia, among them the Hungarians of Burgenland, lost their natural and traditional economic, social and inter-ethnic contacts and became cut off from their traditional market centres (e.g. Sopron, Szombathely). Apart from the economic disaster an even greater psychological and ethnic trauma was caused by the fact that the "iron curtain" and the communist powers in Hungary made the maintenance of previous ties with a Hungarian language environment and institutes of education impossible. The change of power in Hungary put the Hungarians of Burgenland in an awkward situation since "Hungarian" and "communist" had become synonymous in Austrian public opinion. On the other hand, for the Hungarian minority their homeland, which was falling behind Austria in its economic development, was only a symbol of their cultural home and of communism.[6] Thus, it can be understood that the number of those in Burgenland in the 1951 population census declaring Hungarian to be their everyday language had halved (from 10,442 in 1934 to 5,251). A similar fall was recorded among the Hungarians in Vienna of Austrian citizenship, who disguised their Hungarian origins ((1934: 1,042; 1951: 384).

During the economic boom and industrialisation which followed the political treaty creating present-day Austria, and the later withdrawal of Soviet troops from the country (1955), the social mobility of the population (including the Hungarians in Burgenland) increased. This social transformation rapidly disrupted traditional rural ethnic communities which had evolved over centuries. Hungarians who had given up farming or retained it as a part-time occupation moved from villages to industrial centres, where they found themselves in a German speaking environment and became daily or weekly commuters. The abandonment of their birthplace involved an increasing use of German, and in the case of young people, a steady exchange of language and culture.[7] A spectacular loss of the Hungarian language came as a result of a general aversion towards the Hungarian communist system, and an attempt by Hungarians to avoid possible discrimination. The Hungarian language had no economic use and was also lost in a bid to do well at school and in the workplace and, naturally because of mixed marriages. The number of marriages between ethnic Hungarians and Germans accelerated the natural assimilation already within the family framework. In Alsóőr, the most Hungarian village in Burgenland, mixed marriages were 19 % in the period between 1949-1958 and increased to 60.6 % in 1969-1988. The ratio of mixed marriages and factors influencing

---

[5] Baumgartner, G. 1989 "Idevalósi vagyok" - "Einer der hierher gehört". Zur Identität der ungaricshen Sprachgruppe des Burgenlandes — in: Baumgartner, G. et al. (Hg.) Identität und Lebenswelt. Ethnische, religiöse und kulturelle Vielfalt im Burgenland, Prugg Verlag, Eisenstadt, pp.69-86.

[6] Henke, R. 1988 Leben lassen ist nicht genug. Minderheiten in Österreich, Kremayr-Scherian, Wien

[7] Suppan, A. 1983 ibid.

200

Table 36. Change in the ethnic structure of selected settlements of Burgenland (1880 - 1991)

Year	Total population		"Germans"		**Hungarians**		Others	
	number	%	number	%	**number**	%	number	%
Felsőőr - Oberwart								
1880	3,397	100.0	885	26.0	**2,487**	**73.2**	25	0.8
1910	3,912	100.0	842	21.5	**3,039**	**77.7**	31	0.8
1920	4,162	100.0	838	20.1	**3,138**	**75.4**	186	4.5
1923	3,846	100.0	1,162	30.2	**2,664**	**69.3**	20	0.5
1934	4,603	100.0	2,058	44.7	**2,234**	**48.5**	311	6.8
1951	4,496	100.0	2,854	63.5	**1,603**	**36.3**	39	0.2
1961	4,740	100.0	3,011	63.5	**1,630**	**34.4**	99	2.1
1971	5,455	100.0	3,912	71.7	**1,486**	**27.2**	57	1.1
1981	5,715	100.0	4,294	75.1	**1,343**	**23.5**	78	1.4
1991	6,093	100.0	4,210	69.1	**1,592**	**26.1**	291	4.8
Alsóőr - Unterwart								
1880	1,508	100.0	88	5.8	**1,377**	**91.3**	43	2.9
1910	1,464	100.0	63	4.3	**1,393**	**95.2**	8	0.5
1920	1,415	100.0	57	4.0	**1,230**	**86.9**	128	9.1
1923	1,276	100.0	78	6.1	**1,197**	**93.8**	1	0.1
1934	1,267	100.0	93	7.3	**988**	**78.0**	195	14.7
1951	989	100.0	148	15.0	**789**	**79.8**	52	5.2
1961	916	100.0	62	6.8	**795**	**86.8**	59	6.4
1971	859	100.0	104	12.1	**696**	**81.0**	59	6.9
1981	822	100.0	61	7.4	**725**	**88.2**	36	4.4
1991	769	100.0	48	6.2	**669**	**87.0**	52	6.8
Őrisziget - Siget in der Wart								
1880	386	100.0	20	5.2	**362**	**93.8**	4	1.0
1910	333	100.0	16	4.8	**317**	**95.2**	0	0
1920	295	100.0	21	7.1	**271**	**91.9**	3	1.0
1923	300	100.0	28	9.3	**272**	**90.7**	0	0
1934	291	100.0	37	12.7	**253**	**86.9**	1	0.4
1951	262	100.0	217	82.8	**45**	**17.2**	0	0
1961	238	100.0	29	12.2	**209**	**87.8**	0	0
1971	255	100.0	41	16.1	**200**	**78.4**	14	5.5
1981	285	100.0	120	42.1	**165**	**57.9**	0	0
1991	272	100.0	46	16.9	**223**	**82.0**	3	1.1
Felsőpulya - Oberpullendorf								
1880	1,262	100.0	114	9.0	**1,115**	**88.4**	33	2.6
1910	1,327	100.0	66	5.0	**1,241**	**93.5**	20	1.5
1920	1,385	100.0	59	4.3	**1,302**	**94.0**	24	1.7
1923	1,400	100.0	199	14.2	**1,183**	**84.5**	19	1.3
1934	1,838	100.0	563	30.6	**1,227**	**66.8**	48	2.6
1951	1,824	100.0	945	51.8	**863**	**47.3**	16	0.9
1961	2,047	100.0	994	48.6	**1,016**	**49.6**	37	1.8
1971	2,323	100.0	1,462	62.9	**761**	**32.8**	100	4.3
1981	2,422	100.0	1,560	64.4	**724**	**29.9**	138	5.7
1991	2,640	100.0	1,756	66.5	**631**	**23.9**	253	9.6

Sources: 1880, 1900, 1910, 1920: Hungarian census data (mother/native tongue), 1923, 1934: Austrian census data (language affiliation), 1951-1991: Austrian census data (every-day language /"Umgangssprache").
Remark: Felsőpulya includes Középpulya..

natural assimilation were influenced to a large extent by the rate of immigration due to advantageous economic factors, job opportunities, and the geographical position of minority settlements. Most German-speaking settlers had gone to district centres such as Felsőőr and Felsőpulya, which in the first third of the 20th century still had a Hungarian ethnic majority. As a consequence, Hungarians living in these settlements in mixed families numbered 30-38 %.[8] At the time of a survey conducted by L. Somogyi (1964) based on the analyses and evaluations of family names, place of residence, origin and religious affiliation, the number of Hungarians in Burgenland was estimated to be 7,600 (as compared with the 5,642 Hungarians recorded during the 1961 census). People who settled here during the exodus following the 1956 revolution formed only a small number of those leaving their homeland and did not significantly add to the statistical number of Hungarians. On the contrary, owing to accelerated lingual assimilation, unfavourable demographic processes (ageing, mortality) and increasing emigration, the number of people speaking Hungarian as their everyday language (Umgangssprache) decreased from 5,673 to 4,147 between the 1971 and 1981 censuses (a drop from 2.1 % to 1.5 %). Comparing the trends prevailing in Burgenland with the number of Hungarians with Austrian citizenship living in Vienna, with its permanent supply of immigrants, a more favourable change can be observed (1951: 384; 1971: 6,099; 1981: 5,683). During the period between 1981 and 1991, a positive effect of the changes in the political system in Hungary was the increased self-awareness of the Hungarians living in Austria, and the "usefulness" of the Hungarian language. Also, due to an increase in the number of Hungarians settling in Austria following the fall of the "iron curtain", the total number of Hungarians with Austrian citizenship grew by 63.1 % (to 19,638), and that of non-citizens increased by 260.7 % (to 13,821). Non-citizen Vienna residents of Hungarian origin doubled, moreover, in the environs of the Austrian capital and in Lower Austria there was a 7.4-fold increase. The number of autochtonous Hungarians in Burgenland, mainly in Felsőőr and Őrisziget, increased by 23.5 %, while Hungarians with Austrian and other citizenship rose by 63.1 %.

THE PRESENT TERRITORY OF HUNGARIAN SETTLEMENT IN BURGENLAND (ŐRVIDÉK)

At the time of the last Austrian census (1991) the number of people declaring Hungarian to be their everyday language was 33,459 (58.7 of them Austrian citizens). A mere 20.2 % of Hungarians residing in Austria, (i.e. 6,763 persons) live in their indigenous settlement area, in Burgenland. The overwhelming majority of Hungarians can be found scattered not only over the Lajta River area but also in Burgenland. Only 36.7 % of the Hungarian population inhabit the three settlements of Felső Őrség region (Felsőőr, Alsóőr and Őrisziget), forming a small language pocket.

---

[8] Somogyi L. 1966 Die burgenländischen Magyaren in geographischer Sicht, Karl-Franzens Universität, Graz, 279p.

Due to a high number of Hungarians in Burgenland residing in district centres (Felsőőr, Felsőpulya, Kismarton) the ratio of urban dwellers (47.3 %) far exceeded that of the total population (18.2 %) in 1991. 30.4 % of these lived in settlements with 2,000-4,999 inhabitants, while 28.7 % of them inhabited settlements with 5,000-10,000 inhabitants. These are predominantly settlements offering better living conditions, but are more liable to immigration which affects the earlier ethnic pattern. Since the Hungarian majority vanished in Felsőőr and Felsőpulya half a century ago, only 13.2 % of Hungarians in Burgenland are residents of villages (Alsóőr, Őrisziget), where they represent an absolute majority. 63.3 % of them experience considerable German language pressure, living in settlements where their ratio does not reach 25 %. The most populous Hungarian communities of Burgenland are: Felsőőr (1,592), Alsóőr (669), Felsőpulya (631), Kismarton (257), Őrisziget (223) and Boldogasszony (215) *(Fig. 53.)*.

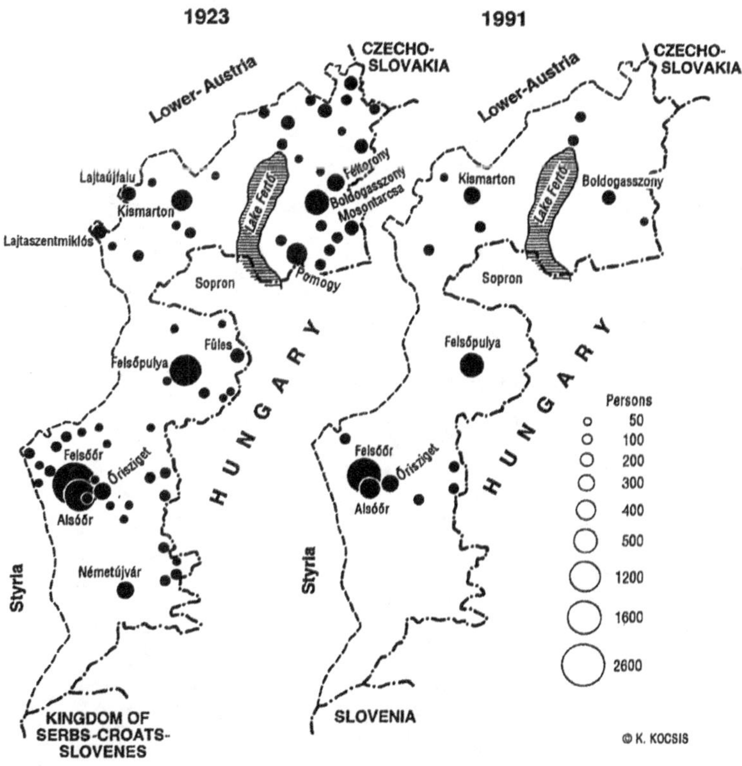

Figure 53. Hungarian communities in Burgenland (1923, 1991)

GEOGRAPHICAL REGISTER

Hungarian and present official (Slovakian, Ukrainain, Rumanian, Serbian, Croatian, Slovenian, German) names with some English remarks.

English abbreviations: R = physical geographical region; PL = plain, lowland; M = mountain, mount; H = hills; B = basin; C = cave; P = plateau; V = valley; PS = pass; S = swamp, marsh, moor; L = lake

SLOVAKIA

Relief names:

Hungarian	*Slovakian*	
Bodrogköz	Medzibodrožie	R
Csallóköz	Žitný ostrov	R
Csilizköz	Čilizská mokraď	R
Dunamenti-alföld	Podunajská nižina	PL
Garammenti-dombság	Hronská pahorkatina	H
Gömbaszögi-barlang	Gombasecká jaskýňa	C
Gömör-Tornai (Szlovák-)-karszt	Slovenský kras	M
Fábiánszög (633 m)	Fabiánka	M
Ipoly-medence	Ipel'ská kotlina	B
Ipolymenti-dombság	Ipel'ská pahorkatina	H
Jávoros	Javorie	M
Karancs-Medves-vidék	Cerová vrchovina	M
Karancs (728 m), Ragács (536 m)	Karanč, Roháč	M
Kassai-medence	Košická kotlina	B
Kelet-Szlovákiai-Alföld	Východoslovenská nižina	PL
Kis-Kárpátok	Malé Karpaty	M
Korponai-fennsík	Krupinská planina	P
Losonci-medence	Lučenecká kotlina	B
Lőcsei-hegység	Levočské vrchy	M
Rima-medence	Rimavská kotlina	B
Rozsnyói-medence	Rožňavská kotlina	B
Selmeci-hegység	Štiavnické vrchy	M
Somoskő	Šomoška	M

Szádelői-völgy	Zádielská dolina	V
Szalánci-(Tokaj-Eperjesi-) hegység	Slánske vrchy	M
Szepesi Magura	Spišská magura	M
Szilicei-fennsík	Silická planina	P
Szlovák-(Gömör-Szepesi-) érchegység	Slovenské rudohorie	M
Tribecs (Zobor 588 m)	Tribeč (Zobor)	M
Vihorlát	Vihorlat	M
Zempléni-hegység (Csókás 469 m)	Zemplínske vrchy (Rozhl'adňa)	M

Hydrographical names:

Hungarian	*Slovakian*
Balog	Blh
Bodrog	Bodrog
Bódva	Bodva
Csermoslya	Čremošná
Dudvág	Dudváh
Duna	Dunaj
Dunajec	Dunajec
Fekete-víz	Čierna Voda
Garam	Hron
Gortva	Gortva
Hernád	Hornád
Ida	Ida
Ipoly	Ipeľ
Kétyi-víz	Kvetnianka
Kis-Duna	Malý Dunaj
Korpona-patak	Krupinica
Kürtös-patak	Krtiš
Laborc	Laborec
Latorca	Latorica
Murány	Muráň
Nyitra	Nitra
Ondava	Ondava
Ósva	Olšava
Párizsi-csatorna	Párižský kanál
Rima	Rimava
Ronyva	Roňava
Sajó	Slaná
Szikince	Sikenica
Tarca	Torysa

Torna	Turna
Turóc	Turiec
Ung	Uh
Vág	Váh
Zsitva	Žitava

Names of historical regions:

Hungarian	*Slovakian*
Abaúj	Abov
Árva	Orava
Bars	Tekov
Gömör	Gemer
Hont	Hont
Kis-Hont	Malohont
Komárom	Komárno
Liptó	Liptov
Nógrád	Novohrad
Nyitra	Nitra
Pozsony	Bratislava, Prešpork
Sáros	Šariš
Szepes, Szepesség	Spiš
Torna	Turna
Trencsén	Trenčín
Turóc	Turiec
Zemplén	Zemplín
Zólyom	Zvolen

Settlement names:

Hungarian	*Slovakian*
Abaszéplak	Košice-Krásna nad Hornádom
Abaújnádasd	Trstené pri Hornáde
Abaújszina	Seňa
Alsóbodok	Dolné Obdokovce
Alsócsitár	Nitra-Štitáre
Alsólehnic	Červený Kláštor
Alsósajó	Nižná Slaná
Alsószecse	Dolná Seč

Alsószeli	Dolné Saliby
Alsózellő	Dolné Zlievce
Ajnácskő	Hajnačka
Appony	Oponice
Aranyosmarót	Zlaté Moravce
Assakürt	Nové Sady
Bakabánya	Pukanec
Bánkeszi	Bánov
Barsbese	Beša
Barslédec, Ladice	Ladice
Bártfa	Bardejov
Bát	Bátovce
Bátorkeszi	Vojnice
Battyán	Boťany
Bazin	Pezinok
Béke	Mierovo
Bélabánya	Banská Belá
Bély	Biel
Béna	Belina
Bény	Bíňa
Besztercebánya	Banská Bystrica
Bodrogmező, Polyán	Poľany
Bodrogszerdahely	Streda nad Bodrogom
Bős	Gabčíkovo
Bussó	Bušince
Buzita	Buzica
Cífer	Cífer
Csáb	Čebovce
Csákányháza	Čakanovce
Csallóközaranyos	Zlatná na Ostrove
Csallóközcsütörtök	Štvrtok na Ostrove
Csata	Čata
Cseklész	Bernolákovo
Cselfalva	Čelovce
Csetnek	Štítnik
Csilizradvány	Čiližská Radvaň
Csíz	Číz
Csörgő	Čerhov
Debrőd	Debraď
Deménd	Demandice
Deregnyő	Drahňov
Dévényújfalu	Bratislava-Devínska Nová Ves
Diósförgepatony	Orehová Potôň
Diószeg	Sládkovičovo

Divény	Divín
Dobóca	Dubovec
Dobsina	Dobšina
Dunacsún	Bratislava-Čuňovo
Dunaszerdahely	Dunajská Streda
Ebeck	Obeckov
Éberhard	Malinovo
Egyházfa	Kostolná pri Dunaji
Ekecs	Okoč
Ekel	Okoličná na Ostrove
Előpatony	Lehnice-Masníkovo
Eperjes	Prešov
Érsekújvár	Nové Zámky
Eszkáros	Skároš
Farnad	Farná
Fél	Tomášov
Feled	Jesenské
Felka	Poprad-Veľká
Felsőfalu	Chvalová
Felsőhosszúfalu	Dlhá
Felsőszecse	Horná Seč
Felsőszeli	Horné Saliby
Fülek	Fiľakovo
Fülekkovácsi	Fiľakovské Kováče
Fülekpilis	Pleš
Fülekpüspöki	Fiľakovo -Biskupice
Galánta	Galanta
Galgóc	Hlohovec
Gálszécs	Sečovce
Garamdamásd	Hronovce-Domaša
Garamszentkereszt	Žiar nad Hronom
Garany	Hraň
Gázlós	Brodské
Ghymes	Jelenec
Girált	Giraltovce
Gömörhosszúszó	Dlhá Ves
Gömörnánás	Gemerský Sad-Nováčany
Gömörsid	Šíd
Gúta	Kolárovo
Gyetva	Detva
Gyügy	Dudince
Hardicsa	Zemplínske Hradište
Hárskút	Lipovnik
Hernádcsány	Čaňa

Hernádtihany	Košice-Ťahanovce
Hódi	Galanta-Hody
Holics	Holíč
Homonna	Humenné
Horvátgurab	Chorvátský Grob
Horvátjárfalu	Bratislava-Jarovce
Igló	Spišská Nová Ves
Illésháza	Nový Život-Eliášovce
Illava	Ilava
Ipolybalog	Balog nad Ipl'om
Ipolyhídvég	Ipel'ské Predmostie
Ipolynyék	Vinica
Ipolyság	Šahy
Ipolyszakállas	Ipel'ský Sokolec
Ipolyvisk	Vyškovce nad Ipl'om
Jánok	Janík
Jászó	Jasov
Jéne	Janice
Jóka	Jelka
Jolsva	Jelšava
Jolsvatapolca	Gemerské Teplice
Kapi	Kapušany
Kárpáthalas	Vištuk
Kassa	Košice
Kassaújfalu	Košice-Košická Nová Ves
Kasza	Košeca
Kátó	Kátov
Kéménd	Kamenín
Késmárk	Kežmarok
Királyhelmec	Král'ovský Chlmec
Kisdobra	Dobrá
Kisgéres	Malý Horeš
Kisperlász	Prihradzany
Kisszalánc	Slančík
Kisszeben	Sabinov
Kisvisnyó	Višňové
Kolon	Koliňany
Komárom	Komárno
Komját	Komjatice
Korompa	Krompachy
Korpona	Krupina
Köbölkút	Gbelce
Kőhegy	Lukovištia
Körmöcbánya	Kremnica

Krasznahorkaváralja	Krasnohorské Podhradie
Kural	Kuraľany
Kürt	Strekov
Lamacs	Bratislava-Lamač
Lasztóc	Lastovce
Lednic	Lednica
Leibic	Kežmarok-Ľubica
Lelesz	Leles
Léva	Levice
Lice	Licince
Losonc	Lučenec
Losoncapátfalva	Opatová
Lőcse	Levoča
Lukanénye	Nenice
Madar	Svodín
Malomszeg, Nyitramalomszeg	Lipová-Mlynský Sek
Marcelháza	Marcelová
Margonya	Marhaň
Mászt	Stupava-Mást
Mecenzéf (Alsó- and Felsőmecenzéf)	Medzev
Megyercs	Čalovec
Meleghegy	Teplý Vrch
Mikolcsány	Gemerský Sad-Mikolčany
Mocsonok	Močenok
Modor	Modra
Mohi	Mochovce
Muzsla	Mužla
Nádszeg	Trstice
Nagyazar	Veľké Ozorovce
Nagybalog	Veľký Blh
Nagycétény	Veľký Cetín
Nagyemőke	Nitra-Veľké Janíkovce
Nagyfödémes	Veľké Uľany
Nagyida	Veľká Ida
Nagykapos	Veľké Kapušany
Nagykövesd	Veľký Kamenec
Nagykürtös	Veľký Krtíš
Nagylég	Lehnice
Nagymagyar	Zlaté Klasy-Rastice
Nagymegyer	Veľký Meder
Nagymihály	Michalovce
Nagyölved	Veľké Ludince
Nagyrőce	Revúca
Nagysalló	Tekovské Lužany

Nagysáros	Veľký Šariš
Nagysenkőc	Šenkvice
Nagysúr	Šúrovce
Nagysurány	Šurany
Nagyszilva	Veľký Slivnik
Nagyszombat	Trnava
Nagytapolcsány	Topoľčany
Nagytárkány	Veľké Trakany
Nagytoronya	Veľká Trňa
Nahács	Naháč
Naszvad	Nasvady
Negyed	Neded
Nemesócsa	Zemianska Olča
Németbél	Veľký Biel-Malý Biel
Németgurab, Magyargurab	Veľký Grob
Németpróna	Nitrianske Pravno
Nyárasd	Topoľníky
Nyitra	Nitra
Nyitracsehi	Nitrany-Čechynce
Nyitragerencsér	Nitra-Hrnčiarovce
Nyitranagykér	Veľký Kýr
Nyitraújlak	Veľké Zalužie
Óbars	Starý Tekov
Ógyalla	Hurbánovo
Ómajor	Majere
Oroszka	Pohronský Ruskov
Oroszvár	Bratislava-Rusovce
Osgyán	Ožďany
Ószombat	Sobotište
Ótura	Stará Tura
Örsújfalu	Komárno-Nová Stráž
Özdöge	Mojzesovo
Palást	Plášťovce
Pálóc	Pavlovce nad Uhom
Pány	Paňovce
Panyidaróc	Panické Drávce
Párkány	Štúrovo
Pécsújfalu	Pečovská Nová Ves
Pelsőc	Plešivec
Pelsőcardó	Ardovo
Perbenyik	Pribeník
Perbete	Pribetá
Perse	Prša
Pográny	Pohranice

Poprád	Poprad
Pozsony	Bratislava
Pozsonyhidegkút	Bratislava-Dúbravka
Pozsonyivánka	Ivanka pri Dunaji
Pozsonyligetfalu	Bratislava-Petržalka
Pozsonypüspöki	Bratislava-Podunajské Biskupice
Pólyi	Poľov
Privigye	Prievidza
Pusztafödémes	Pusté Uľany
Radács	Radatice
Ragyolc	Radzovce
Rimaszécs	Rimavska Seč
Rimaszombat	Rimavska Sobota
Rozsnyó	Rožňava
Sajógömör	Gemer
Sajószentkirály	Kráľ'
Sáró	Šarovce
Sasvár	Šaštín
Selmecbánya	Banská Štiavnica
Selpőc	Šelpice
Sempte	Šintava
Somorja	Šamorín
Somos	Drienov
Sőreg	Šurice
Strázsa	Poprad-Stráže pod Tatrami
Süvete	Šivetice
Szádalmás	Jablonov nad Turnou
Szádudvarnok	Zádielské Dvorniky
Szakolca	Skalica
Szaláncújváros	Slanské Nové Mesto
Szántó	Santovka
Százd	Sazdice
Szenc	Senec
Szentgyörgy	Svätý Jur
Szentistvánfalva	Popudiny
Szepesbéla	Spišská Belá
Szepesszombat	Poprad-Spišská Sobota
Szepesváralja	Spišské Podhradie
Szepsi	Moldava nad Bodvou
Szered	Sereď'
Szilice	Silica
Szilvásújfalu	Slivník
Szimő	Zemné
Szomotor	Somotor

Szőgyén, Magyar- and Németszőgyén	Svodín
Sztropkó	Stropkov
Taksonyfalva	Matúškovo
Tany	Tôň
Tardoskedd	Tvrdošovce
Tasolya	Tašuľa
Tiszacsernyő	Čierná nad Tisou
Tonkháza	Nový Život-Tonkovce
Torna	Turnianské Podhradie
Tornalja	Tornaľa
Tornaújfalu	Nova Bodva-Turnianska Nova Ves
Tornóc	Trnovec nad Váhom
Tótmegyer	Palárikovo
Tőketerebes	Trebišov
Trencsén	Trenčín
Udvard	Dvory nad Žitavou
Ugróc , Zayugróc	Uhrovec
Újbánya	Nová Baňa
Újgyalla	Dulovce
Újlót	Veľké Lovce
Ungpinkóc	Pinkovce
Uzapanyit	Uzovská Panica
Ürmény	Mojmírovce
Vágfarkasd	Vlčany
Vágmagyarád	Trnava-Modranka
Vágpatta	Pata
Vágsellye	Šaľá
Vaján	Vojany
Vajka	Vojka nad Dunajom
Vámosbalog, Alsó- and Felsőbalog	Veľký Blh
Vámosladány	Mýtne Ludany
Varannó	Vranov nad Topľou
Várad	Tekovský Hrádok
Várgede	Hodejov
Várhosszúrét	Krásnohorská Dlhá Luka
Várkony	Vrakúň
Vásárút	Trhové Mýto
Verebély	Vráble
Vilke	Veľká nad Ipľom
Vízkelet	Čierný Brod
Zemplén	Zemplín
Zohor	Zohor
Zólyom	Zvolen
Zselíz	Želiezovce

Zsemlér	Žemliare
Zsére	Žirany
Zsitvabesenyő	Bešenov
Zsitvafödémes	Úľany nad Žitavou
Zsolna	Žilina
Zsolnalitva	Lietava

TRANSCARPATHIA (UKRAINE)

Relief names:

Hungarian	*Ukrainian*	
Alföld (Kárpátontúli-alföld)	Zakarpatska nizovina	PL
Avas	Avaš	M
Borló-Gyil	Veliki Dil	M
Máramarosi-havasok	Horhany, Krasna, Svidovec, Čornohora	M
Nagyszőlősi-hegység	Sevljušska Hora	M
Pojána-Szinyák	Makovicja	M
Tatár-hágó	Jablunickij perevil	PS
Tiszahát	—	R
Vereckei-hágó	Vereckij perevil	PS

Hydrographical names:

Hungarian	*Ukrainian*
Borzsa	Boržava
Latorca	Latorica
Nagyág	Rika
Szernye	Sirne
Talabor	Terebja
Tarac	Teresva
Tisza (Fehér-, Fekete-)	Tisa (Bila-, Čorna)
Ung	Už

Names of certain historical regions:

Hungarian	**Ukrainian**
Bereg	Bereh
Máramaros	Marmaroš
Ugocsa	Uhoča
Ung	Už

Settlement names:

Hungarian	**Ukrainian**
Akli	
Aknaszlatina	Solotvina
Baranya	Baranincy
Barkaszó	Barkasove
Batár	Bratove
Bátyú	Vuzlove, Bateve
Beregdéda	Didove
Beregrákos	Rakošin
Beregsom	Derenkovec
Beregszász	Berehove
Beregszentmiklós	Činadieve
Beregújfalu	Nove Selo
Bótrágy	Batraď
Bustyaháza	Buština
Csap	Čop
Csepe	Čepa
Csikósgorond	Čikoš-Horonda
Csomafalva	Zatisivka
Csongor	Čomanin
Csonkapapi	Popovo
Dercen	Drisina
Eszeny	Eseň
Fancsika	Fančikove
Feketeardó	Čornotisiv
Felsőschönborn, Felsőkerepec	Verchnij Koropec
Fornos	Liskove
Gát	Hat'
Gyertyánliget	Kobilecka Poljana
Huszt	Hust

Ilosva	Iršava
Izsnyéte	Žňatine
Karácsfalva	Karačin
Kerekhegy	Okruhla
Kétgút	Harazdivka
Királyháza	Koroleve
Királymező	Ust' Čorna
Kisbakos	Bakoš
Kisbégány	Mala Bihaň
Kisdobrony	Mala Dobroň
Korláthelmec	Holmec
Kovászó	Kvasove
Kőrösmező	Jasiňa
Leányfalva, Beregleányfalva	Lalove
Makkossjánosi	Ivanivka
Mátyfalva	Matieve
Mezőkaszony	Kosini
Munkács	Mukačeve
Munkácsújfalu, Alsóschönborn	Nove Selo
Nagybakos	Svoboda
Nagybégány	Velika Bihaň
Nagybereg	Berehi
Nagyberezna	Velikij Bereznij
Nagybocskó	Velikij Bičkiv
Nagydobrony	Velika Dobroň
Nagymuzsaly	Mužievo
Nagypalád	Velika Palad'
Nagyszőlős	Vinohradiv
Németkucsova	Kučava
Németmokra	Komsomolsk
Nevetlenfalu	Ďakove
Nyárasgorond	Ňaroš Horonda
Perecsény	Perečin
Pósaháza	Pavsin
Rafajnaújfalu	Rafajlovo
Rahó	Rahiv
Rát	Rativci
Salánk	Šalanki
Szerednye	Seredne
Szernye	Rivne
Szolyva	Svaljava
Szőlősvégardó	Pidvinohradiv
Szürte	Strumkivka
Taracköz	Teresva

Técső	Ťačiv
Tekeháza	Tekove
Tiszabogdány	Bohdan
Tiszacsoma	Čoma
Tiszapéterfalva	Petrove
Tiszasalamon	Solomonove
Tiszaszászfalu	Sasove
Tiszaújlak	Vilok
Ungvár	Užhorod
Vári	Vary
Visk	Viškove
Zápszony	Zapsoň

TRANSYLVANIA (RUMANIA)

Relief names:

Hungarian	*Rumanian*	
Alföld (Nyugati-alföld)	Câmpia Vest	PL
Almás-hegység	Munţii Almăjului	M
Aradi-síkság	Câmpia Aradului	PL
Avas	Munţii Oaşului	M
Barcasági-medence	Depresiunea Bârsei	B
Baróti-hegység (Görgő 1017 m)	Munţii Baraolt (Gurgău)	M
Belényesi-medence	Depresiunea Beiuşului	B
Béli-hegység	Munţii Codru-Moma	M
Bihar-hegység (Bihar 1849 m)	Munţii Bihorului	M
Bodoki-hegység (Kömöge 1241 m)	Munţii Bodoc (Cărpiniş)	M
Borgói-havasok	Munţii Bârgăului	M
Brassói havasok	Munţii Bârsei+Munţii Ciucaş	M
Csukás 1954 m	Ciucaş	
Nagykőhavas 1843 m	Piatra Mare	
Bucsecs	Munţii Bucegi	M
Bükk	Culmea Codrului	M
Cibles	Munţii Ţibleşului	M
Csíki-havasok	Munţii Ciucului+Munţii Tarcăului	M
Tarhavas 1664 m	Grinduşu	
Sajhavasa 1553 m	Gura Muntelului	

Csíki-medence	Depresiunea Ciucului	B
Erdélyi-érchegység	Munţii Metaliferici	M
Érmellék	Câmpia Ierului	PL
Fogarasi-havasok	Munţii Făgăraşului	M
Godján	Munţii Godeanu	M
Görgényi-havasok	Munţii Gurghiului	M
Fancsaltető 1684 m	Fâncelul	
Mezőhavas 1776 m	Saca	
Gutin	Munţii Gutâului	M
Gyalui-havasok	Munţii Gilău+Muntele Mare	M
Gyergyói-havasok	Munţii Giurgeului	M
Siposkő 1567 m	Arbore	
Gyergyói-medence	Depresiunea Giurgeului	B
Hargita	Munţii Harghita	M
Madarasi-Hargita 1800 m	Harghita-Mădăraş	
Kakukkhegy 1558 m	M. Cucului	
Nagycsomád 1301 m	Ciomatul Mare	
Háromszéki-havasok	Munţii Vrancei+Munţii Buzăului	M
Lakóca 1777 m	Lăcăuţi	
Háromszéki-medence	Depresiunea Târgu Secuiesc	B
Kászoni-medence	Depresiunea Plaeşi	B
Kelemeni-havasok	Munţii Călimani	M
Király-erdő	Munţii Pădurea Craiului	M
Királyhágó	Pasul Ciucea	PS
Királykő	Munţii Piatra Craiului	M
Kőhát (Rozsály 1307m)	Munţii Ignuşului (Igniş)	M
Kőrösmenti-síkság	Câmpia Crişurilor	PL
Krassó-Szörényi-érchegység	Munţii Semenicului+	
	Munţii Aninei+M. Dognecei	M
Szemenik	Semenic	
Kudzsiri-havasok	Munţii Şureanu	M
Küküllők-menti-dombság	Podişul Târnavelor	H
Lápos-hegység	Munţii Lăpuşului	M
Lippai-dombság	Podişul Lipovei	H
Lokva-hegység	Munţii Locvei	M
Máramarosi-havasok	Munţii Maramureşului	M
Máramarosi-medence	Depresiunea Maramureşului	B
Meszes-hegység	Munţii Meseş	M
Mezőség	Câmpia Transilvaniei	PL
Nagy-Hagymás-hegység	Munţii Hăşmaşu Mare (Curmături)	M
Nagy-Hagymás 1792 m	Hăşmaşul Mare	
Egyeskő 1608 m	Piatra Singuratică	
Öcsémtető 1707 m	Hăşmaşul Mic	
Nagy-Cohárd 1506 m	Suhard	

Nemere-hegység	Munţii Nemirei	M
Nemere 1649 m	Nemira	
Nagy-Sándor 1640 m	Şandorul Mare	
Páreng-hegység	Munţii Parângului	M
Persányi-hegység (Várhegy 1104 m)	Munţii Perşani (Vf. Cetăţii)	M
Petrozsényi-medence	Depresiunea Petroşani	B
Pojána-Ruszka	Munţii Poiana Ruscăi	M
Radnai-havasok (Ünőkő 2279 m)	Munţii Rodnei (Ineu)	M
Retyezát-hegység	Munţii Retezatului	M
Rétyi-nyír	Mestecănişul de la Reci	R
Réz-hegység	Munţii Plopişului (Şeş)	M
Szár-kő	Munţii Tarcului	M
Szatmári-síkság	Câmpia Someşului	PL
Szebeni-havasok	Munţii Cindrelului	M
Temesi-síkság	Câmpia Timişului	PL
Tordai-hasadék	Cheile Turzii	PS
Torjai-büdösbarlang	Peştera de sulf Turia	C
Torockói-hegység (Székelykő 1128m)	Munţii Trascăului (Piatra Secuiului)	M
Vlegyásza	Munţii Vlădeasa	M
Vulkáni-hegység	Munţii Vâlcanului	M
Zarándi-hegység	Munţii Zărandului	M
Hegyes 798 m	Highiş	
Drócsa 836 m	Drocea	

Hydrographical names:

Hungarian	*Rumanian*
Almás	Almaş
Aranka	Aranca
Aranyos	Arieş
Béga	Bega
Békás	Bicaz
Berettyó	Barcău
Berzava	Birzava
Bodza	Buzău
Borsa	Borşa
Cserna	Cerna
Ér	Ier
Fehér-Kőrös	Crişul Alb
Fekete-Kőrös	Crişul Negru
Feketeügy	Râul Negru

Füzes	Fizeş	
Gyilkos-tó	Lacu Roşu	L
Hortobágy	Hârtibaciu	
Iza	Iza	
Kapus-patak (Kalotaszegen)	Căpuş	
Kapus-patak (Mezőségen)	Lechinţa	
Kászon	Caşin	
Kis-Küküllő	Târnava Mica	
Kis-Szamos (Hideg-, Meleg-Szamos)	Someşul Mic (Someşul Rece,Cald)	
Kölesér	Culişer	
Kraszna	Crasna	
Lápos	Lăpuş	
Ludas	Luduş	
Maros	Mureş	
Medve-tó (Szováta)	Lacu Ursu	L
Mohos-láp	Mlastina Mohoş	S
Nádas	Nadăş	
Nagy-Homoród	Homorodul Mare	
Nagy-Küküllő	Târnava Mare	
Nagy-Szamos	Someşul Mare	
Néra	Nera	
Nyárád	Niraj	
Olt	Olt	
Ompoly	Ampoi	
Pogányos	Pogăniş	
Sajó	Şieu	
Sebes-Kőrös	Crişul Repede	
Szamos	Someş	
Székás	Secaş	
Szent Anna-tó	Lacul Sfânta Ana	L
Sztrigy	Strei	
Tatros	Trotuş	
Temes	Timiş	
Tisza	Tisa	
Tömös	Timiş	
Túr	Tur	
Vargyas	Vârghiş	
Visó	Vişeu	
Zsil	Jiu	

Names of historical regions:

Hungarian	*Rumanian*
Alsó-Fehér	Alba de Jos
Arad	Arad
Aranyosszék	Scaune de Arieş
Bánát	Banat
Beszterce-Naszód	Bistriţa-Nasăud
Bihar	Bihor
Csík	Ciuc
Doboka	Dăbâca
Felső-Fehér	Alba de Sus
Gyergyó	Giurgeu
Háromszék	Trei Scăune
Hunyad	Hunedoara
Kalotaszeg	Călata
Kászon	Caşinu
Kolozs	Cluj
Közép-Szolnok	Solnocul de Mijloc
Kővárvidék	Chioar
Krassó-Szörény	Caraş-Severin
Kraszna	Crasna
Küküllő	Târnava
Máramaros	Maramureş
Maros	Mureş
Szatmár	Satu Mare
Szeben	Sibiu
Szilágy, Szilágyság	Sălaj
Szolnok-Doboka	Solnoc- Dăbâca
Szörény	Severin
Torda	Turda
Zaránd	Zarand

Settlement names:

Hungarian	*Rumanian*
Abrudbánya	Abrud
Ádámos	Adamuş
Ágya	Adea
Aknasugatag	Ocna Şugatag

Ákos	Acăţari
Algyógy	Geoagiu
Alsóbölkény	Beica se Jos
Alsórákos	Racoş
Alvinc	Vânţul de Jos
Anina	Anina
Apáca	Apaţa
Apahida	Apahida
Arad	Arad
Aranyosbánya	Baia de Arieş
Aranyosegerbegy	Viişoara
Aranyosgyéres	Câmpia Turzii
Árapatak	Vâlcele
Árpád	Arpăşel
Árpástó	Braniştea
Avasújváros	Oraşu Nou
Bácsi	Băcia
Bácsfalu	Săcele-Baciu
Bágyon	Bădeni
Balánbánya	Bălan
Balavásár	Bălăuşeri
Balázsfalva	Blaj
Bálványosváralja	Unguraş
Bályok	Balc
Bánffyhunyad	Huedin
Barót	Baraolt
Bátos	Batoş
Batiz	Botiz
Belényes	Beiuş
Belényessonkolyos	Şuncuiş
Belényesújlak	Uileacu de Beiuş
Bélfenyér	Belfir
Béltek	Beltiug
Bereck	Breţcu
Berény	Beriu
Beresztelke	Breaza
Berettyószéplak	Suplacu de Barcău
Beszterce	Bistriţa
Bethlen	Beclean
Bethlenszentmiklós	Sânmiclăuş
Bihar	Biharia
Bihardiószeg	Diosig
Bodola	Budila
Bogártelke	Băgara

Bogdánd	Bogdand
Boksánbánya	Bocşa
Bonchida	Bonţida
Bonyha	Bahnea
Borosjenő	Ineu
Borossebes	Sebiş
Borsa	Borşa
Borszék	Borsec
Bós, Kolozsbós	Boju
Bölön	Belin
Börvely	Berveni
Brassó	Braşov
Buziásfürdő	Buziaş
Bürkös	Bârchiş
Cegőtelke	Ţigău
Csanálos	Urziceni
Csák	Ciacova
Csávás	Ceuaş
Csernakeresztúr	Cristur
Csernátfalu	Săcele-Cernatu
Csernáton	Cernat
Csíkszentdomokos	Sândominic
Csíkszentkirály	Sâncraieni
Csíkszentmárton	Sânmartin
Csíkszenttamás	Tomeşti
Csíkszépvíz	Frumoasa
Csíkszereda	Miercurea Ciuc
Dés	Dej
Désakna	Ocna Dejului
Detta	Deta
Déva	Deva
Dezmér	Dezmir
Dézsánfalva	Dejan
Dicsőszentmárton	Târnaveni
Ditró	Ditrău
Doboka	Dăbâca
Dognácska	Dognecea
Dombos	Văleni
Domokos	Dămăcuşeni
Egeres	Aghireşu
Élesd	Aleşd
Erdőd	Ardud
Erdőfelek	Feleacu
Erdőgyarak	Ghiorac

Erdőszáda	Ardusat
Erdőszentgyörgy	Sângeorgiu de Pădure
Érmihályfalva	Valea lui Mihai
Érmindszent	Ady Endre
Erzsébetbánya	Băiuţi
Erzsébetváros	Dumbrăveni
Etéd	Atid
Facsád	Făget
Fakert	Livada
Farkaslaka	Lupeni
Felőr	Uriu
Felsőbánya	Baia Sprie
Felsővisó	Vişeu de Sus
Felvinc	Unirea
Fogaras	Făgăraş
Fugyivásárhely	Oşorhei
Galócás	Gălăuţaş
Gátalja	Gătaia
Gelence	Ghelinţa
Gernyeszeg	Gorneşti
Gödemesterháza	Stânceni
Görgényszentimre	Gurghiu
Görgényüvegcsűr	Glăjărie
Gyalár	Ghelari
Gyalu	Gilău
Gyanta	Ginta
Gyergyóholló	Corbu
Gyergyóremete	Remetea
Gergyószentmiklós	Gheorgheni
Gyergyótölgyes	Tulgheş
Gyimesbükk	Ghimeş-Făget
Gyimesfelsőlok	Lunca de Sus
Györgyfalva	Gheorghieni
Győröd	Ghiroda
Gyulafehérvár	Alba Iulia
Gyulakuta	Fântinele
Hadad	Hodod
Hadrév	Hădăreni
Hágótőalja	Hagota
Halmágy	Halmeag
Halmi	Halmeu
Haró	Hărău
Hátszeg	Haţeg
Héjjasfalva	Vânători

Holtmaros — Lunca Mureşului
Homoródjánosfalva — Ioneşti
Homoródszentmárton — Mărtiniş
Hosdát — Hăşdat
Hosszúfalu — Săcele-Satu Lung
Hosszúmező — Câmpulung la Tisa
Igazfalva — Dumbrava
Istvánháza — Iştihaza
Jákótelke — Horlacea
Józsefszállás — Iosif
Kalán — Călan
Kalotaszentkirály — Sâncraiu
Kályán, Magyarkályán — Căianu
Kaplony — Căpleni
Kapnikbánya — Cavnic
Kara, Kolozskara — Cara
Karánsebes — Caransebeş
Kászonaltíz — Plăeşii de Jos
Katalin — Cătălina
Kékes — Chiochiş
Kémer — Camăr
Kendilóna — Luna de jos
Kercsed — Stejeriş
Kérő — Băiţa
Kézdimartonos — Mărtănuş
Kézdivásárhely — Târgu Seciuesc
Kisiratos — Iratoşu Mic
Kisjenő — Chişineu Criş
Kiskapus — Copşa Mică
Kisnyégerfalva — Grădinari
Kispereg — Peregu Mic
Kisszécsény — Săceni
Kistécső — Teceu Mic
Kisvarjas — Variaşu Mic
Kóbor — Cobor
Kolozs — Cojocna
Kolozsvár — Cluj-Napoca
Koltó — Coltău
Kommandó — Comandău
Korond — Corund
Kovászna — Covasna
Kőhalom — Rupea
Kökényesd — Porumbeşti
Kökös — Chichiş

Körösbánya	Baia de Criş
Körösfő	Izvoru Crişului
Kőrösjánosfalva	Ioaniş
Köröstárkány	Tărcaia
Kövend	Plăieşti
Kraszna	Crasna
Küküllővár	Cetatea de Baltă
Kürtös	Curtici
Lázári	Lazuri
Lippa	Lipova
Lozsád	Jeledinţi
Lövéte	Lueta
Lugos	Lugoj
Lukafalva	Gheorghe Doja
Lupény	Lupeni
Mádéfalva	Siculeni
Magyarbece	Beţa
Magyarberkesz	Berchez
Magyardécse	Cireşoaia
Magyarfenes	Vlaha
Magyarkecel	Meseşeni de Jos
Magyarlapád	Lopadea Nouă
Magyarlápos	Târgu Lăpuş
Magyarléta	Liteni
Magyarmedves	Urseni
Magyarnemegye	Nimigea
Magyaró	Aluniş
Magyarózd	Ozd
Magyarpécska	Pecica-Rovine
Magyarpéterlaka	Petrilaca de Mureş
Magyarremete	Remetea
Magyarszentmárton	Sânmartinu Maghiar
Magyarszovát	Suatu
Magyarvalkó	Văleni
Magyarvista	Viştea
Majláthfalva	Mailat
Makfalva	Ghindari
Málnás	Mălnaş
Máramarossziget	Sighetu Marmaţiei
Margitta	Marghita
Marosfelfalu	Suseni
Marosfő	Izvoru Mureşului
Maroshévíz	Topliţa
Maroskeresztúr	Cristeşti

Marosludas	Luduş
Marosszentanna	Sântana de Mureş
Marosugra	Ogra
Marosújvár	Ocna Mureş
Marosvásárhely	Târgu Mureş
Marosvécs	Brâncoveneşti
Medgyes	Mediaş
Méhes, Mezőméhes	Miheşu de Câmpie
Méra	Mera
Mezőbaj	Boiu
Mezőbánd	Band
Mezőbodon	Papiu Ilarian
Mezőcsávás	Ceuaşu de Câmpie
Mezőfény	Foieni
Mezőkeszü	Chesău
Mezőpetri	Petreşti
Mezőtelegd	Tileagd
Mezőtelki	Telechiu
Mezőterem	Tiream
Mezőzáh	Zău de Câmpie
Micske	Mişca
Monó	Mânău
Nagyajta	Aita Mare
Nagybacon	Băţanii Mari
Nagybánya	Baia Mare
Nagybodófalva	Bodo
Nagyborosnyó	Boroşneu Mare
Nagycsűr	Şura Mare
Nagyenyed	Aiud
Nagygalambfalva	Porumbenii Mari
Nagyiratos	Iratoşu
Nagykapus	Căpuşu Mare
Nagykároly	Carei
Nagylak	Nădlac
Nagymajtény	Moftinu Mare
Nagymedvés	Medveş
Nagymoha	Grânari
Nagyrápolt	Rapoltu Mare
Nagysármás	Sărmaşu
Nagysomkút	Şomcuta Mare
Nagyszalonta	Salonta
Nagyszeben	Sibiu
Nagyszentmiklós	Sânnicolau Mare
Nagyvárad	Oradea

Nagyzerénd	Zerind
Naszód	Năsăud
Nőricse	Nevrincea
Nyárádremete	Eremitu
Nyárádszereda	Miercurea Nirajului
Olthévíz	Hoghiz
Omor	Roviniţa Mare
Ópécska	Pecica
Oravicabnya	Oraviţa
Ördöngősfüzes	Fizeşu Gherlii
Örményes, Mezőörményes	Urmeniş
Örvénd	Urvind
Ötvösd	Otveşti
Palatka, Magyarpalatka	Pălatca
Palotailva	Lunca Bradului
Páncélcseh	Panticeu
Pankota	Pâncota
Parajd	Praid
Pata, Kolozspata	Pata
Pécska	Pecica
Petrilla	Petrila
Petrozsény	Petroşani
Piski	Simeria
Porgány	Pordeanu
Pósalaka	Poşoloaca
Priszlop	Prislop
Pusztakeresztúr	Cherestur
Pusztaújlak	Uileacu de Criş
Radnót	Iernut
Rákosd	Răcăştia
Resicabánya	Reşiţa
Resinár	Răşinari
Retteg	Petru Rareş (Reteag)
Réty	Reci
Rév	Vadu Crişului
Rónaszék	Coştiui
Rőd	Rediu
Salamás	Şărmaş
Sárköz	Livada
Sarmaság	Şărmăşag
Sáromberke	Dumbravioara
Sárpatak	Şapartoc
Sárvásár	Şaula
Segesvár	Sighişoara

Sepsibükszád	Bixad
Sepsiszentgyörgy	Sfântu Gheorghe
Simonyifalva	Satu Nou /Arad county/
Szabéd	Săbed
Szalárd	Sălard
Szamosardó	Arduzel
Szamosújvár	Gherla
Szaniszló	Sanislău
Szapáryfalva	Ţipari
Szászkabánya	Sasca Montană
Szászlóna	Luna de Sus
Szászrégen	Reghin
Szászsebes	Sebeş
Szászváros	Orăştie
Szatmárhegy	Viile Satu Mare
Szatmárnémeti	Satu Mare
Szatmárudvari	Odoreu
Szecseleváros	Săcele
Szék	Sic
Székelyderzs	Dârjiu
Székelyhíd	Săcueni
Székelykeresztúr	Cristuru Secuiesc
Székelykocsárd	Lunca Mureşului
Székelyudvarhely	Odorheiu Secuiesc
Szentágota	Agnita
Szentegyházas	Vlăhiţa
Szentjobb	Sâniob
Szentleányfalva	Sânleani
Szentmáté	Matei
Szentmihály	Mihai Viteazu
Szépkenyerűszentmárton	Sânmartin
Szerdahely	Miercurea Sibiului
Szilágycseh	Cehu Silvaniei
Szilágynagyfalu	Nuşfalău
Szilágyperecsen	Pericei
Szilágysomlyó	Şimleu Silvaniei
Szilágyzovány	Zăuan
Szinérváralja	Seini
Szováta	Sovata
Sződemeter	Săuca
Sztrigyszentgyörgy	Streisângeorgiu
Talmács, Nagytalmács	Tălmaciu
Tasnád	Tăşnad
Teke	Teaca

Temesrékas	Recaş
Temesvár	Timişoara
Tenke	Tinca
Torda	Turda
Tordaszentlászló	Săvădisla
Tordos	Turdaş
Torja	Turia
Torockó	Rimetea
Torockószentgyörgy	Colţeşti
Torontálkeresztes	Cruceni
Törcsvár	Bran
Tövis	Teiuş
Túrterebes	Turulung
Tusnádfürdő	Băile Tuşnad
Türkös	Săcele-Turcheş
Újegyház	Nocrich
Újmosnica	Moşniţa Nouă
Újszékely	Secuieni
Újszentes	Dumbrăviţa
Uzon	Ozun
Vajdahunyad	Hunedoara
Vajdakamarás	Vaida-Cămăraş
Vajdaszentivány	Voivodeni
Válaszút	Răscruci
Valkó, Valkóváralja	Sub Cetate
Várasfenes	Finiş
Vargyas	Vârghiş
Várkudu	Coldău
Vásáros	Târgovişte
Vasláb	Voşlăbeni
Végvár	Tormac
Verespatak	Roşia Montană
Vice	Viţa
Világos	Şiria
Vinga	Vinga
Visa	Vişea
Vízakna	Ocna Sibiului
Vulkán	Vulcan
Zabola	Zăbala
Zágon	Zagon
Zalatna	Zlatna
Zilah	Zalău
Zimándújfalu	Zimandu Nou
Zselyk	Jeica

Zsibó   Jibou
Zsombolya   Jimbolia

VOJVODINA (YUGOSLAVIA – SERBIA)

Relief names:

Hungarian   *Serbian*

Alföld (Nagyalföld)   Panonska nizija   PL
Bácskai-(Telecskai) löszhát   Telečka   R
Delibláti-homokpuszta   Deliblatska peščara   R
Fruska Gora (Péterváradi-hegység)   Fruška Gora   M
Titeli-fennsík   Titelski breg   P
Verseci-hegység   Vršačke planine   M

Hydrographical names:

Hungarian   *Serbian*

Aranka   Zlatica
Béga   Begej
Csík-ér   Čik
Duna   Dunav
Duna-Tisza-Duna-csatorna   Kanal Dunav-Tisa-Dunav
Fehér-tó (in Bánát)   Belo jezero   L
Kígyós   Plazović
Körös-ér   Kereš
Krassó   Karaš
Krivaja   Krivaja
Ludasi-tó   Ludaško jezero   L
Mosztonga   Mostonga
Palicsi-tó   Palićko jezero   L
Száva   Sava
Temes   Tamiš
Tisza   Tisa

232

Names of historical regions:

Hungarian	**Serbian,-Croatian,-Slovenian**
Bácska (Bácsvidék)	Bačka
Bánát (Bánság)	Banat
Szerémség	Srem

Settlement names:

Hungarian	**Serbian**
Ada	Ada
Alsóittebe	Novi Itebej
Apatin	Apatin
Aracs	Novi Bečej-Vranjevo
Bács	Bač
Bácsfeketehegy,Feketics	Feketić
Bácsföldvár	Bačko Gradište
Bácskertes	Kupusina
Bácskossuthfalva, Ómoravica	Stara Moravica
Bácspalánka	Bačka Palanka
Bácstopolya, Topolya	Bačka Topola
Bajmok	Bajmok
Bajsa	Bajša
Bánmonostor	Banoštor
Basahida	Bašaid
Bezdán	Bezdan
Csantavér	Čantavír
Csóka	Čoka
Csurog	Čurug
Dobrodolpuszta	Dobrodol
Doroszló	Doroslovo
Egyházaskér	Vrbica
Fehértemplom	Bela Crkva
Fejértelep	Šušara
Futak	Futog
Gombos	Bogojevo
Herkóca	Hrtkovci
Hertelendyfalva	Pančevo-Vojlovica
Hódegyháza	Jazovo
Horgos	Horgoš

India	Inđija
Káptalanfalva	Busenje
Karlóca	Sremski Karlovci
Kevevára	Kovin
Kisbelgrád	Mali Beograd
Kisbosznia	Mala Bosna
Kishegyes	Mali Idjoš
Kishomok	Mali Pesak
Kula	Kula
Magyarcsernye	Nova Crnja
Magyarkanizsa	Kanjiža
Magyarmajdány	Majdan
Magyarszentmihály	Mihajlovo
Maradék	Maradik
Martonos	Martonoš
Mitrovica	Sremska Mitrovica
Mohol	Mol
Monostorszeg	Bački Monoštor
Mozsor	Mošorin
Nagybecskerek	Zrenjanin
Nagyfény	Žednik (Stari-, Novi-)
Nagykikinda	Kikinda
Nemesmilitics	Svetozar Miletić
Nyékica	Nikinci
Óbecse	Bečej
Orom	Orom
Oroszlámos	Banatsko Aranđelovo
Pacsér	Pačir
Palánka	Banatska Palanka
Palics	Palić
Pancsova	Pančevo
Péterréve	Bačko Petrovo Selo
Pétervárad	Petrovaradin
Piros	Rumenka
Rábé	Rabe
Ruma	Ruma
Sándoregyháza	Ivanovo
Satrinca	Šatrinci
Szabadka	Subotica
Szaján	Sajan
Székelykeve	Skorenovac
Szenttamás	Srbobran
Szilágyi	Svilojevo
Tamásfalva, Hetény	Hetin

Tavankút	Tavankut
Temerin	Temerin
Tiszakálmánfalva	Budisava
Titel	Titel
Torontáltorda	Torda
Torontálvásárhely	Debeljača
Törökbecse	Novi Bečej
Törökkanizsa	Novi Kneževac
Törzsudvarnok	Banatski Dvor
Újvidék	Novi Sad
Ürményháza	Jermenovci
Verbász	Vrbas
Versec	Vršac
Zenta	Senta
Zentagunaras	Novo Orahovo
Zombor	Sombor
Zsablya	Žabalj

CROATIA

Relief names:

Hungarian	*Croatian*	
Báni-hegység, Baranyahát	Bansko brdo	M
Bilo-hegység	Bilogora	M
Drávamenti-síkság	Podravina	PL
Monoszló	Moslavačka Gora	
Pozsega-medence	Požeška kotlina	
Szávamenti-síkság	Posavina	

Hydrographical names:

Hungarian	*Croatian*
Csázma	Česma
Dráva	Drava
Duna	Dunav

Karasica   Karašica
Kopácsi-rét   Kopački rít   S
Mura   Mura
Száva   Sava
Vuka, Valkó   Vuka

Names of historical regions:

Hungarian	**Croatian**
Baranya (Drávaszög)	Baranja
Muraköz	Međimurje
Szerémség	Srijem
Szlavónia	Slavonija

Settlement names:

Hungarian	**Croatian**
Albertfalu	Grabovac
Almás, Hagymás	Aljmaš
Alsómiholjác	Donji Miholjac
Antunovác	Antunovac Tenjski
Apáti	Opatovac
Berzétemonostor	Nuštar
Baranyabán	Popovac
Baranyaszentistván	Petlovac
Baranyavár	Branjin Vrh
Benge	Šumarina
Bellye	Bilje
Belovár	Bjelovar
Bolmány	Bolman
Boró	Borovo
Bród	Slavonski Brod
Budakóc	Stari Budakovac
Csák	Čakovci
Csáktornya	Čakovec
Csúza	Suza
Dálya	Dalja
Dályhegy	Dalja-Daljska Planina
Dályok	Duboševica

Darázs	Draž
Dárda	Darda
Daruvár	Daruvar
Diakóvár	Đakovo
Erdőd	Erdut
Eszék	Osijek
Főherceglak	Kneževo
Grubisnopolje	Grubišno Polje
Haraszti	Hrastin
Hercegmárok	Gajić
Hercegszőlős	Kneževi Vinogradi
Izsép	Topolje
Kácsfalu	Jagodnjak
Kaporna	Koprivna
Kapronca	Koprivnica
Karancs	Karanac
Keskend	Kozarac
Kiskőszeg	Batina
Kopács	Kopačevo
Kórógy	Korog
Kő	Kamenac
Kőrös	Križevci
Lacháza	Vladislavci
Laskafalu	Čeminac
Laskó	Lug
Légrád	Legrad
Lőcs	Luč
Nagybodolya	Podolje
Nagypisznice	Velika Pisenica
Novszka	Novska
Ójankovác	Stari Jankovci
Pakrác	Pakrac
Pélmonostor	Beli Manastir
Perlak	Prelog
Petárda	Baranjsko Petrovo Selo
Pozsega	Požega
Sepse	Kotlina
Szata	Sotin
Szentlászló	Laslovo
Sziszek	Sisak
Szlatina	Podravska Slatina
Tárnok	Tovarnik
Torjánc	Torjanci
Újbezdán	Novi Bezdan

Újlak | Ilok
Valpó | Valpovo
Varasd | Varaždin
Várdaróc | Vardarac
Verbász | Vrbas
Verőce | Virovitica
Villyó | Viljevo
Vörösmart | Zmajevac
Zágráb | Zagreb
Zsgyála | Žďala

TRANSMURA REGION (SLOVENIA)

Relief names:

Hungarian	*Slovenian*	
Lendvai-hegy	Lendavske gorice	M
Lendvai-medence	Dolinsko	B
Vasi-hegyhát	Goričko	H

Hydrographical names:

Hungarian	*Slovenian*
Kebele-patak	Kobilje
Kerka (Kis-, Nagy-)	Krka (Mala-, Velika-)
Lendva	Lendava
Mura	Mura

Names of historical region:

Hungarian	*Slovenian*
Muravidék (Murántúl)	Pomurje (Prekmurje)

Hungarian	Slovenian
Alsójánosfa	Ivanjševci
Alsólendva	Lendava
Bántornya	Turnišče
Csente	Čentiba
Dobrónak, Lendvavásárhely	Dobrovnik
Felsőlendva	Grad
Göntérháza	Genterovci
Kámaháza	Kamovci
Kebeleszentmárton	Kobilje
Kisfalu	Pordašinci
Lendvahídvég	Mostje
Lendvahosszúfalu	Dolga Vas
Mezővár	Tešanovci
Muraszombat	Murska Sobota
Őrihodos	Hodoš
Pártosfalva	Prosenjakovci
Petesháza	Petišovci
Pince	Pince
Pincemajor	Pince Marof
Radamos	Radmožanci
Rátkalak	Ratkovci
Szárazhegy	Suhi Vrh
Zalagyertyános	Gaberje

BURGENLAND (AUSTRIA)

Relief names:

Hungarian	German	
Fertőzug	Seewinkel	R
Hanság	Waasen	S
Kőszegi-hegység	Günser Gebirge	M
Lajta-hegység	Leitha Gebirge	M
Lánzséri-hegység	Landseer Gebirge	M

Mosoni-síkság	—	PL
Pándorfalvi-fennsík (Fenyér)	Parndorfer Plateau (Heide)	P
Rozália-hegység	Rosaliengebirge	M
Soproni-hegység	Ödenburger Gebirge	M

Hydrographical names:

Hungarian	**German**	
Csáva-patak	Stoober Bach	
Fertő-tó	Neusiedler See	L
Gyöngyös	Güns	
Lajta	Leitha	
Lapincs	Lafnitz	
Pinka	Pinka	
Rába	Raab	
Répce	Rabnitz	
Strém	Strem	
Szék-patak	Zickenbach	
Vulka	Wulka	

Name of historical region:

Hungarian	**German**
Őrség (Felső-Őrség)	Wart

Settlement names:

Hungarian	**German**
Alsóőr	Unterwart
Barátudvar	Mönchhof
Boldogasszony	Frauenkirchen
Borostyánkő	Bernstein
Csajta	Schachendorf
Csáva	Stoob
Darázsfalu	Trausdorf an der Wulka
Darufalva	Drassburg

Doborján	Raiding
Felsőőr	Oberwart
Felsőpulya	Oberpullendorf
Féltorony	Halbturm
Fertőmeggyes	Mörbisch am See
Fraknó	Frochtenstein
Gyanafalva	Jennersdorf
Gyepűfüzes	Kohfidisch
Kabold	Kobersdorf
Királyhida	Bruckneudorf
Kismarton	Eisenstadt
Köpcsény	Kittsee
Lánzsér	Landsee
Léka	Lockenhaus
Locsmánd	Lutzmannsburg
Miklóshalma	Nickelsdorf
Monyorókerék	Eberau
Mosonbánfalva	Apetlon
Mosontarcsa	Andau
Mosontétény	Tadten
Nagyfalva	Mogersdorf
Nagymarton	Mattersburg
Nagysároslak	Moschendorf
Nagyszentmihály	Grosspetersdorf
Németújvár	Güssing
Nezsider	Neusiedl am See
Őrisziget	Siget in der Wart
Pátfalu	Podersdorf
Pinkafő	Pinkafeld
Pomogy	Pamhagen
Rábakeresztúr	Heiligenkreuz im Lafnitztal
Rohonc	Rechnitz
Ruszt	Rust
Sopronkeresztúr	Deutschkreutz
Szentelek	Stegersbach
Szikra	Sieggraben
Tarcsafürdő	Bad Tatzmannsdorf
Városszalónak	Stadt-Schlaining
Vasvörösvár	Rotenturm an der Pinka